W. D. Howells as Critic

The Routledge Critics Series

GENERAL EDITOR: B. C. SOUTHAM, M.A., B.LITT. (OXON.)
*Formerly Department of English, Westfield College,
University of London*

W. D. Howells

as Critic

Edited by

Edwin H. Cady

Professor of English,
Duke University,
Durham, N. Carolina

Routledge & Kegan Paul
London and Boston

First published in 1973
by Routledge & Kegan Paul Ltd
Broadway House, 68–74 Carter Lane,
London EC4V 5EL and
9 Park Street,
Boston, Mass. 02108, U.S.A.
Printed in Great Britain by
W & J Mackay Limited, Chatham

ISBN 0 7100 7676 2

Library of Congress Catalog Card No. 73-83119

In Memoriam
Harry Hayden Clark

General editor's preface

The purpose of the Routledge Critics Series is to provide carefully chosen selections from the work of the most important British and American literary critics, the extracts headed by a considerable Introduction to the critic and his work, to the age in which he was writing, and to the influence and tradition to which his criticism has given rise.

Selections of a somewhat similar kind have always existed for the great critics, such as Johnson, Wordsworth, Arnold, Henry James, and the argument for their appearance in this series is that of reappraisal and re-selection: each age has its own particular needs and desiderata and looks in its especial own way at the writing of the past—at criticism as much as literature. And in the last twenty years or so there has also been a much more systematic and intelligent rereading of other critics, particularly the lesser-known essayists and reviewers of the Victorian period, some of whose writing is now seen to be criticism of the highest order, not merely of historical interest, but valuable to us now in our present reading of nineteenth-century literature, and so informing us in our living experience of literature as well as throwing light upon the state of literature and criticism at particular moments in the past.

B.C.S.

Contents

Chronology

September to New York as free-lance writer; 17 December, accepts Godkin offer as *Nation* commentator and critic.

1866   6 February, accepts offer of assistant editorship of *Atlantic Monthly*, effective 1 March; May, *Atlantic* publishes first of reviews which were to be virtually monthly for ten years and continue sporadically through January 1881 (during these years Howells must have reviewed more than 500 books); October, 'Modern Italian Poets,' *North American Review*; see also April 1867, *inter alia*, as Howells developed Italian themes.

1868   July, 'George William Curtis,' *North American Review*.

1869   May, 'The New Taste in Theatricals,' *Atlantic*.

1871   1 July, becomes editor of the *Atlantic*.

1881   1 February, resigns editorship.

1882   September, 'Mark Twain,' *Century*; November, 'Henry James, Jr.,' *Century*.

1886   January, starts monthly 'Editor's Study,' *Harper's Monthly Magazine*.

1887   1 October, *Modern Italian Poets*.

1891   9 May, *Criticism and Fiction*.

1892   March, last 'Editor's Study.'

1893   December, *My Literary Passions* begins in *Ladies' Home Journal*; ends March 1895.

1895   4 May, column 'Life and Letters' begins, *Harper's Weekly*; June, irregular installments begin of what became *Literary Friends and Acquaintance*, *Harper's Monthly*; 19 October, *My Literary Passions*.

1898   3 February, last regular 'Life and Letters'; 14 May, first weekly column, 'American Letter,' *Literature*.

1899   10 November, last column in *Literature*.

1900   5 May, *Heroines of Fiction* begins in *Harper's Bazar*, ends January 1902; 17 November, *Literary Friends and Acquaintance*; December, begins 'Editor's Easy Chair' column, *Harper's Monthly*; begins monthly critical article for *North American Review*.

1901   26 October, *Heroines of Fiction*.

1902   14 October, *Literature and Life*.

1903   January, ends regular *North American Review* articles but continues to contribute frequently; 13 July, begins column, 'Diversions of the Higher Journalist,' *Harper's Weekly*; 26 December, last 'Diversions of the Higher Journalist,' though pieces for *Weekly* continue until 27 February 1904, and irregularly thereafter.

1907   5 January, 'An Autobiographical view of the *Weekly*,' *Harper's Weekly*; November, 'Recollections of an Atlantic Editorship,' *Atlantic Monthly*.

1910   July–September, 'My Memories of Mark Twain,' *Harper's Monthly*; 10 September, *My Mark Twain*; 15 October, *Imaginary Interviews*.

1915   January, 'Part of Which I was,' *North American Review*; March, 'The Plays of Eugene Brieux,' last *North American Review* article.

1920   April, last 'Editor's Easy Chair'; 11 May, Howells dies in New York City.

Acknowledgments

For permissions to publish from unpublished letters of W. D. Howells I am grateful to the Heirs of William Dean Howells, Professor W. W. Howells, Chairman, who retain all rights in the materials quoted from the letters of Howells to Gosse, 16 November 1882 (owned by the Houghton Library, Harvard University); Howells to Warner, 28 November 1882 (owned by the Watkinson Library, Trinity College, Hartford); and Howells to Matthews (owned by the Butler Library, Columbia University). I am likewise grateful to the Watkinson for permission to use its property. To the Houghton the same, with additional thanks for freedom also to use the communications of Gosse to Howells, 8 and 14 November 1882, of George Otto Trevelyan to Howells, 31 March 1904, and of the anonymous benedictor to Howells, 3 October 1905. Finally, I thank Columbia again for letting me use once more the fine pleasantry of Stephen Crane to Howells, 15 August 1896.

Like all books, this has accrued a number of filial and some avuncular debts while it grew up. Norma Woodard Cady helped as perceptively as she worked faithfully with it for years. Richard Curtis and James D. Gray contributed heartily and shrewdly to the gathering of materials—and Gray straightened me out on the authorship of the famous *Blackwood's* and *London Quarterly* attacks of 1883 on Howells. Each in his own way, George Arms, Don Cook, William M. Gibson, Ronald Gottesman, Clara and Rudolf Kirk, Richard Moody, David Nordloh, Alvin Rosenfeld, Thomas Wortham, and Sam Yellen helped. Some are colleagues and some friends. But, though they all helped, none is of course at all responsible for any error which occurs on the pages beneath this.

E.H.C.

Note on the text

'Jane Austen' (No. 41) is taken, as an exception to rule (see p. 314), from *Heroines of Fiction* on the ground of textual superiority. Every other text is taken from its original magazine or newspaper appearance, with nothing corrected but obvious typographical error. Nos 9, 17, 20 and 21 have quotation marks placed round items of special critical vocabulary; apart from these, titles in quotation marks are Howells's own, and the others have been supplied.

What kind of critic was Howells?

He called himself 'W. D. Howells,' so signing thousands of letters and all his books until in weary age his public and publishers pushed him toward the conventional 'William Dean.' He represents *par excellence* the man of letters, having been successively and repeatedly poet, journalist, travelist, critic, writer of sketches and short stories, novelist, dramatist. As critic he was professedly, sincerely reluctant, complaining that creativity is superior to criticism, that he seldom satisfied himself in criticism, that the critic in him robbed life from the artist, and that to authors in general critics are generally useless.

Yet certain facts conflict with Howells's protestations. He must have been at the least ambivalent, in one voice crying down the criticism he deplored but in another crying it up again. He became an extraordinarily prolific, long-lived critic, publishing his first significant article in 1860 and dying in the midst of work on his last in 1920. During those sixty years he published in sixty-four periodicals and nineteen newspapers, most of it criticism. As the Chronology in this volume shows, he conducted eight periodical columns mainly devoted to literary reviews and comment. He published seven volumes of criticism and more than forty prefaces to other authors' books. Altogether he published substantially more than one, perhaps as much as two millions of words in reviews and literary comment—virtually all of it, as was his habit, somehow contributions to criticism.

I

Howells achieved criticism in what might have been routine reviewing or fluffy gossip because he cared for theory and consciously admired the serious critic. Frequently tendentious, sometimes polemic, he meant always to accomplish something worthy, was therefore tactical and upsetting to readers, and has been often misunderstood, even misrepresented to this day. Only the reading of his criticism, however, not scholarly argument, can lead to understanding of Howells as critic; and it is with that affirmative purpose that the preparation of this volume is undertaken.

It is fair to say of Howells that he thought criticism should be above all serviceable, functional. Though there are many modes, manners, methods, styles, tools, and techniques of criticism, it justifies itself in two goals, both of which help readers, the consumers of literary art. Criticism helps us to read more accurately, more completely. It helps us judge literature, to estimate its worth or importance, more truly. To be serviceable the critic ought, Howells believed, to be essentially taxonomic: skilled but humble, engaging but accurate, broadly informed but personally unobtrusive. But the serious critic must also be morally concerned and responsible. Ideally, in the last analysis, Howells believed in the culture critic, the man of letters intent upon elevating the customs, refining the language, clarifying the motives, helping to raise the quality of the life of the people.

II

Perhaps the oddest misapprehension current about Howells is that which supposes him narrow, superficial, and in effect ignorant. He was in fact almost incredibly informed, sophisticated, and many-minded; in his time an absolute insider, an old professional, long a standard-bearer of the *avant garde*, the friend and ally of the great, the sponsor and patron of the gifted young and friendless, the despair of the entrenched and ancient. As critic he enjoyed the advantages of living at the heart of three worlds. Creatively he had tried or was about to try almost everything literary and he lived in close contact with the world of his peers; he knew art and its life at daily first-hand. Critically he worked in the craft, and multilingually, a long time; and most of his best work he wrote between the ages of fifty and seventy. Commercially, he was in the business of authorship not only as author but as editor, consultant, friend of the great, and a treasured name—he was 'in the know' for half a century.

Howells's sophistication as critic was technical, too. He mastered the modes, knew what each could accomplish, and could wield each to exact, conscious effect. It is always a mistake in a reader to suppose that he is cleverer than Howells. It was also, however, true that Howells as critic was sophisticated in the commercial way. He wrote to be paid by journals which maintained theories of their readership and expected him to appeal to their subscribers. As a professional, Howells obliged. Almost all his criticism, then, like almost all serious criticism—which is nothing if not professional —he shaped to its outlet. His modern reader must attend to this factor in his subtly-adapted, varying styles.

Howells may sometimes seem not at all to be—to the stuffy, portentous, modern sense—a serious critic. Though he maintained the surface of a strolling, personal commentator, of a man of letters *en passant*, his surfaces were protective. They protected the professional in his business relations with outlets. They also, as a necessary, invaluable screen, protected the creative artist. Introducing the Library Edition reprint of essays called *Literature and Life*, Howells noted

the wide, the wild, variety of my literary production in time and space. From the beginning the journalist's independence of the scholar's solitude and seclusion has remained with me, and though I am fond enough of a bookish *entourage*, of the serried volumes of the library shelves, and the inviting breadth of the library table, I am not disabled by the hard conditions of a bedroom in a summer hotel, or the narrow possibilities of a candle-stand, without a dictionary in the whole house, or a book of reference even in the running brooks outside.

I am sure the picture is true, but the comment is uncannily beguiling and self-protective.

As quite another aspect of his sophistication, in fact, what Howells brought with him to the narrow possibilities of that summery 'candle-stand' was broad, exact, international, multilingual learning. He never really went to school, but he read literature in English from Chaucer through Robert Frost and often knew it, as he told one challenging friend, '*au fond.*' He knew Italian and its literature pretty well from Dante through D'Annunzio and seems to have read literary Spanish, French, and German easily and accurately. At the same time, however, he remained not only an American but, as it was then called, a Westerner, with deep concerns for the development of literature and culture in the United States. For that above all he served as a critic. And the thing which interested him most, as it had Jefferson, Emerson, and Whitman, was contemporaneity, culture now and the quality of culture to come.

III

Though it took Howells almost thirty years to assimilate Emerson to himself, his posture as critic proved much the same. Emerson urged on the young men of America a first-hand, an 'original relation.' So did Howells. The hard thing was that their grounds quarreled. The essence of Howells's contemporaneity was to be agnostic and realistic in reductive revolt against the Emersonian faith in ideality. As critic, then, Howells achieved a stance of considerable originality. He became the chief molder and champion of realism and a realistic movement in his country. And the resultant fights, the American aspects of the great Realism War in Western culture at large, turned Howells militant.

In every major critic, as I see him, aesthetics become ethics, then politics, then metaphysics. Howells's ultimate distinction as critic is to have made that major passage under the power of his own vision, sensibility, and imagination, his own theory and his own faith in realism. Whether it is true, as the great *emigré* artist George Grosz thought, that there is or was something in the American atmosphere which makes for realism I do not know. Obviously Howells would have liked that idea. The word 'realism' is protean, very difficult; and I have tried to show how best to make sense of it in a recent book, *The Light of Common Day*, the argument of which I shall not try to recapitulate here. Howells makes good sense for himself in his own terms in the selections below.

The most spectacular feature of Howells's realism was its condemnation —frank, serious, contemptuous—of a false but popular romanticism. People were told, with a force that employed every device from homily to derision to strike home, that the clap-trap they consumed by the car-load was vicious. If they resented that, or, more to the point, if the producers and purveyors of a bad romanticism resented Howells, very well. He then had the positive ideal of a sane and beautiful art to substitute for the false and bad.

To the charge that he was reductive, Howells cheerfully pleaded guilty. His principles of reality were humane, this-worldly, and tough-minded. But the imputation of pessimism he denied. After the fashion of his mind, he could take to himself Emerson's famous defiance of mere rationalism, 'I am always insincere, as always knowing there are other moods.' Like any alert, responsive man, Howells changed his moods with the logic of life and events. No sentimental Pollyanna, he not infrequently felt Jeffersonian—on the whole sanguine about the world's chances. No defeatist, he sometimes felt a Franklinian if not a Swiftian disgust at the obdurate idiocies of human-kind. His criticism reflects both polar moods together with the more con-stant mixed mood, the mood he trusted most.

Agnostically without the Jeffersonian faith in reason, in revolt against all Platonisms, very doubtful about the presence of Jehovah, the realistic sensibility kept a stubborn, desperate, even Hebraic faith in the value and ultimacy of personhood. Howells's realist believed in persons in defiance of monism, whether monism lost men and women in soaring abstraction, the minuet of bloodless categories; or whether it lost them in vortices of blind force and chance. This humanism might be more desperate than that of the Psalmist:

O Lord my God, I cried unto thee and thou has healed me.
O Lord, thou has brought up my soul from the grave; thou has kept me
   alive, that I should not go down to the pit. . . .
What profit is there in my blood, when I go down to the pit? Shall the
   dust praise thee? shall it declare thy truth?

The realist was more desperate but no less humane. He was more desperate because his assurance, if he had any, of the intervening Hand was dim and far indeed, but his faith in personhood stubbornly remained.

For criticism all this issued into a set of terms by which Howells under-took to communicate new ideas, concerns, and attitudes. They nearly set out a paradigm of his criticism, and some are worth adding to anyone's critical vocabulary. Aside from the then conventional terms of literary criticism which Howells used rather conventionally, a glossary of his then special terms would list:

academic	devoted to dead convention.
Altruria	futuristic Utopia where 'synthetized sympathies' replace egotism.
commonplace, the	essence of reality, the one uncommon subject of art.
confidential attitude	habitual intrusion by an authorial persona upon the integrity of fictional illusion.
democracy	political *equality*, a principle of the imagination essential to *realism*.
distinction	vestigial remnant of feudalism, now a *neo-romantic* egotism.
effectism	sacrifice of aesthetic and ethical integrity to induce intense, irresponsible emotions.
equality	cognate with reality, the common and *democracy*— all essential ingredients of the best art.
genius	a delusion.
humanism	ultimate moral, aesthetic concern for common persons.
literosity	self-conscious attention to literary precedent and convention, an imitative yen to appear literary.
neo-romantic	seeking romantic emotional effects in the cynical absence of romantic belief.
photographic	what *realism* is not because realism is not mechanical or cartographic but an art like painting.
realism	the heart of the matter, great imaginative art (too many definitions to quote).
romanticistic, the	see *neo-romantic*.

IV

Howells felt and in some meaningful sense was contemporaneous with the four generations of British authors from the Early Victorians through the Edwardians. With a few notable exceptions, most lamentably Melville, he knew, often intimately, the American authors from long-lived Bryant through the New Poets of 1912. And he was vitally concerned with the coeval Italian, French, Norwegian, Russian, Spanish, and German writers: altogether, 'literary generations' too numerous to list. He introduced to the general literary audience of the English-speaking world a great number of important authors: one set to the Americans, including their own; a variant set, of course, to British readers (including those in the world-wide imperial dependencies). He stood among the pioneer critics introducing, sponsoring, and elucidating Björnson, Cahan, Chesnutt, Clemens, Stephen Crane, Dickinson, Dostoevski, Frederic, Garland, Gorky, Hardy, Harrigan, Herne, Ibsen, Henry and William James, Frank Norris, Tolstoi, Turgenev, Palacio Valdés, Veblen, Verga, and Zola, among others.

The importance of Howells to his large audiences is obvious. It is obvious, that is, that a major influence emanated from Howells for not less than four crucial decades. While certain facts are patent, nobody has systematically studied the reputation or the influence. Several significant books will be written before we can really know how and how much Howells was influential and can understand what the facts mean. In what we now know about the general influence there is no way to discriminate the impact of the fiction from that of the criticism. There lie certain frontiers of knowledge in literary history, and the trails run abruptly into tangles.

We know that Clemens thought his friend the national court of last resort in criticism. We know that James deplored 'The Editor's Study' but regularly sought and got Howells's support. It is no surprise to learn that Crane thought him 'our first critic of course.' But one was not prepared to hear Cable respond to the quarrel over 'Henry James, Jr.' in the spirit of an old Confederate trooper, praising 'the emphatic truth of what you say about the mighty men of a school that would not do for today. Hold that ground. Hold hard.' What does it mean that George Ade, Henry Seidel Canby, Richard Harding Davis, Clyde Fitch, Alice French (Octave Thanet), Lafcadio Hearn, Henry Cabot Lodge, Stuart Merrill, Booth Tarkington, William Allen White—a very mixed bag—paid eager tribute to Howells? What shall we make of the protestations of debt made by Grant Allen, Leonard Merrick, Edward Garnett, and Kipling, as well as Arnold Bennett?

Howells appears to have sensed the meaning of this century to literature, that it would decline as a medium of entertainment but that decline would open the way for 'the serious artist' to aim for the heights. We have still some way to go before we sense the whole meaning of Howells.

A critic's background, 1837–66

Just after the American Civil War, in the middle 1860s, Howells burst upon the critical scene in three distinct roles. Already known as a young, very American poet, a 'Westerner,' he materialized as a smart, innovating New York commentator. But it also appeared that he wrote as a scholar and comparatist, competent in German, conversant with literary Spanish and French, uniquely (for a foreigner) familiar with contemporary Italian literature. He represented the new generation, the new thing: self-tutored, energetic, he was prepared to speak for a new era. And when he had been invited to one of the thrones of native intellectual power, charged to seek out the talents of his generation for the *Atlantic Monthly* and given charge of its commanding book-review columns, he had become altogether a phenomenon. The experience upon which the phenomenon was grounded is worth a brief review.

I

Young Howells, whose father had grown up on the Ohio frontier, himself grew up in the shops where the father printed successive family newspapers. The child could set type (which means working with the letters in mirror image) before he knew how to read. By the age of seven he could set type like a man and worked stints, increasing with age, thereafter. At the age of seventeen he would undertake to write a novel, printed by installments in the paper, composing the text from his head into type as he stood at his case.

Since Howells almost never went to school at all, the shops with their printers' political, literary, and religious gossip formed his grammar school and academy. The papers, featuring literature (usually clipped from 'exchange' papers or magazines), made his best library. And his Welsh-born father, poet, idealist, and reformer, Swedenborgian prophet, quondam author and magazine editor, Utopian, was his teacher, guide, comrade, even psychiatrist. Looking backward, autobiographically, Howells thought he had sprung from a 'reading race,' his father had 'such a decided bent in the direction of literature.' The first chapter of *My Literary Passions* (1895) is

7

'The Bookcase at Home.' Some of Howells's earliest recollections called back the voice of his father reading aloud to the family circle in the evening from books kept on those shelves. Before he could read, the child had heard the poetry of Thomson, Cowper, Burns, Scott, Moore, and Byron.

By the time young Howells turned twelve he had become, as he says, 'a literary creature.' Responding to the atmosphere at home and work, he resolved to master languages, unlock the secrets of history and art, become a scholar, a poet, a man of letters. For a boy locked into bleak, culture-starved villages lost among the forests and raw fields over which the westering edge of civilization had passed before the eyes of his parents, those were daunting ambitions. He was to realize them with the zest and anguish of years of all-out effort, alternating language study with literary composition or reading after a day's work in the print shop or, later, on a reporter's beat.

The stroke of fate was that a boy who almost never went to school transmuted his intense reverie life into a life of letters. When he was not at work and not at play in a boy-life much like that of Tom Sawyer, Howells lost himself in the happy case of books. Reading at that childish random in which destiny lurks, he passed from Goldsmith's histories of Greece and Rome to the *Gesta Romanorum* and thence to a life-long passion, Cervantes. Supported by Irving's *Conquest of Granada*, he determined at the age of eleven to learn Spanish and began, with eventual success, to teach himself from a grammar brought home by a veteran of the Mexican War. The child was formidable. Without masters, libraries, or professional example, at the beginning without tutors, he taught himself language and literature. Just as he taught himself prosody from the rules at the back of *Webster's Dictionary*, so he picked up literary names, works, ideas, and languages wherever he could.

When reaction against editorial sympathy for the slave hounded the father out of Hamilton, Ohio, the adolescent Howells could discover live theater in Dayton, where road-companies played Shakespeare, Kotzebue, and Sheridan, as well as now nameless melodramas, and thirsted to swap tickets for printing. When bankruptcy in Dayton forced the father into the country on an abortive Utopian project, he had time to give his gifted son. There, Howells said, for the first time he grasped 'a literary sense of what I was reading.' When in 1851 it became clear that Utopia was lost once more, the father moved to Columbus, Ohio, where in the midst of studious imitations of Pope, Howells, aged fifteen, published his first poems. And steadily his reading mounted up: Poe, Longfellow, Scott, Marryat, *Uncle Tom's Cabin*, and Ossian became successive passions. He learned about literary conflict and intellectual snobbery from *The Dunciad* and from 'English Bards and Scotch Reviewers.'

All this took place in the secret life of a boy, the confines of family life and a family business, until, at fifteen, Howells was culturally translated. His father's radical convictions and anti-slavery sufferings were rewarded by opportunity in a part of Ohio then culturally almost another world.

In northeastern Ohio, the Western Reserve, the weather was cold and blustering near the shores of Lake Erie, a blue, icy inland sea. And the people were transplanted Yankees. The Western Reserve was an outpost of New England culture, and a lively, radical one. The family became settled and at length prosperous in a town significantly named Jefferson, where the shop put out a newspaper designed to speak for a resident United States Senator and a Congressman who were famous anti-slavery figures. Yankees transplanted perhaps for a generation or two, lately off a raw frontier, with a streak in them of Ethan Allen or Bronson Alcott, the villagers possessed traditions of intense individualism, of experimentation with life and faith. They were not put off by the literary experimenter who in southern Ohio, middle America, had seemed 'a queer boy.'

On the contrary, in Jefferson the village druggist peddled books, and citizens gathered to argue about Dickens and Thackeray, Wordsworth, De Quincey and Byron, Gibbon and Macaulay. Such notes of contemporaneity and fashion were fresh to Will Howells: that people could care about literature! Now he found a friend to share literary passions, and they read Shakespeare together until they had hundreds of lines by heart. Howells read Thackeray, Dickens, Hawthorne, Tennyson. He learned German and soaked his mind in Heinrich Heine, ironist. And now the idea of literary criticism dawned on young Howells after he had discovered Macaulay in tiny Jefferson, Ohio, and began to notice that there regularly came to the office of the *Ashtabula Sentinel* as 'exchanges' copies of the great British quarterlies: *Blackwood's, Edinburgh, London, North British, Westminster*. They taught him a new game, and he read Hazlitt, Hunt, and Lamb; and Poe and Lowell.

II

Though young Howells intended to become a great poet and published poetry in good places, poetry was then as unreliable a ground for a career as now. He fought his way out of the village as a journalist, primarily a political reporter. And there would be a certain irony in the fact that, when asked at age seventy-two to write on 'The Turning Point of My Life', he recognized that the fatefullest pivot turned on his first piece of serious literary criticism. There is significance enough in the fact that even in 1910, when the returns from a long, very productive literary life were mainly in, Howells wished to emphasize more his turning from poetry to prose than his turning to criticism. But that is a different topic.

Meanwhile the story of the turning-point has a lengthy tail, and the implications of its history are important to an understanding of his critical career. Life at home equipped young Howells nicely for success as a political reporter. Happily for him, he came along at what turned out to be a moment of triumph, with whatever perhaps inevitable corruptions, for some of his father's reforming ideals. The libertarian, anti-slavery, anti-imperialist convictions for which the family had suffered after the Mexican War began to prosper politically with the rise of the Republican Party before the Civil War.

Sharing the convictions, Howells prospered, honestly enough, with them. He won a post in the state capital on a newspaper where the clever young men 'fired the Southern heart' with funny paragraphs, and Will Howells could achieve a column called 'News and Humors of the Mail.' The column brought him more than a chance to write occasional book-notices; it opened the way toward professional opportunities and active participation in the social and intellectual life of the provincial capital. As it happened, Columbus, Ohio, at that moment stood apart from the ordinary fresh-water, corn-country state capital. It was loaded with talent. The nation would issue from the Civil War into 'The Ohio Period' in American politics. Political prestige opened the gates to a 'Western' era in the national culture, in which Howells, of course, was to play no minor part. As it was, on the brink of the war, he was surrounded in Columbus by gifted, energetic men and women with an intense, if provincial, devotion to letters.

At the end of 1859 Howells published, in collaboration, a volume of poems which made little difference to anybody but the poets. But after the nomination in May of Abraham Lincoln for the presidency, Howells's ardently Republican publisher saw a vital opportunity and pressed him into service to write a campaign biography of Lincoln which proved to be a turning-point indeed. In official political gratitude, Lincoln would eventually appoint him U.S. Consul to Venice. Immediately, the book gained Howells enough in royalties to stake him to a famous pilgrimage to the East and its literary centers.

There for the first time the future of American letters, which was to be 'Western' or, more accurately, continental, met with the ruling New England present—much of which would shortly belong to the past. On the whole Howells flourished on his trip; but the variations in his happiness were meaningful, virtually diagnostic. In Boston, then the absolute center, as an established if minor *Atlantic Monthly* contributor things went delightfully for Howells with James T. Fields, the great Yankee publisher, and with Lowell, the *Atlantic*'s editor. Lowell took Howells to dinner with Dr Holmes at the Parker House, and Holmes made giddy remarks about the apostolic succession.

If in Boston and, inferentially, Cambridge young Howells swam in cordiality, his experience at Concord, the American Athens of the hour, was mixed. There lived Emerson and Hawthorne and Thoreau, all of whom he was prepared to venerate. They were kind, and he made contact of a sort with Hawthorne. But the great transcendentalists seemed distant, elusive, unavailable in particular to the political passion Howells brought from the West. The truth is that there proved to be what we now call a generation gap fixed between Howells and the major American writers of his father's generation and belief. Perhaps they were too much like his father and repellent to something deep in his sensibility. It was with the professionals of the older generation, the scholars, editors, publishers so different from his quixotic father, that Howells could sympathize.

Certainly, as it turned out, he felt scant sympathy in New York with the resident 'bohemians' of the *Saturday Press*, though he was also among their contributors. Fiery, impecunious, in revolt against the Establishment, they left Howells cold. Also young, also battling for art and its life in America, also in rebellion against conventional standards of belief, of acquisitiveness and careerism, of politics, of popular taste, Howells compared the 'bohemians' with Fields and Lowell and Hawthorne and felt disillusioned. He had heard bad boys ramp around the office before. He shook Walt Whitman's warm hand in Pfaff's Cellar saloon with a puzzled ambivalence, and took the train home to Ohio.

1 'A Hoosier's opinion of Walt Whitman'
1860

Published in the *Ashtabula Sentinel*, 18 July 1860; and in the *Saturday Press*, 11 August 1860.

The title given this essay by the *Saturday Press* was malicious but may have become more so, through ignorance, than the bohemians intended. Howells had made Henry Clapp's magazine equally with Whitman victims of his Heinesque irony; and by his title Clapp meant to spank the Western upstart without, perhaps, knowing that the proper 'Buckeye' of Ohio, the nick-name to which Howells was born, felt entitled to look down upon the Indiana 'Hoosier.'

At any rate, Howells's essay remains important. Many a contemporary commentator on the 1860 *Leaves of Grass* (which Roy Harvey Pearce and his critical school think the truest Whitman) condemned it root and branch. Howells found an effective ironic vehicle for registering at once his deep admiration and his shock. He showed that he understood the aims of *Leaves of Grass*, the history of its reception, and its threat to the established, Tennysonian conventions in which he then wrote verse. He invented a strong tactic for expressing at once his rejection of Whitman's parade of sexual modalities and for acknowledging the virtues he found in a great, revolutionary book. He had learned much from Heine.

Always sympathetic, sometimes actively generous to Whitman personally, Howells was to remain ambivalent about *Leaves of Grass* in commentary extending over not less than a dozen pieces, the last written as late as 1907. Howells's feeling swung strongly toward the positive pole during his most radical years, especially the 1890s when Whitman and his friends began to feel reconciled with Howells. But the ambivalence never resolved itself beyond a truce with Whitman; Howells would never be able to go quite all the way with Walt.

LEAVES OF GRASS.—BY WALT. WHITMAN.—Thayer and Eldrige. Year 85 of the States. (1860–61.)

Who is Walt. Whitman?

The person himself states his character, and replies to this question in the following general terms.

Walt. Whitman, an American, one of the roughs, a kosmos.
Disorderly, fleshy, sensual, eating, drinking, breeding.
No sentimentalist—no stander above men and women, or apart from them.
No more modest than immodest.

This is frank, but not altogether satisfactory. From the journals therefore, and from talk of those who know him, we gather that Walt. Whitman lives in Brooklyn, that he has been a printer, and an omnibus driver, that he wears a red flannel shirt, and habitually stands with his hands in pockets; that he is not chaste nor clean, despising with equal scorn the conventional purity of linen, and the conventional rules of verse; that he is sublime and at the same time beastly; that he has a wonderful brain and an unwashed body. Five years ago, he gave to light the first edition of the *Leaves of Grass*, which excited by its utter lawlessness, the admiration of those who believe liberty to mean the destruction of government, and disgusted many persons of fine feelings. We remember to have seen a brief criticism of the book in dear, dead *Putnam*,[1] by a critic, who seemed to have argued himself into a complete state of uncertainty, and who oracularly delivered an opinion formed upon the model of the judge's charge in Bardell and Pickwick. Ralph Waldo Emerson, however, took by the horns, this bull, that had plunged into the china-shop of poetical literature, threatening all the pretty Dresden ornaments, and nice little cups with gold bands on them; and pronounced him a splendid animal—and left people to infer that he was some such inspired brute as that Jove infurried, when he played Europa that sad trick.

But presently the bull—being a mere brute—was forgotten, and the china-shop was furnished forth anew with delicate wares—new-fashioned dolls, bubble-thin goblets, and dainty match-safes.

Nearly a year ago, the bull put his head through the New York *Saturday Press*' enclosure, and bellowed loud, long and unintelligibly.

The mystery of the thing made it all the more appalling.

The Misses Nancy of criticism hastened to scramble over the fence, and on the other side, stood shaking their fans and parasols at the wretch, and shrieking, 'Beast! beast!'

Some courageous wits attempted to frighten the animal away by mimicry, and made a noise as from infant bulls.

The people in the china-shop shut and bolted their doors.

Several critics petted and patted the bull; but it was agreed that while his eyes had a beautiful expression, and his breath was fragrant with all the meadow-sweetness of the world, he was not at all clean, and in general, smelt of the stables, and like a bull.

But after all, the question remained,—'What does he mean by it?'

It remains yet—now when he stands again in front of the china-shop, with his mouth full of fresh leaves of grass, lilies, clover-heads, buttercups, daisies, cockles, thistles, burrs, and hay, all mingled in a wisp together.

He says:

> I celebrate myself,
> And what I assume you shall assume,
> For every atom belonging to me, as good belongs to you.

And so proceeds, metreless, rhymeless, shaggy, coarse, sublime, disgusting, beautiful, tender, harsh, vile, elevated, foolish, wise, pure and nasty to the four hundred and fifty-sixth page, in a book most sumptuously printed and bound.

If you attempt to gather the meaning of the whole book, you fail utterly.

We never saw a man yet, who understood it all. We who have read it all, certainly do not.

Yet there are passages in the book of profound and subtle significance, and of rare beauty; with passages so gross and revolting, that you might say of them, as the Germans say of bad books—*Sie lassen sich nicht lesen.*[2]

Walt. Whitman is both overrated and underrated. It will not do to condemn him altogether, nor to commend him altogether.—You cannot apply to him the tests by which you are accustomed to discriminate in poetry.

He disregards and defies precedent, in the poetic art. It remains for Time, the all-discerning, to announce his wisdom, or his folly to the future.

Only this: If he is indeed 'the distinctive poet of America,' then the office of poet is one which must be left hereafter to the shameless and the friendless. For Walt. Whitman is not a man whom you would like to know. You might care to see him, to hear him speak, but you must shrink from his contact. He has told too much. The secrets of the soul may be whispered to the world, but the secrets of the body should be decently hid. Walt. Whitman exults to blab them.

Heine in speaking of the confidences of Sterne, and of Jean Paul, says that the former showed himself to the world naked, while the latter merely had holes in his trousers. Walt. Whitman goes through his book, like one in an ill-conditioned dream, perfectly nude, with his clothes over his arm.

NOTES

1 In *Putnam's Monthly Magazine* for September 1856 there had appeared an important review of the 1856 *Leaves of Grass*, unsigned but written by Charles Eliot Norton.
2 'They rather let them alone than read them.'

III

Going abroad made Walt Whitman temporarily irrelevant to Howells. Four years in Venice altered his vision. 'Fancy now,' urged Lowell in review of *Venetian Life* (1866), 'an imaginative young man from Ohio, where the log-hut was but yesterday turned to almost less enduring brick and mortar, set down in the midst of all this almost immemorial permanence of grandeur.' Above all else, his 'eyes' would be quickened by the 'constantly recurring shock of unfamiliar objects.' Being Howells, the young man would work hard to master Italian, both literary and Venetian, would find a tutor in Dante, and would saturate his sensibility more in the strange but common present life of Venice than in its vestiges of almost immemorial grandeur.

The 'good Americans' who go to Paris when they die are those unfortunates who never had the chance to live in Italy. Lucky Howells became an Italophile. And while the scholar in him throve and burgeoned there, the reporter in him changed into a cultural relativist; but the poet quietly declined. He stopped writing poetry soon after he arrived in Venice and could not sell the unpublished verse on hand. Poems came back, he recalled, 'from the magazines of the whole English-speaking world with unfailing promptness,' and he began to wonder if his future were dying. Gradually it dawned on his despair that through his instinct for the contemporary, his passion for the theater, and the intensity of his language studies he had become an authority in a field unknown to Americans. The eager scholar might compensate for the sleeping poet. He wrote a careful article on 'Recent Italian Comedy' for the *North American Review*, sent it to Lowell, then co-editor, and waited.

Lowell's letter of acceptance became a true 'turning-point.' He said, in part: 'Your article is in print, and I was very glad to get it. . . . Write us another article on "Modern Italian Literature," or anything you like. . . . You have enough in you to do honor to our literature. Keep on cultivating yourself.' As Howells recalled forty-five years later,

> I can still see myself coming out of the Gothic landgate of the Palazzo Giustiniani dei Vescovi, where I dwelt in less splendor than might be imagined from its name, receiving Lowell's letter from the postman with my own hand, and knowing it his at a glance by the beautiful super-scription, and tremulously breaking the seal, and then going back up into the palace, and expanding to the utmost measure of its height and breadth.

But after the exhilaration wore off, a meaningful point remained: 'It was a distinct call to the larger criticism which I heard in Lowell's note,' Howells said. 'I had not till now seen myself in the majestic proportions of quarterly reviewer which I had envied other men.' Self-deprecation aside, it was 'a trumpet call to battle.'

That battle became immediate upon Howells's return home in 1865. He had to fight to establish himself and earn his livelihood in the world of American letters. 'I must seek my fortune at the great literary centres,' he had explained to his father from Venice. He went to New York and scratched and scrambled as a free-lance until he 'got a basis' with the great E. L. Godkin on the *Nation*. Idealistic about democracy, Godkin meant to fight for the highest cultural as well as political standards; and his intention made him a believer in serious criticism. Howells turned out to be just his man. Both believed, with Emerson, Hawthorne, Melville, and Whitman, in the necessity of achieving what Tocqueville had insisted could not be had: a spiritually viable democratic culture. Both believed a serious criticism essential to that achievement, though both knew that the people would like it (and buy the *Nation* and sustain the organ of criticism) only if they seasoned the larger criticism with the salt of wit and style.

What Howells achieved as a critic in Venice and New York between 1864 and 1866 was simple but essential: authenticity. As a critic he dis-covered his true temperament and sensibility, his point of view, and thence the ground of his opinions, his judgments of value. The rest was to be growth, development, refinement, and response to the logic of events in the cultural history of his times—but from established grounds. Lacking as yet the terminology and concepts adequate to express his critical personality, he grew into a sophistication of style and insight sufficient to impress Lowell, Norton, Godkin, and, in the end, James T. Fields.

Perhaps five aspects of Howells the critic stand forth from 1864–6:

1   All his yearning for the great world and his Venetian experience to the contrary notwithstanding, he was to remain not merely American but *Western*;

2 his taste, preference, and eyes were to be *contemporaneous*;

3 his mind would run easily in modes *ironic*;

4 he would yearn for the sensible, unpretentious *common* as a good in itself;

5 he would have deep respect for honest, modest *work* (and corresponding contempt for its opposite).

The appropriate hindsight generalization upon those points is that they predict a realist to be. The Western mind struck the first and last notes of 'Recent Italian Comedy.' That essay ends in a talismanic cry of hatred for Austrian imperialism; but it opens in the tone of a Western humorist, expert at playing the innocent at large, who 'has sometimes found a pensive amusement' at the bewilderments of the foreigner groping to locate reality abroad. Taste more than opportunism guided Howells to the significance of comedy in Venice. The drawling detachment of the Western jokester proved a formidable weapon against romantic afflatus, and Howells had guessed it in the studies he was then writing and would collect as *Venetian Life*.

A like conclusion arises from his attention to 'recent' Italian comedy. He rejected out of hand the exotic emotions which led Washington Irving (and the multitude of his heirs) to Europe in order 'to escape, in short,' as Irving explained, 'from the commonplace realities of the present, and lose myself among the shadowy grandeurs of the past.' The impulse Howells perceived in himself was precisely the opposite: to discover himself, if possible, among 'the commonplace realities of the present.' That he found the discovery difficult enough in either Venice or New York accelerated his tendency toward an ironic anti-romanticism and deepened the gap between his tastes and those of his father's generation. A serious criticism, he now felt (and would feel to the end), must reject the formal effects of Whitman's aesthetic absolute and deplore the fact that, for Howells, romantic organicism doomed Whitman to remain a potential, not a realized, poet despite his inherent greatness. In short, the sum of all Howells's experience to age twenty-nine can be expressed as his having arrived at a point of view, a mode of vision, about which he could as yet be less than fully articulate. That point of view was a democratic, common, plain-folks, American way, in Howells's case an aspect of what Arthur O. Lovejoy called 'intellectual anti-intellectualism.' It was a way distinct from the ancient, aristocratic poles of Dionysian or Apollonian vision, yet it was in a sense a middle way between them.

2 'Concerning Timothy Titcomb'[1]
1865

Published in the *Nation*, 23 November 1865.

'Concerning Timothy Titcomb' the New York critic felt no scruples. The notion of a serious criticism coincided with revulsion against violations of his sense of the decencies to inspire Howells to wrath. Writing for Godkin, he wiped J. G. Holland out. In itself that was no great matter, but the incident projects symbolic as well as historic consequences which reveal important things about Howells as critic, about his circumstances, his courage, and his education.

A failed physician who became a popular 'human interest' writer on Samuel Bowles's *Springfield Republican*, Holland and his career were not impossibly like what Howells could have become and done had he stayed in Columbus with the *Ohio State Journal*. Sentimental, folksy, evangelical, moralizing, trite, and superbly unconscious of his pomposity, Holland stood for a mirror inversion of Walt Whitman. As 'Timothy Titcomb,' he wrote novels, novelettes in verse, and 'lectures' aiming to improve the youth of the nation. It can be counted one of the tragedies of American literary history that Dr Holland was the 'man of letters' Emily Dickinson knew best. Perhaps worst of all, Holland was in person a lovable man. Howells hated his literary persona and blew it to rags.

But he made a powerful enemy. From the *Republican* Holland went as a founding editor of *Scribner's Monthly* in 1870 and of the *Century Magazine* in 1881, dying just before the first issue of that great journal appeared. It did not mollify 'the Apostle to the Naïve' when in 1867 Howells in the *Atlantic* laughed at Holland's *Kathrina, Her Life and Mine, in a Poem*. Howells the novelist was pointedly ignored by *Scribner's*, inspiring E. C. Stedman to a pasquinade addressed from the younger to the elder generation:[2]

> H. number I will not review
> The poems of H. number II,
>   Because he can't defend 'em:
> H. number II has nothing done
> With novels of H. number I
>   For fear he must commend 'em!

When, simultaneously with the founding of the *Century*, Howells had resigned from his commitment to the *Atlantic* and Roswell Smith, the publisher, proposed to snap Howells up for the *Century*, Dr Holland declared that he would resign if the invitation were issued. It was perhaps this tempest which led Howells to a moment of his legendary wit:

> Friend, meeting Howells on street: 'Oh, Howells! Have you heard what Dr. Holland says about you?'
> Howells: 'Do you think I have no bosom friends?'

Nevertheless, Howells learned something important about criticism. As he said to a birthday interviewer who inquired about Old New York in 1912 when Howells turned seventy-five, though 'I had performed what I considered a literary duty . . . I can well understand that Dr. Holland was incensed, and after all these years I regret keenly the cruelty of that criticism, however just it may have been.'

Since the 'Country Parson'[3] has been called a prose Tupper, there is, unhappily, nothing left within the whole range of epigram for the characterization of 'Timothy Titcomb.' The situation is perhaps inevitable, but it is not the less desperate. No doubt a future age, should his work descend to posterity, will have the courage and wisdom to express in some comprehensive phrase a sense of their quality; for the present we can only hope to suggest their nature vaguely and unequally.

Fortunately, a great number of readers have already some idea of our author. He has written a good many books, which have had large sales. He has a wide reputation as poet and novelist; and it seems to us he has done his best things in these characters. As a lecturer he is quite as well known, and in the volume before us he publishes the lectures which he has written and delivered during the last six or seven years. These are nine in number, and of such quantity and quality that it exalts our respect for the national sweetness and patience when we consider that they must have each been delivered to popular assemblies at least a score of times.

It might not be without a measure of sadness, however, that we considered this, for the fact suggests uncomfortable ideas of the facility of literary success in this country, and goes far to prove that reputation is the only thing still to be had cheap among us; that while overcoats, butter and eggs, rents and fuel, are exorbitantly dear, fame, like consolidated milk, is within the reach of the humblest resources. But it would be unjust to the public to judge it by what it endures rather than what it likes; and it is doubtful whether the popularity of such writers and lecturers as Mr. Holland is other than apparent. A slovenly and timorous criticism has been the bane alike of readers and of writers, and an order of mind has been allowed to flourish up into a thistly rankness in our literature fit only to browse donkeys. But we doubt greatly whether most people have any genuine appetite for the growth, and we question if even among those to whom harsh dispraise of Mr. Holland would come with almost the shock of a personal affront, there has not sometimes been a suspicion that he was heavy and trite. It would be difficult, certainly, to find anything in these popular lectures which is not dull if new, or old if good. The lecturer himself has sometimes a sense of this, and once expresses the belief that a great deal he has been saying must seem to his audience like the recitation of a schoolroom. We must do him the justice to say, however, that this concession is made in a moment of rare consciousness, and that, for the most part, he rehearses his commonplaces with a dignified carefulness and a swelling port of self-satisfaction inexpressibly amusing. He does not wonder, this eloquent lecturer, he is 'smitten with wonder,' he says, when he thinks 'of the power which bold assumption has in the world,' though we suspect that he is merely smitten with wonder that he should have thought of the tremendous fact; and he might have marvelled at his hearers for submitting to his own pretence of having something wise and novel to tell them. He loves to say 'Now, mark you,' when there is nothing to mark, and is fond of the sort of metaphor which, like bear's meat, grows as you chew upon it, and can neither be swallowed nor ejected. Nothing daunts him, and he does not hesitate to electrify you with the idea, for example, 'that hate is not so good a motive as love, and, thank God! it is not so powerful a motive as love!'

Throughout these lectures Mr. Holland patronizes the good, the true, and the beautiful. He encourages these amiable abstractions, and tries to keep up their spirits by a constant testimony to their good behavior. He is also friendly to the domestic and public virtues; but the great object of his philanthropic condescension is the Christian religion. He cannot say enough in favor of its many winning and useful qualities; and if he sometimes suspects that his platitudes on other subjects might seem like the recitations of schoolboys, he has every reason to believe that his attitude toward our common faith is that of a pedagogue. He wishes to bring this faith out and have its merit recognized, and will never give up his protégée, even though people should think his constancy unfashionable. Religion he finds lamentably absent from politics and society, and, above all, from fashionable literature. He does not find Thackeray Christian, even when he takes 'into account the sulphurous satire which he points with such deadly fire at the very society which makes him fashionable;' and he objects to the pen of Charles Dickens that, although 'thrilling to its nib with the genius which inspires it, he has never written, in good, honest text, the name of Jesus Christ.' The rebuke of worldly-mindedness and vanity and uncharitableness which breaks forth from Thackeray, the unfailing advocacy of the cause of the despised, the poor, and the prisoner in the novels of Charles Dickens, prove nothing of their love of Christianity, because the *name* of Christ is not in their works. Does Mr. Holland wear a crucifix about him? Kingsley, although a traitor to the cause of popular reform, and the inventor of the odious muscular piety of second-rate modern fictions, is Christian, because he calls on the name of the Lord; and Ruskin, who has lately discovered the divine beauty of slavery, is likewise a Christian for the like reason. Mrs. Browning, also, is a Christian writer; and whereas fashionable unchristian writers are doomed to perish, our lecturer is led to the anti-climax of saying: 'The earth is not broad enough, the earth is not deep enough, to bury Mrs. Browning in.'

It may be objected to the censure of such writers as Mr. Holland that, granting their popularity to be factitious, they do a great deal of good to commonplace people; that they reach a large class of hearers and readers who could not be reached by men of genius; that they act as smoked glasses for the weak vision that would else turn away from thought, or, regarding her, would be dazzled to death by her aspect. We desire to give Mr. Holland's admirers and apologists the benefit of this doubt.

NOTES

1 *Plain Talks on familiar Subjects. A Series of Popular Lectures. By T. G. Holland.* New York: Charles Scribner & Co. 1866 [Howells's note].
2 Stedman to Howells, 7 December 1874. In Laura Stedman, *Life and Letters of Edmund Clarence Stedman*, Vol. 1, New York, 1910, pp. 526–7.
3 Scottish Andrew K. H. Boyd (1825–79) wrote the immensely popular *Recreations of a Country Parson*, 1860, and its sequels, which were widely excerpted by American newspapers. Successor 'Country Parsons' continue to this day. *Littell's Living Age* for 6 April 1861 had compared Boyd to Martin Tupper, to the disadvantage of both.

Mr Howells of the *Atlantic*, 1866-81

Though Godkin and Howells made a happy team, they were not to stay together long. Howells was wanted in Boston, and at 'Boston,' meaning mainly Cambridge and the offices of James T. Fields who published the books of all the great New England authors and the *Atlantic Monthly*, they held the keys to national literary prestige. Fields himself came down to recruit Howells for an assistant editorship on the *Atlantic*, offering him not only salary and felicity but power and opportunity. He took over the job on 1 March 1866, his twenty-ninth birthday. Among other duties, Howells was to scout for young talent, soliciting contributions. He was also to review and, as he proved worthy, take charge of the *Atlantic*'s book review columns. He soon proved worthy.

Howells became full editor of the *Atlantic* on 1 July 1871 and resigned his post on 1 February 1881. From the time of his accession to the assistant editorship through the date of his resignation he wrote hundreds of reviews, many of them significant, but few critical essays. Most of the work for what at length became a critical volume, *Modern Italian Poets*, 1887, was written early in the period and published in the *North American Review* or the *Atlantic*. There was a good essay on George W. Curtis in 1868 and the sprightly 'New Taste in Theatricals' of 1869, but after that nothing much but reviews until 1882.

What was significant to Howells as critic about his *Atlantic* years was that they gave him such an education as almost no other post or place than his magazine in Cambridge, Mass., could have furnished an American. Now for the first time in his life he came face to face with the life not of art merely but of ideas strenuously taken. That was partly tradition at this oldest seat of learning in the country, in the long afterglow of Puritanism. 'They take the mind hard in Boston,' Fenimore Cooper had gibed. But it was also because, all suddenly, the sleepy College was transforming itself into a University and the stiff old town was alight with young genius.

Cambridge sparkled with first-rate minds working on or toward the frontiers of knowledge as no comparable group of Americans had worked before. The *Atlantic*'s new man could not have escaped exposure had he failed to measure up. But he did not fail. On the contrary, he took part of the lead in his chosen directions and absorbed a major education in the

23

process. And from that education he began to develop the formed theories of literature and the critical terminology which were to stock the intellectual arsenal of the mature critic.

In the traditions of literary history which stem from Professors Fred Lewis Pattee and Vernon L. Parrington, Howells has been consistently misunderstood for saying that the Cambridge of the 1870s was the perfect home for his spirit. The error of that tradition has been to suppose that Howells referred only to his instructive and supportive friendships with elders in the circle of Longfellow's Dante Club—Appleton, Fields, Dr Holmes, Lowell, Norton, and, of course, Longfellow himself. But if there was hyperbole in Charles Darwin's remarking that in the American Cambridge at Howells's ideal moment there dwelt enough brilliant minds to stock the universities of all England, the saying sprang from lips hardly noted for poesy. Charles Sanders Peirce supposed the proportion of 'superior men in Cambridge at that time' not to be duplicable anywhere.

Like Darwin and Peirce, Howells was by no means thinking only of the luminaries of his father's generation, among whom there was also Henry James, Sr. Into an intermediate age group fell Francis J. Child and Thomas Wentworth Higginson. In Howells's age-bracket there were Brooks and Henry Adams, John Fiske, Justice (to be) Holmes, William and Henry James, Peirce, Thomas Sergeant Perry, and Chauncey Wright. In a still wider circle, bound to Howells by both *Atlantic* contacts and, quite often, shared Western experience, was a group of fellow journalists turned author. They lived at various distances from Cambridge but had a habit of drifting to Boston for meetings of shared conviviality and professional advantage— Henry M. Alden, Thomas Bailey Aldrich, Clemens, Richard Watson Gilder, Bret Harte, John Hay, Ralph Keeler, Clarence King, Stedman, Charles Dudley Warner. Old Western friends like Artemus Ward dropped by. Foreign luminaries were magnetized thither—Hjalmar Hjorth Boyesen lived as Howells's house guest at a time crucial to his career; therefore Björnstjerne Björnson called. Social life throve; intellectual contact was not only frequent but, in a society famous for conversation, often strikingly intimate. People talked freely, that is to say, about the states of their souls.

A decided newness in thought and sensibility, varying somewhat between generations and from person to person, of course, became epidemic in Howells's Cambridge circles and in his generation. To put the situation paradigmatically, everything intellectual history means by 'Darwinism' drove these minds toward the stance of agnosticism. As agnostics they turned away from supernaturalism, whether Hebraic or Platonic, toward forms of humanism. The resultant metaphysical and emotional tensions they resolved as pragmatism in philosophy and realism in art. As Henry Adams rejected the Unitarian optimism of the hereditary 'Boston solution,' Howells, in company with William and Henry James, rejected the romantic idealism of his father and entered upon the newness. Scientists like Asa Gray, Fiske, Peirce, Nathaniel Shaler, Wright, and William James might lead the way, but everyone else marched in the procession after his fashion. From the heart of Cambridge as far as the eye of the age could see, in every intellectually respectable direction the newness flourished.

As Yankee Cantabridgian and as *Atlantic* staffer and then editor, Howells in the 1870s took his intellectual, emotional, and imaginative nutriment from the newness. He began the decade a temperamental, inquiring, experimental proto-realist. During the *Atlantic* period he considered, accepted, and proof-read articles explaining the newness; and he reviewed a number of books dealing with various of its aspects. He reviewed, to take only some of the prominent movers, shakers, and trenders, Agassiz, Auerbach, Björnson, Boyesen, Robert Browning, Clemens, De Forest, George Eliot, Fiske, James, W. E. H. Lecky, William Morris, Ruskin, Taine, Tennyson, and Turgenev. At the same time his own fiction grew, with increasing experimentalism, increasingly toward the international school he increasingly identified as realistic. By the time he gave up his *Atlantic* editorship in 1881 he had become very nearly a doctrinaire realist.

3 'Francesco Dall' Ongaro's *Stornelli*
1868

Published in the *North American Review*, January 1868.
As a critical essay and as a piece to represent Howells's treatment of contemporary Italian literature, 'Francesco Dall' Ongaro's *Stornelli*' is more searching, more intimately informed, and more elegant than 'Recent Italian Comedy.' Needless to say, the translations here of fourteen poems, all but two *stornelli*, constitute a keen sort of criticism. The Howells recognized by Italian literati, treasured by Cambridge Italophiles, and invited to distinguished professorial chairs at Harvard, the Johns Hopkins, Cornell, and elsewhere, is this one.

Dall' Ongaro liked the essay so well it was translated and used as an introduction to his collected *Stornelli politici e non politici*, 1883, which contained a charming *stornello* addressed to Howells.

In the month of March, 1848, news came to Rome of the insurrection in Vienna, and a multitude of the citizens assembled to bear the tidings to the Austrian ambassador, who resided in the ancient palace of the Venetian Republic. The throng swept down the Corso, gathering numbers as it went, and paused in the open space before the Palazzo di Venezia. At its summons, the ambassador abandoned his quarters, and fled without waiting to hear the details of the intelligence from Vienna. The people, incited by a number of Venetian exiles, tore down the double-headed eagle from the portal, and carried it for a more solemn and impressive destruction to the Piazza del Popolo, while a young poet erased the inscription asserting the Austrian claim to the palace, and wrote in its stead the words, 'Palazzo della Dieta Italiana.'

The sentiment of national unity expressed in this legend had been the ruling motive of Francesco Dall' Ongaro's life, and had already made his name famous through the patriotic songs that were sung all over Italy. Garibaldi had chanted one of his *Stornelli* when embarking from Montevideo in the spring of 1848 to take part in the Italian revolutions, of which these little ballads had become the rallying-cries; and if the voice of the people is in fact inspired, this poet could certainly have claimed the poet's long-lost honors of prophecy, for it was he who had shaped their utterance. He had ceased to assume any other sacred authority, though educated a priest, and at the time when he devoted the Palazzo di Venezia to the idea of united Italy, there was probably no person in Rome more unpriestly than he.

Dall' Ongaro was born in 1808, at an obscure hamlet in the district of Oderzo in the Friuli, of parents who were small freeholders. They removed with their son in his tenth year to Venice, and there he began his education for the Church in the Seminary of the Madonna della Salute. The tourist who desires to see the Titians and Tintorettos in the sacristy of this superb church, or to wonder at the cold splendors of the interior of the temple is sometimes obliged to seek admittance through the seminary, and it has doubtless happened to more than one of our readers to behold many little sedate old men in their teens, lounging up and down the cool, humid courts there, and trailing their black, priestly robes over the springing mould. The sun seldom strikes into that sad close, and when the boys form into long files, two by two, and march out for recreation, they have a torpid and melancholy aspect, upon which the daylight seems to smile in vain. They march solemnly up the long *Zattere*, with a pale young father at their head, and then march solemnly back again, sweet, genteel, pathetic spectres of childhood, and re-enter their common tomb, doubtless unenvied by the hungriest and raggedest *biricchino*,[1] who asks charity of them as they pass, and hoarsely whispers 'Raven!' when their leader is beyond hearing. There is no reason to suppose that a boy, born poet among the mountains, and full of the wild and free romance of his native scenes, could love the life led at the Seminary of the Salute, even though it included the study of literature and philosophy. From his childhood Dall' Ongaro had given proofs of his poetic gift, and the reverend ravens of the seminary were unconsciously hatching a bird as little like themselves as might be. Nevertheless, Dall' Ongaro left their school to enter the University of Padua as student of theology, and after graduating took orders, and went to Este, where he lived some time as a teacher of belles-lettres.

At Este his life was without scope, and he was restless and unhappy, full of ardent and patriotic impulses, and doubly restrained by his narrow field and his priestly vocation. In no long time he had trouble with the Bishop of Padua, and, abandoning Este, seems also to have abandoned the Church forever. The chief fruit of his sojourn in that quaint and ancient village was a poem entitled '*Il Venerdì Santo*,'[2] in which he celebrated some incidents of the life of Lord Byron, somewhat as Byron would have done. Dall' Ongaro's poems, however, confess the influence of the English poet less than those of other modern Italians, whom Byron infected so much more than his own nation, that it is still possible for them to speak of him as one of the greatest poets and as a generous man.

From Este, Dall' Ongaro went to Trieste, where he taught literature and philosophy, wrote for the theatre, and established a journal in which, for ten years, he labored to educate the people in his ideas of Italian unity and progress. That these did not coincide with the ideas of most Italian dreamers and politicians of the time, may be inferred from the fact that he began in 1846 a course of lectures on Dante, in which he combated the clerical tendencies of Gioberti and Balbo, and criticised the first acts of Pius IX. He had as profound doubt of Papal liberality as Nicolini, at a time when other patriots were fondly cherishing the hope of a united Italy under an Italian pontiff; and at Rome, two years later, he sought to direct popular feeling from the man to the end, in one of the earliest of his graceful *Stornelli*.

PIO NONO.

Pio Nono is a name, and not the man
  Who saws the air from yonder Bishop's seat;
Pio Nono is the offspring of our brain,
  The idol of our hearts, a vision sweet;
Pio Nono is a banner, a refrain,
  A name that sounds well sung upon the street.

Who calls, 'Long live Pio Nono!' means to call,
Long live our country, and good-will to all!
And country and good-will, these signify
That it is well for Italy to die;
But not to die for a vain dream or hope,
Not to die for a throne and for a Pope!

During these years at Trieste, however, Dall' Ongaro seems to have been also much occupied with pure literature, and to have given a great deal of study to the sources of national poetry, as he discovered them in the popular life and legends. He had been touched with the prevailing romanticism; he had written hymns like Manzoni, and, like Carrer, he sought to poetize the traditions and superstitions of his countrymen. He found a richer and deeper vein than the Venetian poet among his native hills and the neighboring mountains of Slavonia, but we cannot say that he wrought it to much better effect. The two volumes which he published in 1840 contain many ballads which are very graceful and musical, but which lack the fresh spirit of songs springing from the popular heart, while they also want the airy and delicate beauty of the modern German ballads. Among the best of them are two which Dall' Ongaro built up from mere lines and fragments of lines current among the people, as in these later years he has more successfully restored us two plays of Menander from the plots and a dozen verses of each. 'One may imitate,' he says, 'more or less fortunately, Manzoni, Byron, or any other poet, but not the simple inspirations of the people. And *The Pilgrim who comes from Rome* and the *Rosettina*, if one could have them complete as they once were, would probably make me blush for my elaborate variations.' But study which was so well directed, and yet so conscious of its limitations, could not but be of the greatest value; and Dall' Ongaro, no doubt, owes to it his gift of speaking more authentically for the popular heart than any other living poet. That which he has done since shows that he studied the people's thought and expression *con amore*, and in no vain sentiment of dilettanteism, or antiquarian research, or literary patronage.

It is not to be supposed that Dall' Ongaro's literary life had at this period an altogether objective tendency. In the volumes mentioned there is abundant evidence that he was of the same humor as all men of poetic genius must be at a certain time of life. Here are pretty verses of occasion, upon weddings and betrothals, such as people write in Italy; here are stanzas from albums, such as people used to write everywhere; here are didactic lines; here are bursts of mere sentiment and emotion. In the volume of *Fantasie*, published at Florence in 1866, Dall' Ongaro has collected some of the ballads from his early works, but has left out the more subjective effusions. Nevertheless, these are so pleasing of their kind, that we may give here at least one passionate little poem, and not wrong the author.

> If, with delight and love aglow,
>   Thou bendest thy brown eyes on me,
> They darken me to all I know,
>   To all that lives and breathes but thee.
>
> And if thou sufferest me to steal
>   Into my hand the silken skein

Of thy loose tresses, love, I feel
   A chill like death upon my brain.

And if to mine thou near'st thy face,
   My heart with its great bliss is rent;
I feel my troubled breathing cease,
   And in my rapture sink and faint.

Ah! if in that trance of delight
   My soul were rapt among the blest,
It could not be an instant's flight
   To heaven's glory from thy breast.

This is well, we say, in its way, for it is the poetry of the senses, and yet not coarse; but we must take something else that the poet has rejected, from his early volume, because it is in a more unusual spirit than the above-given, and because, under a fantastic name and in a fantastic form, the poet expresses the most tragic and pathetic interest of the life to which he was himself vowed.

THE SISTER OF THE MOON.

Shine, moon, ah shine! and let thy pensive light
   Be faithful unto me:
I have a sister in the lonely night
   When I commune with thee.

Alone and friendless in the world am I,
   Sorrow's forgotten maid,
Like some poor dove abandoned to die
   By her first love unwed.

Like some poor floweret in a desert land
   I pass my days alone;
In vain upon the air its leaves expand,
   In vain its sweets are blown.

No loving hand shall save it from the waste,
   And wear the lonely thing;
My heart shall throb upon no loving breast
   In my neglected spring.

That trouble which consumes my weary soul
   No cunning can relieve,

No wisdom understand the secret dole
　Of the sad sighs I heave.

My fond heart cherished once a hope, a vow,
　The leaf of autumn gales!
In convent gloom, a dim lamp burning low,
　My spirit lacks and fails.

I shall have prayers and hymns like some dead saint
　Painted upon a shrine,
But in love's blessed power to fall and faint,
　It never shall be mine.

Born to entwine my life with others, born
　To love and to be wed,
Apart from all I lead my life forlorn,
　Sorrow's forgotten maid.

Shine, moon, ah shine! and let thy tender light
　Be faithful unto me:
Speak to me of the life beyond the night
　I shall enjoy with thee.

It will here satisfy the strongest love of contrasts to turn from Dall'
Ongaro the poet to Dall' Ongaro the politician, and find him on his
feet, and making a speech at a public dinner given to Richard Cobden
at Trieste, in 1847. Cobden was then, as always, the advocate of free
trade, and Dall' Ongaro was then, as always, the advocate of free
government. He saw in the union of the Italians under a customs-
bond the hope of their political union, and in their emancipation
from oppressive imposts their final escape from yet more galling
oppression. He expressed something of this, and, though repeatedly
interrupted by the police, he succeeded in saying so much as to secure
his expulsion from Trieste.

Italy was already in a ferment, and insurrections were preparing
in Venice, Milan, Florence, and Rome; and Dall' Ongaro, consulting
with the Venetian leaders Manin and Tommaseo, retired to Tuscany,
and took part in the movements which wrung a constitution from the
Grand Duke, and preceded the flight of that cowardly and treacherous
prince. In December he went to Rome, where he joined himself with
the Venetian refugees and with other Italian patriots, like D'Azeglio
and Durando, who were striving to direct the popular mind toward
Italian unity. The following March he was, as we have seen, one of
the exiles who led the people against the Palazzo di Venezia. In the

mean time the insurrection of the glorious Five Days had taken place at Milan, and the Lombard cities, rising one after another, had driven out the Austrian garrisons. Dall' Ongaro went from Rome to Milan, and thence, by advice of the revolutionary leaders, to animate the defence against the Austrians in Friuli. One of his brothers was killed at Palmanuova, and another severely wounded. Treviso, whither he had retired, falling into the hands of the Germans, he went to Venice, then a republic under the presidency of Manin; and here he established a popular journal, which opposed the union of the struggling Republic with Piedmont under Carlo Alberto. Dall' Ongaro was finally expelled, and passed next to Ravenna, where he found Garibaldi, who had been banished by the Roman government, and was in doubt as to how he might employ his sword on behalf of his country. In those days the Pope's moderately liberal minister, Rossi, was stabbed, and Count Pompeo Campello, an old literary friend and acquaintance of Dall' Ongaro, was appointed minister of war. With Garibaldi's consent the poet proceeded to Rome, and used his influence to such effect that Garibaldi was authorized to raise a legion of volunteers, and was appointed general of those forces which took so glorious a part in the cause of Italian independence. Soon after, the Pope fled to Gaeta, and when the Republic was proclaimed, Dall' Ongaro and Garibaldi were chosen representatives of the people. Then followed events of which it is a pang keen as a personal grief to read: the malign force which has to-day done its worst to defeat the aspirations of a generous nation interposed then with fatal success. The troops of the French Republic marched upon Rome, and, after a defence more splendid and heroic than any victory, the city fell. The Pope returned to be that evil the world knows to his people, and all who loved Italy and freedom turned in exile from Rome. The cities of the Romagna, Tuscany, Lombardy, and Venetia had fallen again under the Pope, the Grand Duke, and the Austrians, and Dall' Ongaro took refuge in Switzerland.

Without presuming to say whether Dall' Ongaro has been mistaken in his political ideas, we may safely admit that he was no wiser a politician than Dante or Petrarch. He is an anti-Papist, as these were, and like these he has opposed an Italy of little principalities and little republics. But his dream has been, unlike theirs, of a great Italian democracy, and in 1848–49 he opposed the union of the Italian patriots under Carlo Alberto, because this would have tended to the monarchy which has since proven so fatally dependent upon France. It is to be supposed that many of his hopes were wild; but the schemes of the coldest diplomates are scarcely to be called wise. His projects may have been untenable and unstable; but they have not yet been tried, and in the mean time the most solemn treaties, established upon the faith of the firmest governments, have been repeatedly broken.

But it is not so much with Dall' Ongaro's political opinions that we have to do as with his poetry of the revolutionary period of 1848, as we find in it the little collection of lyrics which he calls *Stornelli*, or 'Starlings,' perhaps because of their simple and familiar character. These commemorate nearly all the interesting aspects of that epoch; and in their wit and enthusiasm and aspiration we feel the spirit of a race, at once the most intellectual and the most emotional in the world, whose poets write as passionately of politics as of love. Arnaud awards Dall' Ongaro the highest praise, and declares him 'the first to formulate in the common language of Italy patriotic songs which, current on the tongues of the people, should also remain the patrimony of the national literature. . . . In his popular songs,' continues this critic, 'Dall' Ongaro has given all that constitutes true, good, and—not the least merit—novel poetry. Metre and rhythm second the expression, imbue the thought with harmony, and develop its symmetry. . . . How enviable is that perspicuity which does not oblige you to re-read a single line to evolve therefrom the latent idea!' And we have no less to admire the perfect art which, never passing the intelligence of the people, is never ignoble in sentiment or idea, but always as refined as it is natural.

We do not know how we could better approach the readers whom we wish to win for our poet, than by first offering this lyric, written when, in 1847, the people of Leghorn rose in arms to repel a threatened invasion of the Austrians.

THE WOMAN OF LEGHORN.

Adieu, Livorno! adieu, paternal walls!
    Perchance I never shall behold you more!
On father's and mother's grave the shadow falls.
    My love has gone under our flag to war;
And I will follow him where fortune calls;
    I have had a rifle in my hands before.

The ball intended for my lover's breast,
Before he knows it, my heart shall arrest;
And over his dead comrade's visage he
Shall pitying stoop, and look whom it can be;

Then he shall see and know that it is I:
Poor boy! how bitterly my love shall cry!

The Italian editor of the *Stornelli* does not give the closing lines too great praise when he declares that 'they say more than all the lament of Tancred over Clorinda.' In this little flight of song, we pass over more tragedy than Messer Torquato could have dreamed in the conquest of many Jerusalems; for, after all, there is nothing so tragic as fact. The poem is full at once of the grand national impulse, and of purely personal and tender devotion. It is very human; and that fluttering, vehement purpose, thrilling and faltering in alternate lines, and breaking into a sob at last, is in every syllable the utterance of a woman's spirit and a woman's nature.

Quite as womanly, though entirely different, is this lament, which the poet attributes to his sister for their brother, who fell at Palmanuova, May 14, 1848.

THE SISTER.
(Palma, May 14, 1848.)

And he, my brother, to the fort had gone,
    And the grenade, it struck him in the breast;
He fought for liberty, and death he won,
    For country here, and found in heaven rest.

And now only to follow him I sigh;
A new desire has taken me to die,—
To follow him where is no enemy,
Where every one lives happy and is free.

All hope and purpose are gone from this woman's heart, for whom Italy died in her brother, and who has only these artless, half-bewildered words of regret to speak, and speaks them as if to some tender and sympathetic friend acquainted with all the history going before their abrupt beginning. We think it most pathetic and natural, also, that even in her grief and her aspiration for heaven, her words should have the tint of her time, and she should count freedom among the joys of eternity.

Quite as womanly again, and quite as different once more, is the lyric which the reader will better appreciate when we remind him how the Austrians massacred the unarmed people in Milan, in January, 1848, and how later, during the Five Days, they murdered their Italian prisoners, sparing neither sex nor age.[3]

THE LOMBARD WOMAN.
(Milan, January, 1848.)

Here, take these gaudy robes and put them by;
    I will go dress me black as widowhood;
I have seen blood run, I have heard the cry
    Of him that struck and him that vainly sued.
Henceforth no other ornament will I
    But on my breast a ribbon red as blood.

And when they ask what dyed the silk so red,
    I'll say, 'The life-blood of my brothers dead.'
And when they ask how it may cleanséd be,
    I'll say, 'O, not in river nor in sea;
Dishonor passes not in wave nor flood;
    My ribbon ye must wash in German blood.'

The repressed horror in the lines,

I have seen blood run, I have heard the cry
    Of him that struck and him that vainly sued,

is the sentiment of a picture that presents the scene to the reader's eye as this shuddering woman saw it; and the heart of woman's fierceness and hate is in that fragment of drama with which the brief poem closes. It is the history of an epoch. That epoch is now past, however; so long and so irrevocably past, that Dall' Ongaro comments in a note upon the poem: 'The word "German" is left as a key to the opinions of the time. Human brotherhood has been greatly promoted since 1848. German is now no longer synonymous with enemy. Italy has made peace with the peoples, and is leagued with them all against their common oppressors.'

We have still another of these songs, in which the heart of womanhood speaks, though this time with a voice of pride and happiness.

THE DECORATION.

My love looks well under his helmet's crest;
    He went to war, and did not let them see
His back, and so his wound is the breast:
    For one he got, he struck and gave them three.
When he came back, I loved him, hurt so, best;
    He married me and loves me tenderly.

> When he goes by, and people give him way,
> I thank God for my fortune every day;
> When he goes by he seems more grand and fair
> Than any crossed and ribboned cavalier:
> The cavalier grew up with his cross on,
> And I know how my darling's cross was won!

We think this unaffected, fresh, and good. The poem, like that of 'La Livornese'[4] and 'La Donna Lombarda,'[5] is a vivid picture: it is a liberated city, and the streets are filled with jubilant people; the first victorious combats have taken place, and it is a wounded hero who passes with his ribbon on his breast. As the fond crowd gives way to him, his young wife looks on him from her window with an exultant love, unshadowed by any possibility of harm;—

> Mi menò a moglie e mi vuol tanto bene![6]

This is country and freedom to her,—this is strength which despots cannot break,—this is joy to which defeat and ruin can never come nigh!

It might be any one of the sarcastic and quick-witted people talking politics in the streets of Rome in 1847, who sees the newly elected Senator—the head of the Roman municipality, and the legitimate mediator between Pope and people—as he passes, and speaks to him in these lines the dominant feeling of the moment:—

THE CARDINALS.

> O Senator of Rome! if true and well
>   You are reckoned honest, in the Vatican,
> Let it be yours His Holiness to tell,
>   There are many Cardinals, and not one man.
>
> They are made like lobsters, and, when they are dead,
> Like lobsters change their colors and turn red;
> And while they are living, with their backward gait
> Displace and tangle good Saint Peter's net.

An impulse of the time is strong again in the following *Stornello*,— a cry of reproach that seems to follow some recreant from a beleaguered camp of true comrades, and to utter the feeling of men who marched to battle through defection, and were strong chiefly in their just cause. It bears the date of that fatal hour when the king of Naples, after a brief show of liberality, recalled his troops from

Bologna, where they had been acting against Austria with the confederated forces of the other Italian states, and when every man lost to Italy was as an ebbing drop of her life's blood.

THE DESERTER.
(Bologna, May, 1848.)

Never did grain grow out of frozen earth;
   From the dead branch never did blossoms start:
If thou lovest not the land that gave thee birth,
   Within thy breast thou bear'st a frozen heart;
If thou lovest not this land of ancient worth,
   To love aught else, say, traitor, how thou art!

To thine own land thou couldst not faithful be,—
Woe to the woman that puts faith in thee!
To him that trusteth in the recreant, woe!
Never from frozen earth did harvest grow:
To her that trusteth a deserter, shame!
Out of the dead branch never blossom came.

And this song, so fine in its picturesque and its dramatic qualities, is not less true to the hope of the Venetians when they rose in 1848, and intrusted their destinies to Daniele Manin.

THE RING OF THE LAST DOGE.

I saw the widowed Lady of the Sea
   Crownéd with corals and sea-weed and shells,
That her long anguish and adversity
   Had seemed to drown in plays and festivals.

I said: 'Where is thine ancient fealty fled?—
Where is the ring with which Manin did wed
His bride?' With tearful visage she:
'An eagle with two beaks tore it from me.
Suddenly I arose, and how it came
I know not, but I heard my bridegroom's name.'
Poor widow! 't is not he. Yet he may bring—
Who knows?—back to the bride her long-lost ring.

The poor Venetians of that day dreamed that San Marco might live again, and the fineness and significance of the poem could not have been lost on the humblest in Venice, where all were quick to beauty and vividly remembered that the last Doge who wedded the sea was named, like the new President, Manin.

We think the *Stornelli* of the revolutionary period of 1848 have a peculiar value, because they embody, in forms of artistic perfection, the evanescent as well as the enduring qualities of popular feeling. They give us what had otherwise been lost, in the passing humor of the time. They do not celebrate the battles or the great political occurrences. If they deal with events at all, it is with events that express some belief or longing,—rather with what people hoped or dreamed than with what they did. They sing the Friulan volunteers, who bore the laurel instead of the olive during Holy Week, in token that the patriotic war had become a religion; they remind us that the first fruits of Italian longing for unity were the cannons sent to the Romans by the Genoese; they tell us that the tricolor was placed in the hand of the statue of Marcus Aurelius at the Capitol, to signify that Rome was no more, and that Italy was to be. But the *Stornelli* touch with most effect those yet more intimate ties between national and individual life that vibrate in the hearts of the Livornese and the Lombard woman, of the lover who sees his bride in the patriotic colors, of the maiden who will be a sister of charity that she may follow her lover through all perils, of the mother who names her new-born babe Costanza in the very hour of the Venetian Republic's fall. And we like the *Stornelli* all the better because they preserve the generous ardor of the time, even in its fondness and excess.

After the fall of Rome, Italy, as we have seen, was no better than a cage for birds of their note; and the poet did not long remain un-molested even in his Swiss retreat. In 1852 the Federal Council yielded to the instances of the Austrian government, and expelled Dall' Ongaro from the Republic. He retired with his sister and nephew to Brussels, where he resumed the lectures upon Dante, interrupted by his exile from Trieste in 1847, and thus supported his family. Three years later, he gained permission to enter France, and up to the spring-time of 1859 he remained in Paris, busying himself with literature, and watching events with all an exile's eagerness. The war with Austria broke out, and the poet seized the long-coveted oppor-tunity to return to Italy, whither he went as the correspondent of a French newspaper. On the conclusion of peace at Villafranca, this journal changed its tone, and being no longer in sympathy with Dall' Ongaro's opinions, he left it. Baron Ricasoli, to induce him to make Tuscany his home, instituted a chair of comparative dramatic literature in connection with the University of Pisa, and offered it to

Dall' Ongaro, whose wide general learning and special dramatic studies peculiarly qualified him to hold it. He therefore took up his abode at Florence, dedicating his main industry to a course of public lectures on ancient and modern dramatic literature, and writing those wonderful restorations of Menander's *Phasma* and *Treasure*, which have been heretofore noticed in an article on 'Recent Italian Comedy.'[7] He has written much on many subjects, and always beautifully. His prose has a peculiar delightfulness; and his poems in the Venetian dialect are among the most charming in that winning patois. A Boston publisher has reprinted one of the popular romances in which he represents the humble life of his native province, and his dramas have nearly all been translated into French and German.

As with Dall' Ongaro literature had always been but an instrument for the redemption of Italy, even after his appointment to a university professorship he did not forget this prime object. In nearly all that he has since written, he has kept the great aim of his life in view, and few of the events or hopes of that dreary period of suspense and abortive effort between the conclusion of peace at Villafranca and the acquisition of Venice have gone unsung by him. Indeed, some of his most characteristic *Stornelli* belong to this epoch. After Savoy and Nice had been betrayed to Napoleon, and while the Italians waited in angry suspicion for the next demand of their hated ally, which might be the surrender of the island of Sardinia or the sacrifice of the Genoese province, but which no one could guess in the impervious Napoleonic silence, our poet wrote:—

THE IMPERIAL EGG.

(Milan, 1862.)

Who knows what hidden devil it may be
   Under yon mute, grim bird that looks our way?—
Yon silent bird of evil omen,—he
   That, wanting peace, breathes discord and dismay.
Quick, quick, and change his egg, my Italy,
   Before there hatch from it some bird of prey,—

Before some beak of rapine be set free,
That, after the mountains, shall infest the sea;
Before some ravenous eaglet shall be sent
After our isles to gorge the continent,—
I'd rather a goose even from yon egg should come,—
If only of the breed that once saved Rome!

When, in 1859, by virtue of the popular vote, the Romagna ceased to be part of Saint Peter's patrimony, and became a province of the kingdom of Italy, the Pope is credibly reported to have turned, in one of his frequent bursts of anger, to a crucifix, with the words of the Psalm, 'Clamavi ad te, et non exaudisti me!'[8] 'So far,' says Dall' Ongaro, who relates this in a note to the following poem,—'so far history. The rest deserves confirmation.' And when the reader remembers how many reasons the poet had, as priest and patriot, to know and hate church-craft, and considers how different after all, is the Christ of church-craft from the Christ of the Gospels, we think he will forgive his seeming profanity for his actual wit.

THE PLEBISCITE.

When all Bologna rose and with one voice
   Chose Victor Emanuel her king and chief,
Mastai turned to Jesus on the cross:
   'I knock and knock,' he said, 'and you play deaf.'

And to his vicar Jesus Christ replies:
'Why, you ask me impossibilities!
Ask for a donkey that shall bend its knees,
Ask a Madonna that shall wink its eyes;
And if these things do honor to our part,
I will oblige you, and with all my heart.
But to reduce Romagna to thy reign,
And make its People become Herd again,
Is not so light a miracle as you'd make it;
I know of no one who could undertake it.'

The flight of the Grand Duke from Florence in 1859, and his conciliatory address to his late subjects after Villafranca, in which by fair promises he hoped to win them back to their allegiance; the union of Tuscany with the kingdom of Italy; the removal of the Austrian flags from Milan; Garibaldi's crusade in Sicily; the movement upon Rome in 1862; Aspromonte,—all these events, with the shifting phases of public feeling throughout that time, the alternate hopes and fears of the Italian nation, are celebrated in the later *Stornelli* of Dall' Ongaro. Since the last was written, Venice has fallen to Italy; but thicker clouds have gathered about the destiny of Rome, for within a month we have seen the failure—

   Ahi, quanto a dir qual' era è cosa dura![9]—

of Garibaldi's rash heroic enterprise. The great line of prose which unites us to Europe, and commonly bears us the prices of the markets and the gossip of the courts, thrilled with a touch of unwonted poetry the other day, when it reported the vanquished champion of humanity as looking 'old, haggard, and disappointed,' on his return from the rout at Monte Rotondo; and we fear that his long-tried friend and comrade could not have the heart to sing now as he sang in 1862, after the affair of Aspromonte:—

TO MY SONGS.

Fly, O my songs, to Varignano fly!
　Like some lost flock of swallows homeward flying,
And hail me Rome's Dictator, who there doth lie
　Broken with wounds, but conquered not, nor dying:
Bid him think on the April that is nigh,
　Month of the flowers and ventures fear-defying.

Or if it is not nigh, it soon shall come,
As shall the swallow to his last year's home,
As on its naked stem the rose shall burn,
As to the empty sky the stars return,
As hope comes back to hearts crushed by regret;—
Nay, say not this to his heart ne'er crushed yet!

We Americans, however, whose right and duty it is not to lose faith in the triumph of a just cause, can, even in its gloomiest hour, accept as prophecy these words from one who believes that liberty can triumph only through the submission of the Church to secular law, and the abolition of all her privileges:—

WILLING OR LOATH.

Willing or loath, the flames to heaven tend,
　Willing or loath, the waters downward flow,
Willing or loath, when lightning strokes descend,
　Crumbles the cliff, and the tower's crest sinks low;
Willing or loath, by the same laws that send
　Onward the earth and sun, the people go.

And thou, successor of Saint Peter, thou
Wilt stop the sun and turn us backward now?
Look thou to ruling Holy Church, for we
Willing or loath fulfil our destiny;

Willing or loath, in Rome at last we meet!
We will not perish at the mountain's feet.

We have already noted the more obvious merits of the *Stornelli*, and we need not greatly insist upon them now. Their defects are equally plain; one sees that their simplicity all but ceases to be a virtue at times, and that at times their feeling is too much intellectualized. Yet for all this we must recognize their excellence, and the skill as well as the truth of the poet. It is very notable with what directness he expresses his thought, and with what discretion he leaves it when expressed. The form is always most graceful, and the success with which dramatic, picturesque, and didactic qualities are blent, for a sole effect, in the brief compass of the poems, is not too highly praised in the epithet of novelty. Nothing is lost for the sake of attitude; the actor is absent from the most dramatic touches, the painter is not visible in lines which are each a picture, the teacher does not appear for the purpose of enforcing the moral. It is not the grandest poetry, but it is true feeling, admirable art.

NOTES

1 Street urchin.
2 Good Friday.
3 'Many foreigners,' says Emilio Dandolo, in his restrained and temperate history of *I Volontarii e Bersaglieri Lombardi*, 'have cast a doubt upon the incredible ferocity of the Austrians during the Five Days, and especially before evacuating the city. But, alas! the witnesses are too many to be doubted. A Croat was seen carrying a babe transfixed upon his bayonet. All know of those women's hands and ears found in the haversacks of the prisoners; of those twelve unhappy men burnt alive at Porta Tosa; of those nineteen buried in a lime-pit at the Castello, whose scorched bodies we found. I myself, ordered with a detachment, after the departure of the enemy, to examine the Castello and neighborhood, was horror-struck at the sight of a babe nailed to a post' [Howells's note].
4 'The Woman of Leghorn.'
5 'The Lombard Woman.'
6 This is line 6 of 'The Decoration,' *supra*.
7 *North American Review* for October, 1864 [Howells's note].
8 'I cried unto thee, and thou heardest me not!' From Psalm 120:1?
9 'Alas, how to say what it was is a hard thing!' Dante, *Inferno* i, 4.

4 Turgenev's *Dimitri Roudine*
1873

Review published in the *Atlantic Monthly*, September 1873.

Among Howells's indispensable resources and allies in Cambridge was Thomas Sergeant Perry, a tireless reader and novelistic polymath with whom Howells shared his early friendship with Henry James. Perry read 'everything,' especially fiction published in French or German. Perry was a weighty force for the newness, particularly the realistic; and one of Perry's great *coups* was to discover and present to the serious American literary community the work of Ivan Turgenev. As *Atlantic* editor Howells in effect presented Perry a career by appointing him chief reviewer for European fiction; but Howells himself reviewed three Turgenev novels: *Smoke* in August 1872, a pioneering date, and *Liza* and *Dimitri Roudine* the next year.

Howells had been moved and instructed by Björnson, but for a crucial decade and a half (1871–85) Turgenev became, he said, 'one of the profoundest literary passions of my life.' That passion affected the development of his fiction from *A Foregone Conclusion* through *The Rise of Silas Lapham*, but it more deeply influenced his thought and taste, and thence his criticism. Howells presents an ideal example of the truth that 'literary influence' is never an active force operating upon a passive subject. Much in Howells's *gestalt* had prepared him to seize with joy upon Turgenev and take great profit from him (rather, for instance, than from Flaubert). The great Russians became his men, Turgenev the earliest.

The nature of the light which shone from Turgenev upon Howells and his path he explained exactly in the last paragraph of this review. Turgenev as author is aloof, never intrusive, he is dramatic and impersonal in method. He presents us complex, half-resolved views of human reality so that 'we come finally to half-respectful compassion; and yet is this not the way it would be in life?' Indeed, is this unmoralized morality not more interesting than a fiction which knows, resolves, analyzes, and finally directs us how to conclude concerning everything? 'Meanwhile we are taught a merciful distrust of our own judgments. . . . It is of the kind of novel which can alone keep the art of fiction from being the weariness and derision of mature readers; and if it is most deeply melancholy, it is also as lenient and thoughtful as a just man's experience of men.' All quietly in tone, Howells was dead serious about every word, and the words were new to American literary comment.

Dimitri Roudine, which Messrs. Holt and Williams have reprinted from the excellent version published in *Every Saturday*, is mainly the study of one man's character, but a character so complex that there is little to ask of the author in the way of a story. In fact, Dimitri Roudine is himself sufficient plot; and the reader is occupied from the moment of his introduction with the skilful development of his various traits, to the exclusion of the other incidents and interests. The other persons of the fiction are of a kind which the reader of Turgénieff's stories may begin to classify in some degree, or at least find in a certain measure familiar. The women are, as usual, very well portrayed, especially the young girl Natalie, whose ignorant trust, courage, love, and adoration for Roudine, changing to doubt and scorn,—whose whole maidenly being,—are expressed in a few scenes and phrases. Her mother, Daria Michaëlovna, is also exceedingly well done. She is of an entirely different type, a woman of mind, as she supposes, with advanced ideas, but really full of the pride of caste, worldly, and slight of intellect, though not wanting in selfish shrewdness or a strong will. The reader ought to note with what delicacy, and yet with what force, Turgénieff indicates, in Alexandra Paulovna, a sweet, placid, self-contained maturity, alike different from the wild fragrance of Natalie's young girlhood and the artificial perfume of Daria's well-preserved middle life; though he could hardly fail to do this, for nothing is more observable in Turgénieff than his success in characterizing the different epochs of womanhood. Volinzoff's conscious intellectual inferiority to Natalie, and his simple, manly love for her are nearly all there is of him; Pigasoff, who peculated in office when younger and who in provincial retirement is a brutal censor of the follies of human nature, is rather a study than an actor in the drama which develops Roudine; and Leschnieff, who promises something in himself, and does really prove of firm and generous stuff, is after all hardly more than a relief and explanation of the principal person. It is he who expresses the first doubt of Roudine after that philosopher has made his appearance at Daria Michaëlovna's, crushing Pigasoff, bewildering and charming Natalie, mystifying Alexandra, and provoking Volinzoff. Leschnieff knew him in his student days, when filial love, friendship, and all real things were lost in his habit of eloquent phrasing; when Roudine was cruelly ungrateful and mean in fact, that he might be magnanimous in the abstract; and the shadow of this dark recollection Leschnieff casts upon Roudine's new friends. He does not wish him to marry Natalie, who, he sees, is fascinated with him; but after Roudine's miserable weakness ends their love and all the others despise him, then Leschnieff does justice to his elevation of ideas and purposes.

[Here follow about 800 quoted words.]

We almost forget, in following this tender yet keen analysis of a pathetic character, that there is really something of a story in the book. Roudine imagines that he loves Natalie, and he wins her brave, inexperienced heart; but when their love is prematurely discovered to her mother, and Natalie comes to him ready to fly with him, to be his at any cost, he is paralyzed at the thought of Daria's opposition. 'We must submit,' he says. The scene that follows, with Natalie's amazement, wounded faith, and rising contempt, and Roudine's shame and anguish, is terrible,—the one intensely dramatic passage in the book, and a masterpiece of literary art which we commend to all students and lovers of that art.

We are not quite sure whether we like or dislike the carefulness with which Roudine's whole character is kept from us, so that we pass from admiration to despite before we come finally to half-respectful compassion; and yet is this not the way it would be in life? Perhaps, also, if we fully understood him at first, his relations to the others would not so much interest us. But do we wholly understand him at last? This may be doubted, though in the mean time we are taught a merciful distrust of our own judgments, and we take Leschnieff's forgiving and remorseful attitude towards him. It may be safely surmised that this was the chief effect that Turgénieff desired to produce in us; certainly he treats the story involved in the portrayal of Roudine's character with almost contemptuous indifference, letting three epilogues limp in after the first rambling narrative has spent itself, and seeming to care for these only as they further reveal the hero's traits. But for all this looseness of construction, it is a very great novel,—as much greater than the novel of incident as *Hamlet* is greater than *Richard III*. It is of the kind of novel which can alone keep the art of fiction from being the weariness and derision of mature readers; and if it is most deeply melancholy, it is also as lenient and thoughtful as a just man's experience of men.

5 Mark Twain's
The Adventures of Tom Sawyer
1876

Review published in the *Atlantic Monthly*, May 1876.

No man but Howells could have been simultaneously the intimate and mentor of both Mark Twain and Henry James. Clemens stood for the Western side of Howells's life, James for its international side. Incapable of meeting, Clemens and James stood apart for more than forty years while Howells loved, admired, delighted in, counseled and served them both. If their separate geniuses now stand taller than his, his was broader than either of theirs.

Howells met the man he was to call 'the Lincoln of our literature' in 1869, when Clemens, 'with his crest of red hair, and the wide sweep of his flaming mustache,' called at the *Atlantic* office to thank the reviewer who had praised *The Innocents Abroad* for artistry, insight, and for good nature in its humor. A fine achievement of Howells as critic, if he had no other, would be the importance of his insistence to Clemens that he realize his potential to be a true artist, no mountebank. Before Howells reviewed *Tom Sawyer* he had persuaded Clemens to think of himself as a serious author, eliciting from him as *Atlantic* contributions first 'A True Story,' 1874, a wonderful achievement in positive realism. Then he coaxed Clemens into entering upon the matter of Mark Twain's greatness, with 'Old Times on the Mississippi,' 1875.

That work of Howells's as friendly editor became an intimate creative sort of criticism, a kind of imaginative magic by which Howells helped liberate an erstwhile 'funny man' from the chrysalis where he had been growing beautiful wings. In their mutual adventures with Tom Sawyer, Howells helped Clemens move toward still another stage of growth. Clemens had earlier progressed from the fine Negro character study of 'A True Story' into the Matter of the Mississippi and at least to the borders of Hannibal. Now by constant solicitation and support, even by labor repaid only in friendship, Howells coached Clemens into mastery of the Matter of Hannibal, a third essential step toward the *Adventures of Huckleberry Finn*.

Mr Howells of the *Atlantic* was able to perform two other sorts of critical service for Clemens by exploiting the weight of his own name and position. Both, interestingly, took for granted the power, the '*authority*,' as Clemens said, of Howells's critical word. Clemens felt safely backed in creative experimentation by Howells's eminence. It was while working on *Tom Sawyer* that he expressed his gratitude (and Mrs Clemens's) that Howells had declared him 'no mere buffoon' but authentically an artist: 'Yours is the recognized critical Court of Last Resort in this country,' he wrote in 1875; 'from its decision there is no appeal.' A month later Howells, having read (and edited) the manuscript of *Tom Sawyer*, declared it 'all exciting and splendid'—and volunteered casually to take care of its critical reception: 'Give me a hint when it's to be out, and I'll start the sheep to jumping in the right places.'[1]

The resultant review not only taught readers forever what to see in *Tom Sawyer*, it established the historical fact that, in train with Aldrich's *Story of a Bad Boy*, Clemens had invented a new genre for American literature, the 'boy-book' as Howells named it to Clemens, a genre to which Howells himself and Garland, Stephen Crane, William Allen White, Owen Johnson, Tarkington, and Sherwood Anderson were all to make important contributions. Howells spotted the evolution from *Tom Brown's Schooldays* through Aldrich to Clemens, identified the genre, named it, and wrote its classic description in his *Atlantic* review. In so doing he fulfilled his own requirements for taxonomical criticism.

Mr. Aldrich has studied the life of *A Bad Boy* as the pleasant reprobate led it in a quiet old New England town twenty-five or thirty years ago, where in spite of the natural outlawry of boyhood he was more or less part of a settled order of things, and was hemmed in, to some measure, by the traditions of an established civilization. Mr. Clemens, on the contrary, has taken the boy of the Southwest for the hero of his new book,[2] and has presented him with a fidelity to circumstance which loses no charm by being realistic in the highest degree, and which gives incomparably the best picture of life in that region as yet known to fiction. The town where Tom Sawyer was born and brought up is some such idle, shabby little Mississippi River town as Mr. Clemens has so well described in his piloting reminiscences, but Tom belongs to the better sort of people in it, and has been bred to fear God and dread the Sunday-school according to the strictest rite of the faiths that have characterized all the respectability of the West. His subjection in these respects does not so deeply affect his inherent tendencies but that he makes himself a beloved burden to the poor, tender-hearted old aunt who brings him up with his orphan brother and sister, and struggles vainly with his manifold sins, actual and imaginary. The limitations of his transgressions are nicely and artistically traced. He is mischievous, but not vicious: he is ready for almost any depredation that involves the danger and honor of adventure, but profanity he knows may provoke a thunderbolt upon the heart of the blasphemer, and he almost never swears; he resorts to any stratagem to keep out of school, but he is not a downright liar, except upon terms of after shame and remorse that make his falsehood bitter to him. He is cruel, as all children are, but chiefly because he is ignorant; he is not mean, but there are very definite bounds to his generosity; and his courage is the Indian sort, full of prudence and mindful of retreat as one of the conditions of prolonged hostilities. In a word, he is a boy, and merely and exactly an ordinary boy on the moral side. What makes him delightful to the reader is that on the imaginative side he is very much more and though every boy has wild and fantastic dreams, this boy cannot rest till he has somehow realized them. Till he has actually run off with two other boys in the character of buccaneer, and lived for a week on an island in the Mississippi, he has lived in vain; and this passage is but the prelude to more thrilling adventures, in which he finds hidden treasures, traces the bandits to their cave, and is himself lost in its recesses. The local material and the incidents with which his career is worked up are excellent, and throughout there is scrupulous regard for the boy's point of view in reference to his surroundings and himself, which shows how rapidly Mr. Clemens has grown as an artist. We do not remember anything in which this propriety is violated, and its preservation adds immensely to the grown-up reader's satisfaction in the amusing and exciting story. There is a boy's love-affair, but it is never treated otherwise than as a boy's love-affair. When the half-breed has murdered the young doctor, Tom and his friend, Huckleberry Finn, are really, in their boyish terror and superstition, going to let the poor old town-drunkard be hanged for the crime, till the terror of that becomes unendurable. The story is a wonderful study of the boy-mind, which inhabits a world quite distinct from that in which he is bodily present with his elders, and in this lies its great charm and its universality, for boy-nature, however human-nature varies, is the same everywhere.

The tale is very dramatically wrought, and the subordinate characters are treated with the same graphic force that sets Tom alive before us. The worthless vagabond, Huck Finn, is entirely delightful throughout, and in his promised reform his identity is respected: he will lead a decent life in order that he may one day be thought worthy to become a member of that gang of robbers which Tom is to organize.

Tom's aunt is excellent, with her kind heart's sorrow and secret pride in Tom; and so is his sister Mary, one of those good girls who are born to usefulness and charity and forbearance and unvarying rectitude. Many village people and local notables are introduced in well-conceived character; the whole little town lives in the reader's sense, with its religiousness, its lawlessness, its droll social distinctions, its civilization qualified by its slave-holding, and its traditions of the wilder West which has passed away. The picture will be instructive to those who have fancied the whole Southwest a sort of vast Pike County, and have not conceived of a sober and serious and orderly contrast to the sort of life that has come to represent the Southwest in literature. Mr. William M. Baker gives a notion of this in his stories, and Mr. Clemens has again enforced the fact here, in a book full of entertaining character, and of the greatest artistic sincerity.

Tom Brown and Tom Bailey are, among boys in books, alone deserving to be named with Tom Sawyer.

NOTES

1 Henry Nash Smith and William M. Gibson, eds., *Mark Twain – Howells Letters*, vol. 1, Harvard, 1960, 67–134.
2 *The Adventures of Tom Sawyer*. By MARK TWAIN. Hartford: American Publishing Co. 1876 [Howells's note].

6 'James's *Hawthorne*'
1880

Published in the *Atlantic Monthly*, February 1880.

As equally the friend and promoter of Henry James, Howells dealt with problems diametrically different from those presented by Clemens. In meaning and importance to Howells the two great friends were as opposite as they were in person irreconcilable, yet of course each complemented one side of Howells himself. Entitled to call himself the original Jacobite, the recipient of some of James's most significant letters, Howells spent almost fifty years struggling to encourage James's development, place his work, raise his literary income, advance his reputation, explain his achievement and, always and above all else, fight to make a dull and gainsaying generation recognize the greatness of the art of Henry James. As early as 1866 Howells delighted to discuss 'the true principles of literary art' with 'young Henry James,' and he pressed Fields to accept more fiction by 'Henry W. James.' As late as 1911 Howells strained to swing the leverage of his name and of his post as President of the American Academy of Arts and Letters to win that Nobel Prize for Henry James which was inexplicably never awarded. And on Howells's deathbed in 1920 he sat writing a last 'Easy Chair' and a last, eloquent justification of 'The American James,' not finished.

From the beginning James stood in relation to Howells in a number of respects the opposite of Clemens: younger, unknown, aesthetic to the point of preciosity, Europeanized, 'mod,' seriously theoretical. As James's career developed his reputation grew certain unpopular dimensions: he seemed snobbish, high-flown, anti-American, 'difficult.' Howells found himself with two genius friends on his critical hands, both members of the same literary generation, his own; both great artists, despite all differences, of the newness; both deserving of the highest recognition and requiring, though for opposite reasons, a critic's fighting help to secure it. Howells struggled to get the world to take Clemens seriously and to take James despite high seriousness.

Though Howells 'discovered' James and remained zealous to promote his name and interest, he was scrupulous not to appear to own him. The life-long colloquy between them often became a debate, and neither hesitated to score, politely of course, off his friend. One needs some background in the literary wars of the age to see that Howells's review effectively supports James's *Hawthorne* by simply ignoring their mutual opponents, the romantic and neo-romantic idealists and 'idealizers' who made Hawthorne their prophet in condemnation of the agnostic realists. James never wrote a more realistic (or embattled) piece of criticism than his *Hawthorne*, and Howells's allied strategy was to give him the palm without so much as mentioning the fight.

The Hawthorne issue upon which the friends divided overtly, crisply, no doubt rested upon the tension each felt within himself between native America and mighty Europe: James was a rather new and anxious expatriate, eager to justify his choice; Howells, repatriated, had cast his lot creative and critical with his turbulent *patria*. Therefore James, echoing Fenimore Cooper and Hawthorne himself, complained of the thin destitution of the artist's cultural aliment at home:

> one might enumerate the items of high civilisation, as it exists in other countries, which are absent from the texture of American life, until it should become a wonder to know what was left. No State, in the European sense of the word, and indeed barely a specific national name. No sovereign, no court, no personal loyalty, no aristocracy, no church, no clergy, no army, no diplomatic service, no country gentlemen, no palaces, no castles, nor manors, nor old country-houses, nor parsonages, nor thatched cottages, nor ivied ruins; no cathedrals, nor abbeys, nor little Norman churches; no great Universities nor public schools—no Oxford, nor Eton, nor Harrow; no literature, no novels, no museums, no pictures, no political society, no sporting class—no Epsom nor Ascot!

What indeed is left? asked Howells: 'we have the whole of human life remaining, and a social structure presenting the only fresh and novel opportunities left to fiction, opportunities manifold and inexhaustible.'

There was a degree of hyperbole in both statements; but that is likely to be so when a man feels the stress of ambivalence and feels compelled to bet his life on one value or the other. With all due allowance for personal and circumstantial differences, the James–Howells relation was as intimate, interesting, and determinative for both friends as the Twain–Howells relation. We shall not comprehend its full range or significance until somebody publishes a Jamesian equivalent to the admirable *Mark Twain–Howells Letters*, a sorely-needed project one fears is blocked by the obstinate monolatry of Professor Leon Edel, the great biographer of James.

Mr. James's book on Hawthorne,[1] in Morley's English Men of Letters series, merits far closer examination and carefuller notice than we can give it here, alike for the interest of its subject, the peculiarity of its point of view, and the charm and distinction of its literature. An

American author writing of an American author for an English public incurs risks with his fellow-countrymen which Mr. James must have faced, and is much more likely to possess the foreigner whom he addresses with a clear idea of our conditions than to please the civilization whose portrait is taken. Forty-six, fifty, sixty-four, are not dates so remote, nor are Salem and Concord societies so extinct, that the people of those periods and places can be safely described as provincial, not once, but a dozen times; and we foresee, without any very powerful prophetic lens, that Mr. James will be in some quarters promptly attainted of high treason. For ourselves, we will be content with saying that the provinciality strikes us as somewhat over-insisted upon, and that, speaking from the point of not being at all provincial ourselves, we think the epithet is sometimes mistaken. If it is not provincial for an Englishman to be English, or a Frenchman French, then it is not so for an American to be American; and if Hawthorne was 'exquisitely provincial,' one had better take one's chance of universality with him than with almost any Londoner or Parisian of his time. Provinciality, we understand it, is a thing of the mind or the soul; but if it is a thing of the experiences, then that is another matter, and there is no quarrel. Hawthorne undoubtedly saw less of the world in New England than one sees in Europe, but he was no cockney, as Europeans are apt to be.

At the same time we must not be thought to deny the value and delightfulness of those chapters on Salem and Brook Farm and Concord. They are not very close in description, and the places seem deliciously divined rather than studied. But where they are used unjustly, there will doubtless be abundant defense; and if Salem or Brook Farm be mute, the welkin will probably respond to the cries of certain critics who lie in wait to make life sorrowful to any one dealing lightly with the memory of Thoreau or the presence of the poet Channing. What will happen to a writer who says of the former that he was 'worse than provincial, he was parochial,' and of the latter that he resembled the former in 'having produced literary compositions more esteemed by the few than by the many,' we wait with the patience and security of a spectator at an *auto da fé*, to see. But even an unimbattled outsider may suggest that the essential large-mindedness of Concord, as expressed in literature, is not sufficiently recognized, although it is thoroughly felt. The treatment of the culture foible and of the colorless aesthetic joys, the attribution of 'a great deal of Concord five and thirty years ago' to the remark of a visitor of Hawthorne that Margaret Fuller 'had risen perceptibly into a higher state of being since their last meeting,' are exquisite,—too exquisite, we fear, for the sense of most Englishmen, and not too fine only for the rarefied local consciousness which they may sting. Emerson is indeed devoutly and amply honored, and there is something particularly sweet and tender in the characterization of such surviving Brook Farmers as the author remembers to have met; but even in speaking of Emerson, Mr. James has the real misfortune to call his grand poem for the dedication of the monument to Concord Fight a 'little hymn.' It is little as Milton's sonnet on Shakespeare is little.

We think, too, that in his conscience against brag and *chauvinism* Mr. James puts too slight a value upon some of Hawthorne's work. It is not enough to say of a book so wholly unexampled and unrivaled as *The Scarlet Letter* that it was 'the finest piece of imaginative writing put forth in' America; as if it had its parallel in any literature. When he comes to speak of the romances in detail, he repairs this defect of estimation in some degree; but here again his strictures seem somewhat mistaken. No one better than Mr. James knows the radical difference between a romance and a novel, but he speaks now of Hawthorne's novels, and now of his romances, throughout, as if the terms were convertible; whereas the romance and the novel are as distinct as the poem and the novel. Mr. James excepts to the people in *The Scarlet Letter*, because they are rather types than persons, rather conditions of the mind than characters; as if it were not almost precisely the business of the romance to deal with types and mental conditions. Hawthorne's fictions being always and essentially, in conception and performance, romances, and not novels, something of all Mr. James's special criticism is invalidated by the confusion which, for some reason not made clear, he permits himself. Nevertheless, his analysis of the several books and of the shorter tales is most interesting; and though we should ourselves place *The Blithedale Romance* before *The House of the Seven Gables*, and should rank it much higher than Mr. James seems to do, we find ourselves consenting oftener than dissenting as we read his judgments. An admirably clear and just piece of criticism, we think, is that in which he pronounces upon the slighter and cheaper *motif* of *Septimius Felton*. But here there are not grounds for final sentence; it is possible, if that book had received the author's last touches, it might have been, after all, a playful and gentle piece of irony rather than a tragedy.

What gives us entire satisfaction, however, is Mr. James's characterization, or illustration, of Hawthorne's own nature. He finds him an innocent, affectionate heart, extremely domestic, a life of definite, high purposes singularly unbaffled, and an 'unperplexed intellect.' The black problem of evil, with which his Puritan ancestors wrestled concretely, in groans and despair, and which darkens with its portentous shadow nearly everything that Hawthorne wrote, has become his literary material; or, in Mr. James's finer and more luminous phrase, he 'transmutes this heavy moral burden into the very substance of the imagination.' This strikes us as beautifully reasonable and true, and we will not cloud it with comment of ours. But satisfactorily as Mr. James declares Hawthorne's personality in large, we do not find him sufficient as to minor details and facts. His defect, or his error, appears oftenest in his discussion of the note-books, where he makes plain to himself the simple, domestic, democratic qualities in Hawthorne, and yet maintains that he sets down slight and little aspects of nature because his world is small and vacant. Hawthorne noted these because he loved them, and as a great painter, however full and vast his world is, continues to jot down whatever strikes him as picturesque and characteristic. The disposition to allege this inadequate reason comes partly from that confusion of the novelist's and the romancer's work of which we have spoken, and partly from a theory, boldly propounded, that it needs a long history and 'a complex social machinery to set a writer in motion.' Hawthorne himself shared, or seemed to share, this illusion, and wrote *The Marble Faun*, so inferior, with its foreign scene, to the New England romances, to prove the absurdity of it. As a romancer, the twelve years of boyhood which he spent in the wild solitudes of Maine were probably of greater advantage to him than if they had been passed at Eton and Oxford. At least, until some other civilization has produced a romantic genius at all comparable to his, we must believe this. After leaving out all those novelistic 'properties,' as sovereigns, courts, aristocracy, gentry, castles, cottages, cathedrals, abbeys, universities, museums, political class, Epsoms, and Ascots, by the absence of which Mr. James suggests our poverty to the English conception, we have the whole of human life remaining, and a social structure presenting the only fresh and novel opportunities left to fiction, opportunities manifold and inexhaustible. No man would have known less what to do with that dreary and worn-out paraphernalia than Hawthorne.

We can only speak of the excellent comment upon Hawthorne's *Old Home*, and the skillful and manly way in which Mr. James treats of that delicate subject to his English audience. Skillful and manly the whole book is,—a miracle of tact and of self-respect, which the author need not fear to trust to the best of either of his publics. There is nothing to regret in the attitude of the book; and its literature is always a high pleasure, scarcely marred by some evidences of hurry, and such *writerish* passages as that in which *sin* is spoken of as 'this baleful substantive with its attendant adjective.'

It is a delightful and excellent essay, refined and delicate in perception, generous in feeling, and a worthy study of the unique romancer whom its closing words present with justice so subtle and expression so rich:—

He was a beautiful, natural, original genius, and his life had been singularly exempt from worldly preoccupations and vulgar efforts. It had been as pure, as simple, as unsophisticated as his work. He had lived primarily in his domestic affections, which were of the tenderest kind; and then—without eagerness, without pretension, but with a great deal of quiet devotion—in his charming art. His work will remain; it is too original and exquisite to pass away; among the men of imagination he will always have his niche. No one has had just that vision of life, and no one has had a literary form that more successfully expressed his vision. He was not a moralist, and he was not simply a poet. The moralists are weightier, denser, richer, in a sense; the poets are more purely inconclusive and irresponsible. He combined in a singular degree the spontaneity of the imagination with a haunting care for moral problems. Man's conscience was his theme, but he saw it in the light of a creative fancy which added, out of its own substance, an interest, and, I may almost say, an importance.

NOTE

1 *Hawthorne.* [Morley's English Men of Letters.] By HENRY JAMES, JR. London: Macmillan & Co. New York: Harper and Brothers. 1880 [Howells's note].

Realism: war declared, 1881–6

The step Howells took in 1881 was bold in the premises. He abandoned the best literary 'basis' in the country and struck out, seeking to better his art, into territory not safely charted for an American career. He resigned his editorship of the *Atlantic Monthly*. The ominous premises were that nobody had yet proved that one could live entirely upon his pen, his creativity, in the United States. Howells had explained to his father from Venice exactly what Henry Clapp of the *Saturday Press* reiterated in 1865: to get along you had to stand upon 'a basis,' like editorship, which paid a weekly salary good enough to sustain author and family while creative work was done around the edges. Not only prestige, unparalleled contacts, an almost automatic market for literary production, a perfect tie-in with a book publisher and an ideal 'basis,' the *Atlantic* had provided almost automatic critical authority. Since Howells left it to devote mature energies to fiction, he wrote little criticism during the ensuing half decade. But of the few prime pieces he did write, one affected the course of literary criticism in both Britain and the United States.

Throughout his critical life, Howells insisted that American literature was 'a condition of English literature,' though he thought the time near at hand when the British author might look to the American for a model. Therefore he felt a sort of tender indignation, as in a lovers' quarrel, when he saw that leadership in the art of fiction had passed at mid-century to the Continent. Looking back from the occasion of the national celebration of his seventy-fifth birthday in 1912, Howells owned that in poetry Britain had kept the ascendancy; but not in fiction. Having acknowledged the fictional primacy of France, he declared:

> There are many kinds of art, but there is only one best kind. . . . Look about you, I say, not only in America, but in England, and you will see that . . . the English, too, have come to the right faith in their latest and greatest work. But we came to this faith first because we had opener minds than the English, and because we brought a willingness to learn of those masters who could teach, because we were somehow instinctively continental. Since then a world of continental art has offered itself to us. Masterpieces have come to us from everywhere—from Norway, from

57

Russia, from Poland, from Spain, from Italy, from Portugal. . . . Our fiction so far as it really exists is of the European and not the English make and the newer English fiction, so far as it really exists, is not of the English, but of the European make, the American make.

British cultural lag in the novel Howells blamed upon a benighted criticism—of the sort that drove Thomas Hardy away from fiction and jailed Henry Richard Vizetelly for publishing *La Terre*. Howells knew that the realist in America ran risks, and looking backward from 1912 he recognized that his own head had rested on the block in 1887-8. But in 1882 he knew only that a violent aesthetic war raged in Paris over the newness—realism in fiction, impressionism in painting. He had no reason then to suppose that what appeared to him to be one among a set of rather casual and promotional articles would make him the prime target in a bitter international quarrel and plunge him for thirty years to come into the Realism War.

It all started innocently with the coincidence of Howells's resignation from the *Atlantic*—so he could refresh his imagination by European residence, especially in Italy; so he could devote full time to fiction—with the conversion of *Scribner's Monthly* into the *Century* under the dynamic leadership of publisher Roswell Smith and (with Holland's death in the midst of the changeover) editor Richard Watson Gilder. The *Century* meant to be and became an international journal. During its first year it featured Matthew Arnold, Thomas Bewick, Robert Browning, Disraeli, Lamb, Newman, F. W. Robertson, Dante Gabriel Rossetti, and Scott, among others. It published Lord Bryce, Carlyle, Mary Cowden-Clarke, Dobson, Gosse, Andrew Lang, F. W. H. Myers, and C. Kegan Paul. In self-gratulation at the end of his first year Gilder bragged of 'the astonishing growth' of his circulation in Great Britain.

Gilder believed, however, that success at home and abroad depended upon holding fast to a 'genuine American quality,' and another of his policies had been expressed in a series of features on American authors: Holland in December 1881 and, progressively through 1882, Cable, Howells (by Perry), Lowell, Thoreau, and Twain (by Howells).

7 'Henry James, Jr.'
1882

Published in the *Century Magazine*, November 1882.

Howells really had no reason to suppose that when he told the obvious truth about James in the first issue of *Century*'s second year, November 1882, it would plunge him into acrimony. He could not know that, at the mediocre levels of British literary journalism, there was a growing determination to ambush the American upstarts.

I

Something would seem to have been darkening Anglo-American cultural relations at the end of 1882, for in retrospect Howells might, had he looked back, have seen that there were storm signals flying. On 26 November he wrote from Switzerland to congratulate Charles Dudley Warner on the essay 'England' which had also appeared in the November *Century*:

> I dare say you have seen how the *Saturday Review* abused it—and how vulgarly and ineffectually. The English are so thin-skinned that they cannot bear a word from us, and yet they produce philosophers, like Matthew Arnold, who without ever having been in America, lecture us on America, and like Spencer who having passed two months of insomnia among us, inform us that republicanism is a failure. Suppose one of us came to England and got himself interviewed so that he could pronounce monarchy a failure!

Whatever the *Saturday Review* was and whether Howells realized his mood or not, it could hardly be denied that he was feeling a bit pugnacious.

Himself an old newspaper man, Howells never inclined to take the press seriously; but even before he wrote Warner he was aware of American papers kicking up a fuss about his James article. And Edmund Gosse, an English literary friend who appears to have been on the Scribner pay-roll, had given him a foretaste of what was to be the extraordinary English reaction to his having dared to say what anyone would now agree to: 'The art of fiction has, in fact, become a finer art in our day than it was with Dickens and Thackeray'; and its 'chief exemplar' is James.

59

On 8 November Gosse wrote, 'So you have demolished poor old Dickens and Thackeray, have you?' and concluded with a postscript:

> MOTTO FOR THE AMERICAN CRITIC
> Ho! the old school! Thackeray, Dickens!
> Throw them out to feed the chickens.—
> Ho! the new school! James and ——
> Lay the flattery on with trowels.
> (Doggerel by a candid friend.)

As it happened, Howells never answered that letter directly, for he had a letter in the mails which crossed with Gosse's and Gosse wrote, less aggressively, on 14 November:

> I think, to speak of the matter quite soberly, that it is our tendency to overrate these writers from national partiality, just as it is your tendency to underrate them for the same reason. . . . I think I shall always do battle with you on your favorite literary stand-point, that the intellectual product of a democracy must be finer than that of a monarchy. I am sure the inmost reason of your dislike to Dickens and Thackeray is that they flourished in a corrupt and pestilent monarchy.

Howells's answer on 16 November suggests a degree of genuine astonishment. He and James have hardly enjoyed trowels full of praise, even from American critics, but 'rather shovels and pitchforks full of blame.' He had thought himself a great admirer of Dickens and Thackeray; and he hoped Gosse could really not 'think me so pitiful as to judge men's art by their political opinions or conditions: if that were the case what should I have to say of Shakespeare or Cervantes, whom I quite prefer to Milton or Landor?' Would Gosse be so kind as to send him the November *Century* 'so I can see what I have been saying of Dickens and Thackeray.' But, as Gosse probably knew, it was too late. At both *Blackwood's* and the *London Quarterly Review* they had rods in pickle for Howells, and in the January 1883 numbers of both reviews the rods sprang out whistling.

II

The early numbers of *The Wellesley Index to Victorian Periodicals, 1824-1900* identify for us the authors who poisoned Howells's relations with Britain and her critics for twenty years. The *Blackwood* article, 'American Literature in England,' was written by Mrs Oliphant; the *Quarterly Review* piece, 'American Novels,' came from Louis John Jennings. It was, as Howells always insisted, a pity that the law of critical anonymity still reigned: how was he to know that his masked attackers were critically insignificant? Mrs Oliphant solicited her job with stated malice, and there is nothing in 'American Novels' to suggest that Jennings felt otherwise.

Both pursued much the same logic as Gosse: it was insufferably cheeky for Howells to cry down the sainted Dickens and Thackeray; it was shocking in him to exalt James; indeed, in praising James he was really glorifying himself; there was no truth in him; these 'Jacobs of literature' had been treated too hospitably, courteously, generously in Britain and it was time to put them in their places. The *Century* crowd were naught but a 'select circle of *puffistes littéraires*,' said Jennings; and Mrs Oliphant settled all sorts of matters by remarking that, 'When a writer of fiction commits himself so terribly as to allege that the art of which he is a professor is finer than the art of Thackeray, the punishment for which he prepares himself is so prodigious that it becomes ridiculous.' She said that she felt it would be too cruel to explain.

The British and the American press, being in the business of selling papers, reprinted, quoted, solicited reactions, cried Howells up on Monday and down on Tuesday, and complained bitterly on Wednesday at the vulgarity of the controversy. The din kept up for a decade. And inevitably the battle involved minds more formidable than those of Jennings or Oliphant. As George Pellew, Howells's brilliant young friend, observed in 1888, 'For a long time a wordy war has raged in the magazines and the newspapers between so-called realists and romanticists. . . . The ground is strewn with dead and dying reputations.' Pellew saw Howells ranged against Saintsbury, Symonds, Lang, and Stevenson—and hastened to Howells's side. 'In the beginning of the century,' Pellew concluded, 'the influence of heredity and the dependence of the individual character upon the social environment were not understood. An honest return, therefore, to the point of view of the early romanticists is now impossible. . . . Human sympathy has broadened, society has become more democratic; a scientific study of history has shown the interdependence of all men, the comparative unimportance of exceptional men, and the all-importance of those commonplace individuals who form the mass of a people.'[1] On that ground the realist stood and fought.

There was no reason why Howells should have been amused at being misrepresented and damned for what he had not said by critics who were either incapable of understanding or unwilling to understand him. The best gauge of his feelings was to register in his 'Editor's Study' counter-attacks on British criticism, the most overt of which appeared in October 1886. Commenting on George Parsons Lathrop's introduction to a poetic anthology, Howells noticed that Lathrop had dared suggest that even Shakespeare sometimes nodded, quoted Lathrop to that effect, then exclaimed in tones of mock panic:

It is we who have italicized those last terrible words.

Does Mr. Lathrop perhaps remember how a few years ago the British Isles were shaken to their foundations, and their literary dependency here quaked.

'Fron one to the other sea,'

and all the dead conventionalities rose to a sitting posture in their graves with horror, because someone casually said that the 'mannerism of Dickens and the confidential attitude of Thackeray would not now be tolerated,' fiction having become 'a finer art than it was in their day'? Has Mr. Lathrop forgotten that awful moment? Are we to have that day of wrath all over again? Mr. Lathrop is a poet, and at times a very charming one: does he realize that he has placed himself in a position to be asked whether he thinks he writes greater poetry than Shakespeare? Is he aware that to many worthy persons he will actually seem to have said so?

Its former occupant might well take pleasure in stepping out of the pillory of which Mr. Lathrop seems emulous, and in turning to heave the first half-brick at him. He is young, and has his best work before him, and brick-bats will do him good, if he keeps on speaking the truth and saying things which, if said on any other subject, would seem the stalest truisms. The world moves—this terrestrial ball—that was settled by science, which knows; the aesthetic world does not move— that was settled by taste, which does not need to know.

Ironies and all other jokes aside, however, these things mattered and Howells knew why he had to fight and take the consequences. As Carl Van Doren said, 'any serious study in the intellectual and spiritual history of America discovers more and more lines converging to the controversies of the decade from 1880 to 1890 when Howells's was the most eloquent voice.'[2]

III

At the risk of too much multiplying commentary, one further consideration should be advanced in connection with this pivotal 'Henry James, Jr.' British critics were not wrong in detecting a certain national hostility in Howells. The truth, as the best of them saw, was that Howells felt an almost classically Freudian ambivalence towards Britain. He loved and hated it simultaneously and with passion. He adhered to a definite Anglophilo-phobia, and of course his emotions played back and forth between the poles.

I do not think that his attitudes and their consequences for him and for many others have been adequately studied, and it cannot be done here. But I think it useful to outline at least the major circumstances. The roots of ambivalence grew in Howells's pluralism of background, typically American but peculiar in its particularity. His immigrant grandfather and father brought with the name the Cymric grudge. Beginning Quakers, the family coped with difficulty on the frontier with the patriotic passions of the American war against Britain of 1812–14. Unstable in the new country and on the Ohio frontier, the Howellses experimented in religions and politics until they came out on balance quite radical. Howells's paternal grandfather became an abolitionist and a Millerite, his father a radical deist and demo-crat who turned Swedenborgian, Free-Soil, Utopian, abolitionist, and original, radical Republican. Howells's mother's people were Indian-fighting Pennsylvania Dutch (Docks) and Irish (Deans). None of these factors inclined an American boy to Anglophilia.

On the other hand, the poets adored at the hearth-side were British. Like every literate American, Howells lived much of his imaginative life in that Britain of the mind which Americans know differently but deeply. Among his 'literary passions' he recorded successively Goldsmith, Scott, Pope, Ossian, Shakespeare, Dickens, Wordsworth, Chaucer, Macaulay, Thackeray, Tennyson, De Quincey, George Eliot, Charles Reade, Trollope, and Hardy. And he knew them well, from repeated readings which gave him a fund of recognition, reference, and recall. As he tried to explain, from the midst of the battle, to his friend Brander Matthews,

> Long before other critics were 'toiling over the problems in college classrooms,' which I have approached in my dotage, I had read every line of Thackeray, and most of him a dozen times; I know him *au fond*, and whether I speak rightly or not, I speak of what I know. Trollope is incomparably the finer and truer artist, and will be so held in the final accounting. He was to me a thoroughly hateful person, at the same time.

And that brings us to the second point. Regardless of whose fault it was, Howells's personal experience of England and the English remained equivocal for much of forty years. To go to England for the first time in 1861 was like visiting a land of dreams, but he found English folk gloating and chuckling over his country's woe in Civil War and eager to impress their sentiments on a young representative of the Union government. After the war he had mixed luck in England on his way home. Carrying a letter of introduction to Anthony Trollope in hopes of help with a publisher (the sort of help to the young for which Howells himself would become famous), he was made to feel the sting of a great man's contempt—and got no help. Yet he found a half-publisher for *Venetian Life*, Trübner; and his eventual British publisher, David Douglas of Edinburgh, became the dearest, most cherished of friends.

Inevitably, as his career grew, Howells won English friends and lovers. But Gosse became a problem. The record now open shows that Gosse, who courted Howells furiously, was often privately hostile; and it is not likely that Howells remained ignorant of this. It was bad luck that Stevenson, so close to James, chose to take arbitrary offence at his own mis-reading of *A Modern Instance*. The whole episode about 'Henry James, Jr.' was worse luck. Still another sort of ill fate rose from a matter of timing. In decades during which Björnson, Taine, Turgenev, Palacio Valdés, and Tolstoi variously sent him messages of admiration and alliance, the fleering voices of Oliphant, Jennings, and Andrew Lang seemed to speak for English opinion.

Only after the turn of the century did relations improve. Then Howells heard from the British readers who loved his work. He went to England with plans to write travel books, and Oxford took advantage of the opportunity to present him an honorary degree at the Encaenia of 1904. That year he heard the gratitude of George Otto Trevelyan 'for the enormous number of hours of keen and unmixed delight which I owe to you.' The next year an anonymous 'bibliographer and ex-reviewer' on colonial sick-leave wrote to bless him for 'alleviating terrible days with the critic's imperishable delight in exquisite prose vitalized by the purest humanitarianism . . . full of the spirit of the Christ, its perception, its sympathy, its delicacy.' Of course Howells was not conquered, but he was reconciled, the war was over. *London Films*, 1906, *Certain Delightful English Towns*, 1906, and *Seven English Cities*, 1909, rank, all together, with *English Traits* and *Our Old Home* and are, if anything, rather more sympathetic towards England, rather more strikingly critical of the United States.

The events of Mr. James's life—as we agree to understand events—may be told in a very few words. His race is Irish on his father's side and Scotch on his mother's, to which mingled strains the generalizer may attribute, if he likes, that union of vivid expression and dispassionate analysis which has characterized his work from the first. There are none of those early struggles with poverty, which render the lives of so many distinguished Americans monotonous reading, to record in his case: the cabin hearth-fire did not light him to the youthful pursuit of literature; he had from the start all those advantages which, when they go too far, become limitations.

He was born in New York city in the year 1843, and his first lessons in life and letters were the best which the metropolis—so small in the perspective diminishing to that date—could afford. In his twelfth year his family went abroad, and after some stay in England made a long sojourn in France and Switzerland. They returned to America in 1860, placing themselves at Newport, and for a year or two Mr. James was at the Harvard Law School, where, perhaps, he did not study a great deal of law. His father removed from Newport to Cambridge in 1866, and there Mr. James remained till he went abroad, three years later, for the residence in England and Italy which, with infrequent visits home, has continued ever since.

It was during these three years of his Cambridge life that I became acquainted with his work. He had already printed a tale—'The

Story of a Year'—in the *Atlantic Monthly*, when I was asked to be
Mr. Fields's assistant in the management, and it was my fortune
to read Mr. James's second contribution in manuscript. 'Would you
take it?' asked my chief. 'Yes, and all the stories you can get from the
writer.' One is much securer of one's judgment at twenty-nine than,
say, at forty-five; but if this was a mistake of mine I am not yet old
enough to regret it. The story was called 'Poor Richard,' and it dealt
with the conscience of a man very much in love with a woman who
loved his rival. He told this rival a lie, which sent him away to his
death on the field,—in that day nearly every fictitious personage had
something to do with the war,—but Poor Richard's lie did not win
him his love. It still seems to me that the situation was strongly and
finely felt. One's pity went, as it should, with the liar; but the whole
story had a pathos which lingers in my mind equally with a sense of
the new literary qualities which gave me such delight in it. I admired,
as we must in all that Mr. James has written, the finished workmanship in which there is no loss of vigor; the luminous and uncommon
use of words, the originality of phrase, the whole clear and beautiful
style, which I confess I weakly liked the better for the occasional
gallicisms remaining from an inveterate habit of French. Those who
know the writings of Mr. Henry James will recognize the inherited
felicity of diction which is so striking in the writings of Mr. Henry
James, Jr. The son's diction is not so racy as the father's; it lacks its
daring, but it is as fortunate and graphic; and I cannot give it greater
praise than this, though it has, when he will, a splendor and state
which is wholly its own.

Mr. James is now so universally recognized that I shall seem to be
making an unwarrantable claim when I express my belief that the
popularity of his stories was once largely confined to Mr. Fields's
assistant. They had characteristics which forbade any editor to refuse
them; and there are no anecdotes of thrice-rejected manuscripts
finally printed to tell of him; his work was at once successful with all
the magazines. But with the readers of *The Atlantic*, of *Harper's*, of
Lippincott's, of *The Galaxy*, of *The Century*, it was another affair. The
flavor was so strange, that, with rare exceptions, they had to 'learn to
like' it. Probably few writers have in the same degree compelled
the liking of their readers. He was reluctantly accepted, partly through
a mistake as to his attitude—through the confusion of his point of
view with his private opinion—in the reader's mind. This confusion
caused the tears of rage which bedewed our continent in behalf of the
'average American girl' supposed to be satirized in Daisy Miller, and

prevented the perception of the fact that, so far as the average American girl was studied at all in Daisy Miller, her indestructible innocence, her invulnerable new-worldliness, had never been so delicately appreciated. It was so plain that Mr. James disliked her vulgar conditions, that the very people to whom he revealed her essential sweetness and light were furious that he should have seemed not to see what existed through him. In other words, they would have liked him better if he had been a worse artist—if he had been a little more confidential.

But that artistic impartiality which puzzled so many in the treatment of Daisy Miller is one of the qualities most valuable in the eyes of those who care how things are done, and I am not sure that it is not Mr. James's most characteristic quality. As 'frost performs the effect of fire,' this impartiality comes at last to the same result as sympathy. We may be quite sure that Mr. James does not like the peculiar phase of our civilization typified in Henrietta Stackpole; but he treats her with such exquisite justice that he lets *us* like her. It is an extreme case, but I confidently allege it in proof.

His impartiality is part of the reserve with which he works in most respects, and which at first glance makes us say that he is wanting in humor. But I feel pretty certain that Mr. James has not been able to disinherit himself to this degree. We Americans are terribly in earnest about making ourselves, individually and collectively; but I fancy that our prevailing mood in the face of all problems is that of an abiding faith which can afford to be funny. He has himself indicated that we have, as a nation, as a people, our joke, and every one of us is in the joke more or less. We may, some of us, dislike it extremely, disapprove it wholly, and even abhor it, but we are in the joke all the same, and no one of us is safe from becoming the great American humorist at any given moment. The danger is not apparent in Mr. James's case, and I confess that I read him with a relief in the comparative immunity that he affords from the national facetiousness. Many of his people are humorously imagined, or rather humorously *seen*, like Daisy Miller's mother, but these do not give a dominant color; the business in hand is commonly serious, and the droll people are subordinated. They abound, nevertheless, and many of them are perfectly new finds like Mr. Tristram in *The American*, the bill-paying father in the 'Pension Beaurepas,' the anxiously Europeanizing mother in the same story, the amusing little Madame de Belgarde, Henrietta Stackpole, and even Newman himself. But though Mr. James portrays the humorous in character, he is decidedly not on humorous terms with his readers; he ignores rather than recognizes the fact that they are both in the joke.

If we take him at all we must take him on his own ground, for clearly he will not come to ours. We must make concessions to him, not in this respect only, but in several others, chief among which is the motive for reading fiction. By example, at least, he teaches that it is the pursuit and not the end which should give us pleasure; for he often prefers to leave us to our own conjectures in regard to the fate of the people in whom he has interested us. There is no question, of course, but he could tell the story of Isabel in *The Portrait of a Lady* to the end, yet he does not tell it. We must agree, then, to take what seems a fragment instead of a whole, and to find, when we can, a name for this new kind in fiction. Evidently it is the character, not the fate, of his people which occupies him; when he has fully developed their character, he leaves them to what destiny the reader pleases.

The analytic tendency seems to have increased with him as his work has gone on. Some of the earlier tales were very dramatic: 'A Passionate Pilgrim,' which I should rank above all his other short stories, and for certain rich poetical qualities, above everything else that he has done, is eminently dramatic. But I do not find much that I should call dramatic in *The Portrait of a Lady*, while I do find in it an amount of analysis which I should call superabundance if it were not all such good literature. The novelist's main business is to possess his reader with a due conception of his characters and the situations in which they find themselves. If he does more or less than this he equally fails. I have sometimes thought that Mr. James's danger was to do more, but when I have been ready to declare this excess an error of his method I have hesitated. Could anything be superfluous that had given me so much pleasure as I read? Certainly from only one point of view, and this a rather narrow, technical one. It seems to me that an enlightened criticism will recognize in Mr. James's fiction a metaphysical genius working to aesthetic results, and will not be disposed to deny it any method it chooses to employ. No other novelist, except George Eliot, has dealt so largely in analysis of motive, has so fully explained and commented upon the springs of action in the persons of the drama, both before and after the facts. These novelists are more alike than any others in their processes, but with George Eliot an ethical purpose is dominant, and with Mr. James an artistic purpose. I do not know just how it should be stated of two such noble and generous types of character as Dorothea and Isabel Archer, but I think that we sympathize with the former in grand aims that chiefly concern others, and with the latter in beautiful dreams that primarily concern herself. Both are unselfish and devoted women, sublimely true to a mistaken ideal in their marriages; but, though they come to this common martyrdom, the original difference in them remains. Isabel has her great weaknesses, as Dorothea had, but these seem to me, on the whole, the most nobly imagined and the most nobly intentioned women in modern fiction; and I think Isabel is the more subtly divined of the two. If we speak of mere characterization, we must not fail to acknowledge the perfection of Gilbert Osmond. It was a profound stroke to make him an American by birth. No European could realize so fully in his own life the ideal of a European *dilettante* in all the meaning of that cheapened word; as no European could so deeply and tenderly feel the sweetness and loveliness of the English past as the sick American, Searle, in 'The Passionate Pilgrim.'

What is called the international novel is popularly dated from the publication of *Daisy Miller*, though *Roderick Hudson* and *The American* had gone before; but it really began in the beautiful story which I have just named. Mr. James, who invented this species in fiction, first contrasted in the 'Passionate Pilgrim' the New World and Old World moods, ideals, and prejudices, and he did it there with a richness of poetic effect which he has since never equalled. I own that I regret the loss of the poetry, but you cannot ask a man to keep on being a poet for you; it is hardly for him to choose; yet I compare rather discontentedly in my own mind such impassioned creations as Searle and the painter in 'The Madonna of the Future' with *Daisy Miller*, of whose slight, thin personality I also feel the indefinable charm, and of the tragedy of whose innocence I recognize the delicate pathos. Looking back to those early stories, where Mr. James stood at the dividing ways of the novel and the romance, I am sometimes sorry that he declared even superficially for the former. His best efforts seem to me those of romance; his best types have an ideal development, like Isabel and Claire Belgarde and Bessy Alden and poor Daisy and even Newman. But, doubtless, he has chosen wisely; perhaps the romance is an outworn form, and would not lend itself to the reproduction of even the ideality of modern life. I myself waver somewhat in my preference—if it is a preference—when I think of such people as Lord Warburton and the Touchetts, whom I take to be all decidedly of this world. The first of these especially interested me as a probable type of the English nobleman, who amiably accepts the existing situation with all its possibilities of political and social change, and insists not at all upon the surviving feudalities, but means to be a manly and simple gentleman in any event. An American is not able to pronounce as to the verity of the type; I only know that it seems probable and that it is charming. It makes one wish that it were in Mr. James's way to paint in some story the present phase of change in England. A titled personage is still mainly an inconceivable being to us; he is like a goblin or a fairy in a storybook. How does he comport himself in the face of all the changes and modifications that have taken place and that still impend? We can hardly imagine a lord taking his nobility seriously; it is some hint of the conditional frame of Lord Warburton's mind that makes him imaginable and delightful to us.

It is not my purpose here to review any of Mr. James's books; I like better to speak of his people than of the conduct of his novels, and I wish to recognize the fineness with which he has touched-in the pretty primness of Osmond's daughter and the mild devotedness of Mr. Rosier. A masterly hand is as often manifest in the treatment of such subordinate figures as in that of the principal persons, and Mr. James does them unerringly. This is felt in the more important character of Valentin Belgarde, a fascinating character in spite of its defects,—perhaps on account of them—and a sort of French Lord Warburton, but wittier, and not so good. 'These are my ideas,' says his sister-in-law, at the end of a number of inanities. 'Ah, you call them ideas!' he returns, which is delicious and makes you love him. He, too, has his moments of misgiving, apparently in regard to his nobility, and his acceptance of Newman on the basis of something like 'manhood suffrage' is very charming. It is of course difficult for a remote plebeian to verify the pictures of legitimist society in *The American*, but there is the probable suggestion in them of conditions and principles, and want of principles, of which we get glimpses in our travels abroad; at any rate, they reveal another and not impossible world, and it is fine to have Newman discover that the opinions and criticisms of our world are so absolutely valueless in that sphere that his knowledge of the infamous crime of the mother and brother of his betrothed will have no effect whatever upon them in their own circle if he explodes it there. This seems like aristocracy indeed! and one admires, almost respects, its survival in our day. But I always regretted that Newman's discovery seemed the precursor of his magnanimous resolution not to avenge himself; it weakened the effect of this, with which it had really nothing to do. Upon the whole, however, Newman is an adequate and satisfying representative of Americanism, with his generous matrimonial ambition, his vast good-nature, and his thorough good sense and right feeling. We must be very hard to please if we are not pleased with him. He is not the 'cultivated American' who redeems us from time to time in the eyes of Europe; but he is unquestionably more national, and it is observable that his unaffected fellow-countrymen and women fare very well at Mr. James's hands always; it is the Europeanizing sort like the critical little Bostonian in the 'Bundle of Letters,' the ladies shocked at Daisy Miller, the mother in the 'Pension Beaurepas' who goes about trying to be of the 'native' world everywhere, Madame Merle and Gilbert Osmond, Miss Light and her mother, who have reason to complain, if any one has. Doubtless Mr. James does not mean to satirize such Americans, but it is interesting to note how they strike such a keen observer. We are certainly not allowed to like them, and the other sort find somehow a place in our affections along with his good Europeans. It is a little odd, by the way, that in all the printed talk about Mr. James—and there has been no end of it—his power of engaging your preference for certain of his people has been so little commented on. Perhaps it is because he makes no obvious appeal for them; but one likes such men as Lord Warburton, Newman, Valentin, the artistic brother in *The Europeans*, and Ralph Touchett, and such women as Isabel, Claire Belgarde, Mrs. Tristram, and certain others, with a thoroughness that is one of the best testimonies to their vitality. This comes about through their own qualities, and is not affected by insinuation or by downright *petting*, such as we find in Dickens nearly always and in Thackeray too often.

The art of fiction has, in fact, become a finer art in our day than it was with Dickens and Thackeray. We could not suffer the confidential attitude of the latter now, nor the mannerism of the former, any more than we could endure the prolixity of Richardson or the coarseness of Fielding. These great men are of the past—they and their methods and interests; even Trollope and Reade are not of the present. The new school derives from Hawthorne and George Eliot rather than any others; but it studies human nature much more in its wonted aspects, and finds its ethical and dramatic examples in the operation of lighter but not really less vital motives. The moving accident is certainly not its trade; and it prefers to avoid all manner of dire catastrophes. It is largely influenced by French fiction in form; but it is the realism of Daudet rather than the realism of Zola that prevails with it, and it has a soul of its own which is above the business of recording the rather brutish pursuit of a woman by a man, which seems to be the chief end of the French novelist. This school, which is so largely of the future as well as the present, finds its chief exemplar in Mr. James; it is he who is shaping and directing American fiction, at least. It is the ambition of the younger contributors to write like him; he has his following more distinctly recognizable than that of any other English-writing novelist. Whether he will so far control this following as to decide the nature of the novel with us remains to be seen. Will the reader be content to accept a novel which is an analytic study rather than a story, which is apt to leave him arbiter of the destiny of the author's creations? Will he find his account in the un-flagging interest of their development? Mr. James's growing popu-larity seems to suggest that this may be the case; but the work of Mr. James's imitators will have much to do with the final result.

In the meantime it is not surprising that he has his imitators. Whatever exceptions we take to his methods or his results, we cannot deny him a very great literary genius. To me there is a perpetual delight in his way of saying things, and I cannot wonder that younger men try to catch the trick of it. The disappointing thing for them is that it is not a trick, but an inherent virtue. His style is, upon the whole, better than that of any other novelist I know; it is always easy, without being trivial, and it is often stately, without being stiff; it gives a charm to everything he writes; and he has written so much and in such various directions, that we should be judging him very in-completely if we considered him only as a novelist. His book of European sketches must rank him with the most enlightened and agreeable travelers; and it might be fitly supplemented from his uncol-lected papers with a volume of American sketches. In his essays on modern French writers he indicates his critical range and grasp; but he scarcely does more, as his criticisms in *The Atlantic* and *The Nation* and elsewhere could abundantly testify.

There are indeed those who insist that criticism is his true vocation, and are impatient of his devotion to fiction; but I suspect that these admirers are mistaken. A novelist he is not, after the old fashion, or after any fashion but his own; yet since he has finally made his public in his own way of storytelling—or call it character-painting if you prefer,—it must be conceded that he has chosen best for himself and his readers in choosing the form of fiction for what he has to say. It is, after all, what a writer has to say rather than what he has to tell that we care for nowadays. In one manner or other the stories were all told long ago; and now we want merely to know what the novelist thinks about persons and situations. Mr. James gratifies this philo-sophic desire. If he sometimes forbears to tell us what he thinks of the last state of his people, it is perhaps because that does not interest him, and a large-minded criticism might well insist that it was childish to demand that it must interest him.

I am not sure that my criticism is sufficiently large-minded for this. I own that I like a finished story; but then also I like those which Mr. James seems not to finish. This is probably the position of most of his readers, who cannot very logically account for either preference. We can only make sure that we have here an annalist, or analyst, as we choose, who fascinates us from his first page to his last, whose narrative or whose comment may enter into any minuteness of detail without fatiguing us, and can only truly grieve us when it ceases.

NOTES

1 'The New Battle of the Books,' *Forum*, 5 (July 1888), 564-73.
2 *The Roving Critic*, 1923, 73.

'The Editor's Study,' 1886–92

Without an editorship but with strong creative impulses welling up in his imagination between 1881 and 1886, Howells wrote a pride of distinctive, increasingly serious novels: *A Modern Instance*, *Indian Summer*, *The Rise of Silas Lapham*, *The Minister's Charge*. Despite the din of critical warfare, it was mainly creative experience which developed his radical allegiance to the newness, realism, and which set him on the threshold of socialist belief. His concern was multiplied by imaginative probing into the human condition under contemporary circumstances, by a series of symbolic personal encounters and subjective responses, and by the results of his fairly systematic investigations of the lives of the industrial poor. It all culminated with his discovery of Tolstoi, who came to him, Howells said repeatedly, with the impact of a religious conversion. But it is worth recording that what Howells took from Tolstoi runs parallel to what he had been taught in his father's home and shop.

I

There was a paradox, inevitably irritating to his opponents, in the situation from which Howells conducted the revolutionary criticism of 1886–92. Late in 1885 he had concluded what he confessed to be an 'incredibly advantageous' contractual arrangement with the biggest, richest publisher in the United States, Harper and Bros. At a period when there was no American income tax and the dollar was worth six if not ten times its current purchasing power, the Harpers paid him $10,000 a year (not counting book royalties): $7,000 to write a novel a year and $3,000 to conduct a new literary column in *Harper's Monthly* to be called 'The Editor's Study.'

Perhaps no other author in the world enjoyed such contractual security (though of course it meant herculean labor), security based merely on the product of his pen. *Harper's Monthly* had a substantial British circulation, and at the Harpers' they were quite as alert to the commercial value of controversy as Gilder at the *Century*. Howells was therefore free to be provocative, even aggressive: 'It's fun banging the babes of Romance about,' he said. It was fun because Howells had stored up fresh insights, exciting new convictions, the emotions of new social concern, and a stock of old literary resentments. In expression his sincerity needed to be channeled only by tactical prudence—and it paid, beautifully.

The time would come when, in deep pain from personal loss, he would find scalping neo-romantics (and being scalped) fun no longer and, having other lives to live, terminate his contract and set a date to 'The Editor's Study.' Meanwhile his column became a landmark in American literary criticism. I think there has never been another to rival 'The Editor's Study' for national and international effect, for freshness and seriousness of ideas, for power in making literary reputations and educating provincial Americans to the work of great foreign authors. He insisted on the centrality of a modern, international school of novelists external to Anglo-American tradition. He fought in season and out for recognition of post-Darwinian, perhaps neo-Christian, convictions of the necessity for human compassion, justice, and solidarity—ideas which in one form or another were at work to change the world, as his opponents would not see.

II

'The Editor's Study,' which made its début in January 1886, took positions tendentiously modern, in fact contemporaneous, American, democratic, realistic, and searching. It became a monument of American literary history, but its principles, aesthetic and moral, retain their own sort of critical vitality today. And in a volume like the present one it is necessary to point out that there have been two schools of thought regarding the proper text in which to set forth Howells's criticism of this crucial period. The elder opinion, mistaken though not unreasonable, was that represented in the only predecessor volume to this one, *Criticism and Fiction and Other Essays, by W. D. Howells*, ed. Clara Marburg Kirk and Rudolf Kirk, New York, 1959. The latter opinion is that first put forward by Everett Carter in *Howells and The Age of Realism*, Philadelphia, 1950.

The elder attitude, shared by most historians of criticism who have studied Howells, presumably based itself on the ancient principle of textual bibliography that the best text is the latest which passed from the hand of the author to the press. On 9 May 1891 the Harpers published *Criticism and Fiction*, a compilation of 'Editor's Study' pieces, none first published later than October 1890 (thus missing seventeen months of the column). The selection and arrangement were made by W. D. Howells and the book regularly published: *ergo*, it could be argued, *Criticism and Fiction* stands for Howells's criticism of the period, is even the standard reference for his best, most interesting critical thought.

But there are difficulties, even lions in the path of that logic. Simply as logic it is challenged, perhaps confuted, by the new logic in textual criticism which flowers from a branch grafted by Fredson Bowers upon a stem of W. W. Greg. In sum, the new logic demands that we know everything we can about a literary text so as to determine its best state and that we reprint for literary study the best of texts even if we have to arrive at it by rejecting demonstrably mistaken alterations made by the author himself. Quite interestingly, Carter disabled *Criticism and Fiction* before the appearance of Greg's famous essay, 'The Rationale of Copy-Text.'

Chapter IV of *Howells and The Age of Realism*, entitled 'Critical Realism,' presents as its fifth section 'The Invalidation of *Criticism and Fiction*.' Here Carter argues cogently, so I think, that in *Criticism and Fiction* Howells confused himself and misled his readers by hastily muddling the book together with 'scissors and pastepot.' Snatching essays out of context, disregarding the genetic order of his ideas, insights and sentiments as they had developed through time, Howells misrepresented his criticism to posterity. It has long seemed to me that Carter's perception was correct, and what we now know about the motive for Howells's undertaking *Criticism and Fiction* argues in Carter's favor. Howells did it because James R. Osgood, his dear friend, old publisher, and former business manager, thought the volume up and persuaded Howells to undertake it because Osgood needed the business. Osgood's bankruptcy in 1885 had put Howells on the market in which the Harpers claimed him, and Osgood had become a representative of the Harpers in London. But it was as 'James R. Osgood, McIlvaine & Co., Publishers, London' that he besought Howells in November 1890 to make a book of 'Editor's Study' pieces and let him have the English rights. Howells loved Osgood and obliged him, but he hustled together a bad compilation.

It is therefore the argument from deadly damage done to Howells's thought and prose by his own rupture of contexts which I find most damning to *Criticism and Fiction*. Carter is right. Two contexts for what Howells said so significantly in 'The Editor's Study' ought to be respected. The first context is local: Howells said each of his best things in the immediate context of considering a particular book, event or idea; and his sense like his prose loses bloom when plucked out of context. The second context is genetic: historically, through personal, literary, social, and intellectual events, Howells changed, developed, deepened, sometimes altered his views during the 135 intense, sometimes tragic months during which he wrote 'Studies'; and his progressions may not be ignored. Neither ought the intimacy, the personal tone and the humor to be sacrificed. The 'Study' essays are often admirable—versatile, light-footed, penetrating, even funny; *Criticism and Fiction* is too polemic, a barrage.

In the last analysis one cannot accept the author's demolition of his true contexts in *Criticism and Fiction*. But if one must then reprint from 'The Editor's Study' itself, it is clear that in a volume such as the present he must select. How shall he select better than Howells himself? By working to do what Howells did not: edit sensitively, and faithfully to the true contexts. 'Studies' were by design familiar in mode, rather rambling and opportunistic, rather newsy. Vital criticism lies in them beside gossip and other relatively unimportant comment. I have tried hard to select as fairly as space permits.

8 Grant's *Personal Memoirs*: the sublimity of the common

1886

From 'The Editor's Study,' *Harper's Monthly*, March and August 1886.

One of Howells's major insights, militantly anti-romantic, perceived what he tendentiously referred to as 'the superiority of the vulgar.' Stated as one of the early, dominant notes in the orchestration of 'The Editor's Study,' this insight said that 'genius' and 'heroism' and 'distinction' were shams. Like Whitman, Howells believed such notions to be vestigial remnants of a feudal, wicked past. Unlike Whitman, he agreed with Clemens's indictment of 'Sir Walter Scottism' in the nineteenth century: revivals of the false sublime revealed the fatuous egotism of the romantic. The revolutionary thing was to see beauty, truth, and goodness in the homely commonplace of plain people. Perfectly original in the arts, such he thought also the distinctively American thing: 'we have heard a great deal about what the American was to be in literature when he once got there. What if this were he—this good form without formality, this inner dignity, this straightforward arrival, this mid-day clearness?'

We have just read a book by one of the greatest captains who ever lived—a plain, taciturn, simple, unaffected soul—who tells the story of his wonderful life as unconsciously as if it were all an every-day affair, not different from other lives, except as a great exigency of the human race gave it importance. So far as he knew, he had no natural aptitude for arms, and certainly no love for the calling. But he went to West Point because, as he quaintly tells us, his father '*rather thought he would go*'; and he fought through one war with credit, but without glory. The other war, which was to claim his powers and his science, found him engaged in the most prosaic of peaceful occupations; he obeyed its call because he loved his country, and not because he loved war. All the world knows the rest, and all the world knows that greater military mastery has not been shown than his campaigns illustrated. He does not say this in his book, or hint it in any way; he gives you the facts, and leaves them with you. But these *Personal Memoirs of U. S.*

Grant, written as simply and straightforwardly as his battles were fought, couched in the most unpretentious phrase, with never a touch of grandiosity or attitudinizing, familiar, homely, even common in style, is a great piece of literature, because great literature is nothing more nor less than the clear expression of minds that have something great in them, whether religion, or beauty, or deep experience. Probably Grant would have said that he had no more vocation to literature than he had to war. He owns, with something like contrition, that he used to read a great many novels; but we think he would have denied the soft impeachment of literary power. Nevertheless, he shows it, as he showed military power, unexpectedly, almost miraculously. All the conditions here, then, are favorable to supposing a case of 'genius.' Yet who would trifle with that great heir of fame, that plain, grand, manly soul, by speaking of 'genius' and him together? Who calls Washington a genius? or Franklin, or Bismarck, or Cavour, or Columbus, or Luther, or Darwin, or Lincoln? Were these men second-rate in their way? Or is 'genius' that indefinable, preternatural quality, sacred to the musicians, the painters, the sculptors, the actors, the poets, and above all, the poets? Or is it that the poets, having most of the say in this world, abuse it to shameless self-flattery, and would persuade the inarticulate classes that they are on peculiar terms of confidence with the deity? No doubt

> The poet in a golden clime was born,
> With golden stars above,

and they are in some sort creditable to our species. If we should have no more poets we might be less glorious as a race, but we should certainly be more modest—or they would. At least a doctrine wholly opposed to the spirit of free institutions and the principles of civil service reform would go out of the world with them; but since we shall probably have them to the end of the story, let us try to rid ourselves of it as we may. There is no Maelstrom sucking down ships and vomiting up bottles with MSS. in them; there is only a bad current off the coast of Norway. There is no 'genius'; there is only the mastery that comes to natural aptitude from the hardest study of any art or science; 'genius' exists chiefly in the fancy of those who hope that some one else will think they have it. The men who do great things as quietly as they do small things do not commend themselves to the imagination as geniuses; there must be something spectacular in them, or they must have some striking foible or vice or disability united with their strength before they can be so canonized. Then for some reason we are expected to recognize them as different in essence from other men, as a sort of psychical aristocracy, born gentle, while the rest of us were born simple.

That which criticism seems most certainly to have done is to have put a literary consciousness into books unfelt in the early masterpieces, but unfelt now only in the books of men whose lives have been passed in activities, who have been used to employing language as they would have employed any implement, to effect an object, who have regarded a thing to be said as in no wise different from a thing to be done. In this sort we have seen no modern book so unconscious as *General Grant's Personal Memoirs*, which is now complete in its second volume. We have already spoken of the first volume, and of the simplicity which distinguished it. The same unimpassioned, singular directness characterizes the story to its end. The author's one end and aim is to get the facts out in words. He does not cast about for phrases, but takes the word, whatever it is, that will best give his meaning, as if it were a man or a force of men for the accomplishment of a feat of arms. There is not a moment wasted in preening and prettifying, after the fashion of literary men; there is no thought of style, and so the style is good as it is in the Book of Chronicles, as it is in the *Pilgrim's Progress*, or in a novel of De Foe's, with a peculiar, almost plebeian, plainness at times. There is no more attempt at dramatic effect than there is at ceremonious pose; things happen in that tale of a mighty war as they happened in the mighty war itself, without setting, without artificial reliefs, one after another, as if they were all of one quality and degree. Judgments are delivered with the same unimposing quiet; no awe surrounds the tribunal except that which comes from the weight and justice of the opinions; it is always an unaffected, unpretentious man who is talking; and throughout he prefers to wear the uniform of a private, with nothing of the general about him but the shoulder-straps, which he sometimes forgets.

We have heard a great deal about what the American was to be in literature when he once got there. What if this were he—this good form without formality, this inner dignity, this straightforward arrival, this mid-day clearness?

9 'Negative Realism': Stevenson, Balzac
1886

From 'The Editor's Study,' *Harper's Monthly*, May 1886.

There may have been something chemically antagonistic between Howells and Robert Louis Stevenson. On the brink of Howells's English visit in 1882, Stevenson committed the literary *gaffe* of misreading *A Modern Instance* as a tract against divorce and the social *gaffe* of informing Howells that therefore he did not wish to know him. Whether friendship would have altered Howells's opinion of Stevenson, however, I think dubious. Long after Stevenson's death, preceded by mutual apology and reconciliation by letter, Howells declined to revise his literary judgment, explaining to an inquiring professor that he 'put Hardy above all the other living English. Stevenson is food for babes—boy babes—in his fiction, though he is a true, rare poet.'

Bracketing Stevenson with Balzac, then, provided Howells a tactic for expressing what I have called 'negative realism'—the realist's attack upon the vision, sensibility, and morality of the romancer, his romance, and thus romanticism, 'the satiric reduction of romantic, Dionysian egoism and glamor.'[1] Strong conviction informed the mockery with which Howells laughed down 'these monsters' Jack the Giant-Killer and Puss in Boots masquerading as reality. Offended taste tempted him to be savage with 'romanticism' in its fantastic, allegorical, and pretentious modes. But seriousness demanded of Howells that he say what he meant by realism; and here he met the demand with one of his fine definitions of what I should call 'positive realism.' The romantic, he said, succeeded upon an exhausted classicism and became obsolete in its turn:

> it remained for realism to assert that fidelity to experience and probability of motive are essential conditions of a great imaginative literature. . . . When realism becomes false to itself . . . and maps life instead of picturing it, realism will perish too. Every true realist . . . feels in every nerve the equality of things and the unity of men. . . . In criticism it is his business to break the images of false gods and misshapen heroes, to take away the poor silly toys that many grown people would still like to play with.

I.

Mr. Robert Louis Stevenson in his new romance, *The Strange Case of Dr. Jekyll and Mr. Hyde*, follows the lines explored by Mr. Edward Bellamy in his romance of *Miss Ludington's Sister*. But the Patent-office abounds in simultaneously invented machinery, and, at any rate, Mr. Stevenson may claim an improvement upon the apparatus of Mr. Bellamy. The American writer supposed several selves in each human being, which died successively and became capable of meeting one another in a different state of existence. Mr. Stevenson immensely simplifies the supposition by reducing these selves to the number of two—a moral self and an unmoral self. The moral self in the *Strange Case* was Dr. Jekyll, who, by the use of a certain drug, liberated Mr. Hyde, his unmoral self or evil principle, in whom he went about wreaking all his bad passions, without the inconvenience of subsequent remorse; all he had to do was to take the infusion of that potent salt, and become the good Dr. Jekyll again. The trouble in the end was that Mr. Hyde, from being at first smaller and feebler than Dr. Jekyll, outgrew him, and formed the habit of coming forth without the use of the salt. Dr. Jekyll was obliged to kill them both.

The romancer cannot often be taken very seriously, we suppose; he seems commonly to be working out a puzzle, and at last to have produced an in ellectual toy; but Mr. Stevenson, who is inevitably a charming and sympathetic writer, and whom we first knew as the author of certain poems full of deep feeling and sincerity, does something more than this in his romance; he not only fascinates, he impresses upon the reader the fact that if we indulge the evil in us it outgrows the good. The lesson is not quite new, and in enforcing it he comes dangerously near the verge of allegory; for it is one of the hard conditions of romance that its personages starting with a *parti pris* can rarely be characters with a living growth, but are apt to be types, limited to the expression of one principle, simple, elemental, lacking the God-given complexity of motive which we find in all the human beings we know.

Hawthorne, the great master of the romance, had the insight and the power to create it anew as a kind of fiction; though we are not sure that *The Scarlet Letter* and the *Blithedale Romance* are not, strictly speaking, novels rather than romances. They do not play with some old superstition long outgrown, and they do not invent a new superstition to play with, but deal with things vital in every one's pulse. We are not saying that what may be called the fantastic romance—

the romance that descends from *Frankenstein* rather than *The Scarlet Letter*—ought not to be. On the contrary, we should grieve to lose it, as we should grieve to lose the pantomime or the comic opera, or many other graceful things that amuse the passing hour, and help us to live agreeably in a world where men actually sin, suffer, and die. But it belongs to the decorative arts, and though it has a high place among them it cannot be ranked with the works of the imagination—the works that represent and body forth human experience. Its ingenuity can always afford a refined pleasure, and it can often, at some risk to itself, convey a valuable truth.

II.

We can be glad of it even in a writer of our time, but it would be hard to forgive a contemporary for a bit of theatricality like that which the new translation of Balzac offers us in *The Duchesse de Langeais*. It is worse, if anything could be worse, than *Père Goriot*—more artificial in motive, more malarial, more oblique in morals. In fact, the inversion of the principles of right and wrong, the appeal made to the reader's sympathy for the man who cannot ruin the married coquette he loves, is as bad a thing as we know in literature. But it has its value as part of the history of Balzac's evolution, which was curiously fitful and retarded. It is a survival of romanticism, and its Sworn Thirteen Noblemen, who abduct the Duchess at a ball and bring her back before supper, and who are pledged to defend and abet each other in all good and ill, are the sort of mechanism not now employed outside of the dime fictions.

It must by no means be supposed, in fine, that because Balzac was a realist, he was always a realist. As a matter of fact, he was sometimes a romanticist as flamboyant as Victor Hugo himself, without Victor Hugo's generous sympathy and noble faith; and we advise the reader that a more depraving book could hardly fall into the hands of the young than *The Duchesse de Langeais*—more false to life, more false to art. It is a pity that it is bound up in the Boston edition with *The Illustrious Gaudissart*, a charming piece of humor and nature.

III.

It is droll to find Balzac, who suffered such bitter scorn and hate for his realism while he was alive, now become a fetich in his turn, to be shaken in the faces of those who will not blindly worship him. But it is no new thing in the history of literature: whatever is established is sacred with those who do not think. At the beginning of the century, when romance was making the same fight against effete classicism which realism is making today against effete romance, the Italian poet Monti declared that 'the romantic was the cold grave of the Beautiful,' just as the realistic is now supposed to be. The romance of that day and the realism of this are in certain degree the same. Romance then sought, as realism seeks now, to widen the bounds of sympathy, to level every barrier against aesthetic freedom, to escape from the paralysis of tradition. It exhausted itself in this impulse; and it remained for realism to assert that fidelity to experience and probability of motive are essential conditions of a great imaginative literature. It is not a new theory, but it has never before universally characterized literary endeavor. When realism becomes false to itself, when it heaps up facts merely, and maps life instead of picturing it, realism will perish too. Every true realist instinctively knows this, and it is perhaps the reason why he is careful of every fact, and feels himself bound to express or to indicate its meaning at the risk of over-moralizing. In life he finds nothing insignificant; all tells for destiny and character; nothing that God has made is contemptible. He cannot look upon human life and declare this thing or that thing unworthy of notice, any more than the scientist can declare a fact of the material world beneath the dignity of his inquiry. He feels in every nerve the equality of things and the unity of men; his soul is exalted, not by vain shows and shadows and ideals, but by realities, in which alone the truth lives. In criticism it is his business to break the images of false gods and misshapen heroes, to take away the poor silly toys that many grown people would still like to play with. He cannot keep terms with Jack the Giant-Killer or Puss in Boots, under any name or in any place, even when they reappear as the convict Vautrec, or the Marquis de Montrivaut, or the Sworn Thirteen Noblemen. He must say to himself that Balzac, when he imagined these monsters, was not Balzac, he was Dumas; he was not realistic, he was romantic.

NOTE

1 See Edwin H. Cady, *The Light of Common Day*, Indiana, 1971, 7 *et passim*.

10 Edward Harrigan: a native, urban, theater of the commonplace
1886

From 'The Editor's Study,' *Harper's Monthly*, July 1886.

As Howells recorded repeatedly, he was passionately fond of the theater and had been given crucial insights into life and literature by the plays of Goldoni in Venice. In an American theater dominated by the fossilized 'well-made play' on the one hand and wildly vacuous romanticisms on the other, Howells naturally became an early Ibsenite. Meanwhile he looked earnestly for something native at home and found it, to his delight, in a New York dramatist who is still a mystery of American dramatic and literary history. Howells spoke, in fact, the most authoritative contemporaneous word we have on the plays of Edward Harrigan.

Harrigan's popularity reached so far that his 'Mulligan Guard March' (1873) was quoted by Kipling in *Kim* (1901). Yet the only Harrigan play now in print appears in Richard Moody, *Dramas from the American Theatre, 1762–1909*, New York, 1966, the substantial introduction to which is much the best general treatment of Harrigan. Howells not only pioneered in his appreciation of Harrigan in 1886, he has kept his primacy. Where the rest of the world purported to see only 'knock-down and slambang,' vulgar fun, Howells saw sensitive registration of reality, artistic integrity, originality—in short, realism.

Harrigan responded, as Moody points out, by coming to conceive of himself in Howellsian terms. His drama, he said in 1889, held the mirror up to 'human nature,' which 'thins out and loses all strength and flavor under the pressures of riches and luxury. It is most virile and aggressive among those who know only poverty and ignorance. It is then the most humorous and odd. . . . In the realism which I employ I believe in being truthful to the laws which govern society as well as to the types of which it is composed. A play-wright drops to a low level when he tries being a moralist, but to a much lower level when he gilds vice and sin and glorifies immorality.'[1]

—One of Howells's key points, precisely.

We will not speak of Mr. Gilbert's exquisite ironies; he is an Englishman, and we are talking now about the American drama, or non-drama; for, in spite of theatres lavishly complete in staging, and with all the sanitary arrangements exemplary—the air changed every fifteen minutes, and artificially refrigerated in the summer—we have still no drama. Yet we have the prospect of something of the kind, and naturally we have it in accordance with the existing conditions. We have an abundance of most amusing sketches and extravaganzas, embodying more or less of our grotesque life; and amongst these, saving the respect of all the gentilities, are Mr. Hoyt's *Rag Baby*, and other absurdities. But, most hopeful of all the promises, we have the plays of Mr. Edward Harrigan. Our one original contribution and addition to histrionic art was negro minstrelsy, which, primitive, simple, elemental, was out of our own soil, and had the characteristics that distinguish autochthonic conceptions. But that is a thing almost of the past, and we have now to do with a novel contribution to the drama, and not to the art of the drama. It is peculiarly interesting, because it is morally, though not materially, the contribution most possible under our peculiar circumstances, for it is the work of a man in whom the instincts of the author combat the theatre's traditions, and the actor's experience censures the author's literary vanity. Mr. Harrigan writes, stages, and plays his pieces; he is his own playwright, manager, and comedian. He has his own theatre, and can risk his own plays in it, simply and cheaply, in contempt of the carpenter and upholsterer. Not that he does treat these useful personages with contempt, but he subordinates them. In his theatre the highly decorated husk and gilded shell are not everything, nor the kernel attenuated to the last degree of innutritiousness. But the setting is at the same time singularly perfect and entirely sufficient. Mr. Harrigan accurately realizes in his scenes what he realizes in his persons; that is the actual life of this city.[2] He cannot give it all; he can only give phases of it; and he has preferred to give its Irish-American phases in their rich and amusing variety, and some of its African and Teutonic phases. It is what we call low life, though whether it is essentially lower than fashionable life is another question. But what it is, it is; and it remains for others, if they can, to present other sides of our manifold life with equal perfection; Mr. Harrigan leaves a vast part of the vast field open. In his own province we think he cannot be surpassed. The art that sets before us all sorts and conditions of New York Irishmen, from the laborers in the street to the most powerful of the ward politicians and the genteelest of the ladies of that interesting race, is the art of Goldoni—the joyous yet conscientious art of the true dramatist in all times who loves the life he observes. The old Venetian filled his scene with the gondoliers, the serving-folk, the fish-women, the trades-people, the quacks, the idlers, the gamesters, of his city; and Mr. Harrigan shows us the street-cleaners and contractors, the grocery-men, the shysters, the politicians, the washer-women, the servant-girls, the truckmen, the policemen, the risen Irishman and Irish woman, of contemporary New York. Goldoni carried through scores of comedies the same characters, the masks of the older drama which he drove from the stage, and Mr. Harrigan instinctively repeats the same personages in his Mulligan series. Within his range the New-Yorker is not less admirable than the Venetian. In fact, nothing could be better than the neatness, the fineness, with which the shades of character are given in Mr. Mulligan's Irish people; and this literary conscientiousness is supplemented by acting which is worthy of it. Mr. Harrigan is himself a player of the utmost naturalness, delicate, restrained, infallibly sympathetic; and we have seen no one on his stage who did not seem to have been trained to his part through entire sympathy and intelligence. In certain moments of *Dan's Tribulations* the illusion is so perfect that you lose the sense of being in the theatre; you are out of that world of conventions and traditions, and in the presence of the facts.

All the Irish aspects of life are treated affectionately by this artist, as we might expect from one of his name; but the colored aspects do not fare so well under his touch. Not all the Irish are good Irish, but all the colored people are bad colored people. They are of the gloomy, razor-bearing variety; full of short-sighted lies and prompt dishonesties, amusing always, but truculent and tricky; and the sunny sweetness which we all know in negro character is not there. We do not wholly object to the one-sided picture; it has its historical value; and so has the contemptuous prejudice of both Irish and negroes for the Italians, which comes out in the *Leather Patch*; that marks an epoch and characterizes a condition.

The *Leather Patch* is not nearly so good as the Mulligan series, though it has very good things in it. The author seems to have labored for incident and effect in a plot, whereas all that the heart asked of him was to keep his delicious Irish folks on the scene and keep them talking. As it is, some passages of the piece are extremely good; and it is as a whole in the good direction. The material is rude, very rude; we repeat that; it is the office or it is the will of this artist to work in that material; but it is the artist and not the material which makes the work of art. The error of the dramatist has been that he has at times not known how to hold his hand; he has given us the whole truth where part of it would have been enough; he might have spared us some shocking suggestions of the undertaking business. At other times he quite forgets his realism: the whole episode of the colored wake, with its plantation spirituals, is real and excellent; but when the old-clothes men and women of Chatham Street join in a chorus, one perceives that the theatre has come to the top, and the poet has lapsed.

In spite of such lapses, however, we recognize in Mr. Harrigan's work the spring of a true American comedy, the beginning of things which may be great things. We have more than intimated its limitations; let us say that whatever its offences, it is never, so far as we have seen it, indecent. The comedies of Edward Harrigan are, in fact, much decenter than the comedies of William Shakespeare.

They are like Shakespeare's plays, like Molière's plays, in being the work of a dramatist who is at the same time a manager and an actor. Possibly this is the only way we can have a drama of our own; it is not a bad way; and it is at least a very natural way. At any rate, loving reality as we do, we cannot do less than cordially welcome reality as we find it in Mr. Harrigan's comedies. Consciously or unconsciously, he is part of the great tendency toward the faithful representation of life which is now animating fiction. . . .

But we feel that we ought to ask the reader's patience with our digression about New York theatres. The real drama is in our novels mostly. It is they chiefly which approach our actual life, and interpret it so far as it has yet been represented to the vast majority of our intelligent public; it is in them alone that a number, only a little less than that majority, will ever see it represented. The theatre is the amusement of the city, of people whose lives are crowded with pleasures and distractions; but the novel is the consolation, the refuge, of the fine spirits that pine in the dulness of small towns, or the monotony of the country, where other intellectual resources are few, and the excitements none. It is therefore of little consequence to the great mass of those who truly love literature whether the theatre is good or bad; they will never see it; they will never suffer from it, or profit by it. We in the great cities long for a renewal of the glories that surrounded it in the days when it was a living interest; but that is an affair of sentiment merely, and it would not greatly matter if the theatre remained always what it has long been—a mere diversion, neither affecting our life, nor affected by it. Perhaps the theatrical drama will never revive. We have noted some signs of renewed respiration, but we should not think it quite cataclysmal if, after a few gasps, it ceased to breathe again. We should certainly regret to see any art perish, but it is for the arts, like the interests, to assert their own vitality and maintain it; and if the drama, with all our lavish love of the theatre, cannot hold its own there, and prosper and advance, as the novel has prospered and advanced, in spite of the unfriendly literary conditions, it simply proves that the drama is an outworn literary form. It cannot be willed back to life by criticism, censured back, or coaxed back. It must take its chances; it must make them.

NOTES

1 Quoted in Moody, 547.
2 i.e. New York.

11 Dostoevski discovered: the 'smiling aspects' issue
1886

From 'The Editor's Study,' *Harper's Monthly*, September 1886.

One of the distinctions of 'The Editor's Study' and its author is that they brought early news of Dostoevski and *Crime and Punishment* to the serious American reader and a less startling but still pioneering Dostoevski criticism to the broader public which read literature in English.

Ironically, the significance of this critique has been overshadowed by a misreading, apparently willfull, which snatched a phrase out of one of the many contexts in *Criticism and Fiction* which Howells himself had twice confused. He destroyed the original context to make the first edition of *Criticism and Fiction* and muddled it further in revision for his Library Edition. Van Wyck Brooks in *The Ordeal of Mark Twain* achieved a libel upon Howells's mind and sensibility which has continued to live in the standard reference, defying reason and evidence for more than a quarter of a century past. Brooks's original motive, modified in his own *New England : Indian Summer*, 1940, and denied in his *Howells, His Life and World*, 1959, answered to the demand of his historical imagination in 1920 that there be some figure to represent the bland, yea-saying and Victorian optimism which Brooks thought had smothered the tragic vision of Clemens.

Brooks selected Howells for his villain and plucked out of context, plucked arbitrarily and unjustifiably from its every context, a phrase which first appeared in section III of this 'Study': 'the more smiling aspects of life, which are the more American.' That phrase he came to treat as an incomplete comparison (as if it occurred in an advertisement for cigarettes) which stood without context and could be properly cited to show that Howells was a timid, neurotically silly, male Pollyanna. Brooks entered the phrase almost indelibly upon American literary history as a false truism.[1]

A glance at the true context will show how Brooks misread. He could not have failed to know that Howells in his own time was regularly attacked for pessimism, even for pessimism in commending such writers as Dostoevski. And Brooks ought to have known how darkly Howells's novels run from *A Modern Instance* forward, how heart-breaking are the poems of *Stops of Various Quills*, how deep became Howells's social alienation from the world of his times, and even what 'The Editor's Study' said repeatedly, e.g.:[2]

Especially in America, where the race has gained a height never reached before, the eminence enables more men than ever before to see how even here vast masses of men are sunk in misery that must grow every day more hopeless, or embroiled in a struggle for mere life that must end in enslaving and imbruting them.

There stood Howells's point. As a realist he saw that American reality was 'more smiling' than the reality of Dostoevski's Russia and that fiction must register the truth. But as a socialist Howells saw that the American 'more smiling aspects,' far from warranting the sleep of inwit, demanded more sensitivity, more responsibility, perhaps even more alarm.

I.

The readers of Tourguéneff and of Tolstoi must now add Dostoïevsky to their list if they wish to understand the reasons for the supremacy of the Russians in modern fiction; and we think they must put him beside these two, and not below either, in moral and artistic qualities. They are all so very much more than realists that this name, never satisfactory in regard to any school of writers, seems altogether insufficient for them. They are realists in ascertaining an entire probability of motive and situation in their work; but with them this is only the beginning; they go so far beyond it in purpose and effect that one must cast about for some other word if one would try to define them. Perhaps humanist would be the best phrase in which to clothe the idea of their literary office, if it could be limited to mean their simply, almost humbly, fraternal attitude toward the persons and conditions with which they deal, and again extended to include a profound sense of that individual responsibility from which the common responsibility can free no one. The phrase does not express that artistry which one feels in them, and it can only group them loosely in a single characteristic; but it certainly hints at what one feels most of all in the latest known of these great masters. At the same time, if it suggests anything of sentimentality, it is wholly and mischievously false. For instance, in *Le Crime et le Châtiment*, which we have just been reading, and which, besides *Les Humiliés et Offensés*, is the only book of Dostoïevsky's yet given in French, the author studies the effect of murder in the assassin, who is brought to confession and repentance by a hapless creature whom poverty has forced to a life of shame. Yet there is nothing of the maudlin glamour of heroism thrown about this pair; Raskolnikoff is the only man who has not been merely brutal to Sonia, and she divines his misery through her gratitude; this done, her one thought, her only hope, is not to help him hide his crime, but to help him own it to the law and to expiate it. She sees that there is no escape for him but this, and her inspiration is not superior to her; it is not from her mind, but from her soul, primitively good and incorrupt, amidst the hideous facts of her life, which, by-the-way, are in nowise brought forward or exploited in the story. Raskolnikoff is not her lover; he becomes so only when his expiation has begun; and the reader is scarcely allowed to see beyond the first breaking down of his egotistic self-justification in the Siberian prison. He has done the murder for which he suffers upon a theory, if not a principle: the theory that the greatest heroes and even benefactors of the race have not hesitated at crime when it would advance their extraordinary purposes or promote their development. He is a student, forced to quit the university by his poverty, and he reasons that it is better he should complete his career, destined, as he feels, to be useful and splendid, than that a certain old woman who keeps a pawnbroker's shop should continue to live and to prey upon the necessities of others. He asks himself which of the extraordinary men who have set the world forward would have stopped at putting her out of his way if he had found it to his advantage, and he kills her and robs her; he kills her half-witted sister too, the harmless thing that comes in upon him and his first victim through the door he has forgotten to lock. His punishment begins with this deed, which he had never counted upon, for the wickedness of the old usuress was largely his defence for taking her off; but it cannot properly be said that Raskolnikoff feels regret or even remorse for his crime until he has confessed it. Till then his terrible secret, which all the accidents and endeavors of the world seem conspiring to tear from him, forms his torment, and almost this alone. His repentance and his redemption begin with his penalty. The truth is a very old one, but what makes this book so wonderful is the power with which it is set forth. The story is not merely an accumulation of incident upon incident, a collection of significant anecdotes, as it might be in the hands of an inferior artist, but a mounting drama, to the catastrophe of which all the facts and characters tend, not mechanically or intentionally, but in the natural and providential way; it is only in the latter half of the story that you suspect a temptation in the author to intensify and to operate. At moments the stress of the story is almost intolerable; the misery of Raskolnikoff is such that you suffer all Sonia's despair when he comes back from the police office without having confessed, and you scarcely breathe till he makes the second attempt and succeeds.

The arrival of his mother and sister in the midst of his wretchedness, to be the loving and trusting witnesses of suffering of which they cannot understand the cause, is merely one of the episodes of the book which penetrate the soul by their reality, by their unsparing yet compassionate truth. But the impressive scenes abound so that it is hard to name one without having seemed to leave a finer one unmentioned. Perhaps there is nothing of higher and nobler strain than that series of passages in which the Judge of Instruction, softened and humanized by the familiarity with crime which hardens so many, tries to bring Raskolnikoff to confess for his own sake the murder which the Judge is sure he committed. Other passages are of a pathos intense beyond anything else that we can remember in fiction, and chief among them, perhaps, are those in which Sonia's stepmother goes mad after her drunken husband's death, and leads her little children, fantastically tricked out in tattered finery, through the street to sing and dance. She is herself dying of consumption; terrible fits of coughing interrupt her ravings, and the weird escapade is the precursor of her death; she ceases to live the same night. Between her and her step-daughter, whom her wild appeal drove to ruin that the others might not starve, there exists an affection which no sense of wrong done and wrong suffered can weaken; their love for each other is a consolation when they have no friend or helper but the impenitent assassin who wreaks upon them the desire to do good, to help some one, which is one of the most subtly divined traits of a soul at war with itself.

It is a lurid chapter of human life certainly, but the light of truth is in it; and in the ghastliest picture which it presents there is the hope, the relief, that human sympathy gives, and everywhere there is recognition of the fact that behind the supreme law is the supreme love, and only there. It is therefore by no means a desperate book, nor a wholly depressing book. It not only clearly indicates the consequences of sin, but it attempts to define their bounds, the limits at which they seem to cease. Raskolnikoff suffers, but we reach the point at which he begins not to suffer. He makes others suffer, but we see where the suffering which his guilt inflicts must naturally end. It leaves him at the outset of a new life, the life of a man who has submitted to punishment, and has thereby won the privilege to repent. It is the reverse of a pessimistic book.

II.

The reader of such a story will hardly be satisfied without knowing something of the author, and in an article of the *Revue des Deux Mondes* for January 15, 1885, M. Eugène-Melchoir de Vogüé will tell him the hardly less tragical story of Dostoïevsky's own life. It seems that he was born at Moscow, in a charity hospital, in 1821, and to the day of his death he struggled with poverty, injustice, and disease. His first book, *Poor People*, which won him reputation and the hope of better things, was followed within a few years by his arrest for Socialism. He was not really concerned in Socialism, except through his friendship for some of the Socialists, but he was imprisoned with them, and after eight months of solitude in the casemate of a fortress—solitude unrelieved by the sight of a friendly human face, or a book, or a pen—he was led out to receive his sentence. All the prisoners had been condemned to death; the muskets were loaded in their presence, and levelled at their breasts; then the muzzles were struck up, and the Czar's commutation of their sentence was read. They were sent to Siberia, where Dostoïevsky spent six years at hard labor. There he made his studies among the prisoners for his book *The Humiliated and the Wronged*, which the French have now translated with *The Crime and the Punishment*. At the end of this time he returned to St. Petersburg, famous, beloved, adored, to continue his struggle with poverty and disease. The struggle was long, for he died only five years ago, when his body was followed to the grave by such a mighty concourse of all manner of people as never assembled at the funeral of any author before. 'Priests chanting prayers; the students of the universities; the children of the schools; the young girl medical students; the Nihilists, distinguishable by their eccentricities of costume and bearing—the men with their shawls, and the women with their spectacles and close-clipped hair; all the literary and scientific societies; deputations from all parts of the empire—old Muscovite merchants, peasants, servants, beggars; in the church waited the official dignitaries, the Minister of Public Instruction, and the young princes of the imperial family. A forest of banners, of crosses, and of crowns waved over this army in its march; and while these different fragments of Russia passed, you could distinguish the gentle and sinister faces, tears, prayers, sneers, and silences, tranquil or ferocious. . . . What passed was the spectacle of this man's own work, formidable and disquieting, with its weakness and its grandeur; in the first rank, without doubt, and the most numerous, his favorite clients, the *Poor People*, *The Humiliated and the Wronged*, even *The Bedeviled*'—these are all titles of his books—'wretched beings happy to have their day, and to bear their defender on the path of glory, but with them and enveloping them all that uncertainty and confusion of the national life such as he has painted it, all the vague hopes that he had roused in all. As the czars of old were said to gather together the Russian earth, this royal spirit had assembled the Russian soul.'

III.

M. Vogüé writes with perhaps too breathless a fervor, but his article is valuable for the light it casts upon the origins of Dostoïevsky's work, and its inspirations and motives. It was the natural expression of such a life and such conditions. But it is useful to observe that while *The Crime and the Punishment* may be read with the deepest sympathy and interest, and may enforce with unique power the lessons which it teaches, it is to be praised only in its place, and its message is to be received with allowances by readers exterior to the social and political circumstances in which it was conceived. It used to be one of the disadvantages of the practice of romance in America, which Haw-thorne more or less whimsically lamented, that there were so few shadows and inequalities in our broad level of prosperity; and it is one of the reflections suggested by Dostoïevsky's book that whoever struck a note so profoundly tragic in American fiction would do a false and mistaken thing—as false and as mistaken in its way as dealing in American fiction with certain nudities which the Latin peoples seem to find edifying. Whatever their deserts, very few American novelists have been led out to be shot, or finally exiled to the rigors of a winter at Duluth: one might make Herr Most the hero of a labor-question romance with perfect impunity; and in a land where journeymen carpenters and plumbers strike for four dollars a day the sum of hunger and cold is certainly very small, and the wrong from class to class is almost inappreciable. We invite our novelists, therefore, to concern themselves with the more smiling aspects of life, which are the more American, and to seek the universal in the individual rather than the social interests. It is worth while, even at the risk of being called com-monplace, to be true to our well-to-do actualities; the very passions themselves seem to be softened and modified by conditions which cannot be said to wrong any one, to cramp endeavor, or to cross lawful desire. Sin and suffering and shame there must always be in the world, we suppose, but we believe that in this new world of ours it is mainly from one to another one, and oftener still from one to one's self. We have death too in America, and a great deal of disagreeable and painful disease, which the multiplicity of our patent medicines does not seem to cure; but this is tragedy that comes in the very nature of things, and is not peculiarly American, as the large, cheerful average of health and success and happy life is. It will not do to boast, but it is well to be true to the facts, and to see that, apart from these purely mortal troubles, the race here enjoys conditions in which most of the ills that have darkened its annals may be averted by honest work and unselfish behavior.

It is only now and then, when some dark shadow of our shameful past appears, that we can believe there ever was a tragic element in our prosperity. Even then, when we read such an artlessly impressive sketch as Mrs. Sarah Bradford writes of Harriet Tubman—once famous as the Moses of her people—the self-freed bondwoman who led three hundred of her brethren out of slavery, and with a price set upon her head, risked her life and liberty nineteen times in this cause; even then it affects us like a tale

> Of old, unhappy, far-off things,
> And battles long ago,

and nothing within the date of actual history. We cannot realize that most of the men and women now living were once commanded by the law of the land to turn and hunt such fugitives back into slavery, and to deliver such an outlaw as Harriet over to her owner; that those who abetted such outlaws were sometimes mulcted to the last dollar of their substance in fines. We can hardly imagine such things now for the purposes of fiction; all troubles that now hurt and threaten us are as crumpled rose leaves in our couch. But we may nevertheless read Dostoïevsky, and especially our novelists may read him, to advantage, for in spite of his terrible picture of a soul's agony he is hopeful and wholesome, and teaches in every page patience, merciful judgment, humble helpfulness, and that brotherly responsibility, that duty of man to man, from which not even the Americans are emancipated.

NOTES

1 But a hopeful trend may have registered itself in the difference between James D. Hart, ed., *The Oxford Companion to American Literature*, third edition, New York, 1956, and Thomas H. Johnson, ed., *The Oxford Companion to*

American History, 1966. Hart climaxes his entry on 'Howells' by asserting that among Howells's critical dicta was 'that truthfulness to American life would inevitably picture the smiling aspects of experience.' Johnson's 'Howells' entry mercifully ignores that weary canard and by implication denies it in saying that Howells 'believed that fiction as an art must deal with what is actual and observable, not what is romanticized or genteel.'

2 'The Editor's Study,' August 1889.

12 Realism: the moral issue
1887

From 'The Editor's Study,' *Harper's Monthly*, April 1887.
It is not likely that any major critic has been more written about by commentators and historians who had not troubled to read him than Howells. One tradition of comment strong in the first half of the present century has been that Howells's morality was simply 'Victorian.' A second tradition has been that he was morally flabby and confused. Neither tradition is true, as this 'Study' demonstrates.

Nothing is now more obvious than that 'Victorian morality' was, in historical fact, anything but simple or unified. Howells's moral thought, far from flabby, was definite, deeply *engagé*, and no more confused than that of any man profoundly concerned with, as Howells liked to say, 'the riddle of the painful earth.'[1] Far from simple and much further from conventional, then, Howells's moral thought sprang from roots personal and familial. Its Swedenborgian bases, in particular, lent it a peculiar character. And it had become by the time of 'The Editor's Study' openly hostile to much of what passed for public morality in the age and in the art surrounding Howells.

I.

It must have been a passage from Vernon Lee's *Baldwin*, claiming for the novel an indefinitely vast and subtle influence on modern character, which provoked the following suggestive letter from one of our readers:

—— , —— Co., MD., *Sept.* 18, 1886.
Dear Sir,—With regard to article IV, in the Editor's Study in the September *Harper*, allow me to say that I have very grave doubts as to the whole list of magnificent things that you seem to think novels have done for the race, and can witness in myself many evil things which they have done for me. Whatever in my mental make-up is wild and visionary, whatever is untrue, whatever is

97

injurious, I can trace to the perusal of some work of fiction. Worse than that, they beget such high-strung and supersensitive ideas of life that plain industry and plodding perseverance are despised, and matter-of-fact poverty, or every-day, commonplace distress, meets with no sympathy, if indeed noticed at all, by one who has wept over the impossibly accumulated sufferings of some gaudy hero or heroine.

Hoping you will pardon the liberty I have taken in addressing you, I remain,

Most respectfully yours, —— ——.

We are not sure that we have the controversy with the writer which he seems to suppose, and we should perhaps freely grant the mischievous effects which he says novel-reading has wrought upon him, if we were not afraid that he had possibly reviewed his own experience with something of the inaccuracy we find in his report of our opinions. By his confession he is himself proof that Vernon Lee is right in saying, 'The modern human being has been largely fashioned by those who have written about him, and most of all by the novelist,' and there is nothing in what he urges to conflict with her claim that 'the chief use of the novel' is 'to make the shrewd and tolerant a little less shrewd and tolerant, and to make the generous and austere a little more skeptical and easy-going.' If he will look more closely at these postulates, we think he will see that in the one she deals with the effect of the novel in the past, and in the other with its duty in the future. We still think that there 'is sense if not final wisdom' in what she says, and we are quite willing to acknowledge something of each in our correspondent.

But novels are now so fully accepted by every one pretending to cultivated taste—and they really form the whole intellectual life of such immense numbers of people, without question of their influence, good or bad, upon the mind—that it is refreshing to have them frankly denounced, and to be invited to revise one's ideas and feelings in regard to them. A little honesty, or a great deal of honesty, in this quest will do the novel, as we hope yet to have it, and as we have already begun to have it, no harm; and for our own part we will confess that we believe fiction in the past to have been largely injurious, as we believe the stage play to be still almost wholly injurious, through its falsehood, its folly, its wantonness, and its aimlessness. It may be safely assumed that most of the novel-reading which people fancy is an intellectual pastime is the emptiest dissipation, hardly more related to thought or the wholesome exercise of the mental faculties than opium-eating; in either case the brain is drugged, and left weaker and crazier for the debauch. If this may be called the negative result of the fiction habit, the positive injury that most novels work is by no means so easily to be measured in the case of young men whose character they help so much to form or deform, and the women of all ages whom they keep so much in ignorance of the world they misrepresent. Grown men have little harm from them, but in the other cases, which are the vast majority, they hurt because they are not true—not because they are malevolent, but because they are idle lies about human nature and the social fabric, which it behooves us to know and to understand, that we may deal justly with ourselves and with one another. One need not go so far as our correspondent, and trace to the fiction habit 'whatever is wild and visionary, whatever is untrue, whatever is injurious,' in one's life; bad as the fiction habit is, it is probably not responsible for the whole sum of evil in its victims, and we believe that if the reader will use care in choosing from this fungus-growth with which the fields of literature teem every day, he may nourish himself as with the true mushroom, at no risk from the poisonous species.

The tests are very plain and simple, and they are perfectly infallible. If a novel flatters the passions and exalts them above the principles, it is poisonous; it may not kill, but it will certainly injure; and this test will alone exclude an entire class of fiction, of which eminent examples will occur to all. Then the whole spawn of so-called unmoral romances, which imagine a world where the sins of sense are unvisited by the penalties following, swift or slow, but inexorably sure, in the real world, are deadly poison: these do kill. The novels that merely tickle our prejudices and lull our judgment, or that coddle our sensibilities, or pamper our gross appetite for the marvellous, are not so fatal, but they are innutritious, and clog the soul with unwholesome vapors of all kinds. No doubt they too help to weaken the mental fibre, and make their readers indifferent to 'plodding perseverance and plain industry,' and to 'matter-of-fact poverty and commonplace distress.'

Without taking them too seriously, it still must be owned that the 'gaudy hero and heroine' are to blame for a great deal of harm in the world. That heroine long taught by example, if not precept, that Love, or the passion or fancy she mistook for it, was the chief interest of a life which is really concerned with a great many other things; that it was lasting in the way she knew it; that it was worthy of every sacrifice, and was altogether a finer thing than prudence, obedience, reason; that love alone was glorious and beautiful, and these were mean and ugly in comparison with it. More lately she has begun to idolize and illustrate Duty, and she is hardly less mischievous in this new rôle, opposing duty, as she did love, to prudence, obedience, and reason. The stock hero, whom, if we met him, we could not fail to see was a most deplorable person, has undoubtedly imposed himself upon the victims of the fiction habit as admirable. With him, too, love was and is the great affair, whether in its old romantic phase of chivalrous achievement or manifold suffering for love's sake, or its more recent development of the 'virile,' the bullying, and the brutal, or its still more recent agonies of self-sacrifice, as idle and useless as the moral experiences of the insane asylums. With his vain posturings and his ridiculous splendor he is really a painted barbarian, the prey of his passions and his delusions, full of obsolete ideals, and the motives and ethics of a savage, which the guilty author of his being does his best— or his worst—in spite of his own light and knowledge, to foist upon the reader as something generous and noble. We are not merely bringing this charge against that sort of fiction which is beneath literature and outside of it, 'the shoreless lakes of ditch-water,' whose miasms fill the air below the empyrean where the great ones sit; but we are accusing the work of some of the most famous, who have, in this instance or in that, sinned against the truth, which can alone exalt and purify men. We do not say that they have constantly done so, or even commonly done so; but that they have done so at all marks them as of the past, to be read with the due historical allowance for their epoch and their conditions. For we believe that, while inferior writers will and must continue to imitate them in their foibles and their errors, no one hereafter will be able to achieve greatness who is false to humanity, either in its facts or its duties. The light of civilization has already broken even upon the novel, and no conscientious man can now set about painting an image of life without perpetual question of the verity of his work, and without feeling bound to distinguish so clearly that no reader of his may be misled, between what is right and what is wrong, what is noble and what is base, what is health and what is perdition, in the actions and the characters he portrays.

The fiction that aims merely to entertain—the fiction that is to serious fiction as the opéra bouffe, the ballet, and the pantomime are to the true drama—need not feel the burden of this obligation so deeply; but even such fiction will not be gay or trivial to any reader's hurt, and criticism will hold it to account if it passes from painting to teaching folly.

More and more not only the criticism which prints its opinions, but the infinitely vaster and powerfuler criticism which thinks and feels them merely, will make this demand. For our own part we confess that we do not care to judge any work of the imagination without first of all applying this test to it. We must ask ourselves before we ask anything else, Is it true?—true to the motives, the impulses, the principles that shape the life of actual men and women? This truth, which necessarily includes the highest morality and the highest artistry—this truth given, the book *cannot* be wicked and cannot be weak; and without it all graces of style and feats of invention and cunning of construction are so many superfluities of naughtiness. It is well for the truth to have all these, and shine in them, but for falsehood they are merely meretricious, the bedizenment of the wanton; they atone for nothing, they count for nothing. But in fact they come naturally of truth, and grace it without solicitation; they are added unto it. In the whole range of fiction we know of no *true* picture of life—that is, of human nature—which is not also a masterpiece of literature, full of divine and natural beauty. It may have no touch or tint of this special civilization or of that; it had *better* have this local color well ascertained; but the truth is deeper and finer than aspects, and if the book is true to what men and women know of one another's souls it will be true enough, and it will be great and beautiful. It is the conception of literature as something apart from life, superfinely aloof, which makes it really unimportant to the great mass of mankind, without a message or a meaning for them; and it is the notion that a novel may be false in its portrayal of causes and effects that makes literary art contemptible even to those whom it amuses, that forbids them to regard the novelist as a serious or right-minded person. If they do not in some moment of indignation cry out against all novels, as our correspondent does, they remain besotted in the fume of the delusions purveyed to them, with no higher feeling for the author than such maudlin affection as the *habitué* of an opium-joint perhaps knows for the attendant who fills his pipe with the drug.

II.

Or, as in the case of another correspondent of the Study, who writes that in his youth he 'read a great many novels, but always regarded it as an amusement, like horse-racing and card-playing,' for which he had no time when he entered upon the serious business of life, it renders them merely contemptuous. His view of the matter may be commended to the brotherhood and sisterhood of novelists as full of wholesome if bitter suggestion; and we urge them not to dismiss it with high literary scorn as that of some Bœotian dull to the beauty of art. Refuse it as we may, it is still the feeling of the vast majority of people for whom life is earnest, and who find only a distorted and misleading likeness of it in our books. We may fold ourselves in our scholars' gowns, and close the doors of our studies, and affect to despise this rude voice; but we cannot shut it out. It comes to us from wherever men are at work, from wherever they are truly living, and accuses us of unfaithfulness, of triviality, of mere stage-play; and none of us can escape conviction except he prove himself worthy of his time—a time in which the great masters have brought literature back to life, and filled its ebbing veins with the red tides of reality. We cannot all equal them; we need not copy them; but we can all go to the sources of their inspiration and their power; and to draw from these no one need go far—no one need really to go out of himself.

Fifty years ago, Carlyle, in whom the truth was always alive, but in whom it was then unperverted by suffering, by celebrity and despair, wrote in his study of Diderot:

> Were it not reasonable to prophesy that this exceeding great multitude of novel-writers and such like must, in a new generation, gradually do one of two things: either retire into the nurseries, and work for children, minors, and semi-fatuous persons of both sexes, or else, what were far better, sweep their novel-fabric into the dust-cart, and betake themselves with such faculty as they have to understand and record what is true, of which surely there is, and will forever be, a whole infinitude unknown to us of infinite importance to us? Poetry, it will more and more come to be understood, is nothing but higher knowledge; and the only genuine Romance (for grown persons), Reality.

If after half a century fiction still mainly works for 'children, minors, and semi-fatuous persons of both sexes,' it is nevertheless one of the hopefulest signs of the world's progress that it has begun to work for 'grown persons,' and if not exactly in the way that Carlyle might have solely intended in urging its writers to compile memoirs instead of building the 'novel-fabric,' still it has in the highest and widest sense already made Reality its Romance. We cannot judge it, we do not even care for it, except as it has done this; and we cannot conceive of a literary self-respect in these days compatible with the old trade of make-believe, with the production of the kind of fiction which is too much honored by classification with card-playing and horse-racing.

NOTE

1 Tennyson, 'The Palace of Art,' 213.

13 Criticism: a decorum of taxonomy
1887

From 'The Editor's Study,' *Harper's Monthly*, June 1887.

It doubtless lay in the nature of his polemic situation—which did become not unlike the symbolic drama Andrew Lang described in his trope of an 'international tennis of flouts and jeers, with Mr. Howells "smashing" at the net'[1]—that Howells felt compelled to define his intention by repeatedly declaring his sense of the nature and function of criticism. He distinguished between criticism itself and the theory of criticism—or the criticism of criticism, etc. He urged the inutility of criticism to the artist and thence the propriety of a fitting humility in the critic. And he concluded that it is a decorum of taxonomy which befits the critic. The critic may justify his existence by personal transparency, a scientific modesty, and by helping the reader to see what kind of literature it is with which reader and critic have to do: nothing more. In the tradition of literary criticism as it was available to Howells, perhaps his implied theory of the critic best conformed itself to the method of Goethe.

I.

Some months ago the Study made occasion to say certain things in praise of American criticism, which, so far as we could observe, displeased most of the American critics. This effect might well have discouraged a less ardent optimist, but, with a courage which we will own we admire, we have clung to our convictions, and should be willing to repeat our unwelcome compliments. They were qualified compliments, if we remember rightly; we should not even now like to commit ourselves to indiscriminate flattery of our fellow-critics; and if we were again to enter upon such dangerous ground, we should prefer to recognize a general amelioration of our dreadful trade on this continent rather than specify improvements. If we were to be quite honest (which is really *not* the best policy in some things), we should say to these brothers of ours that they were still rather apt to behave brutally in behalf of good taste and the best art; and that they were perilously beset by temptations to be personal, to be vulgar, to be arrogant, which they did not always overcome. Perhaps we might go so far as to say that their tone was sometimes ruffianly; though perhaps this would be going too far; perhaps one ought to add that it might not be consciously so. In this home of the amenities, this polite haunt of literary discernment, artistic sensibility, and moral purpose, the critic sometimes appears in the panoply of the savages whom we have supplanted; and it is hard to believe that his use of the tomahawk and the scalping-knife is a form of conservative surgery. It is still his conception of his office that he should assail with bitterness and obloquy those who differ with him in matters of taste or opinion; that he must be rude with those he does not like, and that he ought to do them violence as a proof of his superiority. It is too largely his superstition that because he likes a thing it is good, and because he dislikes a thing it is bad; the reverse is quite possibly the case, but he is yet indefinitely far from knowing that in affairs of taste his personal preference enters very little. Commonly he has no principles, but only an assortment of prepossessions for and against; and we grieve to say that this otherwise very perfect character is sometimes uncandid to the verge of dishonesty. He seems not to mind misstating the position of any one he supposes himself to disagree with, and then attacking him for what he never said, or even implied; the critic thinks this is droll, and appears not to suspect that it is immoral. He is not tolerant; he thinks it a virtue to be intolerant; it is hard for him to understand that the same thing may be admirable at one time and deplorable at another; and that it is really his business to classify and analyze the fruits of the human mind as the naturalist classifies the objects of his study, rather than to praise or blame them; that there is a measure of the same absurdity in his trampling on a poem, a novel, or an essay that does not please him as in the botanist's grinding a plant under-foot because he does not find it pretty. He does not conceive that it is his business rather to identify the species and then explain how and where the specimen is imperfect and irregular. If he could once acquire this simple ideal of his duty he would be much more agreeable company than he now is, and a more useful member of society; though we trust we are not yet saying that he is not extremely delight-ful as he is, and wholly indispensable. He is certainly more ignorant than malevolent; and considering the hard conditions under which he works, his necessity of writing hurriedly from an imperfect examina-tion of far more books, on a greater variety of subjects, than he can even hope to read, the average American critic—the ordinary critic of commerce, so to speak—is very well indeed. Collectively he is more than this; for, as we said once before, we believe that the joint effect of our criticism is the pretty thorough appreciation of any book submitted to it.

II.

The misfortune rather than the fault of our several or individual critic is that he is the heir of the false theory and bad manners of the English school. The theory of that school has apparently been that almost any person of glib and lively expression is competent to write of almost any branch of polite literature; its manners are what we know. The American, whom it has largely formed, is by nature very glib and lively, and commonly his criticism, viewed as imaginative work, is more agreeable than that of the Englishman; but it is, like the art of both countries, apt to be amateurish. In some degree our authors have freed themselves from English models; they have gained some notion of the more serious work of the Continent; but it is still the ambition of the American critic to write like the English critic, to show his wit if not his learning, to strive to eclipse the author under review rather than illustrate him. He has not yet caught on to the fact that it is really no part of his business to exploit himself, but that it is altogether his duty to place a book in such a light that the reader shall know its class, its function, its character. The vast good-nature of our people preserves us from the worst effects of this criticism without principles. Our critic, at his lowest, is rarely malignant; and when he is rude or untruthful, it is mostly without truculence; we suspect that he is often offensive without knowing that he is so. If he loves a shining mark because a fair shot with mud shows best on that kind of target, it is for the most part from a boyish mischievousness quite innocent of malice. Now and then he acts simply under instruction from higher authority, and denounces because it is the tradition of his publication to do so. In other cases the critic is obliged to support his journal's repute for severity, or for wit, or for morality, though he may himself be entirely amiable, dull, and wicked; this necessity more or less warps his verdicts.

The worst is that he is personal, perhaps because it is so easy and so natural to be personal, and so instantly attractive. In this respect our criticism has not improved from the accession of large numbers of ladies to its ranks, though we still hope so much from women in our politics when they shall come to vote. They have come to write, and with the effect to increase the amount of little-digging, which rather superabounded in our literary criticism before. They 'know what they like'—that pernicious maxim of those who do not know what they ought to like—and they pass readily from censuring an author's performance to censuring him. They bring a lively stock of mis-apprehensions and prejudices to their work; they would rather have heard about than known about a book; and they take kindly to the public wish to be amused rather than edified. But neither have they so much harm in them; they too are more ignorant than malevolent.

III.

Our criticism is disabled by the unwillingness of the critic to learn from an author, and his readiness to mistrust him. A writer passes his whole life in fitting himself for a certain kind of performance; the critic does not ask why, or whether the performance is good or bad, but if he does not like the kind, he instructs the writer to go off and do some other sort of thing—usually the sort that has been done already, and done sufficiently. If he could once understand that a man who has written the book he dislikes, probably knows infinitely more about its kind and his own fitness for doing it than any one else, the critic might learn something, and might help the reader to learn; but by putting himself in a false position, a position of superiority, he is of no use. He ought, in the first place, to cast prayerfully about for humility, and especially to beseech the powers to preserve him from the sterility of arrogance and the deadness of contempt, for out of these nothing can proceed. He is not to suppose that an author has committed an offence against him by writing the kind of book he does not like; he will be far more profitably employed on behalf of the reader in finding out whether they had better not both like it. Let him conceive of an author as not in any wise on trial before him, but as a reflection of this or that aspect of life, and he will not be tempted to browbeat him or bully him.

So far as we know, this is not now the carriage of criticism toward authorship in any country but England and her literary colonies. Self-restraint, decency, even politeness, seem to characterize the behavior of critics elsewhere. They may not like an author's work, but they do not for that reason use him with ignominy or insult. Some extreme friends of civilization have insisted that a critic should not write of a book what he would not say to the author personally about it; but this is not possible; it is at least premature, if not a little unreasonable. All that we now suggest is that the critic need not be impolite, even to the youngest and weakest author. A little courtesy, or a good deal, a constant perception of the fact that a book is not a misdemeanor, a decent self-respect that must forbid the civilized man the savage pleasure of wounding, are what we ask for our criticism, as something which will add sensibly to its present lustre; or, if nothing can do that, will at least approach it to the Continental attitude, and remove it from the English.

IV.

We do not really suppose that the inhabitants of the British Islands are all satisfied with their literary criticism; we suspect that many of them must have their misgivings when the *Saturday Review*, for example, calls names and makes faces because some one has, for instance, deplored the survival of the English aristocracy in our time. They must some of them feel that it is not a wholly terrible spectacle; that however right the *Review* may be, its behavior is a little ridiculous. But those islanders are very curious, and in some things quite remote; they may still think the tomtom a powerful argument, and the gourd-rattle the best means of carrying conviction to the minds of men. They may even admire the solemn port of the *Academy* when it knits its classic front and tells an American novelist that 'he is, to say the least, presumptuous' in questioning the impeccability of English fiction. What he would be, if the *Academy* were to say the most, one shrinks from guessing; but apparently the British aristocracy, which reads the British novel so little, and the British novel, which derides the British aristocracy so much, are twin monuments whose perfection no foreigner may doubt, under pain of British criticism's high displeasure.

It is no doubt partially in revolt from this severity that we call in question British criticism itself, and beg American criticism, which is still in the sap, to incline to other ways, to study different methods and different measures. At this stage of the proceedings, with the light of civilization flowing in upon us from the whole European continent, it would be a pity to continue in that old personal, arrogant, egotistical tradition; it would be something more than a pity, it would be a sin; and we tenderly entreat our brethren, from the highest to the lowest, to take thought of the matter, to reason with themselves, and to be warned by the examples which they have hitherto sought to imitate.

V.

Consider, dear friends, what you are really in the world for. It is not, apparently, for a great deal, because your only excuse for being is that somebody else has been. The critic exists because the author first existed. If books failed to appear, the critic must disappear, like the poor aphis or the lowly caterpillar in the absence of vegetation. These insects may both suppose that they have something to do with the creation of vegetation; and the critic may suppose that he has something to do with the creation of literature; but a very little reasoning ought to convince alike aphis, caterpillar, and critic that they are mistaken. The critic—to drop the others—must perceive, if he will question himself more carefully, that his office is mainly to ascertain facts and traits of literature, not to invent or denounce them; to discover principles, not to establish them; to report, not to create.

The history of all literature shows that even with the youngest and weakest author criticism is quite powerless against his will to do his own work in his own way; and if this is the case in the green wood, how much more in the dry! It has been thought by the sentimentalists that criticism, if it cannot cure, can at least kill, and Keats was long alleged in proof of its efficacy in this sort. But criticism neither cured nor killed Keats, as we all now very well know. It wounded, it cruelly hurt him, no doubt; and it is always in the power of the critic to give pain to the author—the meanest critic to the greatest author—for no one can help feeling a rudeness. But every literary movement has been violently opposed at the start, and yet never stayed in the least, or arrested, by criticism; every author has been condemned for his virtues, but in no wise changed by it. In the beginning he reads the critics; but presently perceiving that he alone makes or mars himself, and that they have no instruction for him, he mostly leaves off reading them, though he is always glad of their kindness or grieved by their harshness when he chances upon it. This we believe, is the general experience, modified, of course, by exceptions.

VI.

Then, are we critics of no use in the world? We should not like to think that, though we are not quite ready to define our use. If we were to confess that we had none, we must not say, Let us not be like these English critics; but, Let us not be at all.

More than one sober thinker is inclining at present to suspect that æsthetically or specifically we *are* of no use, and that we are only useful historically; that we may register laws, but not enact them. We are not quite prepared to admit that æsthetic criticism is useless, though in view of its futility in any given instance it is hard to deny that it is so. It certainly seems as useless against a book that strikes the popular fancy, and prospers on in spite of condemnation by the best critics, as it is against a book which does not generally please, and which no critical favor can make acceptable. This is so common a phenomenon that we wonder it has never hitherto suggested to criticism that its point of view was altogether mistaken, and that it was really necessary to judge books not as dead things, but as living things—things which have an influence and a power irrespective of beauty and wisdom, and merely as expressions of actuality in thought and feeling. Perhaps criticism has a cumulative and final effect; perhaps it does some good we do not know of. It apparently does not affect the author directly, but it may reach him through the reader. It may in some cases enlarge or diminish his audience for a while, until he has thoroughly measured and tested his own powers. We doubt if it can do more than that; but if it can do that, we will admit that it may be the toad of adversity, ugly and venomous, from whose unpleasant brow he is to snatch the precious jewel of lasting fame.

We employ this figure in all humility, and we conjure our fraternity to ask themselves, without rancor or offence, whether we are right or not. In this quest let us get together all the modesty and candor and impartiality we can; for if we should happen to discover a good reason for continuing to exist, these qualities will be of more use to us than any others in examining the work of people who really produce something.

NOTE

1 'At the Sign of the Ship,' *Longman's*, 19 (April 1892), 682.

14 Civilization and barbarism, romance and reality: the question of modern civilization
1887

From 'The Editor's Study,' *Harper's Monthly*, September 1887.

Howells came to believe, perhaps correctly, that issues not merely aesthetic or personal but fateful for the whole modern world lay in the bed-rock significance of his realism war. Not like sporting chaff or points at tennis at all, the issues were civilization and its future. In retrospect we know that the futures of Europe and Western culture did stand in the balance in those years tilting toward 1914. Whether he knew the right answers or not, Howells understood the questions. The questions were whether the culture of the West, of which Howells was helping to settle the fact that American culture partook, could respond adequately to the challenges of democracy, population density, popular education, industrialization, urbanism, and technological power. The sphinx of modernism put the riddle, the right answer to which was the creation of a spiritually satisfactory popular culture. The response of Western culture, the First World War, was the wrong reply.

The truly crucial issue for Howells in the latter 1880s, then, was whether he and his movement could win their fight for public taste. In his case, of course, it was the fight for public taste in the United States first and then, as American reformers had dreamed since 1630 when the theocrats of the Massachusetts Bay tried to set their city shining on a hill, for the taste of Great Britain. Though Howells lost like everybody else, his campaign appears, especially in the retrospect of our insistently wistful questions about what happened to us, and why, in the first half of this present century, to have interest and significance.

Not to repeat his argument, which he enforces throughout this 'Study,' it is worth noticing that he regards the larger fight for the public sensibility as a contest between a Dionysian and an Apollonian morality. Since nobody is perfectly civilized, the contention that people 'like melodrama, impossible fiction, and the trapeze' only shows that there is something of Huck Finn in the maturest mind, something of the barbarian in the most cultivated. That we must pay our dues to Brother Ass, however, proves only that we need more cultivation, more light. If democracy is not to go down into the Dionysian, the tragic dark, it must achieve what Tocqueville had said it never could: its own true culture.

As Howells saw the condition of the historical moment, there existed a great international movement toward light and healing, the realism he identified with civilization, though his inclusion of Thackeray, Balzac, Manzoni, Hawthorne, 'or even Walter Scott' among the saints suggests that he excluded no sincere romantic, no serious artist. The real challenge he saw to be what is childish, barbarian, 'neo-romantic' or 'romanticistic,' as he would come to call fake romance. The question was how to create an adequate modernity; and Howells believed in its centrality so seriously that he would blister Max Nordau's *Degeneration* when it appeared.

In retrospect it is easy to know that Howells quickly lost his fight for public taste: he was to admit it as early as 1894. In a broader view it is also evident that by 1914 his fight for civilization had also been lost. The lights went out over Europe one by one, and the culture of the West went down into the Dionysian dark. Do we know whether the Apollonian light will be relit? The questions the witness of Howells asks us are whether we have anything to regret—or to learn.

I.

A writer in a Western periodical has put into convenient shape some common errors concerning popularity as a test of merit in a book. He seems to think, for instance, that the love of the marvellous and impossible in fiction, which is shown not only by 'the unthinking multitude clamoring about the book counters' for fiction of that sort, but by the 'literary elect' also, is proof of some principle in human nature which ought to be respected as well as tolerated. He seems to believe that the ebullition of this passion forms a sufficient answer to those who say that art of all kinds should represent life, and that the art which misrepresents life is feeble art and false art. But it appears to us that a little carefuler reasoning from a little closer inspection of the facts would not have brought him to these conclusions. In the first place, we doubt very much whether the 'literary elect' have been fascinated in great numbers by the fiction in question; but if we supposed them to have really fallen under that spell, we should still be able to account for their fondness and that of the 'unthinking multitude' upon the same grounds, without honoring either very much. It is the habit of hasty casuists to regard civilization as inclusive of all the members of a civilized community; but this is a palpable error. Many persons in every civilized community live in a state of more or less evident savagery with respect to their habits, their morals, and their propensities; and they are held in check only by the law. Many more yet are savage in their tastes, as they show by the decoration of their houses and persons, and by their choice of books and pictures; and these are left to the restraints of public opinion. In fact, no man can be said to be thoroughly civilized or always civilized; the most refined, the most enlightened person has his moods, his moments of barbarism, in which the best, or even the second best, shall not please him. At these times the lettered and the unlettered are alike primitive, and their gratifications are of the same simple sort; the highly culti-vated person may then like melodrama, impossible fiction, and the trapeze as sincerely and thoroughly as a boy of thirteen or a barbarian of any age.

We do not blame him for these moods; we find something instruc-tive and interesting in them; but if they lastingly established them-selves in him, we could not help deploring the state of that person. No one can really think that the 'literary elect,' who are said to have joined the 'unthinking multitude' in clamoring about the book counters for the romances of no-man's land, take the same kind of pleasure in them as they do in a novel of Tolstoi, Tourguénief, George Eliot, Thackeray, Balzac, Manzoni, Hawthorne, Henry James, Thomas Hardy, Palacio Valdés, or even Walter Scott. They have joined the 'unthinking multitude' perhaps because they are tired of thinking, and expect to find relaxation in feeling—feeling crudely, grossly, merely. For once in a way there is no great harm in this; perhaps no harm at all. It is perfectly natural: let them have their innocent debauch. But let us distinguish, for our own sake and guid-ance, between the different kinds of things that please the same kind of people; between the things that please them habitually and those that please them occasionally; between the pleasures that edify them and those that amuse them. Otherwise we shall be in danger of becoming permanently part of the 'unthinking multitude,' and of remaining puerile, primitive, savage. We shall be so in moods and at moments; but let us not fancy that those are high moods or fortunate moments. If they are harmless, that is the most that can be said for them. They are lapses from which we can perhaps go forward more vigorously; but even this is not certain.

Our own philosophy of the matter, however, would not bring us to prohibition of such literary amusements as the writer quoted seems to find significant of a growing indifference to truth and sanity in fiction. Once more, we say, these amusements have their place, as the circus has, and the burlesque, and negro minstrelsy, and the ballet, and prestidigitation. No one of these is to be despised in its place;

but we had better understand that it is not the highest place, and that it is hardly an intellectual delight. The lapse of all the 'literary elect' in the world could not dignify unreality; and their present mood, if it exists, is of no more weight against that beauty in literature which comes from truth alone, and never can come from anything else, than the permanent state of the 'unthinking multitude.'

II.

Yet even as regards the 'unthinking multitude,' we believe we are not able to take the attitude of the writer we have quoted. We are afraid that we respect them more than he would like to have us, though we cannot always respect their taste, any more than that of the 'literary elect.' We respect them for their good sense in most practical matters; for their laborious, honest lives; for their kindness, their good-will; for that aspiration toward something better than themselves which seems to stir, however dumbly, in every human breast not abandoned to literary pride or other forms of self-righteousness. We find every man interesting, whether he thinks or unthinks, whether he is savage or civilized; for this reason we cannot thank the novelist who teaches us not to know, but to unknow, our kind; and we cannot believe that Miss Murfree will feel herself praised by a critic who says she has made her Tennessee mountaineers acceptable to us because she 'has fashioned them as they are not.' We believe that she has made them acceptable for exactly the opposite reason, and has taught us to see the inner loveliness and tenderness, however slight and evanescent, of those poor, hard, dull, narrow lives, with an exquisite sympathy which we are afraid must remain unknown to the lovers of the sweet-pretty. The perfect portrayal of what passes even in a soul whose body smokes a cob-pipe or dips snuff, and dwells in a log hut on a mountain-side, would be worth more than all the fancies ever feigned; and we value Miss Murfree's work for the degree in which it approaches this perfection. It is when she seems to have drawn upon romance and tradition rather than life for her colors that we have wished her to 'give us her mountain folk as she saw them before her fancy began to work upon them.' This may be 'babbling folly,' and 'sheer, unmixed nonsense'; our critic is so sure of himself as to be able to call it so; but we venture to reaffirm it. It appears to us that the opposite position is one of the last refuges of the aristocratic spirit which is disappearing from politics and society, and is now seeking to shelter itself in æsthetics. The pride of caste is becoming the pride of taste; but as before, it is averse to the mass of men; it consents to know them only in some conventionalized and artificial guise. It seeks to withdraw itself, to stand aloof; to be distinguished, and not to be identified. Democracy in literature is the reverse of all this. It wishes to know and to tell the truth, confident that consolation and delight are there; it does not care to paint the marvellous and impossible for the vulgar many, or to sentimentalize and falsify the actual for the vulgar few. Men are more like than unlike one another: let us make them know one another better, that they may be all humbled and strengthened with a sense of their fraternity. Neither arts, nor letters, nor sciences, except as they somehow, clearly or obscurely, tend to make the race better and kinder, are to be regarded as serious interests; they are all lower than the rudest crafts that feed and house and clothe, for except they do this office they are idle; and they cannot do this except from and through the truth.

III.

A more temperate critic than the one we have been quoting deplores in a New York journal the danger which attends the new fiction of the South from its prompt and easy success. He calls himself a Southerner, and he thinks it would be well if there were a school of Southern criticism for the censure of Southern literature; but at the same time he is disposed to defend this literature against a charge which we agree with him cannot lie against it alone. It has been called narrow, and he asks: 'Is not the broadest of the new American fiction narrow, when compared, as it should be compared, with the authors of Russian fiction, French fiction, English fiction? Is there a living novelist of the North whose largest boundaries do not shrink to pitiful dimensions when put by the side of Tolstoi's or Balzac's, or Thackeray's?'

We do not know certainly whether a Southerner thinks narrowness a defect of Northern fiction or not, but upon the supposition that he does so, we remind him that both Thackeray and Balzac are dead, and that our recent novelists might as well, for all purposes of argument, be compared with Cervantes and Le Sage. Moreover, Balzac is rather a narrow writer in each of his books, and if we are to grant him breadth we must take him in the whole group which he required to work out his *comédie humaine*. Each one of Mr. Henry James's books is as broad as any one of Balzac's; and we believe his *Princess Casamassima* is of a scope and variety quite unknown to them. Thackeray, to be sure, wandered through vast spaces, but his greatest work was concerned with the very narrow world of English society; his pictures of life outside of society were in the vein of caricature. As for Tolstoi, he is the incomparable; and no novelist of any time or any tongue can fairly be compared with him, as no dramatist can fairly be compared with Shakespeare. Nevertheless, if something of this sort is absolutely required, we will instance Mr. J. W. De Forest, in his very inadequately named *Miss Ravenel's Conversion*, as presenting an image of American life during the late rebellion, both North and South, at home and in the field, which does not 'shrink to pitiful dimensions' even when 'put by the side of Tolstoi's' *War and Peace*; it is an admirable novel, and spacious enough for the vast drama glimpsed in it. Mr. Cable's *Grandissimes* is large enough to reflect a civilization; and Mr. Bishop, in *The Golden Justice* and *The House of a Merchant Prince*, shows a feeling for amplitude in the whole design, as well as for close and careful work in the details.

The present English fiction is as narrow as our own; and if a Southerner had looked a little farther abroad he would have found that most modern fiction was narrow in a certain sense. In Italy he would have found the best men writing novels as brief and restricted in range as ours; in Spain the novels are intense and deep, and not spacious; the French school, with the exception of Zola, is narrow; the Norwegians are narrow; the Russians, except Tolstoi, are narrow, and the next greatest after him, Tourguénief, is the narrowest great novelist, as to mere dimensions, that ever lived, dealing nearly always with small groups, isolated and analyzed in the most American fashion. In fine, the charge of narrowness accuses the whole tendency of modern fiction as much as the American school. But we do not by any means allow that this superficial narrowness is a defect, while denying that it is a universal characteristic of our fiction; it is rather, for the present, a virtue. Indeed, we should call the present American work, North and South, thorough, rather than narrow. In one sense it is as broad as life, for each man is a microcosm, and the writer who is able to acquaint us intimately with half a dozen people, or the conditions of a neighborhood or a class, has done something which cannot in any bad sense be called narrow; his breadth is vertical instead of lateral, that is all; and this depth is more desirable than horizontal expansion in a civilization like ours, where the differences are not of classes, but of types, and not of types either so much as of characters.

A new method was necessary in dealing with the new conditions, and the new method is world-wide, because the whole world is more or less Americanized. Tolstoi is exceptionally voluminous among modern writers, even Russian writers; and it might be said that the *forte* of Tolstoi himself is not in his breadth sidewise, but in his breadth upward and downward. *The Death of Ivan Illitch* leaves as vast an impression on the reader's soul as any episode of *War and Peace*, which indeed can only be recalled in episodes, and not as a whole. In fine, we think that our writers may be safely counselled to continue their work in the modern way, because it is the best way yet known. If they make it true, it will be large, no matter what its superficies are; and it would be the greatest mistake to try to make it big. A big book is necessarily a group of episodes more or less loosely connected by a thread of narrative, and there seems no reason why this thread must always be supplied. Each episode may be quite distinct, or it may be one of a connected group; the final effect will be from the truth of each episode, not from the size of the group.

IV.

Take, for instance, a number of studies like *A Humble Romance, and Other Stories*, by Miss Mary E. Wilkins, and you have the air of simple village life as liberally imparted as if all the separate little dramas were set in a single frame and related to one another. The old maids and widows aging and ailing and dying in their minute wooden houses; the forlorn elderly lovers; the simple girls and youths making and marring love; the husbands and wives growing apart and coming together; the quarrels and reconciliations; the eccentricities and the heroisms; the tender passions and true friendships; the funerals and weddings; the hates and spites; the injuries; the sacrifices; the crazy consciences; the sound commonsense—are all suggested and expressed in a measure which, we insist, does not lack breadth, though each sketch is like the sentences of Emerson, 'an infinitely repellent particle,' and will have nothing to do with any other, so far as community of action is concerned. Community of character abounds: the people are of one New England blood, and speak one racy tongue. It might all have been done otherwise; the lives and fortunes of these villagers might have been interwoven in one texture of narrative; but the work would not necessarily have gained breadth in gaining bulk. Breadth is in the treatment of material, not in the amount of it.

The great picture is from the great painter not from the extensive canvas. Miss Wilkins's work could hardly have given a wider sense of life in a Yankee village and the outlying farms if it had greater structural unity. It has unity of spirit, of point of view, of sympathy; and being what the author intended, we ask no other unity of it; many 'broader' views lack this unity which is so valuable. Besides, it has humor of a quaint, flavorous sort, it has genuine pathos, and a just and true respect for the virtues of the life with which it deals. We are tempted to give some passages illustrative of a very remarkable freshness in its description; they are abundant, but perhaps we had better content ourselves by referring the reader to the opening of the touching sketch, 'A Far-away Melody.' What is notable in all the descriptions is the absence of literosity; they are as unrhetorical as so many pictures of Tourguénief's, or Björnson's, or Verga's, and are interesting proofs of the fact that the present way of working is instinctive; one writer does not learn it from another; it is in the time, in the air, and no critic can change it. When you come to the motives of these little tales, the simplicity and originality are not always kept; sometimes they ring false, sentimental, romantic; but even then they are true in the working out of character, though this does not redeem them from the original error. For the most part, however, they are good through and through, and whoever loves the face of common humanity will find pleasure in them. They are peculiarly American, and they are peculiarly 'narrow' in a certain way, and yet they are like the best modern work everywhere in their directness and simplicity. They are somewhat in the direction of Miss Jewett's more delicate work, but the fun is opener and less demure, the literature is less refined, the poetry is a little cruder; but there is the same affectionate feeling for the material, a great apparent intimacy with the facts, and a like skill in rendering the Yankee parlance. We have our misgivings, however, about 'thar' and 'whar' on New England tongues, though we are not ready to deny that Miss Wilkins heard them in the locality she evidently knows so well.

V.

We own our misgiving with misgiving; for so clever a writer has probably thought upon this point already. We do not suppose infallibility in clever writers; but we do suppose a greater intelligence concerning their own work than any critic can bring to it; their ignorance even may be more valuable than his information; it may keep them at least from attempting to do their own work in some one else's way, and that is a great matter. In fact, if our present literary condition were bad, North or South, we should have no such hope of its improvement from criticism as the Southerner whom we have been quoting. In his belief that severity of censure would avail much, he advises Southern writers to turn from the mistaken kindness of Northern editors, and if they cannot get wholesome castigation from their Southern contemporaries, to go back to Poe, 'and take from his critical writings a certain standard of originality, contempt of mediocrity, and passion for beauty.' But we doubt if it is possible to take any such standard, contempt, and passion from Poe, who, with great talent, had a perversity, arrogance, and wilfulness that render him wellnigh worthless as a censor of others' work, and a mechanical ideal that disabled him from doing any very noble work of his own. He was of his time, and his tales and poems remain a part of literary history; but if they were written to-day, most of them could not be taken seriously. Do not go to Poe, we should say to our Southern writers if we felt it our office to instruct them, but go to Life. Do not trouble yourselves about standards or contempts or passions; but try to be faithful and natural; and remember that there is no greatness, no beauty, which does not come from truth to your own knowledge of things. In the mean time, that 'standard of mere acceptableness at the hands of the great Northern magazines' which a Southerner laments as ruinous to Southern writers is, to our thinking, the best critical standard they could have; and although these magazines certainly do 'publish almost monthly, poems or short stories which never live as literature,' this does not disable them as criterions. At least three-fifths of the literature called classic, in all languages, no more lives than the poems and stories that perish monthly in our magazines. It is all printed and reprinted, generation after generation, century after century; but it is not alive; it is as dead as the people who wrote it and read it, and to whom it meant something, perhaps; with whom it was a fashion, a caprice, a passing taste. A superstitious piety preserves it, and pretends that it has æsthetic qualities which can delight or edify; but nobody really enjoys it, except as a reflection of the past moods and humors of the race, or a revelation of the author's character; otherwise it is trash, and often very filthy trash, which the present trash at least is not. The 'standard of mere acceptableness at the hands of the great Northern magazines' is a very high standard. They are not perfect; but there is an even texture in the quality of their literature which so wide a variety of literature has never presented before. They are made with conscience and intelligence, and with an instinctive preference for what is most modern as, upon the whole, the best. Any Southern writer who contributes to them may be sure that their editors will be the first to know when he is repeating himself, when he is standing still, and when he is going backward, and may confidently await their warning signal.

The whole field of human experience was never so nearly covered by imaginative literature in any age as in this; and American life especially is getting represented with unexampled fulness. It is true that no one writer, no one book, represents it, for that is not possible; our social and political decentralization forbids this, and may forever forbid it. But a great number of very good writers are instinctively striving to make each part of the country and each phase of our civilization known to all the other parts; and their work is not narrow in any feeble or vicious sense. The world was once very little, and it is now very large. Formerly, all science could be grasped by a single mind; but now the man who hopes to become great or useful in science must devote himself to a single department. It is so in everything—all arts, all trades; and the novelist is not superior to the universal rule against universality. He contributes his share to a thorough knowledge of groups of the human race under conditions which are full of inspiring novelty and interest. He works more fearlessly, frankly, and faithfully than the novelist ever worked before; his work, or much of it, may be destined never to be reprinted from the monthly magazines; but if he turns to his book-shelf and regards the array of the British or other classics, he knows that they too are for the most part dead; he knows that the planet itself is destined to freeze up and drop into the sun at last, with all its surviving literature upon it. The question is merely one of time. He consoles himself, therefore, if he is wise, and works on; and we may all take some comfort from the thought that most things cannot be helped. Especially a movement in literature like that which the world is now witnessing cannot be helped; and we could no more turn back and be of the literary fashions of any age before this than we could turn back and be of its social, economical, or political conditions.

15 The artificial, ideal, academic grasshopper

1887

From 'The Editor's Study,' *Harper's Monthly*, December 1887.

Though Howells had little enough to say of Ruskin and in certain ways their intellectual temperaments were mutually exclusive, nevertheless he first read Ruskin with Venice all about him and must in the long run have been influenced in both social and aesthetic thought. In general the necessary strategy of a realist led him to reject the transcendentalism of any romantic organicist. As Emerson put it so purely, the romantic idealist said, 'Particular natural facts are symbols of particular spiritual facts.' Then he exclaimed, 'Behold!' The realist, sad agnostic, replied, 'My eyes are dim, I cannot see. Where is your spiritual fact? Your natural fact I perceive. Let us see it clearly, in full natural truth and beauty. Come to think of it, who ever saw it so before?'

Like the coeval Impressionist painters, Howells identified the obsolete romantic with the Academic and the Academic with meaninglessness, the 'dead conventionalities.' Taking a hint from Hippolyte Taine, he invented a dry mock of a trope for dramatizing his insight and set it brilliantly within smaller gems of quotation from great names whom no anti-realist could despise: Michelangelo, Burke, Goethe. The trope has long been famous, but in its original context one can see that Howells set it forth in a superb critical essay.

I.

The question of a final criterion for the appreciation of art, or of a 'unity of taste,' which Mr. J. Addington Symonds treated with so much reason, in the passage quoted from his last volumes[1] in the Study for November, is one that perpetually recurs to those interested in any sort of æsthetic work. The reader will remember that Mr. Symonds held, in brief, that simplicity and naturalness and honesty were the lasting tests; moods and tastes and fashions change, people fancy now this and now that; but what is unpretentious and what is

121

true is enduringly beautiful and good, and nothing else is so. This is not saying that fantastic and monstrous and artificial things do not please; everybody knows that they do please immensely for a time, and then, after the lapse of a much longer time, they have the charm of the *rococo*. Nothing is more curious than the fascination that fashion has. Fashion in women's dress, almost every fashion, is somehow delightful, else it would never have been the fashion; but if any one will look through a collection of old fashion plates, he must own that most fashions have been ugly. A few, which could be readily instanced, have been very pretty, and even beautiful, but it is doubtful if these have pleased the greatest number of people. The ugly delights as well as the beautiful, and not merely because the ugly in fashion is associated with the young loveliness of the women who wear the ugly fashions, and wins a charm from them, not because the vast majority of mankind are tasteless, but for some cause that is not perhaps ascertainable. It is quite as likely to return in the fashions of our clothes, and houses and furniture, and poetry and fiction and painting, as the beautiful, and it may be from an instinctive or a reasoned sense of this that some of the extreme naturalists now refuse to make the old discrimination against it, or to regard the ugly as any less worthy of celebration in art than the beautiful; some of them, in fact, seem to regard it as rather more worthy, if anything. Possibly there is no absolutely ugly, no absolutely beautiful; or possibly the ugly contains always an element of the beautiful better adapted to the general appreciation than the more perfectly beautiful. This is a hazardous and somewhat discouraging conjecture, but we offer it for no more than it is worth; and we do not pin our faith to the saying of one whom we heard denying, the other day, that a thing of beauty was a joy forever. He contended that Keats's line should have read, 'Some things of beauty are sometimes joys forever,' and that any assertion beyond this was hazardous.

II.

We should, indeed, prefer another line of Keats's, if we were to profess any formulated creed, and should feel much safer with his 'Beauty is Truth, Truth Beauty,' than even with our friend's reformation of the more quoted verse. It brings us back to the solid ground taken by Mr. Symonds, which is not essentially different from that taken in a book read last summer, at the season when the newspaper noticers of the magazines suppose their conductors to be sharing the luxurious disoccupation of the daily journalists. It was at that season when these children of inspiration invariably announce that the July *Century* or *Atlantic* or *Harper* betrays the enervating influences of the weather in the lax and flimsy character of its contents (the number having actually been made up in the eager air of early May, when the sleepless energies of the editor were irritated to their highest activity by the conviction that the winter was going to last forever); and at the same time there came to us a carefully marked paragraph assuring us, in the usual confident and unsparing terms, that we were mistaken in supposing that literature should be true to life—'it should be true to art.' Out of the envious spirit which will be readily attributed to us we suppress the name of the newspaper; but there is no reason why we should withhold that of the book, which every reader of taste will suppose an intimacy with, as we should ourselves have done six months ago. It was the great Mr. Burke's *Essay on the Sublime and the Beautiful*—a singularly modern book, considering how long ago it was wrote (as the great Mr. Steele would have written the participle a little longer ago), and full of a certain well-mannered and agreeable instruction. In some things it is of that droll little eighteenth-century world, when philosophy had got the neat little universe into the hollow of its hand, and knew just what it was, and what it was for; but it is quite without arrogance; it is not even so confident as the newspaper which we are keeping back the name of. It will be seen that Mr. Burke differs radically with this other authority, which, however, he unwittingly owns to be of the sort called critical, and might almost be supposed to have had prophetically in mind. 'As for those called critics,' he says,

they have generally sought the rule of the arts in the wrong place; they have sought among poems, pictures, engravings, statues, and buildings; *but art can never give the rules that make an art*. This is, I believe, the reason why artists in general, and poets principally, have been confined in so narrow a circle; they have been rather imitators of one another than of nature. Critics follow them, and therefore can do little as guides. I can judge but poorly of anything while I measure it by no other standard than itself. *The true standard of the arts is in every man's power; and an easy observation of the most common, sometimes of the meanest things, in nature, will give the truest lights*, where the greatest sagacity and industry that slights such observation must leave us in the dark, or, what is worse, amuse and mislead us by false lights.

III.

If this should happen to be true—and it certainly commends itself to our acceptance—it might portend an immediate danger to the vested interests of criticism, only that it was written a hundred years ago; and we shall probably have the 'sagacity and industry that slights the observation of nature' long enough yet to allow most critics the time to learn some more useful trade than criticism as they pursue it. Nevertheless, we are in hopes that the communistic era in taste foreshadowed by Burke is approaching, and that it will occur within the lives of men now overawed by the foolish old superstition that literature and art are anything but the expression of life, and are to be judged by any other test than that of their fidelity to it. The time is coming, we trust, when each new author, each new artist, will be considered, not in his proportion to any other author or artist, but in his relation to the human nature, known to us all, which it is his privilege, his high duty, to interpret. 'The true standard of the artist is in every man's power,' already as Burke says; Michelangelo's 'light of the piazza,' the glance of the common eye, is and always was the best light on a statue; Goethe's 'boys and blackbirds' have in all ages been the real connoisseurs of berries; but hitherto the mass of common men have been afraid to apply their own simplicity, naturalness, and honesty to the appreciation of the beautiful. They have always cast about for the instruction of some one who professed to know better, and who browbeat wholesome common-sense into the self-distrust that ends in sophistication. They have fallen generally to the worst of this bad species, and have been 'amused and misled' (how pretty that quaint old use of *amuse* is!) 'by the false lights' of critical vanity and self-righteousness. They have been taught to compare what they see and what they read, not with the things that they have observed and known, but with the things that some other artist or writer has done. Especially if they have themselves the artistic impulse in any direction they are taught to form themselves, not upon life, but upon the masters who became masters only by forming themselves upon life. The seeds of death are planted in them, and they can produce only the still-born, the academic. They are not told to take their work into the public square and see if it seems true to the chance passer, but to test it by the work of the very men who refused and decried any other test of their own work. The young writer who attempts to report the phrase and carriage of every-day life, who tries to tell just how he has heard men talk and seen them look, is made to feel guilty of something low and unworthy by the stupid people who would like to have him show how Shakespeare's men talked and looked, or Scott's, or Thackeray's, or Balzac's, or Hawthorne's, or Dickens's; he is instructed to idealize his personages, that is, to take the life-likeness out of them, and put the literary-likeness into them. He is approached in the spirit of the wretched pedantry into which learning, much or little, always decays when it withdraws itself and stands apart from experience in an attitude of imagined superiority, and which would say with the same confidence to the scientist: 'I see that you are looking at a grasshopper there which you have found in the grass, and I suppose you intend to describe it. Now don't waste your time and sin against culture in *that* way. I've got a grasshopper here, which has been evolved at considerable pains and expense out of the grass-hopper in general; in fact, it's a type. It's made up of wire and card-board, very prettily painted in a conventional tint, and it's perfectly indestructible. It isn't very much like a real grasshopper, but it's a great deal nicer, and it's served to represent the notion of a grass-hopper ever since man emerged from barbarism. You may say that it's artificial. Well, it *is* artificial: but then it's ideal too; and what you want to do is to cultivate the ideal. You'll find the books full of my kind of grasshopper, and scarcely a trace of yours in any of them. The thing that you are proposing to do is commonplace; but if you say that it isn't commonplace, for the very reason that it hasn't been done before, you'll have to admit that it's photographic.'

IV.

As we said, we hope the time is coming when not only the artist, but the common, average man, who always 'has the standard of the arts in his power,' will have also the courage to apply it, and will reject the ideal grasshopper wherever he finds it, in science, in literature, in art, because it is not 'simple, natural, and honest,' because it is not like a real grasshopper. But we will own that we think the time is yet far off, and that the people who have been brought up on the ideal grass-hopper, the heroic grasshopper, the impassioned grasshopper, the self-devoted, adventureful, good old romantic card-board grass-hopper, must die out before the simple, honest, and natural grass-hopper can have a fair field. We are in no haste to compass the end of these good people, whom we find in the mean time very amusing. It is delightful to meet one of them, either in print or out of it—some sweet elderly lady or excellent gentleman whose youth was pastured on the literature of thirty or forty years ago—and to witness the confidence with which they preach their favorite authors as all the law and the prophets. They have commonly read little or nothing since, or, if they have, they have judged it by a standard taken from these authors, and never dreamt of judging it by nature; they are destitute of the documents in the case of the later writers; they suppose that Balzac was the beginning of realism, and that Zola is its wicked end; they are quite ignorant, but they are ready to talk you down, if you differ from them, with an assumption of knowledge sufficient for any occasion. The horror, the resentment, with which they receive any question of their very peccable literary saints is to be matched only by the frenzy of the *Saturday Review* in defending the British aristocracy; you descend at once very far in the moral and social scale, and anything short of offensive personality is too good for you; it is expressed to you that you are one to be avoided, and put down even a little lower than you have naturally fallen.

These worthy persons are not to blame; it is part of their intellectual mission to represent the petrifaction of taste, and to preserve an image of a smaller and cruder and emptier world than we now live in, a world which was feeling its way toward the simple, the natural, the honest, but was a good deal 'amused and misled' by lights now no longer mistakable for heavenly luminaries. They belong to a time, just passing away, when certain authors were considered authorities in certain kinds, when they must be accepted entire and not questioned in any particular. Now we are beginning to see and to say that no author is an authority except in those moments when he held his ear close to Nature's lips and caught her very accent. These moments are not continuous with any authors in the past, and they are rare with all. Therefore we are not afraid to say now that the greatest classics are sometimes not at all great, and that we can profit by them only when we hold them, like our meanest contemporaries, to a strict accounting, and verify their work by the standard of the arts which we all have in our power, the simple, the natural, and the honest.

NOTE

1 *The Renaissance in Italy.*

16 From Emerson to Tolstoi
1888

From 'The Editor's Study,' *Harper's Monthly*, February 1888.

Perhaps, as I have said before, because they too much confronted him with his need to revolt against his well-loved father, Howells long remained ambivalent, uncomfortable with the great American romantics. About Whitman, as we have seen, he felt always in conflict. In and out of New York for twenty-five years while Melville lived there, Howells apparently did not meet him; and Howells reviewed *Battle-Pieces* in 1866 with none of the sympathy he would have brought to that poetry by 1890. At Concord in 1860 Howells was baffled by the Thoreau with whom he had come to exult in mutual enthusiasm for John Brown. And as youthful admirer, then as editor, even as a fellow member of The Saturday Club, Howells felt eluded by Emerson. Of the elder set, only Lowell, an equivocal romantic, and Henry James, Sr., briefly almost a surrogate father, made Howells comfortable.

By the time he wrote the February 1888 'Editor's Study' (probably in October 1887), however, Howells felt ready to come to terms with the elder generation. Now he had the wherewithal for accommodation. Whoever thinks Howells's mind squeamish might contemplate his conclusion that it was supremely Emerson's 'impersonality . . . which makes him now and always our neighbor and our friend, the most imaginable person of his day'; to appreciate Emerson's rejection of romantic ego-fixation, he suggested, let the reader meditate

> the wisdom through which the mass of our stupidity and selfishness may finally be civilized into indifference to those questions, through a sense of duty to others. In a period still reeking with gross romantic individualism, when so many were straining to retch out the last rinsings of their sick egotism upon their fellows, he stood hale and serene and sane, elect and beautiful in every aspect of his mind.

Perhaps Howells's diction had been influenced by thinking of Henry James, Sr., in the context, but it might also have been affected by the transit of his mind from Emerson to Whitman. Aesthetic revolt, Howells now thinks, Emerson's own artistic 'impatience of smoothness and regularity, his joy in a fractured surface,' made him appreciate Whitman's form. Now, at last, Howells is ready to approve Whitman's poetic. But not, he perceives, Whitman's ultimate morality: Tolstoi's is greater, truer. If the two 'masters . . . are the same in aesthetic effect,' they nevertheless stand 'at opposite poles morally': Whitman stands for Dionysian 'rapture' and release; 'the Russian's is the cry of the soul for help against the world and the flesh.'

Thus Howells arrives at an aesthetic which becomes an ethic: the test is 'literary consciousness,' literosity. Tolstoi seems almost the only writer without it. Whitman, Thackeray, Dickens, Gogol, even Daudet (and all humorists and therefore, of course, Howells himself) are 'literose.' Next to Tolstoi, Verga, Palacio Valdés (sometimes), William Hale White ('Mark Rutherford'), Maupassant, and occasionally Mary Wilkins Freeman possess 'simplicity,' a virtue almost as difficult as purity.

It was another fine essay, another sacrificed in *Criticism and Fiction*.

I.

We have seldom read a biography in which life and character appeared with more completeness than in Mr. James Elliot Cabot's *Memoir of Ralph Waldo Emerson*. The work must have been all the more difficult because the life was so uneventful, and the character so essentially undramatic. Of course Mr. Cabot has allowed both to express themselves in Emerson's abundant letters and journals, but he has not abandoned his office to these, and what he has to say of Emerson from time to time, in comment and summary, is no less valuable for a right understanding of Emerson than what Emerson says of himself. Often it is more valuable, for Emerson still needs an apostle to the Gentiles. The literary merit of the book, which to our present thinking is always the least merit of a good book, is of a sort as uninsistent as Emerson could have wished that of a record of his life to be, and that is perhaps saying all that one need say of the clear style, the unaffected manner, and the candid attitude.

There is the advantage in the last that it leaves you assured of the estimates you form in Emerson's favor throughout; you feel that nothing has been done to force your liking or your duty to that illuminated conscience which Emerson was from first to last. He was the final and pre-eminent Puritan, with all that made Puritanism mean and harsh, cruel and hateful, eliminated from his righteous and gentle spirit; and this is what Mr. Cabot's memoir enables you to perceive in almost the same measure as if you had known the man. It was inevitable that such a man, with the defects as well as the virtues of his qualities, should seem placed out of time. He was, indeed, so much ahead of his time in his perceptions that we have not yet lived long enough to know how modern they were.

His sympathies perhaps lagged a little. He was not a man who *felt* his way; he had to *see* it; though when once he saw it, lions might be in it, but he went forward. His indifference to consequences came partly from his impersonality; he was so much an idealization of the ordinary human being that his fears were attenuated, like his sympathies. This again was Puritanism, which had so wholly died out of his creed that almost at the outset of his clerical career he found it impossible to go on making formal prayers in the pulpit, or administering the communion. Then he promptly turned his back upon this career, though with many a longing, lingering look over his shoulder for some ideal Church in which these functions would not be insisted on.

His evolution as an antislavery reformer is an even more interesting illustration of these facts of his character. When he was a very young man he came in contact with slavery in Florida, where he had gone one winter for his health; but he does not seem to have felt the horror, the crime of it, so much as he discerned its gross unreason, its inconsistency, its absurdity; and he was repelled from the abolitionists at first by his dislike of violence, even in convictions, and of the very appearance of disorder. But when once he had taken the measure of the affair with that telescopic eye of his, and had intellectually compassed its whole meaning to the very furthest and finest implication, his whole nature solidified against slavery. The man in whom conscience and intellect were angelically one perceived that the law and order which defied justice and humanity were merely organized anarchy, and that as a good citizen he could have no part in them. When the Fugitive Slave Bill became a law, 'There is an infamy in the air,' he said, at the indignation meeting in Concord. 'I wake in the morning with a painful sensation, which I carry about all day, and which, when traced home, is the ignominy which has fallen on Massachusetts.' It is a 'filthy law,' 'a law which no man can obey, or abet the obeying, without loss of self-respect, or forfeiture of the name of gentleman.' Later, at a Kansas relief meeting in Cambridge, he advised 'the sending of arms to the settlers in Kansas for resistance to the pro-slavery raids from Missouri.' After Harper's Ferry he said that if John Brown should suffer, he would 'make the gallows glorious like the cross,' but he omitted this and other passages from the republished lecture, 'distance of time,' says his biographer, 'having brought the case into juster perspective.' With the light of our own time, and the modern improvements of the 'perfection of reason' as applied by the courts, he might see cause to modify other expressions; but he spoke in days when good men thought that their sense of justice was pre-eminently binding upon their consciences, and brought all laws and decisions that conflicted with this sense into lasting discredit with those whom their teachings schooled.

II.

Emerson, though not one of the earliest, became easily one of the first of those men, and no doubt many a gray-bearded youth can remember with us the liberating thrill of his words, beautiful as sculptured marble, vivid as flame. Was it the poetry or the humanity which touched us most? Both, equally, we think; for again these were angelically one in the man, who could not have been a poet for beauty's sake alone, although he feigned that beauty was sufficient in and to itself. In humanity, as in his theories of what literature should be to us, Emerson is still the foremost of all our seers, and will be so a hundred years hence. He seems in these sorts to be almost a disembodied force, but this is an illusion of his extreme impersonality. It ought not to be necessary to explain that his intellectual coldness, which, whenever he would,

Burned frore, and frost performed the effect of fire,

did not chill his affectional make-up. Tender and faithful son, and loving servant of his widowed mother's narrow circumstance, he was always a devoted husband, and the fondest as well as wisest of fathers; but he found it difficult to make his shy heart go out beyond the bounds of kinship and old friendship. The gentlest of men could sometimes be as infinitely repellent a particle as one of his own sentences, and he whimsically confesses to his diary that while he gets on well enough with Man, he finds it hard to meet men half-way or upon common ground. Now we are beginning to know that there is no such thing as Man, that there are only men, but Emerson can, with all his shrinking from men, best teach us how to treat them, with a view to their highest good. Mr. Matthew Arnold gave him supreme praise when he said that those who wished to live in the spirit must go to Emerson, though many worthy persons were aggrieved that he should have said Emerson was not so great a poet as this, not so great an essayist as that, not so great a philosopher as the other. To live in the spirit is the lesson of his life as well as of his literature; his whole memory strengthens and purifies. You learn from it that one who lives in the spirit cannot be unfaithful to the smallest rights or interests of others; cannot ignore any private obligation or public duty without shame and pain.

Every new thing, every new thought, challenged him: abolition, Brook Farm, Walt Whitman: he was just to each, and, with Emerson, as with all high souls, to be just was to be generous. He was for a long time supposed to be the exemplar of Transcendentalism. People who did not know what he meant said that he meant Transcendentalism, and as nobody ever quite knew what Transcendentalism meant, they again said that it meant Emerson. But mental dimness was as foreign to him as moral dimness; all that he says is impatient, is tense with meaning.

> While self-inspection sucked its little thumb,
> With 'Who am I?' and 'Wherefore did I come?'

Emerson was deeply employed in meditating the wisdom through which the mass of our stupidity and selfishness may finally be civilized into indifference to those questions, through a sense of duty to others. In a period still reeking with gross romantic individualism, when so many were straining to retch out the last rinsings of their sick egotism upon their fellows, he stood hale and serene and sane, elect and beautiful in every aspect of his mind. It is his impersonality, the quality that made him cold and unseizable to so many—it is this which makes him now and always our neighbor and our friend, the most imaginable person of his day. The value of Mr. Cabot's memoir is that it lets that sculpturesque figure grow fully upon you; and yet, even after reading this memoir, we should like to recur, for something more of color and warmth, to Henry James, Sen.'s incomparably vivid and suggestive essay on Emerson.[1] Written from the heartiest liking and the most tingling resentment of his elusiveness, the keenest perception, and the strictest limitations, and expressed from a lexicon peculiar to the author, this essay is of really unique value in the literature of biography.

III.

Perhaps Mr. Cabot imparts the same sense of Emerson, but the degree is wanting; and he has not touched at all one of the most interesting facts, from a literary point of view, in Emerson's history. His perception of the great and fruitful elements in Walt Whitman's work, when the *Leaves of Grass* first appeared, was long suffered to weigh with the public as unqualified praise; but Mr. Whitman has himself finally done justice to Emerson's exceptions. They concerned what may be called the manners, if not the morals, of Mr. Whitman's poetry; and we think they are still valid; but there is no doubt that Emerson felt a keen sympathy with the æsthetic revolt so courageously embodied in its form. His own verse, in a certain beautiful lawlessness, expresses now and again his impatience of smoothness and regularity, his joy in a fractured surface, a broken edge, his exultation in a pace or two outside the traces. Mostly, however, the freedom of his thoughts sufficed him; he submitted their utterance to the conventional measures; yet he could foresee the advantages of bringing poetry nearer to the language and the carriage of life, as Mr. Whitman's work seemed promising to do; and it was characteristic of him that he should not stint his congratulations to the author.

We have been thinking of them in connection with a passage of a recent criticism in the *World* newspaper reviewing one of the late translations of Tolstoi. The writer has discovered that 'the Russian absolutely ignores all rules, all efforts at an artistic roundness and finish. He finds life without artistic roundness, and he draws it as he sees it. There is no composition, no grouping, merely stern verity.' This cannot greatly surprise any reader of the Study; perhaps that reader will not even find wholly novel the assertion that beside this verity the realism 'of the extremest French and American apostles shrinks into bald convention.' But this is true, as a rule, and we are glad to have the *World*'s critic say it and feel it, while we commend Mr. Whitman's work, both in verse and prose, as a signal exception to this rule.

As a whole we do not commend it, and for the very reason that we do commend Tolstoi as a whole. The American's frankness is, on its moral side, the revolt of the physical against the ascetic; the Russian's is the cry of the soul for help against the world and the flesh. The American is intolerant of all bonds and bounds, and he bursts them with a sort of Titanic rapture; the Russian's devotion to the truth is so single that he is apparently unconscious of the existence of limitations; but both of these masters, at opposite poles morally, are the same in æsthetic effect.

IV.

The question as to whether American writers or French writers can ever approach the directness of the Russian writers is one which involves the much larger question of literary consciousness. Walt Whitman's rebellion was itself a confession of this consciousness; and we ought to recognize that Tolstoi alone, even among Russian writers, seems wholly without it. Some philosophers have attempted to explain his unconsciousness upon the theory that he has the good fortune to write in a language and land without a literary past, and is therefore wholly untrammelled by tradition; but these must have counted without the fact that Gogol, the father of Russian naturalism, who wrote fifty years ago, was as full of literary consciousness as Thackeray or Dickens. They ignore another fact, namely, that perhaps the book which most nearly approaches the simplicity of Tolstoi is *I Malavoglia*, by the Italian Verga, who has a literary past running back almost indefinitely. Near to this we think we should place *Maximina*, by Valdés, the Spaniard, who derives also from a remote literary antiquity. The only alloy in its unconsciousness is the humor which pervades it, and which perhaps disables the unconsciousness of the best American work, consciousness being the very essence of humor. Amongst Englishmen the author of the *Revolution in Tanner's Lane* and the *Mark Rutherford* books must be counted for his simplicity and directness. Amongst the French masters Daudet is always literose; and half the time Zola gives you the sense of book-making; the Goncourts are sincere, but still a little conscious; the repulsive masterpieces of Maupassant are as free from posing at least as Tolstoi's work.

If we come to the Americans, it is without the courage to make a very confident claim for any but the latest beginners, a Southerner here and there, and such a Northerner as Miss Wilkins, who, however, cannot always be trusted. We have something worse than a literary past: we have a second-hand literary past, the literary past of a rich relation. We are, in fact, still literary colonists, who are just beginning to observe the aspects of our own life in and for themselves, but who preserve our English ancestors' point of view, and work in their tradition.

Yet the future is ours if we want it, and we have only to turn our backs upon the past in order to possess it. Simplicity is difficult; some of the sophisticated declare it impossible at this stage of the proceedings; but it is always possible to be unaffected, just as it is to be morally honest, to put our object before ourselves, to think more of the truth we see than of our poor little way of telling it, and to prize the fact of things beyond the effect of things. What if, after all, Tolstoi's power came from his conscience, which made it as impossible for him to caricature or dandify any feature of life as to lie or cheat? What if he were so full of the truth, and so desirous to express it for God's sake and man's sake, that he would feel the slightest unfaithfulness to it a sin? This is not wholly incredible of such a man, though it is a hard saying for those who write merely from the low artistic motive long vaunted as the highest.

NOTE

1 *Literary Remains of Henry James.* Edited by WILLIAM JAMES [Howells's note].

17 Zola, Tolstoi, and 'the pessimistic'
1888

From 'The Editor's Study,' *Harper's Monthly*, March 1888.

It is almost enough to say of this essay that it shows that, in the same period during which Vizetelly was made a martyr in the same cause, Howells positively commended *La Terre* to the attention of the serious reader. But he did more. He bracketed Zola with his idolized Tolstoi, and he called attention to the fact that both masters demanded that the serious reader be required to face what Unamuno has since taught us to call the tragic vision of life.

I.

Mr. H. C. Lea's *History of the Inquisition of the Middle Ages* is one of those books whose significance does not cease even with the suggestion of the remotest relations of its subject to the life of the period. One would read it to less than its whole purport if he failed to grasp the fact that underlying the cruelty of the Catholic Church in dealing with heresy were the primitive passions which stirred the heart of the Cave Dweller, and which still animate civilization in its social, commercial, and political rivalries and competitions. History, when it is wisely written, is both record and prophecy in its deeper implications. The aspects and forms change, but the motives remain the same, refined, indeed, and unconsciously masked, yet essentially what they were ever since one man found himself physically or mentally stronger than another, and sought to confirm his advantages by his brother's lasting subjection. He has never lacked the best reasons for this. The proofs that his self-seeking is for his brother's good are always so abundant that he is rarely driven to an open and cynical profession of an egoistic intention. In fact, when it comes to this with him, he is near to being a better man, for he then becomes intolerable to himself. But as long as he can make believe with any hopeful measure of success that he is somehow serving God, or humanity, or society, by the exploitation of his fears for his supremacy, by his lust of dominion, his state is not hopeful. We need not go far afield for exemplifications; if we cannot find them in our own hearts, we may see them in the lives of our neighbors all round us. The difference between the persecuting spirit of the past and the persecuting spirit of the present is largely a difference of ideals, of ends. . . . There is in the course of history something more than the suggestion that evil dies of the mortal sting which it inflicts and that it defeats those who employ it, in accomplishing itself.

II.

It will be interesting to know how this happened with the evil known as the Inquisition, with that fulness of detail which we may expect in Mr. Lea's second and third volumes, announced to complete the work projected in his first. In the mean time some of the questions involved will present themselves to the reader of Zola's latest and perhaps awfulest book, *La Terre.* Filthy and repulsive as it is in its facts, it is a book not to be avoided by the student of civilization, but rather to be sought and seriously considered. It is certainly not a book for young people, and it is not a book for any one who cares merely for a story, or who finds himself by experience the worse for witnessing in literature the naked realities of lust and crime. This said, it is but fair to add that it legitimately addresses itself to scientific curiosity and humane interest. The scene passes in that France where the first stirring of a personal conscience once promised a brilliant race the spiritual good which triumphant persecution finally denied it; and it is not wholly gratuitous to suppose that we see in the peasants of *La Terre* effects of the old repressions which stifled religious thought among them, and bound all their hopes, desires, and ambitions to the fields they tilled. When the Revolution came, it came too late to undo the evil accomplished, and the immediate good that it did included another evil. It justly gave to the peasant the ownership of the land, but it implanted in him the most insatiable earth-hunger ever known in the world. This creature, this earth-fiend whom Zola paints, is superstitious, but cynically indifferent to religion, and apparently altogether unmoral; lustful and unchaste, but mostly saved from the prodigal vices by avarice that spares nothing, relents to no appeal, stops at no wrong, and aspires only to the possession of land, and more land, and ever more land. This is the prevailing type, varied and relieved by phases of simple, natural good in a few of the characters; and the Church, so potent against the ancestral heresy, struggles in vain against the modern obduracy, in the character of the excellent priest, who is the only virtuous person in the book. The story is a long riot of satyr-lewdness and satyr-violence, of infernal greed that ends in murder, of sordid jealousies and cruel hates; and since with all its literary power, its wonderful force of realization, it cannot remain valuable as literature, but must have other interest as a scientific study of a phase of French life under the Second Empire, it seems a great pity it should not have been fully documented. What are the sources, the proofs, of this tremendous charge against humanity, in those simple conditions, long fabled the most friendly to the simple virtues? This is the question which the reader, impatient if not incredulous of all this horror, asks himself when he has passed through it.

III.

He must ask it also at the end of that curious narrative drama of Tolstoi's, known to us as yet only in the French version of *La Puissance des Ténèbres*. This too deals with peasant life, and with much the same hideous shames and crimes as *La Terre*. The main difference —but it is a very great one—is that the Russian peasant, wicked as he is, is not so depraved as the French peasant; he has a conscience; he is capable of remorse, of repentance, of expiation. It is true that one of the *muzhiks*, to whose amendment the drama is addressed, and to a group of whom Tolstoi read it for their criticism, declared that the principal person, after accomplishing his purposes, would not have owned his crimes or wished to suffer for them as his one hope of escape from self-torment; but we may suppose this opinion the effect of restricted observation, and may safely trust the larger and deeper knowledge of the author. We should again, however, like to have the documentary proofs in the case, and should feel more hopeful of the good to be done among the muzhiks by the play if we felt sure that they would recognize it as a true picture. In the mean time they are not likely to know much about it; the censorship has forbidden its representation in Russia, and it remains for the consideration of such people of other countries as know how to read.

Whether much is done to help those whose life is depicted in fiction is a question which no one is yet qualified to answer, fiction has only so very recently assumed to paint life faithfully, and most critics still claim that it is best for it not to do so. It is said that the stories of Erckmann-Chatrian, by their fidelity to the abominations and horrors of war, have had the effect of weakening the love of military glory in the French people; and the books of the pastor Bitzius, who wrote fifty years ago—under the pseudonym of Jeremias Gotthelf—stories as intensely realistic as any of the present day, are claimed to have wrought a great reform in the manners and morals of the Bernese peasants, whom he photographed in their own dialects. But we suspect that fiction, like the other arts, can only do good of this kind indirectly; when it becomes hortatory, it is in danger of becoming dull, that is to say, suicidal.

18 Matthew Arnold
1888

From 'The Editor's Study,' *Harper's Monthly*, July 1888.

It seems a pity that Howells's essay on Matthew Arnold is so little known because it is one of his best literary essays and extraordinarily self-definitive. The final use, after all, of criticism to the reader is to help him decide what is or is not for him—and so help him to discover who is there behind his eyes. By the same token, the good of reading a foreign author is much the same as the chief good of travel or foreign residence: they teach us to see the realities of home.

Howells knew his Arnold and defined himself largely in opposition. He understood Arnold's American commentary and grew to the point where he could admit its cogency. But by that same token once more, Arnold mainly helped Howells in his personal solution of the grand task of the American imagination which Benjamin Townley Spencer has studied elegantly under a revealing title, *The Quest for Nationality*. The basic demand made upon every American imagination by what Henry James called 'the immense, complex drama' of the national life is that he shall decide what is to be for him the true America. There is a fine, un-written volume on the mind and work of W. D. Howells to be based upon his Arnold essay. And its key waits in the calm irony of his remarking:

> So far from feeling cast down by Mr. Arnold's failure to detect distinc-tion in a nation which has produced such varied types of greatness in re-cent times as Lincoln, Longfellow, Grant, Emerson, John Brown, Mrs. Stowe, Hawthorne . . . we are disposed to a serene complacency by it.

A like vision would inform his little-known but important radical essays of 1894–1903.

I.

It has been interesting to note the effect of Matthew Arnold's death upon a people whom his criticism had just irritated against him. The sad event cut short many expressions of resentment, and even turned to kindness the more difficult mood of those who were disposed to laugh at him. It restored the perspective in which we had seen him before he came to us, and enabled us again to value his censure aright. Upon the whole, the impression which Americans had received from him personally was not one of great dignity, and though this was partly the result of that mischievous license of the reporters which he complained of, it was also partly due to something in his own mental make-up and attitude. He became, in a certain degree, one of our national jokes, and he suffered a slight with those who most deplored the injustice done him by this fate. Something of D'Oyly Carte, and association with the management of Mr. Oscar Wilde's mission and Messrs. Gilbert and Sullivan's comic operas; something of the ignominy of subjection to calls of 'Louder!' at his half-heard lectures; something of the malicious pleasure men take in finding an arbiter of taste saying things in bad taste, and a wise person committing indiscretions, contributed to his lapse as a cult among us; but we must not deny that this happened also because we are an irreverent people, and find from time to time a pleasure in trampling on the idols we set up. Now, however, that is all past; death has made it impossible for us to rail or smile at the man whose presence could not always command our homage, and we can freely admit his greatness in literature and his good-will toward a perverse generation. Even while we perceive that his observation of our life wanted breadth and depth and finality, we must acknowledge that in its superficial way, and as far as it went, it was mainly just. We cannot deny that we are a loud and vain and boastful nation; that our reporterized press is often truculently reckless of privacy and decency; that our local nomenclature is beggarly in its poverty and horribly vulgar, and that tens of thousands of our places seem to have been named with less sense and less taste than dogs and horses are named; that our cabs and hotels are expensive; that a moderate income does not go so far here as in England; and that to the average person of culture we must be less entertaining than almost any other nation. We are not picturesque, and we are not splendid. Our towns, when they are tolerably named, are not varied in their characteristics, and our civilization, as a means of pleasure to polite people of limited means and of sympathies narrowed to their own class, with the historic ideals of beauty and grandeur, is very much of a failure. Mr. Arnold might have said with some truth that we have not even been equal to our political and economic opportunities; we cannot be particularly proud of our legislatures and administrations; the relations of capital and labor in our free democracy are about as full of violence as those in any European monarchy; we have wasted the public lands which we won largely by force and fraud, and we are the prey of many vast and corrupting monopolies. Perhaps any other Aryan race could have done as well as we have done with our liberties and resources; and if the future is still ours, the present is by no means without its danger and disgrace.

II.

Yet some good things we have done, some great things achieved, and among these is the abolition of that 'distinction' which Mr. Arnold found wanting in our life. We have noticed a disposition among the critics of his criticism to dispute the fact, but it is his only stricture upon our conditions which we should gladly accept as true. If we have really got rid of distinction of the sort he seems to prize, we have made a great advance on the lines of our fundamental principles. If we understand it aright, distinction of the sort that shows itself in manner and bearing toward one's fellow-men is something that can exist only through their abeyance, not to say their abasement. Our whole civilization, if we have a civilization of our own, is founded upon the conviction that any such distinction is unjust and deleterious, and our whole political being is a protest against it. In every way our history has said that a game of that kind was not worth the candle, and that human nature was better in itself than any aristocratic extract or decoction from it. One of the truths which Americans have always held to be self-evident was that a man, if he was honest, was not only privileged, but was in duty bound, to look other men in the face, with eyes as nearly upon the same level as congenital differences would allow. The fear with most Americans to whom this truth is precious has been that our social structure was not responsive to our political ideal; that the snobbishness, more or less conscious, which alone makes distinction possible was at least microscopically present in our composition. But if an observer like Mr. Arnold, accustomed to distinction as it shows itself in European civilization, was unable to perceive it here—if he could find great ability, power, goodness, in our noted men, and every virtue except distinction, we may reasonably console ourselves with the hope that snobbishness is also absent from all Americans not corrupted by the evil communications of the Old World.

So far from feeling cast down by Mr. Arnold's failure to detect distinction in a nation which has produced such varied types of greatness in recent times as Lincoln, Longfellow, Grant, Emerson, John Brown, Mrs. Stowe, Hawthorne, not to name many others eminent in art and science and finance, we are disposed to a serene complacency by it. Here, we may say, with just self-gratulation, is positive proof that we have builded better than we knew, and that our conditions, which we have always said were the best in the world, have evolved a type of greatness in the presence of which the simplest and humblest is not abashed. Somehow, the idea that we call America has realized itself so far that we already have identification rather than distinction as the fact which strikes the foreign critic in our greatness. Our notable men, it seems, are notable for their likeness to their fellow-men, and not for their unlikeness; democracy has subtly but surely done its work; our professions of belief in equality have had their effect in our life; and whatever else we lack in homogeneity, we have in the involuntary recognition of their common humanity by our great men something that appears to be peculiarly American, and that we think more valuable than the involuntary assumption of superiority, than the distinction possible to greatness, among peoples accustomed to cringe before greatness.

III.

We have come to this rather lately, and we fear we have not come to it so fully as Mr. Arnold would have the world believe. But we may see the progress we have made in the right direction by the study of our own past, and especially of that formative period when the men who invented American principles had not yet freed themselves from the influence of European traditions. We spoke in a recent Study of the character of Franklin, and we think of him now as the most modern, the most American, among his contemporaries. Franklin had apparently none of the distinction which Mr. Arnold lately found lacking in us; he seems to have been a man who could no more impose upon the imagination of men used to abase themselves before birth, wealth, achievement, or mastery in any sort, as very many inferior men have done in all times, than Lincoln or Grant. But he was more modern, more American, than any of his contemporaries in this, though some of them were of more democratic ideals than he. His simple and plebeian past made it impossible for a man of his common-sense to assume any superiority of bearing, and the unconscious hauteur which comes of aristocratic breeding, and expresses itself at its best in distinction, was equally impossible to him. It was very possible, however, with other men as ardently and unselfishly patriotic and as virtuous as he, and distinction was not wanting to the men of the Republic's early days. Washington had it, and Hamilton; Jefferson tried hard not to have it; but Burr had it, and Hancock had it; and most of the great men whom New York contributed to that period of our history had it; and of course the Carolinians, as far as they were eminent. Above all, Gouverneur Morris had it, and he had it for the very reason that Franklin hadn't it, because he was well-born, because he was brought up in the heart of a rich, gay, patrician society, because all the foolish things which have been done since the world began to differentiate men from men socially had been done for him in the full measure of the Colonial possibilities.

In the brilliant sketch which Mr. Theodore Roosevelt has written of Morris's brilliant career (it is among the very best of Mr. Morse's 'American Statesmen' series) the reader may study one of the most interesting characters of our history, with the advantages of a most suggestive, intelligent, and comprehensive authority, and it will be his own fault if he fails of that finer meaning of the book which is sometimes tacit even for the writer of it. The one thoroughly admirable thing in Morris, his prompt and unfailing patriotism, in which he was as American as his antitype, Franklin, remains the consolation of such as cannot admire his other qualities. These were the qualities of a brave, truthful, generous, impulsive, yet clear-headed aristocrat; and his greatness was limited chiefly by his want of sympathy with men outside of his own class. His services were given freely and fearlessly to his country; yet what he did for nationality, for democracy, was done somewhat from that curious inverted pride which is a common foible of the aristocratic temperament. In his long mission to France he saw too much of the nobility and too much of the mob for a man of his make to believe fully in either: he wrote of both with contemptuous sarcasm: but at home he was of those who distrusted the popular initiative, while foreseeing the future greatness of the country which that initiative could alone promote. In private life he was at least as blameless as Franklin, if that is not saying very much; he was not scrupulous about women, and he had those traits of a man of the world which all silly women admire, and some sensible women admire sillily. When a young man he lost a leg by an accident which his own coxcombry provoked, but he bore his misfortune through life with uncomplaining dignity and with bitter irony in about equal parts. His courage was cavalieresque, but he had an eighteenth century skeptical spirit, and he was neither saintly nor exactly heroic. In spite of his foibles, he was a man of great common-sense, and though he took himself seriously as a 'gentleman,' he did not take himself solemnly; he was too critical to be altogether disdainful. His political services were general rather than particular; as a statesman he forecast the material rather than the political future of the country, and the social future growing out of it; he would not have liked or trusted modern Americanism any more than Mr. Arnold, to whom, if he could have appeared, he would certainly have appeared distinguished. Distinction, in fact, is what one feels throughout in regard to Gouverneur Morris, and in the end one feels that if he had been less distinguished he would have been greater; he would have been a lesson and an incentive, which, with all the respect his qualities inspire, one can hardly say that he was. Did his distinction, that effect of waning traditions, that result of the misfortune of being born with all the advantages, keep him just short of the highest usefulness to his generation as well as ours? Probably Mr. Arnold would not think so; but all the same, as a historical figure, he remains more decorative than structural; that is, the Revolution could have been without such a man as Morris infinitely easier than without such a man as Franklin. He was a brilliant finial, but the temple of our liberties in no wise rests upon him.

IV.

Far be it from us to say anything against the decorative in its place. It is something that we cannot afford to lose out of life; but somehow it must be had at less cost than hitherto, and we must not mistake it for anything vital. It is valuable, in a way it is even important, but it is not vital, and in our haste to be finer and politer than our critics will allow us to be, we ought not to seek it at the cost of anything vital, of anything that keeps men humble and simple and brotherly, the greatest with the meanest. Except as distinction can grow out of an absolutely unassuming attitude, and the first man among us appear distinguished from the rest only by his freedom from any manner of arrogation, we are much better without it. The distinction that abashes and dazzles, this is not for any people of self-respect to cultivate or desire; and we mean here precisely the best distinction that Mr. Arnold can mean. We do not mean the cheap and easy splendor of the vulgar aristocrat or plutocrat, but that far subtler effect in lives dedicated to aims above the common apprehension, and apart from the interests and objects of the mass of men; we mean the pride of great achievement in any sort, which in less fortunate conditions than ours betrays itself to the humiliation of meaner men. The possessor of any sort of distinction, however unconscious he may be of the fact, has somewhere in his soul, by heredity, or by the experience of his superiority, the spark of contempt for his fellow-men; and he is for that reason more deplorable than the commonest man whom his presence browbeats. If our civilization is so unfavorable to the expression of contempt that Mr. Arnold could find no distinction among our great men, then we may hope that in time it may be wholly quenched.

We are so far from taking his discovery ill of him that we cheerfully excuse to it his failure to detect the existence of literature and art among us. Comparisons are odious, as we found ourselves when Mr. Arnold compared Emerson to his disadvantage with several second-rate British classics, and we will not match painter with painter, architect with architect, sculptor with sculptor, poet with poet, to prove that our art and literature are at least as good as those of present England. In some points we might win and in others lose, but in any case it would be an idle game. What we should like to do, however, is to persuade all artists intending greatness in any kind among us that the recognition of the fact pointed out by Mr. Arnold ought to be a source of inspiration to them, and not discouragement. We have been now some hundred years building up a state on the affirmation of the essential equality of men in their rights and duties, and whether we have been right or been wrong the gods have taken us at our word, and have responded to us with a civilization in which there is no distinction perceptible to the eye that loves and values it. Such beauty and such grandeur as we have is common beauty, common grandeur, or the beauty and grandeur in which the quality of solidarity so prevails that neither distinguishes itself to the disadvantage of anything else. It seems to us that these conditions invite the artist to the study and the appreciation of the common, and to the portrayal in every art of those finer and higher aspects which unite rather than sever humanity, if he would thrive in our new order of things. The talent that is robust enough to front the everyday world and catch the charm of its work-worn, care-worn, brave, kindly face, need not fear the encounter, though it seems terrible to the sort nurtured in the superstition of the romantic, the bizarre, the heroic, the distinguished, as the things alone worthy of painting or carving or writing. The arts must become democratic, and then we shall have the expression of America in art;

and one reproach which Mr. Arnold is half right in making us shall have no justice in it. The implication of his censure was not so much that we had no literature or no art, as that we had nothing that was strictly American in either; but even in this he seems to have been speaking without the documents. Here and there a man has detached himself from tradition, and has struck something out of our life that is ours and no other's. Of late this has been done more and more in our fiction, which, if we were to come to those odious comparisons, we need not be afraid to parallel book for book with contemporary English fiction; and no one can look at Mr. St. Gaudens's head of Sherman in the Academy and fail to see how possible the like achievement is in sculpture—at least to a St. Gaudens. It has no distinction, in Mr. Arnold's sense, no more distinction than he would have found in the great soldier's actual presence, but it seems to express the grandeur of a whole people, a free people, friendly, easy, frank, and very valiant. . . .

VI.

There is a lovely prose poem of Tourguénief's, telling how he went into a church when a boy, and knelt down beside a peasant. Suddenly it rushed into the boy's mind that this man was Jesus Christ, and for a while he could not look round at his companion for awe of his own hallucination; when he did so, there was only the plain, common man. Then it was borne in upon him that Christ was really like that poor peasant when he was on earth, and only a plain, common man. There is, indeed, no evidence that the founder of our religion struck his contemporaries as 'distinguished,' and there is considerable proof in the record of his doings and sayings that he would hardly have valued distinction in others.

We need not at least impute it to ourselves as a serious moral shortcoming if we are without it, and we may find some consolation in the fact that we have in a measure realized the Christian in the democratic ideal. There is something sweet, something luminous, in the reflection that apparently there is in the ordinary American the making of the extraordinary American; that the mass of our people were so near to such great men as Grant and Lincoln in sympathy and intelligence that they could not be awed from them to the distance that lends distinction. It was the humane and beneficent effect of such grandeur as theirs that it did not seem distinguished, but so natural that it was like the fulfilment of the average potentiality.

19 Sex in literature

1889

From 'The Editor's Study,' *Harper's Monthly*, June 1889.

One day we shall have a book on the reputation of W. D. Howells which, properly done, will be marvelously revealing. For not less than a century until now, the man has had the power to precipitate in his critics sharply self-revealing reactions. By decades, generations and schools, his critics, lovers and haters, have defined themselves in response to him. As Edward Marshall put it in 1894, there has been scant moderation:[1]

> The remark of a critic to me a few weeks ago was: 'There is no middle ground with Howells—people think him either a master or an ass.' That is literally true. . . . Everybody that reads in America knows something about Howells and likes or dislikes him.

On no point has controversy more raged about Howells than about his treatment of sexuality in fiction and criticism. And the odd fact, very revealing of critics, is the conflict of their passions. Howells's reputation seems to have swung directly from intimations of his 'dirtiness' to damnation of his 'Victorianism.'

Low points in the one retrogression were such as the review of *The Rise of Silas Lapham* (*Catholic World*, November 1885) which called Howells's attitude that of a 'scientific decadence' which brought him at last to 'a scene that, for hopeless depravity both in the author and subject, out-Zolas Zola.' Howells's logic, complained the reviewer, 'is the progress from man to apes, from the apes to the worms, from the worms to bacteria, from bacteria to—mud. It is the descent to dirt.' In the same month the *Andover Review*, avowedly devoted to promoting Calvinist orthodoxy, carried a review by Hamilton Wright Mabie which opined that attention to such themes as Howells's evidenced 'a mental or a moral disease' because the new realism 'is, in a word, practical atheism applied to art.' Mabie, like others among Howells's attackers, was a friend. Another friend, even protégé, Maurice Thompson, came to damn Tolstoi as a publicity-seeking 'crank' who 'writes novels as dirty and obscene as the worst part of Walt Whitman's *Leaves of Grass*, and as coarse and vulgar and tedious as so-called realism can be made.' Howells he condemned as a corrupter of the national morality for commending Zola and Tolstoi to the country. He

147

characterized realism as 'a literary decadence' devoted to 'defaming woman-kind,' then moved to its criticism:[2]

> One of the striking tricks common to contemporary realists is that of simulating a cordial good-humor and a perfect sincerity while nagging at the life-cords of the most sacred things. For instance if the realist be a critic he will never fail to close up even his most favorable estimate of a book with a jolly sneer which he is sure will go to the very soul of the author.

So much for friends.

But William Roscoe Thayer, writing 'The New Story-Tellers and the Doom of Realism' in 1894 (*Forum*), was no friend. He attacked Howells as a critical propagandist for 'foreign ... moral filth,' one who 'swallowed Tolstoi's *Kreutzer Sonata* and Zola's *La Terre*, and smacked his lips, bidding us all do likewise.' He pilloried realism as 'Epidermism,' reducing 'literature, art, and morals to anarchy,' with 'much' in its pages 'that is nasty (under the plea of "science"), and much that is morbid, and more that is petty.' Little as he sounds it, Thayer was an intellectually distin-guished Bostonian, socially prominent and well-connected—a dangerous enemy. It was in failing to convince such personalities that Howells's 'Editor's Study' campaign failed, in the last analysis. And problems of sexuality in the arts figured centrally in the argument.

There shines a fascinating side-light in Thomas Russell Sullivan, a Boston novelist. On 6 May 1891 he attended the third performance of James A. Herne's experimental play *Margaret Fleming* but walked out after the third act when Mrs Herne, playing Margaret, took out her breast on stage to suckle Fleming's new-born illegitimate child, the mother of the plot having died. His 'gorge rose,' Sullivan confessed to his diary. It is not so easy as might be supposed to say what revolted Sullivan. Surely it was not the breast—or even its dramatic suggestion—for mothers suckling babes in, for instance, railroad waiting rooms were then a common, inevitable phenomenon; and there was no bar to any well-behaved, non-smoking male's sitting on the 'Ladies' side. But nothing could be clearer than that critic Ludwig Lewisohn was simply ignorant when he declared Howells to have been so sexually neurotic as to fall into 'a kind of negative frenzy at the slightest suggestion of man's mammalian nature.'[3] The scheme for producing *Margaret Fleming* in Boston originated with Howells, and he served as its most prominent sponsor—as Sullivan complained.

Why, then, all Howells's caution about 'the Young Girl' and 'Anglo-Saxon decency'? If under conventions of decency, was there not a strong line of sexuality for any mature reader to find in Howells's fiction? As criticism has repeatedly shown, there was. Did he not seek to popularize Zola, Tolstoi, Palacio Valdés, even Maupassant? Writing in November 1902 on 'What Should Girls Read?' for *Harper's Bazar*, what did he answer? Almost anything: 'It is the experience of life which brings the knowledge of good and evil, and without the experience the darkest passages of race biography are without effect upon the ingenuous mind. Innocence gathers only honey in the fields where experience sucks poison from the same flowers.' A young girl's most dangerous reading is the newspaper's 'Woman's Page.' Whence the problem?

The answers seem to be complex and less than satisfactory. As with many a basic problem, much depends at last upon faith. Certainly the D. H. Laurentian faith of the twenties or the Norman Mailerian faith of the fifties that free sexuality would make for great art and the salvation of the race has failed. Literature, cinema, theater could not be 'freer,' and what seems now in danger is the survival of potency in the sophisticated population. And where is greatness? Better 'decency,' hypocrisy, and potency than *The Naked Lunch*? It has become at any rate debatable, as perhaps it was not twenty years ago.

As to Howells's motives, they were partially moral: Swedenborg taught the beauty and goodness of 'conjugial love' but the damnation of sexual egotism—and Howells equated romanticism with self-regard. They were partially tactical and commercial: he wrote for respectable family magazines, fought for artistic principles to which he thought 'passion' irrelevant—and he knew from hard editorial experience what havoc moral indignation in the readership wreaked upon the subscription list. He was compelled to defend himself against the Thompsons and Thayers of his world. Even as we post-Freudians, as a pre-Freudian he had his doubts and ambivalences —and good reason for them. A hundred 'Freudian' critics to the contrary notwithstanding, there is not a simple answer.

I.

One of the great newspapers the other day invited the prominent American authors to speak their minds upon a point in the theory and practice of fiction which had already vexed some of them. It was the question of how much or how little the American novel ought to deal with certain facts of life which are not usually talked of before young people, and especially young ladies. Of course the question was not decided, and we forget just how far the balance inclined in favor of a larger freedom in the matter. But it certainly inclined that way; one or two writers of the sex which is somehow supposed to have purity in its keeping (as if purity were a thing that did not practically concern the other sex, preoccupied with serious affairs) gave it a rather vigorous tilt to that side. In view of this fact it would not be the part of prudence to make an effort to dress the balance; and indeed we do not know that we were going to make any such effort. But there are some things to say, around and about the subject, which we should like to have some one else say, and which we may ourselves possibly be safe in suggesting.

II.

One of the first of these is the fact, generally lost sight of by those who censure the Anglo-Saxon novel for its prudishness, that it is really not such a prude after all; and that if it is sometimes apparently anxious to avoid those experiences of life not spoken of before young people, this may be an appearance only. Sometimes a novel which has this shuffling air, this effect of truckling to propriety, might defend itself, if it could speak for itself, by saying that such experiences happened not to come within its scheme, and that, so far from maiming or mutilating itself in ignoring them, it was all the more faithfully representative of the tone of modern life in dealing with love that was chaste, and with passion so honest that it could be openly spoken of before the tenderest bud at dinner. It might say that the guilty intrigue, the betrayal, the extreme flirtation even, was the exceptional thing in life, and unless the scheme of the story necessarily involved it, that it would be bad art to lug it in, and as bad taste as to introduce such topics in a mixed company. It could say very justly that the novel in our civilization now always addresses a mixed company, and that the vast majority of the company are ladies, and that very many, if not most, of these ladies are young girls. If the novel were written for men and for married women alone, as in continental Europe, it might be altogether different. But the simple fact is that it is not written for them alone among us, and it is a question of writing, under cover of our universal acceptance, things for young girls to read which you would be put out-of-doors for saying to them, or of frankly giving notice of your intention, and so cutting yourself off from the pleasure —and it is a very high and sweet one—of appealing to these vivid, responsive intelligences, which are none the less brilliant and admirable because they are innocent.

III.

One day a novelist who liked, after the manner of other men, to repine at his hard fate, complained to his friend, a critic, that he was tired of the restriction he had put upon himself in this regard; for it is a mistake, as can be readily shown, to suppose that others impose it. 'See how free those French fellows are!' he rebelled. 'Shall we always be shut up to our tradition of decency?'

'Do you think it's much worse than being shut up to their tradition of indecency?' said his friend.

Then that novelist began to reflect, and he remembered how sick the invariable motive of the French novel made him. He perceived finally that, convention for convention, ours was not only more tolerable, but on the whole was truer to life, not only to its complexion, but also to its texture. No one will pretend that there is not vicious love beneath the surface of our society; if he did, the fetid explosions of the divorce trials would refute him; but if he pretended that it was in any just sense characteristic of our society, he could be still more easily refuted. Yet it exists, and it is unquestionably the material of tragedy, the stuff from which intense effects are wrought. The question, after owning this fact, is whether these intense effects are not rather cheap effects. We incline to think they are, and we will try to say why we think so, if we may do so without offence. The material itself, the mere mention of it, has an instant fascination; it arrests, it detains, till the last word is said, and while there is anything to be hinted. This is what makes a love intrigue of some sort all but essential to the popularity of any fiction. Without such an intrigue the intellectual equipment of the author must be of the highest, and then he will succeed only with the highest class of readers. But any author who will deal with a guilty love intrigue holds all readers in his hand, the highest with the lowest, as long as he hints the slightest hope of the smallest potential naughtiness. He need not at all be a great author; he may be a very shabby wretch, if he has but the courage or the trick of that sort of thing. The critics will call him 'virile' and 'passionate'; decent people will be ashamed to have been limed by him; but the low average will only ask another chance of flocking into his net. If he happens to be an able writer, his really fine and costly work will be unheeded, and the lure to the appetite will be chiefly remembered. There may be other qualities which make reputations for other men, but in his case they will count for nothing. He pays this penalty for his success in that kind; and every one pays some such penalty who deals with some such material. It attaches in like manner to the triumphs of the writers who now almost form a school among us, and who may be said to have established themselves in an easy popularity simply by the study of exotic shivers and fervors. They may find their account in the popularity, or they may not; there is no question of the popularity.

IV.

But we do not mean to imply that their case covers the whole ground. So far as it goes, though, it ought to stop the mouths of those who complain that fiction is enslaved to propriety among us. It appears that of a certain kind of impropriety it is free to give us all it will, and more. But this is not what serious men and women writing fiction mean when they rebel against the limitations of their art in our civilization. They have no desire to deal with nakedness, as painters and sculptors freely do in the worship of beauty; or with certain facts of life, as the stage does, in the service of sensation. But they ask why, when the conventions of the plastic and histrionic arts liberate their followers to the portrayal of almost any phase of the physical or of the emotional nature, an American novelist may not write a story on the lines of *Anna Karenina* or *Madame Bovary*. *Sappho* they put aside, and from Zola's work they avert their eyes. They do not condemn him or Daudet necessarily, or accuse their motives; they leave them out of the question; they do not want to do that kind of thing. But they do sometimes wish to do another kind, to touch one of the most serious and sorrowful problems of life in the spirit of Tolstoi and Flaubert, and they ask why they may not. At one time, they remind us, the Anglo-Saxon novelist did deal with such problems—De Foe in his spirit, Richardson in his, Goldsmith in his. At what moment did our fiction lose this privilege? In what fatal hour did the Young Girl arise and seal the lips of Fiction, with a touch of her finger, to some of the most vital interests of life?

Whether we wished to oppose them in their aspiration for greater freedom, or whether we wished to encourage them, we should begin to answer them by saying that the Young Girl had never done anything of the kind. The manners of the novel have been improving with those of its readers; that is all. Gentlemen no longer swear or lie drunk under the table, or abduct young ladies and shut them up in lonely country houses, or so habitually set about the ruin of their neighbors' wives, as they once did. Generally, people now call a spade an agricultural implement; they have not grown decent without having also grown a little squeamish, but they have grown comparatively decent; there is no doubt about that. They require of a novelist whom they respect unquestionable proof of his seriousness, if he proposes to deal with certain phases of life; they require a sort of scientific decorum. He can no longer expect to be received on the ground of entertainment only; he assumes a higher function, something like that of a physician or a priest, and they expect him to be bound by laws as sacred as those of such professions; they hold him solemnly pledged not to betray them or abuse their confidence. If he will accept the conditions, they give him their confidence, and he may then treat to his great honor, and not at all to his disadvantage, of such experiences, such relations of men and women as George Eliot treats in *Adam Bede*, in *Daniel Deronda*, in *Romola*, in almost all her books; such as Hawthorne treats in the *Scarlet Letter*; such as Dickens treats in *David Copperfield*; such as Thackeray treats in *Pendennis*, and glances at in every one of his fictions; such as Mrs. Gaskell treats in *Ruth Barton*; such as most of the masters of English fiction have at some time treated more or less openly. It is quite false or quite mistaken to suppose that our novels have left untouched these most important realities of life. They have only not made them their stock in trade; they have kept a true perspective in regard to them; they have relegated them in their pictures of life to the space and place they occupy in life itself, as we know it in England and America. They have kept a correct proportion, knowing perfectly well that unless the novel is to be a map, with everything scrupulously laid down in it, a faithful record of life in far the greater extent could be made to the exclusion of guilty love and all its circumstances and consequences.

We justify them in this view not only because we hate what is cheap and meretricious, and hold in peculiar loathing the cant of the critics who require 'passion' as something in itself admirable and desirable in a novel, but because we prize fidelity in the historian of feeling and character. Most of these critics who demand 'passion' would seem to have no conception of any passion but one. Yet there are several other passions: the passion of grief, the passion of avarice, the passion of pity, the passion of ambition, the passion of hate, the passion of envy, the passion of devotion, the passion of friendship; and all these have a greater part in the drama of life than the passion of love, and infinitely greater than the passion of guilty love. Wittingly or unwittingly, English fiction and American fiction have recognized this truth, not fully, not in the measure it merits, but in greater degree than most other fiction.

V.

Who can deny that it would be incomparably stronger, incomparably truer, if once it could tear off the habit which enslaves it to the celebration chiefly of a single passion, in one phase or another, and could frankly dedicate itself to the service of all the passions, all the interests, all the facts? Every novelist who has thought about his art knows that it would, and we think that upon reflection he must doubt whether his sphere would be greatly enlarged if he were allowed to treat freely the darker aspects of the favorite passion. But, as we have shown, the privilege, the right to do this is already perfectly recognized. This is proved again by the fact that serious criticism recognizes as masterworks (we will not push the question of supremacy) the two great novels which above all others have moved the world by their study of guilty love. If by any chance, if by some prodigious miracle, any American should now arise to treat it on the level of *Anna Karenina* and *Madame Bovary*, he would be absolutely sure of success, and of fame and gratitude as great as those books have won for their authors.

But what editor of what American magazine would print such a story?

Certainly we do not think any one would; and here our novelist must again submit to conditions. If he wishes to publish such a story (supposing him to have once written it), he must publish it as a book. A book is something by itself, responsible for its character, which becomes quickly known, and it does not necessarily penetrate to every member of the household. The father, or the mother may say to the child, 'I would rather you wouldn't read that book'; if the child cannot be trusted, the book may be locked up. But with the magazine and its serial the affair is different. Between the editor of a reputable English or American magazine and the families which receive it there is a tacit agreement that he will print nothing which a father may not read to his daughter, or safely leave her to read herself. After all, it is a matter of business; and the insurgent novelist should consider the situation with coolness and common-sense. The editor did not create the situation; but it exists, and he could not even attempt to to change it without many sorts of disaster. He respects it, therefore, with the good faith of an honest man. Even when he is himself a novelist, with ardor for his art and impatience of the limitations put upon it, he interposes his veto, as Thackeray did in the case of Trollope when Trollope approached the forbidden ground.

It does not avail to say that the daily papers teem with facts far fouler and deadlier than any which fiction could imagine. That is true, but it is true also that the sex which reads the most novels reads the fewest newspapers; and, besides, the reporter does not command the novelist's skill to fix impressions in a young girl's mind or to suggest conjecture. All this is very trite; it seems scarcely worth saying; and it appears pathetically useless to answer in the only possible way the complaint of the novelist that in the present state of the book trade it is almost impossible to get an audience for an American novel. That seems very likely, but, dear friend, your misfortune begins far back of the magazine editor. If you did not belong to a nation which would rather steal its reading than buy it, you would be protected by an international copyright law, and then you might defy the magazines and appeal to the public in a book with a fair hope of getting some return for your labor on it. But you *do* belong to a nation that would rather steal its reading than buy it, and so you must meet the conditions of the only literary form with which stolen literature cannot compete. The American magazine much more than holds its own against anything we can rob the English of. Perhaps it is a little despotic, a little arbitrary; but unquestionably its favor is essential to success, and its conditions are not such narrow ones. You cannot deal with Tolstoi's and Flaubert's subjects in the absolute artistic freedom of Tolstoi and Flaubert; since De Foe, that is unknown among us; but if you deal with them in the manner of George Eliot, of Thackeray, of Dickens, of society, you may deal with them even in the magazines. There is no other restriction upon you. All the horrors and miseries and tortures are open to you; your pages may drop blood; sometimes it may happen that the editor will even exact such strong material from you. But probably he will require nothing but the observance of the convention in question; and if you do not yourself prefer bloodshed he will leave you free to use all sweet and peaceable means of interesting his readers.

Believe us, it is no narrow field he throws open to you, with that little sign to keep off the grass up at one point only. Its vastness is still almost unexplored, and whole regions in it are unknown to the fictionist. Dig anywhere, and do but dig deep enough, and you strike riches; or, if you are of the mind to range, the gentler climes, the softer temperatures, the serener skies, are all free to you, and are so little visited that the chance of novelty is greater among them.

NOTES

1 'A Great American Writer,' *Philadelphia Press*, 15 April 1894, 27.
2 'The Analysts Analyzed,' *Critic*, n.s. 3 (10 July 1885), 19–22; and the *Literary World*, 18 (3 September 1887), 281–2.
3 Ludwig Lewisohn, *Expression in America*, New York, 1932, 244.

20 'Neo-romanticism,' the 'romanticistic' 1889

From 'The Editor's Study,' *Harper's Monthly*, September 1889.
One of the inevitable but important results of Howells's quest for realism was his coinage of critical terms as he came to new ideas which struggled for expression. Among the terms he coined none carried more weight of implication than 'neo-romantic.' Equivalent to another, more awkward term, 'the romanticistic,' Howells's 'neo-romantic' expressed a pointed historical insight. It was, that is, one thing to have been a Wordsworth, Coleridge, or Keats, an Emerson or Hawthorne, a Whitman or Thoreau, a genuine believer in romantic aesthetics. But it was altogether different to manipulate romantic chills, thrills, levitations, and all the weirdness of 'the light that never was' and do it cynically, without conviction or commitment. To operate ramshackle machinery to induce artificial emotions and call them 'romantic' Howells thought 'romanticistic.' One who did so without romantic faith he called 'neo-romantic.' The terms were and are penetrating and of use in keeping our ideas clear, our aesthetic responses clean.

Or, at the end of the ends, and if we must come very low in our defence of one[1] we own a favorite with us, he is at the worst not writing from a theory, which seems to be what works Mr. William Sharp an injury in his *Romantic Ballads and Poems of Phantasy*. Mr. Sharp believes that 'there is a romantic revival imminent in our poetic literature,' as 'in pure fiction the era of romance as opposed to pseudo-realism is about to begin, if the tide be not already well on the flow,' and he appears to have set himself rather consciously to take it in the direction of fortune. Or perhaps it is his preface coming before his poems that gives this impression; very possibly the poems were written first, and the preface imagined from them. In any case, he thinks much may be done with 'the weird, the supernatural,' and he is hard upon those whose ballads are of blue china and the like rather than of white ladyes and the like. He may be right; the children still tell ghost stories; but we remind the reader that romanticism was the expression of a world-mood; it was not merely literary and voluntary; it grew naturally out of the political, social, and even economical conditions at the close of the eighteenth century. It was a development of civilization, and not simply a revulsion from the classicistic literary fashions which it replaced, or it could not have gone so deep in the lives of men as it did. In its day it was noble and beautiful; it lifted and widened the minds of people; it afforded them a refuge in an ideal world from the failure and defeat of this. To assume that we can have it back on any such terms as Mr. Sharp imagines seems to belittle a world-mood to a study-mood, a closet-mood; to narrow its meaning, to take it from humanity and give it to the humanities. Romanticism belonged to a disappointed and bewildered age, which turned its face from the future, and dreamed out a faery realm in the past; and we cannot have its spirit back because this is the age of hopeful striving, when we have really a glimpse of what the earth may be when Christianity becomes a life in the equality and fraternity of the race, and when the recognition of all the facts in the honest daylight about us is the service which humanity demands of the humanities, in order that what is crooked may be made straight, and that what is wrong may be set right. The humanities are working through realism to this end, not consciously, for that is not the way of art, but instinctively; and they will not work to that other end, because, so far as it was anywise beautiful or useful, it was once for all accomplished by the romanticists of the romantic-istic period.

So it seems to us, but we may be wrong. What we are sure of is that in reacquainting ourselves with the weird and the supernatural, as they are seriously addressed to the reader's sensation in Mr. Sharp's ballads, we have failed to experience that agreeable condition of goose-flesh which we knew in our romantic youth, and which we understand to be the intentional and exemplary state of the neo-romanticist of whatever age. Mr. Sharp's *Weird of Michael Scott*, the wizard who accidentally burns up his own soul, which he happens to find outside his body, is a Weird that leaves us quite cold, though we own to have experienced rather a fine thrill in reading the poem of the Willis Dancers, those youths and maids who have died unloved, and whose spirits meet in phantasmal wooing above the church-yard mould. The suggestive theme is treated with delicate insight, and with a tender-ness which gains nothing when it attempts to express 'passion.'

Perhaps we do scanty justice to Mr. Sharp's poetry in our dissent from his theory; one of the evils of having very firm convictions is that you want to deny all merit to people who have different ones. Mr. Sharp is by no means a narrow-minded critic, and he has a word of warning for those who think the importance of a work of art lies in the subject rather than the treatment; he reminds them that noble or ignoble is in the mind of the artist, not in the material he works in. He is so reasonable in this that we would like to call his notice, and that of others who are nowadays asking a good deal of the imagination, to a passage concerning the true nature and office of that mental attribute. The passage is from Isaac Taylor's *Physical Theory of another Life*, and is in explanation of his preference of analysis for his attempted exploration of the unknown. 'Plainly,' he says, 'it is not the imagination that can render us aid in conceiving of a new and different mode of existence, *since this faculty is but the mirror of the world around it, and must draw all its materials from things actually known.* It may exalt, refine, ennoble, enrich what it finds, and it may shed over all the splendor of an effulgence such as earth never actually sees; yet it must end where it began, in compounding elements and in recombining forms furnished to its hand; *and if ever it goes or seems to go beyond these limits, the product is grotesque or absurd, not beautiful: there is no grace or charm in that which trenches upon the actual forms of nature.'*

It seems to us we have here a reason why a generation like the present, so rich in the experience of the past as to have really ascertained two or three æsthetic principles, should not revert in its poetry and fiction to the inspirations of romanticism, which belonged to the childhood and the second-childhood of the world, when people believed in the grotesque creatures of their own imaginations, and then when they made-believe in them. The whole affair seems very simple and plain. All the machinery of romanticism, so far as it involves the superstitions, helpless or voluntary, of either epoch, is grown finally ramshackle; and for our own part, we cannot see why it is any more reverend than an idol which has become a doll, or any more capable of resuscitation in the awe or the sentiment of grown people. Nobody, we suppose, would ask us to go back and believe in, or make-believe in, the knights and ladies, pages and squires, hinds and minstrels, of romance, as at all like the real ones who once existed; and it is rather hard to be asked to toy again with the wizards and the phantoms, the weirds and the wraiths, that never existed. Once we believed in them, and once we made-believe in them. Is not that enough? Or are we to make-believe again? How tiresome! Why not go back and do pastorals a third time? Or is there some law of the mind that suffers one reversion of this sort, but forbids two?

[Here Howells devotes a short section to Sharp's collection of *American Sonnets*.]

But we find ourselves recalled from the pleasure of praising Mr. Sharp's *American Sonnets* to our grievance with him concerning a romantic revival, by Dr. S. Weir Mitchell's suggestive treatment of the old superstition of the elixir of life in his new poem, *The Cup of Youth*. Here the poet evolves from the subject qualities which appeal in the highest degree to the imagination without overtaxing your modern capacity by asking you to suppose his own acceptance of the superstition; whereas, if we understand the neo-romanticists aright, he should have pretended to make himself a party to it. Uberto, the inventor of the elixir in *The Cup of Youth*, might have really drunk it off, and in his return to youth abandoned to loveless old age the wife who had devoted her life to him. But this would have been a fruitless effect in the reader's mind; it would have been recognized, and then it would have ceased. As it is, the group of people sketched remain living in our thoughts: the selfish seeker after the secret of renewed existence, defeated and mocked in the very moment when he was to have triumphed, by the girl who spills the draft and avenges the poor old wife, and then finds her own punishment in the rejection and disavowal of her deed, to which the wife's pity of her pitiless husband's suffering moves her. Here are real motives that go far deeper than any make-belief could reach; they touch that feeling for all the actors in the little drama which the wise view of any human situation must evoke, and which plays from one to another in equal interest. Here is the truly imaginative treatment of a romantic theme; that is, the scientific treatment, which can alone dignify it. What was vital in it is suggested; the mere husk is still left for the fancy of any neo-romanticist to batten on. In some such sort Dr. Holmes has dealt with recondite phases of our common nature, and has given them the last charm for the imagination by refusing to deal with them in the spirit of make-belief, by keeping himself an impartial spectator. In the same sort Hawthorne himself achieved his highest effects; and with that delicate smile of his cast a final discredit on the superstition he had been playing with. But no such tricksy gleam remains upon the tragedy which our poem has sketched: the picture at the close perpetuates a moment of poignant pathos.

NOTE

1 Madison Cawein, a Kentucky poet, whose *Accolon of Gaul* has just been reviewed.

21 'Effectism'
1889

From 'The Editor's Study,' *Harper's Monthly*, November 1889.
With the background of his Iberian literary passions since childhood, Howells took a special pleasure in discovering and publicizing Spanish realists—Galdós, Emilia Pardo-Bazan, Juan Valera, and especially Armando Palacio Valdés. By that serendipity which occurs to the well-prepared, Howells came upon Palacio Valdés in 1885 and in the 'Study' for April 1886 praised *Marta Y Maria* as an example to merely 'clever' American writers of 'what fiction may be at its best.' Of course, he continued,

> it is a realistic novel; it is even by an author who has written essays upon realism, and who feels obliged, poor fellow, in choosing a theme which deals with the inside rather than the outside of life, to protest that the truth exists within us as well as without . . . and that the beautiful and the noble also lie within the realm of reality. We should ourselves go a little farther, and say that they are to be found nowhere else.

Astonished and delighted, Palacio Valdés wrote to thank Howells, and eventually they developed a correspondence of solid significance to literary history (Howells writing Italian replies to Palacio Valdés's Spanish letters). Correspondence ripened into friendship, a sense of international literary alliance, even collaboration. The relationship would amply repay careful study—a study which would be much illuminated if the papers of Palacio Valdés and Howells's letters to him could be found.

There is more than a possibility that Howells had planted, either through 'The Editor's Study' (which he gave Palacio Valdés ample reinforcement to read with care) or in correspondence, the idea of 'effectism' if not the term. At any rate, as this 'Study' shows, his Spanish friend supplied the material for a climax to his columns of December 1887 ('the grasshopper') and September 1889 ('neo-romanticism'). The fine new term and Palacio Valdés's crushing attack on 'effectism' provided Howells an elegant device for getting at the neo-romantics whether they masqueraded as pseudo-realists or pseudo-romancers.

Howells translated the preface to *Sister San Sulpice* to say:

> It is entirely false that the great romantic, symbolic, or classic poets

modified nature; such as they have expressed her they felt her. . . .
Only those falsify her who, without feeling classic or romantic wise, set
about being classic or romantic, wearisomely reproducing the models of
former ages. . . . The principal cause of the decadence of contemporary literature is . . . the vice . . . called *effectism*, or the itch of
awaking at all cost in the reader vivid and violent emotions, which
shall do credit to the invention and originality of the writer.

Or, in short, one of the Continental masters established perfectly for
Howells one of the primary points he was striving to make to the Anglo-
American literary world. What counts is not that Realist in the Middle
Ages meant Idealist. Integrity and authenticity count. Living vitally in
your own times, seeing with your own eyes and speaking in your own voice
count.

So much for Palacio Valdés. Howells could be content to demand in his
own voice of the English critics why they could learn nothing from Jane
Austen, why they fought for factitious standards. He was, of course, never
more militant.

I.

How a better fashion can ever change for a worse; how the ugly can
come to be preferred to the beautiful; in other words, how an art
can decay, is a question which has often been approached, if not
actually debated in this place. We do not know that we expect to
debate it now; in the hurry of month after month, when the toe of
September comes so near the heel of August, and March galls the
kibe of February, the time never seems to arrive when the Study can
really sweep and garnish itself, and quiet down to a season of serene
inquiry upon such a point. At best it appears able only to cast some
fitful gleams upon it, and then have its windows broken by all the
little wanton boys of newspaper criticism, who like to throw stones
at the light wherever they see it. The cost the Study is at in the mere
matter of putty and glass, after one of their outbreaks, is such as
would discourage a less virtuous apartment; but with the good
conscience we have, and the faith we cherish that these *gamins* may
yet grow up to be ashamed of themselves, we cheerfully pay the
expense, and trim the lamp anew, and set it again where those who care
may come to it. If they are not a great many, they are all the closer
friends, perhaps, for being few; and it is in a kind of familiar intimacy
that we turn to them with a question like that we have suggested. It
has been coming up in our mind lately with regard to English fiction

and its form, or rather its formlessness. How, for instance, could people who had once known the simple verity, the refined perfection of Miss Austen, enjoy anything less refined and less perfect?

With her example before them, why should not English novelists have gone on writing simply, honestly, artistically, ever after? One would think it must have been impossible for them to do otherwise, if one did not remember, say, the lamentable behavior of the people who support Mr. Jefferson, and their theatricality in the very presence of his beautiful naturalness. It is very difficult, that simplicity, and nothing is so hard as to be honest, as the reader, if he has ever happened to try it, must know. 'The big bow-wow I can do myself, like any one going,' said Scott, but he owned that the exquisite touch of Miss Austen was denied him; and it seems certainly to have been denied in greater or less measure to all her successors. But though reading and writing come by nature, as Dogberry justly said, a taste in them may be cultivated, or once cultivated, it may be preserved; and why was it not so among those poor islanders? One does not ask such things in order to be at the pains of answering them one's self, but with the hope that some one else will take the trouble to do so, and we propose to be rather a silent partner in the enterprise, which we shall leave mainly to Señor Armando Palacio Valdés.

II.

This delightful author will, however, only be able to answer our question indirectly from the essay on fiction with which he prefaces his last novel, and we shall have some little labor in fitting his saws to our instances. It is an essay which we wish every one intending to read, or even to write, a novel, might acquaint himself with; and we hope it will not be very long before we shall have it in English, together with the charming story of *The Sister of San Sulpizio*, which follows it. In the mean time we must go to the Spanish for some of the best and clearest things which have been said of the art of fiction in a time when nearly all who practise it have turned to talk about it.

Señor Valdés is a realist, but a realist according to his own conception of realism; and he has some words of just censure for the French naturalists, whom he finds unnecessarily, and suspects of being sometimes even mercenarily, nasty. He sees the wide difference that passes between this naturalism and the realism of the English and Spanish; and he goes somewhat further than we should go in condemning it. 'The French naturalism represents only a moment, and an insignificant part of life. . . . It is characterized by sadness and narrowness. The prototype of this literature is the *Madame Bovary* of Flaubert. I am an admirer of this novelist, and especially of this novel; but often in thinking of it I have said, How dreary would literature be if it were no more than this! There is something anti-pathetic and gloomy and limited in it, as there is in modern French life;' but this seems to us exactly the best possible reason for its being. We believe with Señor Valdés that 'no literature can live long without joy,' not because of its mistaken æsthetics, however, but because no civilization can live long without joy. The expression of French life will change when French life changes; and French naturalism is better at its worst than French unnaturalism at its best. 'No one,' as Señor Valdés truly says, 'can rise from the perusal of a naturalistic book . . . without a vivid desire to escape' from the wretched world depicted in it, 'and a purpose, more or less vague, of helping to better the lot and morally elevate the abject beings who figure in it. Natural-istic art, then, is not immoral in itself, for then it would not merit the name of art; for though it is not the business of art to preach morality, still I think that, resting on a divine and spiritual principle, like the idea of the beautiful, it is perforce moral. I hold much more immoral other books which, under a glamour of something spiritual and beau-tiful and sublime, portray the vices in which we are allied to the beasts. Such, for example, are the works of Octave Feuillet, Arsène Hous-saye, Georges Ohnet, and other contemporary novelists much in vogue among the higher classes of society.'

III.

But what is this idea of the beautiful which art rests upon, and so becomes moral? 'The man of our time,' says Señor Valdés, 'wishes to know everything and enjoy everything; he turns the objective of a powerful equatorial toward the heavenly spaces where gravitate the infinitude of the stars, just as he applies the microscope to the infini-tude of the smallest insects; for their laws are identical. His experience, united with intuition, has convinced him that in nature there is neither great nor small; all is equal. All is equally grand, all is equally just, all is equally beautiful, because all is equally divine,' as the Study has before now perhaps sufficiently insisted. But beauty, Señor Valdés explains, exists in the human spirit, and is the beautiful effect which it receives from the true meaning of things; it does not matter what the things are, and it is the function of the artist who feels this effect to impart it to others. We may add that there is no joy in art except this perception of the meaning of things and its communication; when you have felt it, and told it in a poem, a symphony, a novel, a statue, a picture, an edifice, you have fulfilled the purpose for which you were born an artist.

The reflection of exterior nature in the individual spirit, Señor Valdés believes to be the fundamental of art. 'To say, then, that the artist must not copy but create is nonsense, because he can in no wise copy, and in no wise create. He who sets deliberately about modifying nature, shows that he has not felt her beauty, and therefore cannot make others feel it. The puerile desire which some artists without genius manifest to go about selecting in nature, *not what seems to them beautiful, but what they think will seem beautiful to others*, and rejecting what may displease them, ordinarily produces cold and insipid works. For, instead of exploring the illimitable fields of reality, they cling to the forms invented by other artists who have succeeded, *and they make statues of statues, poems of poems, novels of novels*. It is entirely false that the great romantic, symbolic, or classic poets modified nature; such as they have expressed her they felt her; and in this view they are as much realists as ourselves. In like manner if in the realistic tide that now bears us on there are some spirits who feel nature in another way, in the romantic way, or the classic way, they would not falsify her in expressing her so. Only those falsify her who, without feeling classic wise or romantic wise, set about being classic or romantic, wearisomely reproducing the models of former ages; and equally those who without sharing the sentiment of realism, which now prevails, force themselves to be realists merely to follow the fashion.'

The pseudo-realists, in fact, are the worse offenders, to our thinking, for they sin against the living; whereas those who continue to celebrate the heroic adventures of Puss in Boots and the hair-breadth escapes of Tom Thumb, under various aliases, only cast disrespect upon the immortals, who have passed beyond these noises.

IV.

The ingenious English magazinist who has of late been retroactively fending the works of Tolstoi and Dostoyevsky from the last days of that saint of romance, George Sand, as too apt to inspire melancholy reflections in a lady of her life and literature, and who cannot rejoice enough that her dying hours were cheered by the writings of that reverend father in God, Alexander Dumas, *père*, would hardly be pleased, we suppose, with all the ideas of Señor Valdés concerning the novel, its nature, and its function, in modern life. 'The principal cause,' the Spaniard says, 'of the decadence of contemporary literature is found, to my thinking, in the vice which has been very graphically called *effectism*, or the itch of awaking at all cost in the reader vivid and violent emotions, which shall do credit to the invention and originality of the writer. This vice has its roots in human nature itself, and more particularly in that of the artist; he has always something feminine in him, which tempts him to coquet with the reader, and display qualities that he thinks will astonish him, as women laugh for no reason, to show their teeth when they have them white and small and even, or lift their dresses to show their feet when there is no mud in the street. . . . What many writers nowadays wish, is to produce an effect, grand and immediate, to play the part of *geniuses*. For this they have learned that it is only necessary to write exaggerated works in any sort, since the vulgar do not ask that they shall be quietly made to think and feel, but that they shall be startled; and among the vulgar of course I include the great part of those who write literary criticism, and who constitute the worst vulgar, since they teach what they do not know. . . . There are many persons who suppose that the highest proof an artist can give of his fantasy is the invention of a complicated plot, spiced with perils, surprises, and suspenses; and that anything else is the sign of a poor and tepid imagination. And not only people who seem cultivated, but are not so, suppose this, but there are sensible persons, and even sagacious and intelligent critics, who sometimes allow themselves to be hoodwinked by the dramatic mystery and the surprising and fantastic scenes of a novel. They own it is all false; but they admire the imagination, what they call the "power" of the author. Very well; all I have to say is that the "power" to dazzle with strange incidents, to entertain with complicated plots and impossible characters, now belongs to some hundreds of writers in Europe; while there are not much above a dozen who know how to interest with the ordinary events of life, and with the portrayal of characters truly human. If the former is a talent, it must be owned that it is much commoner than the latter. . . . If we are to rate novelists according to their fecundity, or the riches of their invention, we must put Alexander Dumas above Cervantes,' says Señor Valdés; but we must never forget that Dumas brought distraction if not peace to the death-bed of a woman who would probably have been unpleasantly agitated by those Russian authors who are apt to appeal to the imagination through the conscience.

'Cervantes,' Señor Valdés goes on to say, 'wrote a novel with the simplest plot, without belying much or little the natural and logical course of events. This novel, which was called *Don Quixote*, is perhaps the greatest work of human wit. Very well, the same Cervantes, mischievously influenced afterward by the ideas of the vulgar, who were then what they are now and always will be, attempted to please them by a work giving a lively proof of his inventive talent, and wrote the *Persiles and Sigismunda*, where the strange incidents, the vivid complications, the surprises, the pathetic scenes, succeed one another so rapidly and constantly that it really fatigues you. . . . But in spite of this flood of invention, imagine,' says Señor Valdés, 'the place that Cervantes would now occupy in the heaven of art, if he had never written *Don Quixote*,' but only *Persiles and Sigismunda*!

From the point of view of modern English criticism, which likes to be melted, and horrified, and astonished, and blood-curdled, and goose-fleshed, no less than to be 'chippered up' in fiction, Señor Valdés were indeed incorrigible. Not only does he despise the novel of complicated plot, and everywhere prefer *Don Quixote* to *Persiles and Sigismunda*, but he has a lively contempt for another class of novels much in favor with the gentilities of all countries. He calls their writers 'novelists of the world,' and he says that more than any others they have the rage of *effectism*. 'They do not seek to produce effect by novelty and invention in plot . . . they seek it in character. For this end they begin by deliberately falsifying human feelings, giving them a paradoxical appearance completely inadmissible. . . . Love that disguises itself as hate, incomparable energy under the cloak of weakness, virginal innocence under the aspect of malice and impudence, wit masquerading as folly, etc., etc. By this means they hope to make an effect of which they are incapable through the direct, frank, and conscientious study of character.' He mentions Octave Feuillet as the greatest offender in this sort among the French, and Bulwer among the English; but Dickens is full of it (Boffin in *Our Mutual Friend* will suffice for all example), and the present loathsome artistic squalor of the English drama is witness of the result of *effectism* when allowed full play.

V.

But what, then, if he is not pleased with Dumas, who was sovereign for George Sand in sickness, and is good enough for the ingenious English magazinist in health, or with the *effectists* who delight genteel people at all the theatres, and in most of the romances, what, we ask, will satisfy this extremely difficult Spanish gentleman? He would pretend, very little. Give him simple, life-like character; that is all he wants. 'For me, the only condition of character is that it be human, and that is enough. If I wished to know what was human, I should study humanity.'

But, Señor Valdés, Señor Valdés! Do not you know that this small condition of yours implies in its fulfilment hardly less than the gift of the whole earth, with a little gold fence round it? You merely ask that the character portrayed in fiction be human; and you suggest that the novelist should study humanity if he would know whether his personages are human. This appears to us the cruelest irony, the most sarcastic affectation of humility. If you had asked that character in fiction be superhuman, or subterhuman, or preterhuman, or intrahuman, and had bidden the novelist go, not to humanity, but the humanities, for the proof of his excellence, it would have been all very easy. The books are full of those 'creations,' of every pattern, of all ages, of both sexes; and it is so much handier to get at books than to get at men; and when you have portrayed 'passion' instead of feeling, and used 'power' instead of common-sense, and shown yourself a 'genius' instead of an artist, the applause is so prompt and the glory so cheap, that really anything else seems wickedly wasteful of one's time. One may not make one's reader enjoy or suffer nobly, but one may give him the kind of pleasure that arises from conjuring, or from a puppetshow, or a modern stage play, and leave him, if he is an old fool, in the sort of stupor that comes from hitting the pipe; or if he is a young fool, half crazed with the spectacle of qualities and impulses like his own in an apotheosis of achievement and fruition far beyond any earthly experience. If one is a very great master in that kind, one may survive to be the death-bed comfort of a woman who is supposed to have needed medicining of a narcotic kind from a past of inedifying experiences, and even to be the admiration of an ingenious English magazinist who thinks fiction ought to do the office of hyoscyamus or bromide of potassium.

But apparently Señor Valdés would not think this any great artistic result. Like Emerson, he believes that 'the foolish man wonders at

the unusual, but the wise man at the usual,' that 'the perception of
the worth of the vulgar is fruitful in discoveries.' Like Emerson, he
'asks, not for the great, the remote, the romantic'; he 'embraces the
common,' he 'sits at the feet of the familiar and the low.' Or, in his
own words, 'Things that appear ugliest in reality to the spectator who
is not an artist, are transformed into beauty and poetry when the
spirit of the artist possesses itself of them. We all take part every day
in a thousand domestic scenes, every day we see a thousand pictures
in life, that do not make any impression upon us, or if they make any
it is one of repugnance; but let the novelist come, and without betray-
ing the truth, but painting them as they appear to his vision, he
produces a most interesting work, whose perusal enchants us. That
which in life left us indifferent, or repelled us, in art delights us. Why?
Simply because the artist has made us see the idea that resides in it.
Let not the novelists, then, endeavor to add anything to reality, to
turn it and twist it, to restrict it. Since nature has endowed them with
this precious gift of discovering ideas in things, their work will be
beautiful if they paint these as they appear. But if the reality does not
impress them, in vain will they strive to make their work impress
others.'

VI.

Which brings us again, after this long way about, to the divine Jane
and her novels, and that troublesome question about them. She was
great and they were beautiful because she and they were honest and
dealt with nature nearly a hundred years ago, as realism deals with
it to-day. Realism is nothing more and nothing less than the truthful
treatment of material, and Jane Austen was the first and the last of
the English novelists to treat material with entire truthfulness.
Because she did this, she remains the most artistic of the English
novelists, and alone worthy to be matched with the great Scandinavian and Slavic and Latin artists. It is not a question of intellect,
or not wholly that. The English have mind enough; but they have not
taste enough; or rather their taste has been perverted by their false
criticism, which is based upon personal preference, and not upon
principle; which instructs a man to think that what he likes is good,
instead of teaching him first to distinguish what is good before he
likes it. The art of fiction, as Jane Austen knew it, declined from her
through Scott, and Bulwer, and Dickens, and Charlotte Brontë, and

Thackeray, and even George Eliot, because the mania of romanticism had seized upon all Europe, and these great writers could not escape the taint of their time; but it has shown few signs of recovery in England, because English criticism, in the presence of the Continental masterpieces, has continued provincial and special and personal, and has expressed a love and a hate which had to do with the quality of the artist rather than the character of his work. It was inevitable that in their time the English romanticists should treat, as Señor Valdés says, 'the barbarous customs of the Middle Ages, softening and disfiguring them, as Walter Scott and his kind did'; that they should 'devote themselves to falsifying nature, refining and subtilizing sentiment, and modifying psychology after their own fancy,' like Bulwer and Dickens, as well as like Rousseau and Madame de Staël, not to mention Balzac, the worst of all that sort at his worst. This was the natural course of the disease; but it really seems as if it were their criticism that was to blame for the rest: not, indeed, for the performance of this writer or that, for criticism can never affect the actual doing of a thing; but for the esteem in which this writer or that is held through the perpetuation of false ideals. The only observer of English middle-class life since Jane Austen worthy to be named with her was not George Eliot, who was first ethical and then artistic, who transcended her in everything but the form and method most essential to art, and there fell hopelessly below her. It was Anthony Trollope who was most like her in simple honesty and instinctive truth, as unphilosophized as the light of common day; but he was so warped from a wholesome ideal as to wish at times to be like the caricaturist Thackeray, and to stand about in his scene, talking it over with his hands in his pockets, interrupting the action, and spoiling the illusion in which alone the truth of art resides. Mainly, his instinct was too much for his ideal, and with a low view of life in its civic relations and a thoroughly *bourgeois* soul, he yet produced works whose beauty is surpassed only by the effect of a more poetic writer in the novels of Thomas Hardy. Yet if a vote of English criticism even at this late day, when all continental Europe has the light of æsthetic truth, could be taken, the majority against these artists would be overwhelmingly in favor of a writer who had so little artistic sensibility, that he never hesitated on any occasion great or small, to make a foray among his characters, and catch them up to show them to the reader and tell him how beautiful or ugly they were; and cry out over their amazing properties.

Doubtless the ideal of those poor islanders will be finally changed.

If the truth could become a *fad* it would be accepted by all their 'smart people,' but truth is something rather too large for that; and we must await the gradual advance of civilization among them. Then they will see that their criticism has misled them; and that it is to this false guide they owe, not precisely the decline of fiction among them, but its continued debasement as an art.

22 *A Connecticut Yankee at the Court of King Arthur*
1890

From 'The Editor's Study,' *Harper's Monthly*, January 1890.

It was no accident that Howells began his review of what he thought Clemens's best book with reference to studies in comparative culture. Himself well trained by long thought about the contrasts between America and Italy and between the West and New England, he was keenly aware of the significance of cultural relativity. He understood that one of the modes of literary criticism is culture criticism. And his examination of Clemens's masterpiece, a fantasy but a classic of negative realism, allies itself solidly to his earlier essays on Grant and Matthew Arnold. Howells was determined to have an American, a viable democratic culture. And he believed that Clemens's *Connecticut Yankee* made a solid contribution.

Like banging the babes of romance about, cutting down the post-Tennysonian effectists Howells thought salutary fun. So he thought laughing out of countenance the aristocracies, the militaries, the fortified immunities, and the organized snobberies of the world. But the last and greatest of Clemens's achievements Howells thought his power to command our shame at injustice and our compassion for human pain. He wanted desperately to believe, to make it true, that 'this kind of humor' was indeed 'the American kind,' which, 'employed in the service of democracy, of humanity, began with us a long time ago'; and to make it true Howells invoked one of the great American icons: 'in fact Franklin may be said to have torn it with the lightning from the skies.'

I.

From time to time the Study has done its poor endeavors for a more courteous behavior on the part of literary criticism. If it has not taught this so much by practice as by precept, that is the misfortune of much other instruction; but it is not wholly disabling; and in view of Mr. Philip Gilbert Hamerton's recent essays comparing the *French and English*, the Study has the courage to go even further and commend the spirit of comity in international criticism which his book is such an admirable example of. It was on the point of our pen to write that it was an altogether novel thing in its kind; but we remembered *English Traits* in time, and we remembered Mr. Bryce's *American Commonwealth*. Mr. Hamerton's comparison is not so full of insight as the first, for it is no offence to say Mr. Hamerton is not Emerson; and it is not so comprehensive as the last. But it abounds in opinions agreeably reasoned from the uncommon experience of an Englishman who has spent the greater part of his life in France; and one cannot read it without a various edification. . . .

The chapter on Purity will most surprise Anglo-Saxon readers; but the chapter on Caste is of even more interest, and it is of almost unique value both in temper and in substance, for it describes without caricature, in a democratic commonwealth, and on the verge of the twentieth century, an ideal of life entirely stupid, useless, and satisfied, and quite that which Mark Twain has been portraying in his wonder-story of *A Connecticut Yankee at the Court of King Arthur*. Mr. Hamerton's French noble of the year 1890 is the same man essentially as any of that group of knights of the Round Table, who struck Mr. Clemens's delightful hero as white Indians. In his circle, achievement, ability, virtue, would find itself at the same disadvantage, without birth, as in that of Sir Launcelot. When you contemplate him in Mr. Hamerton's clear, passionless page, you feel that after all the Terror was perhaps too brief, and you find yourself sympathizing with all Mr. Clemens's robust approval of the Revolution.

II.

Mr. Clemens, we call him, rather than Mark Twain, because we feel that in this book our arch-humorist imparts more of his personal quality than in anything else he has done. Here he is to the full the humorist, as we know him; but he is very much more, and his strong, indignant, often infuriate hate of injustice, and his love of equality, burn hot through the manifold adventures and experiences of the tale. What he thought about prescriptive right and wrong, we had partly learned in *The Prince and the Pauper*, and in *Huckleberry Finn*, but it is this last book which gives his whole mind. The elastic scheme of the romance allows it to play freely back and forward between the sixth century and the nineteenth century; and often while it is working the reader up to a blasting contempt of monarchy and aristocracy in King Arthur's time, the dates are magically shifted under

him, and he is confronted with exactly the same principles in Queen
Victoria's time. The delicious satire, the marvellous wit, the wild,
free, fantastic humor are the colors of the tapestry, while the texture
is a humanity that lives in every fibre. At every moment the scene
amuses, but it is all the time an object-lesson in democracy. It makes
us glad of our republic and our epoch; but it does not flatter us into a
fond content with them; there are passages in which we see that the
noble of Arthur's day, who battened on the blood and sweat of his
bondmen, is one in essence with the capitalist of Mr. Harrison's day
who grows rich on the labor of his underpaid wagemen. Our incomparable humorist, whose sarcasm is so pitiless to the greedy and
superstitious clerics of Britain, is in fact of the same spirit and intention as those bishops who, true to their office, wrote the other day
from New York to all their churches in the land: 'It is a fallacy in
social economics, as well as in Christian thinking, to look upon the
labor of men and women and children as a commercial commodity, to
be bought and sold as an inanimate and irresponsible thing. . . . The
heart and soul of a man cannot be bought or hired in any market, and
to act as if they were not needed in the doing of the world's vast work
is as unchristian as it is unwise.'

Mr. Clemens's glimpses of monastic life in Arthur's realm are
true enough; and if they are not the whole truth of the matter, one
may easily get it in some such book as Mr. Brace's *Gesta Christi*, where
the full light of history is thrown upon the transformation of the world,
if not the church, under the influence of Christianity. In the mean
time, if any one feels that the justice done the churchmen of King
Arthur's time is too much of one kind, let him turn to that heart-
breaking scene where the brave monk stands with the mother and
her babe on the scaffold, and execrates the hideous law which puts her
to death for stealing enough to keep her from starving. It is one of
many passages in the story where our civilization of to-day sees itself
mirrored in the cruel barbarism of the past, the same in principle, and
only softened in custom. With shocks of consciousness, one recognizes in such episodes that the laws are still made for the few against
the many, and that the preservation of things, not men, is still the
ideal of legislation. But we do not wish to leave the reader with the
notion that Mr. Clemens's work is otherwise than obliquely serious.
Upon the face of it you have a story no more openly didactic than *Don
Quixote*, which we found ourselves more than once thinking of, as we
read, though always with the sense of the kindlier and truer heart of
our time. Never once, we believe, has Mark Twain been funny at the

cost of the weak, the unfriended, the helpless; and this is rather more than you can say of Cid Hamet ben Engeli. But the two writers are of the same humorous largeness; and when the Connecticut man rides out at dawn, in a suit of Arthurian armor, and gradually heats up under the mounting sun in what he calls that stove; and a fly gets between the bars of his visor; and he cannot reach his handkerchief in his helmet to wipe the sweat from his streaming face; and at last when he cannot bear it any longer, and dismounts at the side of a brook, and makes the distressed damsel who has been riding behind him take off his helmet, and fill it with water, and pour gallon after gallon down the collar of his wrought-iron cutaway, you have a situation of as huge a grotesqueness as any that Cervantes conceived.

The distressed damsel is the Lady Corisande; he calls her Sandy, and he is troubled in mind at riding about the country with her in that way; for he is not only very doubtful that there is nothing in the castle where she says there are certain princesses imprisoned and persecuted by certain giants, but he feels that it is not quite nice: he is engaged to a young lady in East Hartford, and he finds Sandy a fearful bore at first, though in the end he loves and marries her, finding that he hopelessly antedates the East Hartford young lady by thirteen centuries. How he gets into King Arthur's realm, the author concerns himself as little as any of us do with the mechanism of our dreams. In fact the whole story has the lawless operation of a dream; none of its prodigies are accounted for; they take themselves for granted, and neither explain nor justify themselves. Here he is, that Connecticut man, foreman of one of the shops in Colt's pistol factory, and full to the throat of the invention and the self-satisfaction of the nineteenth century, at the court of the mythic Arthur. He is promptly recognized as a being of extraordinary powers, and becomes the king's right-hand man, with the title of The Boss; but as he has apparently no lineage or blazon, he has no social standing, and the meanest noble has precedence of him, just as would happen in England to-day. The reader may faintly fancy the consequences flowing from this situation, which he will find so vividly fancied for him in the book; but they are simply irreportable. The scheme confesses allegiance to nothing; the incidents, the facts follow as they will. The Boss cannot rest from introducing the apparatus of our time, and he tries to impart its spirit, with a thousand most astonishing effects. He starts a daily paper in Camelot; he torpedoes a holy well; he blows up a party of insolent knights with a dynamite bomb; when he and the king disguise themselves as peasants, in order to learn the real life of the people, and are taken and sold for slaves, and then sent to the gallows for the murder of their master, Launcelot arrives to their rescue with five hundred knights on bicycles. It all ends with the Boss's proclamation of the Republic after Arthur's death, and his destruction of the whole chivalry of England by electricity.

We can give no proper notion of the measureless play of an imagination which has a gigantic jollity in its feats, together with the tenderest sympathy. There are incidents in this wonder-book which wring the heart for what has been of cruelty and wrong in the past, and leave it burning with shame and hate for the conditions which are of like effect in the present. It is one of its magical properties that the fantastic fable of Arthur's far-off time is also too often the sad truth of ours; and the magician who makes us feel in it that we have just begun to know his power, teaches equality and fraternity in every phase of his phantasmagory.

He leaves, to be sure, little of the romance of the olden time, but no one is more alive to the simple, mostly tragic poetry of it; and we do not remember any book which imparts so clear a sense of what was truly heroic in it. With all his scorn of kingcraft, and all his ireful contempt of caste, no one yet has been fairer to the nobility of character which they cost so much too much to develop. The mainly ridiculous Arthur of Mr. Clemens has his moments of being as fine and high as the Arthur of Lord Tennyson; and the keener light which shows his knights and ladies in their childlike simplicity and their innocent coarseness throws all their best qualities into relief. This book is in its last effect the most matter-of-fact narrative, for it is always true to human nature, the only truth possible, the only truth essential, to fiction. The humor of the conception and of the performance is simply immense; but more than ever Mr. Clemens's humor seems the sunny break of his intense conviction. We must all recognize him here as first of those who laugh, not merely because his fun is unrivalled, but because there is a force of right feeling and clear thinking in it that never got into fun before, except in *The Biglow Papers*. Throughout, the text in all its circumstance and meaning is supplemented by the illustrations of an artist who has entered into the wrath and the pathos as well as the fun of the thing, and made them his own.

III.

This kind of humor, the American kind, the kind employed in the service of democracy, of humanity, began with us a long time ago; in fact Franklin may be said to have torn it with the lightning from the skies. Some time, some such critic as Mr. T. S. Perry (if we ever have another such) will study its evolution in the century of our literature and civilization; but no one need deny himself meanwhile the pleasure we feel in Mr. Clemens's book as its highest development. His keen-tempered irony is something that we can well imagine Franklin enjoying.

23 Patent, mechanical criticism vs. James A. Herne

1890

From 'The Editor's Study,' *Harper's Monthly*, June 1890.

Still another nice trope for the defects and dangers of bad criticism Howells developed as 'the Miller Coupler and Buffer' patterns of convention in drama and dramatic criticism. If the critic comprehends nothing but dead, artificial, cut-and-dried methods of playwriting, if he sympathizes with nothing else and damns everything else, he converts managers and the public to his view and forces live drama off the stage and stifles actors and dramatists. The Miller Coupler and Buffer may be efficient—author mechanically hooks the conventionalities together into plays and critic mechanically hooks conventionalities together into reviews—but it is the death of art.

A playwright *not* dead, Howells notices, is Herne. *Drifting Apart* shows signs of real life within its machinery. Herne is a man to watch. As we know, Herne responded. In Stephen Crane's phrase for his own response, Herne also joined 'Howells and Garland . . . in the beautiful war,' making another of Howells's platoon of allies, though Herne, born in 1839, was nearly Howells's age. Like Garland, Herne took up Henry George's single tax panacea for social justice and took up Ibsen. Though he had the active help of Howells and Garland with *Margaret Fleming*, it failed repeatedly and disastrously. Fortunately for Herne, he persevered with *Shore Acres*.

When at last *Shore Acres* succeeded, it became a triumph for Howells's school. One reviewer, contrasting it with *Margaret Fleming*, wrote: 'The latter play, Zolaesque in motive and Ibsenesque in treatment, is realistic and repellent; the former is realistic and attractive.' The general notion was that Herne had discovered an American realism, and he is said to have made a million dollars from *Shore Acres*. One hopes Howells could smile.

I.

In spite of the vigilance of our dramatic criticism, which has shown such unwearied perseverance in undervaluing whatever was native or novel in the efforts of our playwrights, we really seem to be pretty well on our way toward the promise of an American comedy. We do not like to put the case more strongly than this, because even yet we have moments when we can scarcely credit the fact, the disparity between the opposing forces is so great.

On the one side, we have long had a large body of gentlemen trained to a profound misconception of their office, and deeply grounded in a traditional ignorance of the essence and nature of the drama, writing every night about the theatres, and more and more believing in themselves and their ideal of what a play ought to be, without reference to what life was. The criticisms which they have thus produced between church-yard-yawning and cock-crowing, with the advantages of a foreman behind and a night editor before, hurrying them up for their copy, have been such as must surprise the sympathetic witness by their uniform confidence and severity; but they have not in great measure carried, even to the most generous compassion, the evidences of fitness for the censorship assumed. These gentlemen have sometimes been able to tell us what good acting is, for they have seen a great deal of acting; but here their usefulness has too often ended; not certainly by their fault, for no man can be justly blamed for not telling more than he knows. Many of them know what a French play is, for they have seen enough adaptations of French plays to have learned to admire their extremely neat carpentry, and their carefully adjusted and brilliantly varnished sections, which can be carried to any climate, and put together and taken apart as often as you like, without making them less representative of anything that ever was in the world. They have been struck with the ingenious regularity of the design in these contrivances; they have seen how smoothly they worked, and they have formed such dramatic theories as they have from dramas in which situation links into situation, and effect into effect, upon lines of such admirable rigidity that it is all as unerring as making up a train of cars with the Miller Coupler and Buffer. But it would be wrong to say that many of these gentlemen apparently know anything of the contemporary Italian drama, Spanish drama, Russian drama, German drama, Norwegian drama; and it would be still more unjust to accuse them, upon the proofs their work has given, of knowing anything of the true functions of any drama, or caring at all for the life which all drama should represent.

On the other hand, opposed to this powerful body of critical gentlemen, whose discipline is so perfect that they often seem to think as one man, and sometimes even as no man at all, we have had a straggling force of playwrights and managers disheartened by a sense of their own want of conformity to the critical ideal, and by a guilty consciousness of preferring the realities they have seen and known in America to the artificialities which exist in the Miller Coupler and Buffer pattern of French drama. These poor fellows have not only been weakened by a knowledge of their inferiority in numbers and discipline to the critics (who count about a hundred to every manager, and a thousand to every playwright), but they have had a fear that there was something low and vulgar in their wish to see American life in the theatre as they have seen it in the street, and the counting-house, and the drawing-room, as they have even seen it in the novel. They have been so much unnerved by this misgiving that they have not yet ventured to be quite true to life, but have only ventured, so far, to offer us a compromise with unreality, which we can praise at most for the truth which could not well be kept out of it.

II.

We say kept out of it; but this may be an appearance only, and it may be that there is all the truth present that there could be got in. The new American play is still too much of the old Miller Coupler and Buffer pattern. We think we discern in it the evidences of a tripartite distrust, which we hope and believe it will outlive; but as yet we should say that the playwright fears the manager, the manager fears the public, and the public fears itself, and ventures to like what it enjoys only with the youthful diffidence which our public has concerning everything but its material greatness. Then this nascent drama of ours is retarded in its development by a fact necessarily present in all evolution. The men whose skill and training would enable them to give it an early maturity are themselves in a process of evolution, which they will probably never complete, because they have not fully the courage of their convictions. Their work will remain after them, for younger men to finish—a fact always interesting in any history of the æsthetic arts, but a little pathetic to witness in the course of its realization. The very men who are now doing our best work will hardly live to do the still better work they are making possible. But the future is not our affair, and we are not going merely to find fault with the present. On the contrary, we fancy that we shall be blamed for praising it too much, and that those who hope nothing may have some reason to reproach us for hoping anything. But such is the uncritical nature of the Study that when anything has given it a pleasure it cannot help being grateful. If it is too grateful, the balance can always be trimmed with the reluctances of those who think it a weakness to own they have been pleased, and a sign of superiority to withhold their thanks. The gentlemen who mostly write the dramatic criticisms, in fact, prove their right to condemn a new play in nothing so much as in allowing its defects to hide its merits, and in magnifying these as the trophies of their own victory over the playwright. A grudging and sneering concession of something funny here and pretty there, of something that touched, something that thrilled, in what was after all not a play, because a true play always has a Miller Coupler and Buffer at each end of every act, goes a great way with our simple-hearted public, which likes hash because it prefers to know what it is eating. With shame we confess we do not know how to practise this fine reticence in praise, this elegant profusion in censure, but we always try our best to hint our little reserves concerning matters before us; and if we have been too lavish in our recognition of the high per-fection of our dramatic criticism, we will try to be blind to some of the more obvious inadequacies of our dramatic literature.

III.

We could note enough of these in Mr. James A. Herne's drama of *Drifting Apart*. It did not seem to us well to represent the events in two acts of a serious play as occurring in a dream; but there was much in the simplicity and naturalness of the action which consoled us for this mechanical contrivance. Other things were not simple and not natural: the death of the starving child, affecting as it was at the time, was a forced note, with that falsetto ring which the death of children on the stage always has, though the little creature who played the scene played it so wonderfully; but the passages between the desperate mother and the wretched father, whose drunken dream prefigures the potential future shown in these acts, are of a most truthful pathos, and are interpreted with that perfect apprehension of the dramatist's meaning which is by no means the sole advantage that comes from acting one's own play. Mr. and Mrs. Herne, who take respectively the parts of husband and wife in a drama which they must have largely constructed together, are both artists of rare quality. Mrs. Herne has the flashes of power that transcend any effect of her husband's exquisite art; but this art is so patient, so beautiful, so unerring, that upon the whole we must praise him most. It never falters, never wanders; it is always tenderly sympathetic. In those dream passages it has a sort of dumb passion that powerfully moves, and in the lighter moments of the opening and closing acts it delights with a humorous playfulness which never forgets itself to farce. It perfectly fits the plain and simple story of the Gloucester fisherman, whose tempter overcomes him on Christmas Eve, and who returns home drunk to his wife and mother, and falls into a heavy sleep, and forecasts all the calamity of the two ensuing acts in his nightmare; but one readily believes that it would be equal to the highest demand upon it, speaking even after the manner of dramatic critics. We ourselves think that no more delicate effect could be achieved than that it makes in the homeliest scenes of the play; and if we speak of that passage in which the man talks out to the two women in the kitchen from the little room adjoining, where he is putting on his best clothes for Christmas, and whimsically scolds them for not being able to find his things, and intersperses his complaints with bits of gossip and philosophy and drolling, it is without the least hope of persuading artificial people of the value of such an episode, but with full confidence that no genuine person can witness it without feeling its charm.

IV.

The play has its weak points, as we have hinted. The author has by no means broken with tradition; he is apt to get the stage to help him out at times when nature seems reluctant in serving his purpose; but upon the whole he has produced a play fresh in motive, pure in tone, high in purpose, and very simple and honest in method. He is one of whom much better things may be reasonably expected, and we do not think he will disappoint even a great expectation. Born and bred to the theatre, he brings an intimate knowledge of its possibilities to his twofold interpretation of life as a dramatist and as an actor. He has that double equipment in art which, from Shakespeare down, has given the finest results.

24 The critics in Altruria: a Christmas masque

1890

From 'The Editor's Study,' *Harper's Monthly*, December 1890.

Not surprisingly in view of his increasing social sympathies, Howells fell into a habit of composing the December 'Editor's Study' about Christmas literature and considerations of the meaning of the holiday and its true keeping. For 1890, however, it seems clear that he recalled one of the pleasant traditions of the Old England's literary Christmas and created a masque. It was traditional that a masque should be moral, and Howells chose two immoral targets: the literary pirates who should be curbed by International Copyright; the international guild of literary critics. Copyright, at least in its nineteenth-century meaning, has long been an accomplished fact and a dead issue. But Howells's little Masque of Critics retains relevance.

This 'Study' also marks Howells's invention of the Utopian commonwealth which he would employ, with every variation upon irony from the playful to the tragic, as a foil for Social-Darwinist America.[1] He built an obvious bridge to the visionary tradition with allusions to Tennyson's 'Locksley Hall':

Till the war-drum throbbed no longer and the battle-flags were furled,
In the Parliament of Man, the Federation of the world.

But he hinted at the flavor of his own ideas and sensibility by coining 'the Synthetized Sympathies of Altruria,' where sweet charity displaces egotism. There the Last of the Romanticists and the Anonymous Critic become one with Punch and Judy.

I.

The Study could scarcely believe its windows.

It knew that this was the witching Christmas-time, when, if ever, the literary spirit begins to see visions, with morals hanging to them like the tails of kites; and to dream dreams of a sovereign efficacy in reforming vicious lives.

But the Study was so strongly principled against things of this sort that it was not willing to suppose itself the scene of even the most edifying hallucination. It rubbed its large French plate panes to a crystal clearness, sacrificing the beautiful frost-work on them without scruple, and peered eagerly into the street, emptied of all business by the holiday.

II.

The change which had passed upon the world was tacit, but no less millennial. It was plainly obvious that the old order was succeeded by the new; that the former imperfect republic of the United States of America had given place to the ideal commonwealth, the Synthetized Sympathies of Altruria. The spectacle was all the more interesting because this was clearly the first Christmas since the establishment of the new status.

The Study at once perceived that what it beheld from its windows was politically only a partial expression of the general condition; that the Synthetized Sympathies formed a province of the Federation of the World, represented by a delegation eager to sacrifice their selfish interests in the Parliament of Man, but was not by any means the centre of things. The fact was not flattering to the Study's patriotic pride, but upon reflection the Study was aware of a supreme joy in not having its patriotic pride flattered.

Every aspect of 'this new world which was the old' attracted the Study, but being a literary Study, and not a political or economical Study, its interest was soon centred in the literary phases of the millennial epoch. These were of every possible character, and their variety was so great that it was instantly evident how hopeless it would be to note them all.

But one thing that struck the Study with peculiar force was the apparent reconciliation of all the principles once supposed antagonistic, the substitution of emulation for rivalry, the harmonization of personal ambitions in a sweet accord of achievement for the common good. It was not exactly the weather for floral displays, but among the festive processions which poured into the public square under the Study's windows was one of Dramatic Critics wreathed with rosebuds, and led in flowery chains by a laughing band of Playwrights, who had captured these rugged natures, and had then persuaded them to see that they could themselves hope to live only by uniting with the playwrights in the endeavor for the beautiful. The critics had been taught to realize that if they kept on killing off the playwrights at the old rate they would soon have no plays to write about, and must themselves starve to death. The playwrights had first appealed to their instinct of self-preservation, and had then convinced their reason that they had no hope but in recognizing and fostering the good in our infant drama, and that one critic who perceived this was much greater than the aggregate of many who could not.

From time to time the procession paused to allow the critics and playwrights to clasp hands and publicly avow a lasting friendship. After them came in long file the Literary Critics, accompanied each by the poet, novelist, historian, or essayist whom he had most deeply injured, and to whom he was linked by a band of violets. The Study understood that these flowers were chosen by the critics themselves, out of all the products of the vegetable kingdom, as best expressive of the critics' modest and shrinking character. They paced with downcast eyes, and were every few steps openly overcome by the honor of walking in those fragrant bands with Creative Authors. These encouraged and supported them, and when the critics would have gone down before them and acknowledged their inferiority and unworthiness, the Creative Authors would not suffer it, but consoled them with the assurance that they too had their uses in the literary world, in noting and classifying its phenomena, and that their former arrogance and presumption would not be counted against them, now they were truly penitent. Each of the critics bore his name and that of the journal he wrote for distinctly inscribed on a badge worn over his heart.

Suddenly, on the flank of this friendly troop of authors and critics, there appeared at no great distance two figures. The first was that of an extremely decrepit old man, dressed to a fantastic youthfulness, with his hair and beard washed to a saffron tint that was not in the least golden. His costume was out of the rag-bag of all epochs, and on his head he wore a wreath of paper flowers.

The other was armed as to his head in a huge helmet like that of the *secutor* who fights with the *retiarius*[2] in the Roman arena, and his face was completely hidden; his body was covered with a suit of scale armor, as the Study at first imagined; to learn later that the scales were a natural expression of the wearer's serpentine nature. Instead of a sword he carried a repeating rifle in his hand, and from time to time he dropped a panel of tall fence from his shoulder to the ground, and crouching behind it fired at some author in the procession.

Horrified at this outrage, which no one seemed inclined to inter-fere with, the Study threw up one of its windows, and called to a boy who was passing on the pavement below: he proved to be the very boy whom Old Scrooge sent to buy the turkey when he woke from his fearful dream and found it was nothing but a dream.

'Our good boy,' said the Study, finding the vocative of the editorial plural absurd, but clinging to it with its well-known fondness for tradition—'Our good boy, will you tell us what is the meaning of that abominable person's behavior in firing into the procession? Is he a Pinkerton man, and does he mistake it for a parade of strikers? Who is he, anyway, and that grotesque simulacrum with him?'

'Those fellows?' asked the boy. 'Oh! the one in front is the Last of the Romanticists, telling the same old story; and the other is the Anonymous Critic, firing blank-cartridges at authors. It's Christmas, you know, and they let the poor old fellows out to amuse themselves.'

[The remainder of this section is a lengthy skit concerned with International Copyright.]

III.

The Study now observed that the authors and critics had all disap-peared from the square, and that the Last of the Romanticists and the Anonymous Critic were poking about in its emptiness in a forlorn and aimless manner. The Romanticist sank down on the curb-stone and fell asleep with his head dropped between his knees; his paper-flower wreath tumbled into the gutter. The Anonymous Critic removed his helmet and revealed his death's-head; he took out a black buccaneer's flag from the helmet and wiped the perspiration from his skull. 'Hot work,' he said, looking round for the boy.

But even the boy had vanished; and now the square was given up to a series of allegorical interludes. The first of these was the Identifica-tion of the Real and the Ideal. The two principles appeared hand in hand, like Tweedledum and Tweedledee in *Through the Looking-glass*, and at once began their great transformation act, by passing into and out of each other with such lightning-like rapidity that they were soon no longer distinguishable. The moment this result had been accomplished, an electric transparency appeared above the consolidation with the legend, *Which is which?* The Romanticist continued to sleep audibly, and the Anonymous Critic said, 'Give it up.' Then the Real and the Ideal bowed together, and separately withdrew.

The True and The Beautiful now entered the square together, and performed their famous *pas seul à deux*. This was not so difficult as it seems when put in words; for The True and The Beautiful are one and the same; only The True is the one, and The Beautiful is the same. They faced the Study windows first as The True, and after performing their dance in that character, wheeled half round and appeared as The Beautiful, in the manner of the person who used to dance as the soldier and the sailor on the stage. Over their head flashed out the words, 'Beauty is truth, truth beauty.'

The Anonymous Critic read the legend aloud, and then murmured vindictively, 'Keats! I did for *him* pretty thoroughly, anyway.'

'Oh, no!' the Study retorted. 'You did your worst, but after all you didn't kill Keats. You hurt him, but he took you very philosophically, at a time when you were very much more regarded than you are now.'

It is the nature of the Anonymous Critic not to be able to bear the slightest contradiction. He raised his weapon and immediately fired a blank-cartridge at the Study windows, putting on his helmet at the same time to avoid recognition. The report woke the Last of the Romanticists, who scrambled to his feet exclaiming, 'Saved, saved! They are saved at last!'

'Who are saved?' asked the Study, with unbroken windows.

'The good old-fashioned hero and heroine. Didn't you hear the minute-gun at sea? He arrived with his raft just as her bark was sinking. He fired one shot, and the miscreant relaxed his hold from her fainting form, and fell a corpse at her feet. The sharp clap of thunder, preceded by a blinding flash, revealed the path they had lost, and they stood at the castle gate. The retainers joined in a shout that made the welkin ring, and the brave cow-boy rode into their midst with the swooning châtelaine on the mustang behind him, while the Saracens and Apaches discharged a shower of arrows, and then fled in all directions. That shot, which proclaimed the suicide of the gambler, in order to give his body for food to the starving companions he had fleeced in the snow-bound Sierras, was the death-knell of the commonplace. Here they come, dying for each other! Ah, that is something *like*! What abundant action! What nobility of motive! What incessant self-sacrifice! No analysis *there*!'

The Study could never understand exactly how it was managed, but in the antics of the fantastic couple who now appeared it was somehow expressed that the youth was perpetually winning the maiden by deeds of the greatest courage and the most unnecessary and preposterous goodness, while the maiden enacted the rôle of the slave at once of duty and of love. When she was not wildly throwing herself into her lover's arms, she was letting him marry another girl, though she knew it would make him unhappy, because she believed the other girl wanted him.

'Ah,' sighed the Anonymous Critic, '*there* is profound knowledge of the heart for you! What poetry! What passion!'

[At this point the column modulates back to the copyright theme and so to the ritual awakening of 'the Study' from its 'dream'.]

NOTES

1 See Clara and Rudolf Kirk, eds, *The Altrurian Romances*, vol. xx of *A Selected Edition of W. D. Howells*, Bloomington, Indiana, 1968.
2 The nimble Roman gladiator who fought with net and trident.

25 Emily Dickinson announced
1891

From 'The Editor's Study,' *Harper's Monthly*, January 1891.

Emily Dickinson's editor Thomas H. Johnson concluded that critical response to the first publication of her *Poems* on 12 November 1890 consisted largely of 'numerous hostile reviews' but that 'What surprised everybody, the editors and publishers most of all, was the continuous demand for new printings, especially in the wake of so many unfavorable reviews.'[1] Though not every review was hostile, one ought not to be immodest about the influence of the critical Court of Last Resort. Perhaps sales might have been strong even if Howells had not praised Dickinson's poetry, 'its rarity, its singular worth,' acclaiming it 'a distinctive addition to the literature of the world' at length and with perspicuous quotation in 'The Editor's Study.'

The proper claim to be made here for Howells as critic is that he proclaimed Emily Dickinson's greatness from the first instant. He went on reading, loving, and quoting her for years thereafter. It appears to be true that he liberated the power of poetic creativity in Stephen Crane by reading Dickinson to him. Perhaps there are few more vital claims to critical significance than the power to discern greatness in one poet and to seed it into another poet's imagination.

The strange *Poems of Emily Dickinson* we think will form something like an intrinsic experience with the understanding reader of them. They have been edited by Mrs. Mabel Loomis Todd, who was a personal friend of the poet, and by Colonel T. W. Higginson, who was long her epistolary and literary acquaintance, but only met her twice. Few people met her so often, as the reader will learn from Colonel Higginson's interesting preface, for her life was mainly spent in her father's house at Amherst, Massachusetts; she seldom passed its doors, and never, for many years, passed the gates of its grounds. There is no hint of what turned her life in upon itself, and probably this was its natural evolution, or involution, from tendencies inherent in the New England, or the Puritan, spirit. We are told that once a year

189

she met the local world at a reception in her father's house; we do not know that there is any harm in adding, that she did not always literally meet it, but sometimes sat with her face averted from the company in another room. One of her few friends was Helen Hunt Jackson, whom she suffered to send one of her poems to be included in the volume of anonymous pieces which Messrs. Roberts Brothers once published with the title of *A Masque of Poets*. Whether the anonymity flattered her love of obscurity or not, it is certain that her darkling presence in this book was the occasion of her holding for many years a correspondence with its publishers. She wrote them, as the fancy took her, comments on their new books, and always enclosed a scrap of her verse, though without making any reference to it. She never intended or allowed anything more from her pen to be printed in her lifetime; but it was evident that she wished her poetry finally to meet the eyes of that world which she had herself always shrunk from. She could not have made such poetry without knowing its rarity, its singular worth; and no doubt it was a radiant happiness in the twilight of her hidden, silent life.

The editors have discharged their delicate duty toward it with unimpeachable discretion, and Colonel Higginson has said so many apt things of her work in his introduction, that one who cannot differ with him must be vexed a little to be left so little to say. He speaks of her 'curious indifference to all conventional rules of verse,' but he adds that 'when a thought takes one's breath away, a lesson on grammar seems an impertinence.' He notes 'the quality suggestive of the poetry of William Blake' in her, but he leaves us the chance to say that it is a Blake who had read Emerson who had read Blake. The fantasy is as often Blakian as the philosophy is Emersonian; but after feeling this again and again, one is ready to declare that the utterance of this most singular and authentic spirit would have been the same if there had never been an Emerson or a Blake in the world. She sometimes suggests Heine as much as either of these; all three in fact are spiritually present in some of the pieces; yet it is hardly probable that she had read Heine, or if she had, would not have abhorred him.

Here is something that seems compact of both Emerson and Blake, with a touch of Heine too:

> I taste a liquor never brewed,
> From tankards scooped in pearl;
> Not all the vats upon the Rhine
> Yield such an alcohol!

Inebriate of air am I,
And debauchee of dew,
Reeling, through endless summer days,
From inns of molten blue.

When landlords turn the drunken bee
Out of the foxglove's door,
When butterflies renounce their drams,
I shall but drink the more!

Till seraphs swing their snowy hats,
And saints to windows run,
To see the little tippler
Leaning against the sun!

But we believe it is only seeming; we believe these things are as wholly her own as this:

The bustle in a house
The morning after death
Is solemnest of industries
Enacted upon earth,—

The sweeping up the heart,
And putting love away
We shall not want to use again
Until eternity.

Such things could have come only from a woman's heart to which the experiences in a New England town have brought more knowledge of death than of life. Terribly unsparing many of these strange poems are, but true as the grave and certain as mortality. The associations of house-keeping in the following poem have a force that drags us almost into the presence of the poor, cold, quiet thing:

'TROUBLED ABOUT MANY THINGS.'

How many times these low feet staggered,
Only the soldered mouth can tell;
Try! can you stir the awful rivet?
Try! can you lift the hasps of steel?

Stroke the cool forehead, hot so often,
Lift, if you can, the listless hair;
Handle the adamantine fingers
Never a thimble more shall wear.

Buzz the dull flies on the chamber window;
Brave shines the sun through the freckled pane;
Fearless the cobweb swings from the ceiling—
Indolent housewife, in daisies lain!

Then in this, which has no name—how could any phrase nominate its weird witchery aright?—there is the flight of an eerie fancy that leaves all experience behind:

I died for beauty, but was scarce
Adjusted in the tomb,
When one who died for truth was lain
In an adjoining room.

He questioned softly why I failed.
'For beauty,' I replied.
'And I for truth,—the two are one;
We brethren are,' he said.

And so, as kinsmen met a night,
We talked between the rooms,
Until the moss had reached our lips,
And covered up our names.

All that Puritan longing for sincerity, for veracious conduct, which in some good New England women's natures is almost a hysterical shriek, makes its exultant grim assertion in these lines:

REAL.

I like a look of agony,
Because I know it's true;
Men do not sham convulsion,
Nor simulate a throe.

The eyes glaze once, and that is death.
Impossible to feign
The beads upon the forehead
By homely anguish strung.

These mortuary pieces have a fascination above any others in the book; but in the stanzas below there is a still, solemn, rapt movement of the thought and music together that is of exquisite charm:

New feet within my garden go,
New fingers stir the sod;

A troubadour upon the elm
Betrays the solitude.

New children play upon the green,
New weary sleep below;
And still the pensive spring returns,
And still the punctual snow!

This is a song that sings itself; and this is another such, but thrilling
with the music of a different passion:

SUSPENSE.

Elysium is as far as to
The very nearest room,
If in that room a friend await
Felicity or doom.

What fortitude the soul contains,
That it can so endure
The accent of a coming foot,
The opening of a door!

The last poem is from the group which the editors have named
'Love'; the other groups from which we have been quoting are
'Nature,' and 'Time and Eternity'; but the love poems are of the same
piercingly introspective cast as those differently named. The same
force of imagination is in them; in them, as in the rest, touch often
becomes clutch. In them love walks on heights he seldom treads,
and it is the heart of full womanhood that speaks in the words of this
nun-like New England life.

Few of the poems in the book are long, but none of the short,
quick impulses of intense feeling or poignant thought can be called
fragments. They are each a compassed whole, a sharply finished point,
and there is evidence, circumstantial and direct, that the author
spared no pains in the perfect expression of her ideals. Nothing, for
example, could be added that would say more than she has said in four
lines:

Presentiment is that long shadow on the lawn
Indicative that suns go down;
The notice to the startled grass
That darkness is about to pass.

Occasionally, the outside of the poem, so to speak, is left so rough, so rude, that the art seems to have faltered. But there is apparent to reflection the fact that the artist meant just this harsh exterior to remain, and that no grace of smoothness could have imparted her intention as it does. It is the soul of an abrupt, exalted New England woman that speaks in such brokenness. The range of all the poems is of the loftiest; and sometimes there is a kind of swelling lift, an almost boastful rise of feeling, which is really the spring of faith in them:

> I never saw a moor,
> I never saw the sea;
> Yet know I how the heather looks,
> And what a wave must be.
>
> I never spoke with God,
> Nor visited in heaven;
> Yet certain am I of the spot
> As if the chart were given.

There is a noble tenderness, too, in some of the pieces; a quaintness that does not discord with the highest solemnity:

> I shall know why, when time is over,
> And I have ceased to wonder why;
> Christ will explain each separate anguish
> In the fair school-room of the sky.
>
> He will tell me what Peter promised,
> And I, for wonder at his woe,
> I shall forget the drop of anguish
> That scalds me now, that scalds me now.

The companionship of human nature with inanimate nature is very close in certain of the poems; and we have never known the invisible and intangible ties binding all creation in one, so nearly touched as in them.

If nothing else had come out of our life but this strange poetry we should feel that in the work of Emily Dickinson America, or New England rather, had made a distinctive addition to the literature of the world, and could not be left out of any record of it; and the interesting and important thing is that this poetry is as characteristic of our life as our business enterprise, our political turmoil, our demagogism, our millionairism.

NOTE

1 Thomas H. Johnson, *The Poems of Emily Dickinson*, Harvard, 1955, I, xlvi–xlvii. But see also R. W. Franklin, *The Editing of Emily Dickinson*, Madison, 1967, 26–7.

26 William James's *Psychology*
1891

From 'The Editor's Study,' *Harper's Monthly*, July 1891.

As Howells was to show dramatically in his recognition of Thorstein Veblen, among his important critical functions was to discover and publicize major contributions to intellectual history. In retrospect it is not easy to believe that William James remained without public reputation until 1891 and publication of *The Principles of Psychology*; but until that time he was hardly more than a lively Harvard professor. To Howells, of course, William was as old if not so intimate a friend as Henry. Howells, who belonged with Henry to the literary set among the Cambridge wits of 1870, had not only seen William, who belonged to the scientific but metaphysical set, with some regularity in social life but shared deeply in a mutual consciousness of belonging to a generation with an understood difference from its fathers.

As the metaphysical set resolved the generational stresses in 'pragmatism,' the literary set resolved them in 'realism,' and they participated knowingly in a joint sensibility. It is also true that pragmatism and realism may be said to have moved on lines of inner necessity toward a shared psychologism. Therefore William James's pre-philosophic masterpiece, his *Psychology*, excited Howells because it lighted before him the path in which his feet were already set.

As Howells kept saying, one of the central features of realistic fiction was its concentration on character, not incident; persons, not plot. But a predictable paradox set in against the realist as he worked deeper into humane reality: his dramatic, external method began to war against his concern for inwardness. In spite of himself the logic of his work drove him toward psychology. But when he at length turned to psychology he met surprise: the study of the spirit of man had been snatched away from the old idealists and had set the new idealizers at defiance. Realism began to transform itself toward post-realism—toward, for instance, stream oi consciousness writing.

When Howells reviewed James's *Psychology* he had already written an extraordinary novelette, pre-Freudian, of course, but psychiatric, *The Shadow of a Dream*, 1890. His creative imagination understood where realism was going, though he would still be a pioneering critic a decade

196

and more later when he could identify what had been going on in fiction. As the taxonomist of the moment, however, he was prepared to identify and enjoy a great book at first reading and describe it so as to make its light and pleasure available to his own reader.

I.

We suppose it would be rather damaging to Professor William James with other scientists to show that in his volumes on *The Principles of Psychology* he writes with a poetic sense of his facts, and with an artistic pleasure in their presentation. We must content ourselves with a far less positive recognition of the charming spirit, the delightful manner, and the flavorous and characteristic style of the work. There are moments when he brings to the intellectual strain of the subject the relief of a humorous touch; when he gives the overtaxed faculties a little vacation, and invites the sympathies of the reader to a share in the inquiry. It has so long been the custom to call a certain friendly and consciously fallible attitude 'human' that we are reluctant to proclaim his relation to his theme as distinctly 'human,' yet the epithet comes unbidden to the pen in attempting to label his performance. After all, it is perhaps as well to use it; perhaps it is as well to admit frankly that the treatise has often those graces and attractions which we have hinted at. There are many other times when it has none of them, and when the author's attitude is so severely scientific, so pitilessly exigent of the reader's co-operation, so remorselessly indifferent to his mental repose, as to be distinctly inhuman. But it must be said of Professor James that he has not only not tried to deny his theme the æsthetic and ethical interest it inherently has for every one having a mind, or thinking he has one, but has been willing to heighten it. In this way it must be admitted that he has come dangerously near writing a 'popular' book. It is not exactly 'summer reading'; the two vast volumes, aggregating some fourteen hundred octavo pages, would not go easily into the pocket or the hand-bag; they will probably not be found in competition with the fiction of the news stands; we could not imagine their being 'lapped out' by the train-boy. But there is no doubt that several of the chapters, such as those on Habit, The Consciousness of Self, Memory, Imagination, Instinct, Will, and Hypnotism, can appeal successfully to people of average culture; and that throughout the work there are passages which may be read aloud to the tenderest female, so lightly and agreeably are some of the most difficult problems of the soul handled in them. We say soul, but we really mean mind, for although psychology took its name from being the 'science of the human soul,' it has now decided that the question of the soul is really no part of its business: the mind only—its attributes, conditions, phenomena—is dealt with; the soul is left out of the account.

Not that as to the existence or the destiny of such a constituent of human nature this science denies anything. On the contrary, in Professor James's work there is a perceptible sympathy and regard for the theories of it; but the inquiry is not with them. The field is vast enough, and the way obscure enough without them; and one impression that remains to the unscientific reader of Professor James's work is that it has not yet been explored, or mapped except at a few points. With one's self always at hand, with one's fellow-creatures swarming upon one, with all human history behind one, a collection of 'infinitely repellent particles' of fact is the sum of psychological industry. The talk is not only about, but round about, the human mind, which it penetrates here and there and wins a glimpse of unsayable things. The fascination of the quest forever remains, and it is this fascination which Professor James permits his reader to share. It could not be said that he has a philosophical system to establish; his philosophical system is his method of collating and presenting discoveries made, and suggesting conclusions from them, and he is always so frank, so tolerant, that you feel he would willingly consider a different inference, if you made it, and would be gladly interested in it. Nothing could be more winning than the informality of his discourse; it captivates the average human being to find that the study of his mind is not necessarily allied to a frigid decorum. Those who know the rich and cordial properties of the philosophical writings of Henry James the elder, will find a kindred heartiness in the speculations of his son, and will be directly at home with him. The ground, of course, is absolutely different; nothing seems further from psychology than theology.

The book is so full of proofs of what we have been trying to say that it seems absurd to cast in the line at one place rather than another, but perhaps the chapter on Will is more abundantly illustrative than some others, though we do not know that such a passage as the following is one of the most illustrative in it: 'Men do not differ so much in their mere feelings and conceptions. Their notions of possibility and their ideals are not as far apart as might be argued from their different fates. No class of them have better sentiments or feel more constantly the difference between the higher and the lower path in life than the hopeless failures, the sentimentalists, the drunkards, the schemers, the "dead-beats," whose life is one long contradiction between know-ledge and action, and who, with full command of theory, never get to holding their limp characters upright. No one eats of the fruit of the tree of knowledge as they do; as far as moral insight goes, in compari-son with them, the orderly and prosperous Philistines whom they scandalize are suckling babes. And yet their moral knowledge, always there, grumbling and rumbling in the background—discerning, commenting, protesting, longing, half resolving—never wholly resolves, never gets its voice out of the minor into the major key, or its speech out of the subjunctive into the imperative mood, never breaks the spell, never takes the helm into its own hands. In such characters as Restif and Rousseau, it would seem as if the lower motives had all the impulsive efficacy in their hands. The more ideal motives exist alongside of them in profusion; and the consciousness of inward hollowness that accrues from habitually seeing the better only to do the worse, is one of the saddest feelings one can bear with him through this vale of tears.'

It will have been perceived from this how much the moral aspect of the facts ascertained interests the writer, who feels their value not only as a moralist but as an artist; he cannot help stating his mind about them picturesquely. This must commend him to the general reader, who, although he may, and probably will, forget about the dark underlying premises of the luminous conclusions that delight him, cannot fail to be greatly stimulated and strengthened by the whole philosophy of the book. It would be hard for us, at least, to find a more important piece of writing in its way than the chapter on Habit; it is something for the young to read with fear and hope, the old with self-pity or self-gratulation, and every one with recognition of the fact that in most things that tell for good or ill, and much or little in life, we are creatures of our own making. It would be well for the reader to review this chapter in the light of that on the Will, where the notion of free-will is more fully dealt with. In fact the will of the weak man is *not* free; but the will of the strong man, the man who has *got the habit* of preferring sense to nonsense and 'virtue' to 'vice,' is a *freed* will, which one might very well spend all one's energies in achiev-ing. It is this preference which at last becomes the man, and remains permanent throughout those astounding changes which every one finds in himself from time to time. 'Every thought we have of a given fact,' Mr. James says, 'is, strictly speaking, unique, and only bears a resemblance of kind with our other thoughts of the same fact. When the identical fact recurs, we *must* think of it in a fresh manner, see it under a somewhat different angle, apprehend it in different relations from those in which it last appeared. And the thought by which we cognize it is the thought of it-in-these-relations, a thought suffused with the consciousness of all that dim content. Often we are ourselves struck at the strange differences in our successive views of the same thing. We wonder how we ever could have opined as we did last month about a certain matter. We have outgrown the possibility of that state of mind, we know not how. From one year to another we see things in new lights. What was unreal has grown real, and what was exciting is insipid. The friends we used to care the world for are shrunken to shadows; the women, once so divine, the stars, the woods, and the waters, how now so dull and common; the young girls that brought an aura of infinity, at present hardly distinguishable existences; the pictures so empty; and as for the books, what *was* there to find so mysteriously significant in Goethe, or in John Mill so full of weight? Instead of all this, more zestful than ever is the work, and fuller and deeper the import of common duties and of common goods.'

We can safely leave to the reader the implications of this admirable thought. If Psychology in this work is treated philosophically rather than scientifically, there can be no question but it is treated profoundly and subtly, and with a never-failing, absolute devotion to the truth. This fidelity is as signal in it as the generosity of the feeling, the elevation of the thought, the sweetness of the humanity which characterize it. If the book does not establish a theory, if it confesses the tentative, adolescent quality of a science which is as old as the race, and as young as the latest human consciousness, it is all the same a rare contribution to knowledge, and a treasury of suggestion which any cultivated intelligence can profit by. It is necessarily inconclusive in many ways, and very likely Psychology can never be a science as some other sciences are, but must always remain a philosophy. If this is so, it can change its mind with less confusion to the unlearned than they feel when they are told that all they have been taught by the highest scientific authorities is mistaken. It can so continue the possession of all who love wisdom, however far off, however wanting in the self-knowledge where all wisdom centres.

II.

What a work like Mr. James's (if there is another like it) does for the unscienced reader is to give him the habit of looking at his mental qualities and ingredients as materials of personality with which his conscience can the more hopefully deal, the more distinctly they are ascertained. It comes to an ethical effect, to suggestion for the ideal social life, with only rather more direct instruction than astronomy has.

27 Hamlin Garland, *Main-Travelled Roads*

1891

From 'The Editor's Study,' *Harper's Monthly*, September 1891.

Not to repeat previous comment, hundreds of pages of ill-informed criticism of Howells, some of it famous, invalidate themselves by comparison with the implications of Howells's praise as 'fine art' of short stories 'full of the bitter and burning dust, the foul and trampled slush of the common avenues of life: the life of the men who hopelessly and cheerlessly make the wealth that enriches the alien and the idler, and impoverishes the producer.'

There remains a book of prime interest to be written on the relations of Howells and Garland. To put it briefly, Garland served for many years as Howells's prime disciple, prophet, recruiter, and advance agent. He personally converted, as Howells would not attempt to do, various members of the Howells school. He published his own version of the literary gospel according to Howells as *Crumbling Idols*, 1894. But the really significant fact is that the stories Howells praised in *Main-Travelled Roads*, which critics think the peak of Garland's achievement, became what they are because Howells cajoled, entreated, even hammered at Garland to be himself, see with his own eyes, speak with his own voice.

When dealing with other minds, Howells took the same stance as Emerson. They both demanded of the young men of America an immediate, authentic contemporaneity. The difference between Emerson's 'Self-Reliance' or 'The Problem' and Howells's criticism, published or spoken to his young men, is metaphysical, epistemological, a matter of faith and vision. In the American 1890s, as Donald Pizer, the best of Garland and Norris critics, has recently said, the key to literary understanding is 'The Centrality of Howells.'[1]

At present we have only too much to talk about in a book so robust and terribly serious as Mr. Hamlin Garland's volume called *Main-Travelled Roads*. That is what they call the highways in the part of the West that Mr. Garland comes from and writes about; and these stories are full of the bitter and burning dust, the foul and trampled slush of the common avenues of life: the life of the men who hopelessly and cheerlessly make the wealth that enriches the alien and the idler, and impoverishes the producer. If any one is still at a loss to account for that uprising of the farmers in the West, which is the translation of the Peasant's War into modern and republican terms, let him read *Main-Travelled Roads* and he will begin to understand, unless, indeed, Mr. Garland is painting the exceptional rather than the average. The stories are full of those gaunt, grim, sordid, pathetic, ferocious figures, whom our satirists find so easy to caricature as Hayseeds, and whose blind groping for fairer conditions is so grotesque to the newspapers and so menacing to the politicians. They feel that something is wrong, and they know that the wrong is not theirs. The type caught in Mr. Garland's book is not pretty; it is ugly and often ridiculous; but it is heart-breaking in its rude despair. The story of a farm mortgage as it is told in the powerful sketch 'Under the Lion's Paw' is a lesson in political economy, as well as a tragedy of the darkest cast. 'The Return of the Private' is a satire of the keenest edge, as well as a tender and mournful idyl of the unknown soldier who comes back after the war with no blare of welcoming trumpets or flash of streaming flags, but foot-sore, heart-sore, with no stake in the country he has helped to make safe and rich but the poor man's chance to snatch an uncertain subsistence from the furrows he left for the battle-field. 'Up the Coulé,' however, is the story which most pitilessly of all accuses our vaunted conditions, wherein every man has the chance to rise above his brother and make himself richer than his fellows. It shows us once for all what the risen man may be, and portrays in his good-natured selfishness and indifference that favorite ideal of our system. The successful brother comes back to the old farmstead, prosperous, handsome, well dressed, and full of patronizing sentiment for his boyhood days there, and he cannot understand why his brother, whom hard work and corroding mortgages have eaten all the joy out of, gives him a grudging and surly welcome. It is a tremendous situation, and it is the allegory of the whole world's civilization: the upper dog and the under dog are everywhere, and the under dog nowhere likes it.

But the allegorical effects are not the primary intent of Mr. Garland's work: it is a work of art, first of all, and we think of fine art; though the material will strike many gentilities as coarse and common. In one of the stories, 'Among the Corn Rows,' there is a good deal of burly, broad-shouldered humor of a fresh and native kind; in 'Mrs.

Ripley's Trip' is a delicate touch, like that of Miss Wilkins; but Mr. Garland's touches are his own, here and elsewhere. He has a certain harshness and bluntness, an indifference to the more delicate charms of style; and he has still to learn that though the thistle is full of an unrecognized poetry, the rose has a poetry too, that even over-praise cannot spoil. But he has a fine courage to leave a fact with the reader, ungarnished and unvarnished, which is almost the rarest trait in an Anglo-Saxon writer, so infantile and feeble is the custom of our art; and this attains tragical sublimity in the opening sketch, 'A Branch Road,' where the lover who has quarrelled with his betrothed comes back to find her mismated and miserable, such a farm wife as Mr. Garland has alone dared to draw, and tempts the broken-hearted drudge away from her loveless home. It is all morally wrong, but the author leaves you to say that yourself. He knows that his business was with those two people, their passions and their proba-bilities. He shows them such as the newspapers know them.

NOTE

1 *American Thought and Writing: The 1890's*, Boston, 1972, 34–109.

28 The quest for nationality
1891

From 'The Editor's Study,' *Harper's Monthly*, November 1891.

As late in American cultural history as the onset of World War II the American critic, too often the American writer, felt bedeviled by the question of cultural, or literary nationality. American vulnerability to the question constituted perhaps the last vestige of colonial and provincial doubt about American relations to the concert of European, of Western culture. Had Americans achieved full membership? For a ridiculously long time the hostile European demanded, 'Where is your Dante? Where is your Shakespeare?' And the defensive American replied, in effect, 'We have Niagara Falls!' It did not seem to help much to point out that the question was about as silly as the answer: there had, after all, been only one Dante and one Shakespeare in all the history of Western culture, and the American man of letters could justly claim both as intrinsic to his own heritage.

One of the difficulties to which the American defendant seems to have been irrationally vulnerable was that characteristically the hostile European felt more concern for European political issues than he felt for disinterested justice. No doubt the American hyper-sensitivity (which sold hostile cultural commentary handsomely in the American market) rooted itself in the provincial inferiority which succeeded upon colonial dependency in Americans. The questions, complex indeed, have been studied brilliantly by Benjamin T. Spencer in *The Quest for Nationality: An American Literary Campaign, from the beginnings to 1892*; and there is good hope of its sequel for the current century.

Toward the end of his 'Editor's Study' campaign Howells decided, however, that nationality was no longer enough. He demonstrated that one could slice up the European carper with an edge of ironic acerbity keener than ever. But he concluded that it no longer much mattered: 'The great and good things in literature nowadays are not the national features, but the universal features.' He pointed out, long before the coinages of 'highbrow' and 'lowbrow,' or 'redskin' and 'pale-face,' or 'pop' and 'élitist' as notions of literary history, the American antithesis of 'two tendencies, apparently opposite, but probably parallel: one a tendency toward an elegance refined and polished, both in thought and phrase,

205

almost to tenuity; the other a tendency to grotesqueness, wild and extravagant, to the point of anarchy.'

But at the last he wished to exercise his irony, bitingly critical, upon Americans who rendered his warfare nugatory because they merely did not care. The plutocracy kept its eyes desperately averted from reality. The great mass of citizens longed for gentility: 'If we have had to dig, or if we are many of us still digging, that is reason enough why we do not want the spade brought into the parlor.' His campaign for American taste, the national sensibility, had been lost.

I.

From time to time there comes a voice across the sea, asking us in varied terms of reproach and entreaty, why we have not a national literature. As we understand this voice, a national literature would be something very becoming and useful to us as a people, and it would be no more than is due the friendly expectation of the English witnesses of our destitution, who have denied from the beginning that we ever could have a national literature; and proved it. The reasons which they still address to our guilty consciousness in demanding a national literature of us are such and so many that the American who reads their appeals must be a very hardened offender if he does not at once inwardly resolve to do all he can to have one. For our own part, we scarcely know how to keep our patience with the writers who have as yet failed to supply us with it. We are personally acquainted with a dozen Americans who could any one of them give us a national literature, if he would take the pains. In fact, we know of some Englishmen who could produce a very fair national literature for us. All they would have to do would be to write differently from those American authors whose works have failed to embody a national literature, and then they would create for us a literature of unmistakable nationality. But with a literature of their own to maintain, it is too much to ask this of them, and we should not hope for help from English writers, except in the form of advice and censure. We ought to be very glad to have so much, but whether we are glad or not we are likely to have it, for there is nothing mean about Englishmen when it comes to advice and censure; and if we cannot get them to make a national literature for us, we had better learn from them how to make it ourselves.

II.

We do not understand the observers of our literary poverty to deny that in certain qualities and colors we have already something national in literature. Perhaps if they were to extend the field of their knowledge a little in the direction of their speculations they might discover that we had something more positive than these colors and qualities; but it never was necessary for an Englishman to know anything of American affairs before writing about them. Here and there an Englishman, like Mr. Bryce, takes the trouble to inform himself, but we do not fancy he is the more acceptable or edifying to his countrymen on that account; and the fact remains that he really need not do it. In treating of American literature the English critic's great qualification is that he should be master of the fact that Mr. Walt Whitman is the only American who writes like Mr. Walt Whitman. It must be owned that the English critic works this single qualification very hard; he makes it go a long way; but we do not blame him for his thrifty use of it; and we should be sorry to quarrel with the simple economy of the inference that we have not a national literature in the proportion that we do not write like Mr. Whitman. If this will serve the turn of the English writer with the English public, why should he be at any greater pains in the matter?

Usually the English writer is not at any greater pains, and the extravagance of knowing something more than what is necessary to such an inference is rare. Even Mr. Watts, who has lately exposed our literary lack to the world in *The Nineteenth Century*, and Mr. Quiller-Couch, who has blamed our literary indifference to the workingman in *The Speaker*, do not go much beyond this inference in their philosophization of our case. Yet, if we were to allow ourselves to bandy words with our betters, we think we might make a suggestion in the interest of general criticism which would perhaps advantage them.

III.

In the first place we should like to invite observation to the fact that for all æsthetic purposes the American people are not a nation, but a condition. They are the old, well-known Anglo-Saxon race, affected and modified by the infusion of other strains, but not essentially changed by these, and not very different from the English at home except in their political environment, and the vastness of the scale of their development. Their literature, so far as they have produced any, is American-English literature, just as the English literature is English-European, and it is as absurd to ask them to have a literature wholly their own as to ask them to have a language wholly their own. In fact, we have noted that where our language does differ from that of the mother English, or grandmother English, the critics who wish us to have a national literature are not particularly pleased. They call our differences Americanisms, and they are afraid of their becoming the language of the whole race.

They ought to be very careful, then, not to chide us too severely for our lack of a national literature. If ever we should turn to and have one, there might be a serious risk of its becoming the literature of the whole race. There is no great danger of an event so mortifying at present, and we merely intimate its possibility as a warning to our critics not to press us too hard. If things should ever come to that pass, we notify them that not only will the American parlance become the English language, but it will be spelled according to Noah Webster. The 'traveller' will have to limp along on one *l*, and the man of 'honour' will no longer point with the pride of long descent to the Norman-French *u* in his last syllable.

IV.

In the mean time we wish to ask our critics if they have not been looking for American literature in the wrong place; or, to use an American expression which is almost a literature in itself, whether they have not been barking up the wrong tree. It appears to us that at this stage of the proceedings there is no such thing as nationality in the highest literary expression; but there is a universality, a humanity, which is very much better. There is no doubt, judging from the enterprising character of our people in other respects, that if we had not come upon the scene so very late in the day we should have had a literature of the most positive nationality in form as well as spirit. It is our misfortune rather than our fault to have arrived when all the literary forms were invented. There remained nothing for us to do but to invent literary formlessness, and this, we understand, is what the English admire Mr. Whitman for doing; it is apparently what they ask of us all. But there is a curious want of variety in formlessness; the elements are monotonous; it is their combinations that are infinitely interesting; and Mr. Whitman seems to have exhausted the resources of formlessness. We cannot go on in his way without servile imitation; the best we can do, since we cannot be national in form, is to be national in spirit and in ideal, and we rather think that in many good ways we are unmistakably so. This is evident from the comparison of any American author with any English author; the difference of qualities is at once apparent; and what more of nationality there might be would, we believe, come of error. There may once have been a time in the history of literature when nationality was supremely desirable: the nationality which expressed itself in the appropriation of forms; but in our time this is not possible, and if it were we think it would be a vice, and we are, above all, virtuous. The great and good things in literature nowadays are not the national features, but the universal features. For instance, the most national fiction at present is the English, and it is the poorest, except the German, which is not at all; while the Russian and the Spanish, the Norwegian and the Italian, the French and the American, which are all so much better, are distinguished by what they have in common rather than by what they have in severalty. The English, who have not felt the great world-movement towards life and truth, are national; those others who have felt it are universal; and perhaps the English critics could be more profitably employed in noting how much the American fiction resembles the Continental fiction than in deploring its want of that peculiarity which renders their own a little droll just now.

Besides, it seems to us that even if we were still in the dark ages when nationality seemed a valuable and admirable thing in itself, they would not find it in our literature in the way they have taken. In any research of the kind we think that the question is not whether this thing or that thing in an author is American or not, but whether upon the whole the author's work is such as would have been produced by a man of any other race or environment. We do not believe that any American writer of recognized power would fail to be found national, if he were tried by this test; and we are not sure but the general use of such a test would result in the discovery of an American literature commensurate in weight and bulk with the emotions of the warmest patriot. The distinctive character of a man's face resides in that complex called his looks; and the nationality of a literature is embodied in its general aspect, not in its particular features. A literature which had none of these would be remarkable for their absence, and if it were produced by one people more than any other would be the expression of their nationality, and as recognizable from its negativity as if it abounded in positive traits.

We do not know, however, that our censors reproach our literature for a want of positivity. Their complaint seems rather to be that it is inadequate to a people who are otherwise so prodigious and original. It strikes them that it is but a small and feeble voice to be the utterance of such a lusty giant; they are listening for a roar, and they hear something very like a squeak, as we understand them. This disappoints them, to say nothing worse; but perhaps it is only our voice changing, and perhaps it would not sound like a squeak if it came from a less formidable body, say San Marino, or Andorra, or even Switzerland. We ought to consider this and take comfort from the possibility, while we taste the tacit flattery in their expectation of a roar from us; from a smaller republic our comparatively slight note could very well pass for a roar, and from a younger one for a mature utterance.

What it is, it is; and it is very probably the natural expression of our civilization, strange as the fact may appear. Our critics evidently think that the writers of a nation can make its literature what they like; but this is a fallacy: they can only make it what the nation likes, involuntarily following the law of environment.

It has been noted that our literature has always been distinguished by two tendencies, apparently opposite, but probably parallel: one a tendency toward an elegance refined and polished, both in thought and phrase, almost to tenuity; the other a tendency to grotesqueness, wild and extravagant, to the point of anarchy. The first has resulted in that delicate poetry which is distinctively American, and in that fiction which has made itself recognized as ours, wherever it is liked or disliked. The last has found its outcome in our peculiar species of humor, which no one can mistake for any other, not even for the English imitations of it. Our literature has these tendencies because the nation has them, and because in some measure each and every American has them. It would take too long to say just how and why; but our censors may rest assured that in this anomalous fact exists the real nationality of our literature. They themselves have a half perception of the truth when they accept and advance Walt Whitman as the representative of our literature. With a supreme passion for beauty, and impatient of all the trammels and disguises of art, he is eager to seize and embrace its very self. For the most part the effort is a failure; the divine loveliness eludes him, and leaves only a 'muddy vesture of decay' in his grasp. He attains success often enough to make good his claim to the admiration the English yield him, and he misses it often enough to keep the more intelligent American observer in doubt. We understand better than they how and why Walt

Whitman is; we perceive that he is now and again on the way to the way we should all like to find; but we know his way is not the way. At the same time we have to own that he is expressive of that national life which finds itself young and new in a world full of old conventions and decrepit ideals, and that he is suggestive if not representative of America. But he is no more so than the most carefully polished writer among us. He illustrates the prevalence of one of our moods, as Longfellow, say, illustrates the other. No one but an American could have written the poetry of Whitman; no one but an American could have written the poetry of Longfellow. The work of both is a part of that American literature which also embraces the work of Mark Twain and of Lowell, of Artemus Ward and of Whittier, of Bret Harte and of Emerson, of G. W. Cable and of Henry James, of Miss Murfree and of O. W. Holmes, of Whitcomb Riley and of T. B. Aldrich.

V.

The great difficulty with America is that she has come to her consciousness at a moment when she feels that she ought to be mature and full-grown, the Pallas among the peoples, with the wisdom of a perfectly trained owl at her bidding. It will not do to be crude when the farthest frontier has all the modern improvements, and the future is penetrated at every point by the glare of an electric. If we are simple we must know it; if we are original, it must be with intention and a full sense of originality. In these circumstances we think we have done not so badly in literature. If we listen to our censors, in generals we shall probably do still better. But we do not think we shall do better by heeding them in details. We would not have any considerable body of our writers set about writing novels and poems concerning the life of toil, which Mr. Quiller-Couch says we have neglected; because in the first place Mr. Quiller-Couch seems to speak from rather a widespread ignorance of the facts; and because in the last place the American public does not like to read about the life of toil; and one of the conditions of producing an American literature is that it shall acceptably address itself to the American public. Nearly all the Americans are in their own persons, or have been in those of their fathers or grandfathers, partakers of the life of toil; and anything about it in literature is to them as coal is to Newcastle, or corn-bread to a Kentuckian. They have had enough of it. What they want is something select, something that treats of high life, like those English novels which have chiefly nourished us; or something that will teach us how to escape the life of toil by a great stroke of business, or by a splendid marriage. What we like to read about is the life of noblemen or millionaires; that is our romance; and if our writers were to begin telling us on any extended scale of how mill hands, or miners, or farmers, or iron-puddlers really live, we should very soon let them know that we did not care to meet such vulgar and commonplace people. Our well-to-do classes are at present engaged in keeping their eyes fast shut to the facts of the life of toil, and in making believe that the same causes will not produce the same effects here as in Europe; and they would feel it an impiety if they were shown the contrary. Our finest gentilities do not care anything about our literature; they have no more concern in it than they have in our politics. As for the people who are still sunk in the life of toil, they know enough of it already, and far more than literature could ever tell them. They know that in a nation which honors toil, the toiler is socially nothing, and that he is going from bad to worse quite as if the body politic had no interest in him. What they would like would be some heroic workman who superhumanly triumphs over his environment and marries the boss's daughter, and lives idle and respected ever after. Almost any class of readers would like a hero of that mould; but no class, and least of all his fellows, would like the life of a workman shown in literature as it really is, and his condition painted as hopeless as the condition of ninety-nine workmen out of every hundred is. The life of toil will do very well for nations which do not honor toil, to read about; but there is something in the very reverence we have for it that renders the notion of it repulsive to us. This is very curious; we do not attempt to explain it; but we can promise the foreign observer that he need not look for American literature in that direction. The life of toil! It is a little too personal to people who are trying to be ladies and gentlemen of elegant leisure as fast as they can. If we have had to dig, or if we are many of us still digging, that is reason enough why we do not want the spade brought into the parlor.

Free-lance, 1892–1900

Since the events surrounding Howells's leaving 'The Editor's Study' have been the subject of conflicting interpretations, perhaps it is best to record them in his own words both retrospective and contemporaneous. In 1912 he contributed a long, important sketch of his relations to the firm for a centenary volume entitled *The House of Harper*, and said, beginning here with his final conversations with J. W. Harper in 1885:

> Then he made a set at me for something I had hitherto absolutely refused to do; which was to write a department in the *Magazine* every month, covering the whole ground of reviewing and book-noticing. Mr. Alden had proposed this to me by letter, and I had distinctly objected to it as forming a break in my fictioning; I should have to unset myself from that, and reset myself for it, and the effect would be very detrimental to me as a novelist. I still think I was right, and that turning aside to critical essaying at that period of my career, when all my mind tended to fictioning, had the effect I feared. A novelist should be nothing but a novelist, which, of course, includes being a moralist if he is a man of any conscience; in art a man cannot serve two masters more than in religion. But in vain I urged my reasons against the insistence of the amiable chief, who went and came, after the manner of his talk, until I gave way. Then we had a little more talk, and it was understood that I was to make the department what I liked and to call it what I liked. My dear and honored predecessor in the 'Easy Chair' was then doing his beautiful work in that department, as well as writing his unrivaled leaders in the *Weekly* and Mr. Harper skilfully led up to what a man might or might not say in the Harper periodicals. There appeared to be a very few things: the only one I remember was that he might not deal, say, with the subject of capital punishment which the House probably agreed about with Mr. Curtis, but at my approach to which it 'rang a little bell.' The phrase pleased me, and I readily consented to leave that matter untouched, not foreseeing that I should, within the next year, write a letter of ironical praise of the good old gallows-tree, then being supplanted by the electric chair, and that Mr. Curtis should print it in the *Weekly* without a tinkle from the little bell.

This is as good a place as any to recognize the good business, to put it on the lowest ground, with which the House left me free to say what I pleased on whatever topic I chose to talk about. Their tolerance put me on my conscience, and I tried to catch the tinkle of the little bell when it was not actually sounded. There was, indeed, one moment when I would not have obeyed its behest, and that was when I protested against the condemnation of the Chicago anarchists as a grotesque perversion of law. My protest was not printed in any of the Harper periodicals, but I suppose it was as distasteful to the House as it was to the immeasurable majority of the American people. It raised a storm about my head, but no echo of the tempest ever reached me from Franklin Square any more than if the House there had quite agreed with me that it was wrong to hang five men for a murder never proved against one of them, because they were violently spoken enthusiasts. The case has already been revised by history, and I cannot feel here-after in my position as I did then; but I cannot cease to remember the magnanimous forbearance of the House in the affair with regard to me.

I was already having trouble enough from my attitude in the 'Editor's Study,' as I had called my new department. From the first it was a polemic, a battle. I detested the sentimental and the romantic in fiction, and I began at once to free my mind concerning the romanticists, as well dead as alive. As I could not in conscience spare either age or sex the effect of my reasons, I soon had every lover of romanticism hating me and saying I had said worse things about it than I had ever said, whatever I had thought. In fact, I carefully kept myself from person-alities; but that did not save me from them either on this shore of the sea or the other. I remember one English reviewer beginning a notice of my book of *Criticism and Fiction*, which grew out of 'The Study' essays, by saying, 'This man has placed himself beyond the pale of decency,' and then, in proof, going on to behave indecently toward me. But that is all past; and since then one of the bitterest of my English enemies has generously written me that I was quite right in what I was always saying about romanticism, if not the romanticists. I am not sure that I was, now; but I was sure then, and I was so sure that I did not much mind the abuse showered upon me, though I would always have liked praise better. When after six years' warfare I gave up writing 'The Study' I talked the matter over with J. Henry Harper, who had mean-while assumed the position left vacant by the retirement of Joseph W. Harper, and I owned that it had been a rigorous experience which I was very willing to have end. I had felt that I had something to say in behalf of the truth, and I had conscientiously said it. I believe that we agreed the effect had been injurious to my books, which had not been so well liked or so much bought as they had before I began my long fight. The worst of it I did not then perceive, or know that my long fight had been a losing fight; I perceive now that the monstrous rag-baby of romanticism is as firmly in the saddle as it was before the joust began, and that it always will be, as long as the children of men are childish.

As I have suggested, some interpretations of this account seem a shade melodramatic. Tired of the fray, Howells said as much to his publishers and found them disenchanted too. As happens between authors and publishers, cold words passed. After each side had made itself plain, there were relenting efforts to explain and be reconciled, but they did not restore the 'Study.' Neither did Howells give up. Most of his best criticism was still to be written, and one motive for relinquishing 'The Editor's Study' lay in what looked like a superb chance at greater freedom and resource. An apparently radical-minded millionaire offered him not a column but a whole magazine.

By intense, reasoned conviction, Howells habitually told the truth about himself. If he could not tell the truth, he kept still. As with any man, he sometimes misremembered or confused things, but I know of no instance in which he can be convicted of falsehood. Late in 1891, with the end of 'The Editor's Study' in sight, he gave two interviews which he treated as opportunities to tell his public the facts. The first interview went to a reporter for the *Boston Daily Advertiser*, who recorded Howells as saying:[1]

> When my agreement [with the Harpers] comes to an end at the close of this year, I shall begin my work as an editor on the *Cosmopolitan*. I got very interested in the 'Study' of *Harper's*, and I have said in it all I wanted to say at present in a critical way. . . . Nevertheless, it was the finest opportunity ever offered a man to say what he wanted to say, and I am satisfied with my opportunity. Mr. Alden is an ideal editor and allowed me to write as I chose.

Still more significant, as 'authorized,' was Hamlin Garland's interview published in Boston's leading paper on New Year's Day. Garland took as his principle of relevance the assertion that 'Mr. Howells has come to stand for the most vital and progressive principle in American literature and to have him again assume editorial charge of a magazine means a great deal to the conservative as well as the more radical wing of our literary public.' Since the 'more radical wing' was bound to care more, however, and it was Garland who wrote, one may suppose that Howells thought it important to emphasize that he had not been forced out of the 'Study' but was going on to better things. Garland paraphrased, while interpreting, Howells as saying that:[2]

> He had placed himself on record, as his friends all know, at a great sacrifice. It seemed vitally necessary that at this stage of our literary development the school of truth should have fuller representation in current criticism, and, great as the sacrifice was, we all saw how much it meant to American literature.

But the interruption to his story writing grew greater, and the work of writing these monthly papers hung over him, as any set work will, doubling the amount of friction with which it should have been produced. Hard as it was, he continued this work until it seemed to him that the principle of literary progress had been stated. . . . Unquestionably Mr. Howells will be a greater power than ever in the radical wing of American literature, and do his great work at less cost to himself.

With whatever allowance for rhetoric, Garland interpreted Howells correctly. But as might have been foretold, the *Cosmopolitan* venture worked out poorly. Howells thought he had acquired freedom to operate a popular 'magazine that reflects the most characteristic and progressive art and criticism in America' (as Garland said). Its millionaire owner supposed he had bought a famous name and would enjoy telling Howells what he might and might not do. Charles Eliot Norton had warned Howells that the *Cosmopolitan* thrived on 'the nitrous oxide gas of second-rate vulgarity.' Apparently Walker balked at efforts to change the atmosphere; and Howells, who had begun work amid fanfares of exultant publicity on 1 March, resigned as of 30 June and became a free-lance once more.

With Howells free, the Harpers rushed back with proposals finally declined because Howells felt that he could no longer bear being corralled into 'a department.' With no need to general a war, however, he found himself released into more, better, and often no less embattled criticism. During these years he wrote *My Literary Passions*, conducting it much like 'a department' for the *Ladies' Home Journal* (1893-5); *Literary Friends and Acquaintance* (irregular installments, 1895-1900, mostly in *Harper's Monthly*); and conducted two light-cavalry columns ('Life and Letters,' *Harper's Weekly*, 1895-8; and 'American Letter' in *Literature*—a British magazine owned by the Harpers, which also had an American issue—1898-9).

The tradition that Howells as critic went soft, retrospective, and subservient to 'old Cambridge'—the essentially Parringtonian tradition—based itself on *Literary Friends and Acquaintance* and contented itself with ignorance of the other and voluminous criticism Howells wrote and published after *Criticism and Fiction*. The enemy of Max Nordau, the champion of Ibsen, Tolstoi, Zola, Edward Bellamy, Thorstein Veblen, Stephen Crane, and Abraham Cahan, and of the Black writers Paul Lawrence Dunbar and Charles W. Chesnutt was anything but 'acquiescent' during the 1890s. In the advance toward Modernism he was already ahead of some of the arrogancies who were to scorn him thirty years later.

NOTES

1 Spencer H. Coon, 'Mr. Howells Talks,' *Boston Daily Advertiser*, 26 December 1891, 3.
2 Hamlin Garland, 'Mr. Howells's Plans,' *Boston Evening Transcript*, 1 January 1892, 6.

29 'Degeneration'
1895

Published in *Harper's Weekly*, 13 April 1895.

Max Nordau became one of the sensations, one of the curiosities of the age. Edwin Arlington Robinson's 'A Poem for Max Nordau,' for instance, constitutes, perhaps deliberately, a puzzle. Written with essential lines in sounding, shrewdly-colored nonsense, it can be read, with equal force, as mockery either of Nordau or of Nordau's 'degenerates.' Howells, who understood Nordau's campaign, made it clear why and how he thought Nordau impossible. As critic he could have found no more emphatic way to identify himself with emerging Modernism.

I.

Whether the amusing madman who fancies himself the only sane person in a world of lunatics has ever really been found in the asylums, or not, I do not know: probably not; he is a little too dramatic, a little too obvious; but one gets rather a vivid notion of him in reading Dr. Max Nordau's book on *Degeneration*. The book is not worth speaking of in itself, or for itself, but it is not altogether idle to speak of a thing so many people are reading, or making believe to read. Like most other German books it is not easy to read, even in an English translation, and even among German books it is hard to read because of a certain heavy emptiness, which seems a peculiar property of its author. Besides, he is offensive in manner, and writes a vulgar, noisy style; he stamps about, and shouts, and calls names; so that when you dismiss the notion of the amusing madman, you are not sure that Dr. Nordau is altogether sober. If you begin to talk of him, you fall into his vice of abusiveness, as I am doing now.

II.

The philosophy of this book, if not very profound, is not original

217

either. He is frank in at least one thing, and openly owns his debt to Professor Lombroso, whose *Insanity and Genius*, and whose *Delinquent Man* have inspired him to the study of mental and moral decay among the modern masters in literature and art. His claim to recognition is that he has carried the Lombrosian theories and methods into regions hitherto unexplored, and has found them full of maniacs and malefactors. The richness of his find will not be surprising to any one who knows the Lombrosian theories and methods, and has witnessed the ease with which the good professor discovers whatever he looks for; and I am not amazed at the haul Dr. Nordau is able to make with a net to which everything that comes is fish. Not such monsters alone as Tolstoi, Ibsen, Zola, Ruskin, Wagner, Verlaine, Maeterlinck, Swinburne, Rossetti, are captured as degenerates, and shown as proofs of Dr. Nordau's second-hand hypotheses, but every realist, symbolist, moralist, mystic, is equally useful to him. They are all instances and examples, and if they are not so apt as he could wish, they can be readily made so. After his bad manners, nothing is so noticeable in Dr. Nordau as his dishonesty, or if it is not worth while to call it by so serious a name, his shuffling. Sometimes this is very impudent, or very ignorant, as when he alleges in proof of Rossetti's degeneracy his use of certain words as a burden in one of his poems; this trick of the old balladists he finds an unmistakable mark of degeneracy in the modern poet who frankly employs it. Again and again in his study of Tolstoi and of Ibsen, if the facts fairly stated will not square with his theory, the author does not mind misstating them. He makes a great show of convicting Ibsen of scientific inaccuracy in dealing with heredity, but after reading a little of Dr. Nordau you want some other doctor's word for what he says. It may be so, but if it is like some other things he says, it may not be so; it may be no truer that the dramatist is mistaken in giving a name to Oswald's malady in *Ghosts* than that there is a parallel between the flight of Nora in *A Doll's House* and the flight of Hjalmar in *The Wild Duck*. Dr. Nordau may be forcing the diagnosis as well as the parallel; and when you have witnessed his misrepresentations of Tolstoi's artistic intention in matters so clear and simple that you cannot think it merely stupid, you must dismiss him as a person wholly unfit to make the study he attempts.

In fact one cannot deal seriously with him. His philosophy is no philosophy at all; the theories and methods which he borrows are those which perpetually put the cart before the horse; his performances are feats of cheap legerdemain which a little attention will discover. At first he seems to be simply a bad-tempered, ill-mannered man in the presence of intellectual conditions which he dislikes, with no other way of venting his hate but to bully and abuse everybody about. The note of insincerity, however, is so insistent throughout, that you end by feeling that even his bluster is put on, and that he is only a clever quack advertising himself. There is not, so far as I can recall, a criticism of his own that is worth the smallest consideration, and the criticism which he quotes is mean and low. He quotes a great deal of criticism which does not apply to what he is saying, apparently in the hope that the reader may be fooled into thinking that it applies; when he calls some one a degenerate, he reports as proof what an unfriendly reviewer says to his disadvantage. This method may be scientific, but it is not moral, and I doubt very much if it is scientific.

The most interesting fact in regard to his book is that it has made any stir in the world, and Dr. Nordau's success here, where a great many people are now reading his book, is another proof of the advantage of living in Europe, so far as America is concerned. To be sure, he did not write for us or at us, but we attend all the more deferentially when people are indifferent. If some ill-conditioned American had written his senseless and worthless book, we should scarcely have troubled ourselves to say that it was senseless and worthless, far less tried to prove it. But it comes to us with authority, coming across seas, and it comes from Germany, where if the critical thinking is somewhat slow, it is believed to be deep and thorough; and we cannot help asking ourselves if there is not something in it. That is what makes me wish to whisper the reader, Dear, simple-souled brother American, there is nothing whatever in it, nothing in its whole five hundred and sixty insufferable pages that you need worry yourself about for a moment. If it were an honest book, which it is not in a single line, it would be in itself the only proof of the intellectual degeneration of our time which the author is able to give; for then you would see in it the spectacle, pathetic and curious enough, of a philistine spirit, so besotted with error as to attempt with its yardsticks and steelyards to measure and weigh the work in ethics and æsthetics of some of the sublimest men who have ever lived. But as it is, it has not so much as this melancholy interest, and we have to get at the unconsciousness behind the author's consciousness before we find anything even of value as materials. What Dr. Nordau really does is to offer himself as an example of that cunning, dishonest, unscrupulous degenerate, well known to alienists, who devotes his powers, abnormally active in disease, to the arts of illusion and deceit. In this quality, Professor Lombroso might very well collect him.

III.

As to the question of any other degeneration in our time it is altogether absurd. The world, in its thinking and feeling, was never so sound and sane before. There is a great deal of fevered and foolish thinking and feeling about thinking and feeling, as there always has been and will be, but there is no more of it than ever. It is no part of my business to defend the nineteenth century, and if I thought the noble mood of its last years merely a death-bed repentance, and not an effect of all the former events of the ages, I should not rejoice in it. Dr. Nordau himself is able to see that there really is no such thing as a *fin de siècle* spirit; but the race is in a certain mood, and the century is near its end, and so the phrase serves as well as another. The only question is whether the mood is a good one, and I have already expressed my sense of it.

I believe it is extremely well to have the underpinning of sentiment and opinion examined, from time to time, and this is what our age above all others has done. It is not a constructive or a reconstructive age, as compared with some other epochs, but it is eminently critical, and whatever is creative in it, is critically creative. It is very conscious, it not only knows, but it keenly feels what it is about. It is not for nothing, it is not blindly or helplessly that it has tried this or that, that it has gone forward to new things or reverted to old things. It experiments perpetually, but not empirically; knowledge and greater knowledge are the cause and effect of all that it has done in the arts as well as the sciences.

If we stand at the end of things, we also stand at the beginning; we are the new era as well as the old. It is not at all important that certain things have fulfilled themselves and passed away; but it is very important that certain others have just begun their fulfilment, and it is these that we are to judge our time by. Our condition is that of a youth and health unknown to human thought before, and it is an excellent thing that with these we have so much courage; if it were only the courage of youth and health it would be well; but it is in fact the courage of a soul that is as old as the world.

A great many good, elderly minded people think it dreadful Ibsen should show us that the house we have lived in so long is full of vermin, that its drainage is bad, that the roof leaks and the chimney smokes abominably; but if it is true, is it not well for us to know it? It is dreadful because it is so, not because he shows it so; and the house is no better because our fathers got on in it as it is. He has not done his work without showing his weakness as well as his strength, and as I do not believe in genius in the miraculous sense, I am not at all troubled by his occasional weakness. It is really no concern of mine whether he solves his problems or not; generally, I see that he does not solve them, and I see that life does not; the longer I live the more I am persuaded that the problems of this life are to be solved elsewhere, or never. It is not by the solution of problems that the moralist teaches, but by the question that his handling of them suggests to us respecting ourselves. Artistically he is bound, Ibsen as a dramatist is bound, to give an æsthetic completeness to his works, and I do not find that he ever fails to do this: to my thinking they have a high beauty and propriety; but ethically he is bound not to be final; for if he forces himself to be final in things that do not and cannot end here, he becomes dishonest, he becomes a Nordau. What he can and must do ethically, is to make us take thought of ourselves, and look to it whether we have in us the making of this or that wrong; whether we are hypocrites, tyrants, pretenders, shams conscious or unconscious; whether our most unselfish motives are not really secret shapes of egotism; whether our convictions are not mere brute acceptations; whether we believe what we profess; whether when we force good to a logical end we are not doing evil. This is what Ibsen does; he gives us pause; and in that bitter muse he leaves us thinking not of his plays, but of our own lives; not of his fictitious people, but of ourselves. If we find ourselves all right we can go ahead with a good conscience, but never quite so cocksure afterwards.

IV.

He does in the region of motive pretty much the same work that Tolstoi does in the region of conduct. If he makes you question yourself before God, Tolstoi makes you question yourself before man. With the one you ask yourself, Am I true? With the other you ask yourself, Am I just? You cannot release yourself from them on any other terms. They will neither of them let you go away, feeling smoothly self-satisfied, patronizingly grateful, smugly delighted, quite charmed. If you want that feeling, you must go to some other shop for it, and there are shops a plenty where you can get it. Both of these great writers now and then overrun each other's province, for their provinces are not very separable, except by a feat of the fancy, though if the reader wishes a distinction between them, I have offered one. I should say, however, that Ibsen dealt with conduct in the ideal, and Tolstoi in the real. How shall I behave with regard to myself? How shall I behave with regard to my neighbor? I imagine that in either case the answer would be the same. It is only the point of view that is different.

As far as any finality is concerned, Tolstoi is no more satisfactory than Ibsen; that is to say, he is quite as honest. He does not attempt to go beyond Christ, who bade us love the neighbor, and cease to do evil; but I suppose this is what Dr. Nordau means by his mysticism, his sentimentality. In fact, Tolstoi has done nothing more than bring us back to the gospels as the fountain of righteousness. Those who denounce him cannot or will not see this, but that does not affect the fact. He asks us to be as the first Christians were, but this is difficult, and it has been so difficult ever since the times of the first Christians, that very few of the later Christians have been at all like them. Even in his most recent crusade, his crusade against the chauvinism which we miscall patriotism, he only continues that warfare against the spirit of provinciality which Christianity began. He preaches no new doctrine, he practises no new life. It is all as old as Calvary; it is the law and life of self-sacrifice. This was and always will be to the Jews a stumbling block, and to the Greeks foolishness: but it is nothing mystical. There is nothing mystical in Tolstoi's books; as far as they are fictions they are the closest and clearest transcripts of the outer and inner life of man; as far as they are lessons in the form of allegory or essay, they are of the simplest and plainest meaning. His office in the world has been, like Ibsen's, to make us look where we are standing, and see whether our feet are solidly planted or not. What is our religion, what is our society, what is our country, what is our civilization? You cannot read him without asking yourself these questions, and the result is left with you. Tolstoi's solution of the problem in his own life is not the final answer, and as things stand it is not the possible answer. We cannot all go dig in the fields, we cannot all cobble peasant's shoes. But we can all do something to lift diggers and cobblers to the same level with ourselves, to see that their work is equally rewarded, and that they share fully with the wisest and the strongest in the good of life. We can get off their backs, or try to get off, and this, after all, is what Tolstoi means us to do.

V.

There is the same mixture of weakness in his power that qualifies the power of Ibsen, and makes his power the more admirable. There are flaws enough in his reasoning; he is not himself the best exponent of his own belief; there is no finality in his precept or his practice. On the other hand, his work has the same æsthetic perfection as Ibsen's, and as an intellect dealing imaginatively with life, he is without a rival. There is the like measure of weakness in Zola, whom Dr. Nordau chooses as the type of realist, with much the same blundering wilfulness that he chooses Ibsen as the type of ego-maniac, and Tolstoi as the type of mystic. Zola never was a realist in the right sense, and no one has known this better, or has said it more frankly than Zola himself. He is always showing, as he has often owned that he came too early to be a realist; but it was he who imag-ined realism, in all its sublime, its impossible beauty, as Ibsen imag-ined truth, as Tolstoi imagined justice. One has to deal with words that hint rather than say what one means, but the meaning will be clear enough to any one capable of giving the matter thought. What Zola has done has been to set before us an ideal of realism, to recall the wandering mind of the world to that ideal, which was always in the world, and to make the reader feel it by what he has tried to do, rather than by what he has done. He has said, in effect, You must not aim in art to be less than perfectly faithful; and you must not lie about the fact any more than you can help. Go to life; see what it is like, and then tell it as honestly as possible. Above all he has shown us what rotten foundations the most of fiction rested on, and how full of malaria the whole region was. He did not escape the infection himself; he was born in that region; the fever of romanticism was in his blood; the taint is in his work. But he has written great epics, and the time will come when it will be seen that he was the greatest poet of his day, and perhaps the greatest poet that France has produced.

VI.

These men are chief of those whom Dr. Nordau has attempted to characterize as degenerates. Of course, he is preposterous, and he is naturally all the worse for knowing that he is preposterous. His proposition is purely fantastic, and if he had some grace of humor in him, one could imagine him amusing himself equally well by turning his proposition round, and maintaining that the real degenerates were great intellects. He could bring quite as much proof that the insane asylums are centres of a wholesome mental activity, as he has brought to show that the people who have led their age are madmen. There is nothing in the tone of his book to make one feel that he could not argue to this effect with quite as much sincerity as to the other.

In fact, Dr. Nordau has the air throughout of trying to see what effect a certain pose will have with the reader. Apparently, he thought the time had come when such a book as he has written might make a noise, and he seems so little serious, that I feel it rather hard to have accused him of insincerity; one ought not to accuse such an obvious pretender of insincerity; there is a kind of unfitness in it; a superfluity.

30 'The Ibsen Influence'
1895

Published in *Harper's Weekly*, 27 April 1895.

In one language or another, New York play-goers have had the chance of seeing four or five of the most characteristic of Ibsen's plays, within rather less than as many years. *Hedda Gabler* was given in German several seasons ago; *Ghosts* was played twice in English winter before last; *A Doll's House* was done in English last winter at the Empire Theatre, and in French this winter by Madame Réjane, and within the past fortnight Mr. Beerbohm Tree has enabled us to realize, from his admirable presentation of *The Enemy of the People*, that the least dramatic of Ibsen's pieces is the most dramatic piece on the stage, when compared with the work of any other author. One must not forget to speak of the first act of *Little Eyolf*, which was performed lately by the pupils of the Berkeley Dramatic School: or perhaps I might better say this fragment performed itself, for the theatrical strength of Ibsen is so great that, like Maeterlinck, he supplies much deficiency in the players, and succeeds in spite of them. I do not mean that the pupils of the Dramatic School were not praiseworthy; in some things they were even excellent; and they were at no moment so false to his world as the great French actress who Gallicized him, and rendered Nora as a cocodette.[1]

The Réjane performance of the play was a prodigious testimony to its vitality; anything less robust must have perished in such handling; but this lived through it, and remained at last an effect of pathos and tragedy. The translation was, as is usual with things translated in the French taste, a paraphrase, and the play was badly cut, so as to leave some of the best things out, and to send Nora out into the world unaccounted for by those finely shaded motives which render her self-exile peremptory; and I am not sure that the pathos and the tragedy were not, after all, a lingering effect from the play as it was given last winter by Mrs. Maddern Fiske and Mr. Courteney Thorpe. There was a certain hard nervousness at times in Mrs. Fiske's realization of Nora, and a want of what we have to call repose, which took from the pleasure of it; but she had truly divined the character, and one felt that in a further study of the part she would have more fully identified herself with it; but Mr. Thorpe's Helmer was a portrayal of the philistine egotist which left nothing to be asked in perfection of accent. It was a piece of acting surpassed only by his Oswald in *Ghosts*, which was a revelation of powers thitherto unhinted in the light roles we had always known him in. He stood forth at once a great tragedian, as new in kind as the hapless wretch whose most pitiable sort he made a personal anguish to every beholder. It was upon the whole one of the most modern things, that is to say one of the best things, I have ever seen upon the stage—that haunt of the decrepitudes and imbecilities of the past; and it imparted a vast hope, a deep consolation. Mr. Thorpe showed his quality in his perfect simplicity, and his willing subjection to the dramatist, and I have only the wish to praise him; but, after all, what one felt was the greatness of Ibsen's conception. The dramatist obtruded himself no more than the actor; they were both there to express a most important conviction in ethics and in æsthetics, and they were jointly absent, as far as any personal effect was concerned. For one of those moments so rare in the theatre the spectator had a sense of absolute drama. Each sharer in that great theatrical event, the very greatest I have ever known, did well, and some of them more than well; and perhaps Mr. Thorpe surpassed the rest of the players as Oswald surpassed the rest of the characters only in embodying the supreme interest—

The sorrow's crown of sorrows—

of the son on whom the father's sins are visited, and who suffers and perishes under our eyes for the misdeeds done before his birth.

I was sensible of some such effect of absolute drama in the performance of *Hedda Gabler*, the next strongest of the Ibsen plays, as I have seen them, after *Ghosts*. Here the playing was very equal, too, and of a very high level in its equality; and though the distinguished actress—I forget her distinguished name—who took the part of Hedda was of course the chief figure on the scene, it was not because she was doing so much better than the others, as because she was embodying to the ear and eye that type of perverse jealousy, devilish greed of power, and reckless hate which the author had conceived in *Hedda Gabler*.

Again, the other night, when I saw Mr. Beerbohm Tree as Dr. Stockmann, in *The Enemy of the People*, I thought neither of Mr. Beerbohm Tree nor of Ibsen; I thought of the great-hearted, imperfect man who dares to be true when every motive and interest but the highest tempts him to be false, and who stands alone, an outcast in his native town, and branded an enemy of the people, rather than betray the trust which as a man of science and a man of honor he holds from a power far higher than the people's. I was aware, beyond this, of the marvellous skill with which the notion of this man was got before the mind of the spectator, by the simplest means, in the barest terms, and in language so plain and common that nothing of it remained with me afterwards but the last words of Stockmann's crucial experience distilling itself in the phrase, 'He is the strongest man who stands most alone.'

The Enemy of the People is the play of Ibsen's which appeals more intimately than any other to the intelligence of an American audience in some ways. The situation in the Norwegian town where the action passes is the image in little of our own vast political hypocrisy. The boss is there in his ruthless power; the truckling journalist is there; the respectable citizen, arrogating to his selfishness the credit of all the virtues, is there; the economico-political ring is there; where Tammany never was heard of, Tammany is! The house recognized the facts with applause at certain points; and in the medicinal baths which have created the prosperity of the town, and which Stockmann may not attempt to rescue from pollution without imperilling its prosperity, or putting its tax-payers to great expense, the spectators must have seen one of those vested interests whose aspect we know so well. But I suppose that otherwise the play could not appeal to us. We are too sophisticated for its simple and natural effects; we want action, we want character, we want incident, as we call the usual hysterics and heroics, and I fancy that the average playgoer would hardly feel that he had got his money's worth, though there is something to be said for the scene of the public meeting where Stockmann is choked off, and for the moment when he gathers up the stones after the mob has broken his windows. But this is hardly enough; there is no love interest in the play; nobody is married or courted in or out of wedlock; no faltering wife is 'saved' from herself; no intending seducer is melodramatically persuaded to leave his potential victim 'pure.' Besides, when we go to the theatre we wish to be amused, in the sense of being tickled or lulled; and incontestibly Ibsen neither tickles nor lulls. You are obliged to think of what you see before you, and to put yourself in the place of people so like yourself that it is not easy to pull yourself out again. If this is the case with a political and social satire like *The Enemy of the People*, it is much more the case with such studies of motive and responsibility as *Ghosts*, and the *Doll's House*, and *Hedda Gabler*, and *Little Eyolf*.

I am not thinking, therefore, of any great acceptance for Ibsen himself on our stage, but for Ibsenism there is already great acceptance, and there will be greater and greater, for he is the master who has more to say to our generation in the theatre than any other, and all must learn his language who would be understood hereafter. The chief trait of his speech, as I have intimated, is its simplicity, and this has impressed itself upon the diction of the new playwrights very noticeably already. Of course, that sort of simplicity is a common tendency of our time, but it is Ibsen who has felt it more than any other, and who has, I think, imparted it in some measure to all who have studied him. Both the theatre and the drama have studied Ibsen, and are studying him more and more; dramatic criticism itself is deigning to look at him a little; but not nearly so much as the drama and the theatre, perhaps because it need not; like 'genius' it knows without learning. The drama and the theatre feel his simplicity in every way—his simplicity of thought and sense, as well as his simplicity of speech. So far as I have spoken with actors who have played Ibsen, I find that without exception, almost, they like to play him, because he gives them real emotions, real characters to express, and they feel in him the support of strong intentions. They have to forget a good deal that they have learned in the school of other dramatists. They have to go back, and become men and women again before Ibsen can do anything with them, or they with him; but when they have once done this, their advance toward a truer art than they have ever known is rapid and unerring. It is very interesting to hear a stage-manager, who has helped them remand themselves to this natural condition, talk of their difficulties in reaching it, when they are most willing and anxious to reach it. They have really to put away from them all that they have learned of artificial and conventional for the stage; everything but their technical skill is a loss, but this is an immense advantage, for Ibsen understands the stage, as perhaps no other dramatist has understood it; and in his knowledge and sympathy with the stage the actor feels a support which he can fully trust. He can implicitly believe that whatever he finds in the dialogue or the direction is fully and positively meant, and that he cannot go wrong if he is true to them. It is not possible to play Ibsen so badly as to spoil him if the actor obeys him; if he obeys him intelligently and skilfully the highest effect is unfailing; but if he merely obeys him blindly and ignorantly, a measure of success is sure to follow. For this reason I have never seen a play of Ibsen's which I felt to be a failure; the Réjane performance of the *Doll's House* was nearer a failure than any other, because the French stage seemed unwilling to obey Ibsen at all.

The influence of Ibsen on the theatre is very interesting, but it is not so important as his influence on the drama. I think the reader of Ibsen will be able to trace his influence in the work of any of the modern English playwrights, or at least I do not think I have deceived myself in imagining that I trace it in the plays of Mr. Pinero, or Mr. Shaw, or Mr. Jones. I do not mean that they have imitated him, or have slavishly followed him, but that they have learned from him a certain way of dealing with material; and I do not mean that they deal with life altogether as he does, or even largely, but only that each one does so in some degree. I could wish that they dealt with it altogether as he does in their choice of the problems they treat, or that they would treat such problems as concern conduct rather than such as concern action. The problem which a play of Ibsen hinges upon is as wide as the whole of life, and it seeks a solution in the conscience of the spectator for the future rather than the present; it is not an isolated case; it does not demand what he would do, or would have done, in a given event; and this is what makes the difference between him and the modern English playwrights. In morals, a puritanic narrowness cramps all our race, which will not suffer us to get beyond the question of personality; but Ibsen always transcends this, and makes you feel the import of what has happened civically, socially, humanly, universally. In *Ghosts*, for instance, who is to blame? You feel that nothing but the reconstitution of society will avail with the wrong and the evil involved.

But the new dramatists have learned from Ibsen to deal with questions of vital interest, and to deal with them naturally, and, on the whole, pretty honestly. For the rest, I should say that it would not be safe or just (what is unjust is never quite safe, I suppose,) to say at which point you felt his influence. So much in the tendency of any time is a common effect from common causes, that it is not well to attribute this or that thing to this or that man. All the Elizabethan dramatists wrote somewhat like Shakespeare, and Shakespeare is the greatest of them all; and yet it would not be easy to prove that he was otherwise their master. I should not undertake to prove that the modern English drama was of the school of Ibsen, except as Ibsen is the greatest of the moderns. But I find much in the new plays that makes me think of him: situations, questions, treatment, motive, character, diction. They lack his poetry, but they have much of the same art, and it appears that we can get on without poetry in plays, but not without art. But whether they have their common traits in common with him because of their contemporaneity, and are like him because they are of the same century and the same modern circumstance, I am not ready to say; and so if I were really driven to the wall, and had to point out absolute instances of his influence in them or die, I should perhaps withdraw the word influence; and then go away thinking my own thoughts. He is above all a moralist, and they are all, more or less effectually, moralists both in the larger and the lesser sense.

NOTE

1 A little cocotte (a bit of a whore).

31 'Dialect in Literature'
1895

From 'Life and Letters,' *Harper's Weekly*, 8 and 22 June 1895.

As a two-part paper published in Howells's 'Life and Letters' column, this is important for its specific comment (announcing Crane's *Maggie*, for instance) and for its exploration of a still-tangled general topic. Not only because he possessed 'the documents,' as he says, through a wide range but also because he had lived vitally through one of the major movements toward serious experiment with the common speech, Howells came to the question with authority. His ear was excellent, and his interest had been long sustained—as witness his cogent correspondence with Clemens over 'A True Story,' the Twain piece mentioned by Howells.

Perhaps it is worth pointing out that of the writers to whom Howells turned as 'documents,' he was personally well-acquainted with a number, might easily have discussed dialect in literature with many (and assuredly did so with some) among them: Murfree, Cable, Riley, Wilkins, Artemus Ward, Lowell, Stowe, Cooke, Spofford, Jewett, Harte, Hay, Clemens, Garland, Wister, Crane, Harrigan, James, Palacio Valdés, and Boyesen. The seriousness with which Howells and his circle took dialect Clemens high-lighted in 'Fenimore Cooper's Literary Offenses,' a major critique in the mode of negative realism. Several of the 'offenses against literary art' Clemens charged against Cooper have to do with the way his people talk. The 'rules' require: 'that when the personages of a tale deal in conversation, the talk shall sound like human talk, and be talk such as human beings would be likely to talk in the given circumstances . . . and help out the tale, and stop when the people cannot think of anything more to say'; and 'that when a personage talks like an illustrated, gilt-edged, tree-calf, hand-tooled, seven-dollar Friendship's Offering in the beginning of a paragraph, he shall not talk like a Negro minstrel in the end of it.'

The point, as Howells thought, was not to 'render' dialect for purposes of effectism but to bring actual language into literature to present human actuality. He even considered writing criticism in live language, as he told an interviewer:

The colloquial style is best for a writer . . . we say 'don't,' and I think it should so stand in print. . . . I thought at one time I would write the

Study papers for *Harper's* with all these natural contractions. But a friend told me I was doing so many unorthodox things that if I did this, too, people would say I was a crank, and I desisted.

His coupling of 'crank' with 'desisted' ought not to be supposed inadvertent.

Applying the fruits of long reading, talking, and of course personal experimentation, exploiting his extraordinary range, Howells showed how one might get a number of first-rate critical returns from a couple of simple-seeming columns. Perhaps the subtlest was his paragraph on Stephen Crane: it stands now as the first national attention given to a great writer's maiden masterpiece. In June 1895 no one could know that by Christmas *The Red Badge of Courage*, published in the fall, would have made the author famous. Howells could only try.

In speaking last week of that arrest of interest on the part of the public in the work of Miss Murfree, or Charles Egbert Craddock, which at present seems to me better than it has ever been, I ventured to suggest that it had unjustly suffered through the disgust for 'dialect' which has undoubtedly overtaken the general reader. In a certain measure, and in a certain kind, perhaps the very highest kind, I do not think the general reader is worth minding, and I should be the last to urge any one who had a conscience in his work, to do his conscience the least violence for the general reader's sake. That would be a dismal error, and a misdeed that would pretty surely fail of its effect if the effect were the general reader's pleasure; for if there is anything clearly ascertained concerning the general reader it is that you never can tell what will please him. He is quite like a spoiled child in not knowing what he wants, but unhappily he is like a spoiled child also in knowing what he does not want, and what he does not want now, and has not wanted for a year or two past, is dialect. He has 'got tired' of it, as he says, and whether his fancy for it, if he ever had a fancy for it, may return hereafter or not, there is no question but he is still tired of it, at this speaking. Though he is not worth minding, æsthetically, numerically he is important, and the writer who wishes to use dialect in the expression of character must decide whether he will get on without the general reader, for if he uses it, he may make sure that in his present temper the general reader will get on without him.

I.

I suspect that the general reader does not always know what dialect is, and that he classes with the carefully distinguished local accents and locutions reported in the pages of such artistic observers of life as Lowell, Mr. Cable, Mr. Page, Mr. Riley, Miss Murfree, or Miss Wilkins, the wild grotesqueries of Artemus Ward and Petroleum V. Nasby in spelling. Probably, if he would or could acquaint himself with the difference, he would find that he had been suffering less from dialect that he supposed, and more from orthographic buffoonery; but I fancy he is in no mood to be instructed on this point; and at any rate I shall not attempt his enlightenment.

Lowell himself wrought in both kinds which the general reader sometimes supposes to be one and all dialect, and he amused himself perhaps as much with the chaotic spelling in Hosea Biglow's letters, as with the subtly shaded accents of the vernacular in his poems. He always loved to indulge a whim, and he gave himself license in the mere burlesque of the one which he would never have permitted himself in the serious artistry of the other. I have a fancy, which I will not offer for anything more, that the trick of grotesque orthography was the invention of Thackeray, who in the *Yellowplush Papers* was, at any rate, the first to use it elaborately. It was easily caught, and it naturally spread to a country where the thing easily caught has more value than anywhere else, and where the general mind is so uncritical that it could be accepted for a long time as something of real significance. But now, I believe, the fun of bad spelling amuses no more; the best spelling of English is so ridiculous that it is a wonder it was ever thought droll to caricature it: and I don't believe that if Artemus Ward himself came back to us he could make us laugh with his wildest burlesques of the lexicon.

II.

It was inevitable that the use of dialect should grow with the wider diffusion of the impulse to get the whole of American life into our fiction. This impulse, partly conscious and partly unconscious, is what has given us the rank we shall be found hereafter to have taken in the literature of our age, and which, whether it has given us great American novels or not, has expressed the national temperament, character, and manner with a fulness not surpassed by contemporary fiction in the case of any other people. It may be said to have begun where our literature began, in New England, and Lowell's accurate and exquisite study of the Yankee dialect in the *Biglow Papers* was the first work of the kind that was truly artistic, or of the effect that I mean. Before Hosea Biglow was, of course Sam Slick was, but one cannot feel that Sam Slick was to the manner born, and the Nova-Scotian author's Connecticut parlance if sometimes well found was often not very true.

There is some dialect of the genuine sort in Mrs. Stowe's *Oldtown Folks*, and Mrs. Rose Terry Cooke had a good ear for Yankee parlance, and reported it delightfully in her New England stories: stories always so good that I grieve to have them the least forgotten. Mrs. Phelps Ward has handled it well, and so has Mrs. Prescott Spofford; though we think of these writers first for other things. Without turning to one of her books I should not be ready to say whether Miss Jewett employs much dialect or not. I have an impression that she imparts the spirit of Yankee parlance without too much insisting upon the letter; an accent here and there suggests it, and a characteristic phrase gives the touch of color that charms. I have a like impression concerning Miss Wilkins, but I have the impression too that she actually uses dialect rather more than Miss Jewett does.

In fact, apart from Lowell in the *Biglow Papers*, I do not know that the Yankee dialect has been much studied by the native writers, though now and then an Englishman has used it at second hand, as mistaken souls among us have now and then used the Scottish dialect. The next attempts at dialect among our writers seem to have been made in California, where forms of the Pike found their way into Mr. Bret Harte's stories and poems along with cockneyisms naturalized out of Dickens. A truer Pike was a little later studied by Mr. John Hay in his ballads; but I do not think that the Southwestern parlance which goes generically by that name has been cultivated much farther in literature. Mr. Cable's ever-delightful use of the Creole accents and forms followed in order of time, I believe, and these remain, to my thinking, almost the most delicately managed of all the experiments in dialect which our prose authors have made. Even with our stupid orthography, which is so false to its office that it is impossible to write in English the commonest vowel sound of the language so that it cannot be mistaken for some other, though there are half a dozen ways of writing it, Mr. Cable has contrived to spell the speech of his Creole characters so that you know just how they spoke. He had noticed that in a dialect or patois each person permits himself to characterize the common speech, and so he varies the English of one Creole from that of another, and he marks the distinction of white Creole from colored Creole. There is something very charming in all this, and the underlying study is concealed by an air of the greatest ease and naturalness.

Another phase of French-English parlance has been much more recently studied by Mr. William McClennan, in his sketches of Canadian life and character. These are mostly in monologue, or in the speech of a supposed narrator, who is native to the dialect used, and nothing could be more delicate than the perfection with which its peculiarities are touched and turned to the light. But I suspect that the very conscience with which the work was done told against it with the general reader, who could have borne with a few sentences of dialect here and there, but was impatient of a perfection veiled from him in the strange locutions which formed the whole texture of the little stories. Then, they had the misfortune to come after he had begun to 'get tired' of dialect, and they never won the recognition which they merited. But the reader interested in such things cannot do better than compare them with the passages of Creole dialect in Mr. Cable's stories, for a sense of their equal fineness as studies of a kindred parlance.

Mr. Cable's performance has been emulated by that of two other writers, like himself Southerners, among whom dialect has been studied with a fresh interest no longer possible to New-Englanders. The two writers I mean are, of course, Mr. Joel Chandler Harris in the Uncle Remus stories, and Mr. Thomas Nelson Page in his several sketches of Virginia negro character. I ought also to speak of at least one brief essay in negro dialect by Mark Twain, who in the limits of a little story supposed to be told by an old negress has philosophized it as thoroughly as any of the others.

I do not know any Southerner who has given the local dialects of the American whites so well as Miss Murfree. As you read you feel sure that those people spoke as she has represented their speech, and that so much of their character dwells in their parlance that if she had made them speak otherwise or less faithfully to their usage, much that is precious would have been lost. A flavor, an aroma would have escaped in the translation that now enriches the reader's sense of them, like the breath of the woods and hills where their quaint, remote, pathetic life passes.

The middle West and the Northwest seem not to have any speech of their own so strongly local that it characterizes the section by a difference from the speech of the East and the South, which colonized it with their accents as well as their populations. Yet in Indiana one of the most sensitive of our observers has found a parlance in which he has cast some of the sweetest and finest verse which can be called American. Without the poetry of James Whitcomb Riley our literature would be so much the poorer that it seems idle to state the fact; and if the passion for writing in dialect had done no more than inspire the dialect poems he has given us, I should think it richly worth all the sufferings of the general reader. He has more perfectly mastered his instrument than any writer of dialect verse since Lowell, and I do not know why one should not frankly place him with Lowell as equally master in that kind.

Mr. Hamlin Garland has given us the notion of something native in the vernacular of rural Wisconsin, but the speech of his characters is too largely the speech of the rustic in the West everywhere to be accepted as a distinct variety; and the talk that Mr. Owen Wister is now reporting in his stories of the Far West is much the same frontier talk we have been accustomed to in earlier writers. He makes it the vehicle of the wild passions and strenuous emotions he deals with so admirably, but it strikes me rather as a verification of something partly known already than a discovery of something new and different. Not that I think such a discovery would have been in any wise more meritorious than such a verification; and in fact I accept it with the greater gratitude because it is what it is.

I referred last week to the work done in 'tough' New York dialect by the author of the Chimmie Fadden stories, but this had been anticipated by Mr. Stephen Crane in a story called *Maggie, a Girl of the Streets*, which was printed some years ago, but could not be said to have been published, so wholly did it fail of recognition. There was reason for this in its grim, not to say grimy truth, and in the impossibility to cultured ears of a parlance whose texture is so largely profanity. All its conscience and all its art could not save it, and it will probably remain unknown, but it embodied perhaps the best tough dialect which has yet found its way into print. That dialect has been spoken much longer on the stage in the comedies of Mr. Harrigan, and it may be heard by any listener in the streets of certain quarters of the city. Those who have not studied it, or listened to it attentively, can have little notion how greatly the common pronunciation of our language has been corrupted by the mixture of races in the poorer quarter, and how a whole glossary of new words has sprung up from the rank life of that mixture. I remember once following rather a long passage of conversation between two characters in one of Mr. Harrigan's plays, and scarcely understanding one word out of three; and I have often heard phrases in the streets of New York which in accent and texture were as strange to me as some whose speakers did not believe themselves to be speaking English.

III.

A very pretty argument could be made to prove that the tendency of the English spoken among us is towards heterogeneity, rather than homogeneity, but I am not going to make it, for fear I should be tempted to force some conclusions without the documents. But I should really like to say something more of dialect, or rather to account for its use, and justify it. I am not sure that I always like to read it; but I think I should have lost much without some effects which it has accomplished in the representation of our national life; and I am sure that the sympathies of every artist in fiction will be with the writers whom a change of the general reader's mood could deprive of one of the great resources of their art, and would leave to show in dry and lifeless paraphrase the racy thought and vital feeling of the characters who naturally express themselves in dialect.

The week before last I had something to say of the use of dialect in imaginative literature, which I fancied did not quite exhaust the subject. I recur to it with an interest which I hope the reader will share, and which I hope will support him through what else I have to say of it.

I.

One reason why the general reader is impatient of 'dialect,' I suppose, is that he rarely notices peculiarities in the speech of people about him, and so fancies dialect an invention of the author's to harass and perplex him. If there is something very marked, he will vaguely feel it, but the more delicate differences, which interest the observer, are quite lost upon him. He would not perceive that most people speak ungrammatically, and that the talk of those who speak grammatically is almost incredibly loose and slovenly. Talk, indeed, has not yet been faithfully reported in literature by those who ought to be its carefulest students, the novelists and dramatists. Stage talk has been and largely is ludicrously unlike life talk, though now the theatre is beginning to take some account of the way people really express themselves. But in novels, and very good novels, written by artists who ought to have had a conscience against it, cultivated persons are represented as saying, Will you not, Am I not, Is he not, though nobody but a half-bred prig ever dreams of using those artificial forms in actual parlance. It is all of a piece with the convention which still obliges us to write the language without any of the contractions we always use in speaking. We write, Did not, Cannot, Would not, Is not, Will not, when we are telling something to be read, but we say Didn't, Can't, Wouldn't, Isn't, and Won't, when we are telling something to be heard; and the contractions are infinitely more graceful and vigorous than the conventional forms. In fact, anything else in talking would be absurd; and from time to time there is an effort to liberate the language of literature from the constraint that the language of life threw off so long ago that no man's memory runs back to the time of its bondage. The lighter literature of the eighteenth century abounds in these endeavors, and even some of the graver; even the verse of Pope and Young. But they were confined to a word or two; the plunge was never bold enough; and in our own time we are not even so far on the way to a free use of the spoken forms. Emerson, to be sure, said 'Tis, in very colloquial moments, but that was perhaps because people seldom say 'Tis any more, and the form had an archaic charm. Now and then Mr. Henry James imparts a thrill of hope by writing a contraction in his narrative, and you think that the good time is coming under the lead of an unquestionable master of English; but presently you find him conforming, like the rest, as if the attempt to break away from tradition were useless.

In reporting dialogue, however, most writers avail themselves of vernacular usage to give an air of reality to their scene, and write the contractions which we all speak, unless, indeed, they are writing romance, when they instinctively feel that the formality of the accepted book-language is more in keeping with the wholly artificial frame. Hawthorne even had his people, or some of them, say Methinks, and they would almost as probably have said Methinks in life, as they would have said I will not, and Have you not, and He did not, and all the rest of it. But I believe we shall not always write the language in the present preposterous fashion, any more than we shall spell it as we now do; and that when we begin to write it as we speak it, we shall all be astonished and overjoyed, we who read as well as we who write, at its grace and ease.

In the meanwhile, I think that I can recognize in the use of dialect a tendency to the final freedom I hope for. The writer who has once used it, and felt his way through it to the life that language has on the lips of men, will never willingly abandon it; and I should not be altogether surprised if in the end he persuaded the general reader to bear with it. I can imagine the pleasure such a writer must feel in telling a whole story in dialect, in the person of some supposed narrator; but I do not think this pleasure can be greater, and I can see no reason why it should be greater, than that we should all have if we wrote the language naturally, or as we speak it.

II.

The use of dialect in modern literature is very modern, I think, and does not much antedate the present century. To be sure, Shakespeare makes his clowns talk like clowns, but their parlance is suggested, rather than represented, and after all there is very little of it. As in the talk of Thomas Hardy's country folks, the personal rather than the provincial character of the speaker is suggested; and this is no doubt the ideal treatment of the vernacular in literature. But if the writer feels that there is something of life which cannot be so imparted to the reader, he does well to represent the speaker's parlance more fully. Perhaps it was the cultivation of the Scottish dialect in poetry by Burns, and in prose by Scott, that gave the impulse toward writing dialect which has at last made the general reader tired. But this would not account for it in other languages and other lands, though there is no telling how quickly and intimately the different literatures influence one another.

The writer who seems to me above all others the master of the colloquial style in dialogue is Carlo Goldoni, who not only wrote entire comedies in dialect, but in his Italian comedies made his Venetians speak Venetian, with subtle distinctions between the accents of the city and of such a near-lying dependence as Chioggia. In Switzerland, the first great realist, Jeremias Gotthelf, as Pastor Bitzius called himself, wrote his novels of peasant life in the peasant dialect of the Canton of Berne; but as I know them only in the French translations, which, of course, do not reproduce the dialect, I am unable to judge of his fidelity in the work, though I have not the least doubt of it. In English fiction I have no very vivid impressions of dialect between Scott and Dickens, yet I know that Miss Edgeworth's Irish tales are full of it. Miss Austen, as far as I remember, eschews it altogether; and we must not, I suppose, call Fanny Burney's report of class vulgarisms dialect. No more can we class with dialect study the careful writing of thieves' slang which occupied the novelists of a much later day, and seems to have received even serious attention from Bulwer in his more youthful romances. When we come down to our own time, there is both the effect and the fact of dialect in George Eliot; but in Trollope there is not even the effect of it. There is a good deal of it in Charles Reade, but I should be afraid that he got it up for the occasion rather than knew it from the lips of men; I have no proof of this, though. Mr. William Black suggests the Highland speech delightfully, but self-denyingly. Long before these writers the tribe of Irish novelists, represented by Lover and Lever, abounded in dialect, or at least brogue, and perhaps the Irish accent has been more heard in fiction than the negro, even; both are easy to do.

The vernacular of Dickens's people never seems to me quite trustworthy; he had not a good ear, and he had no scruple in perverting or inventing forms, if it suited his purpose. I fancy that his best and truest dialect writing is to be found in *Hard Times*, though he indulged in it everywhere in his novels. Thackeray's burlesque of the speech of serving men was always pure caricature; and Hardy appears to be the English novelist who reports the parlance of the common people with most liking and conscience. Wherever you come upon it in his books it is delightful; though, as I said, it is an imitation of their fashion of speech rather than a reproduction of it.

This is apparently the case with Giovanni Verga in his sketches of Sicilian life, and in his beautiful story of *The House by the Medlar Tree*. I do not think that the modern Italian writers have studied the provincial parlances at all in the degree that Goldoni did, and I know of very little Italian work in dialect among their later novelists. I am not saying there is none, but merely that I am ignorant.

In the Spanish novelists, whom I know a little better, I find a disposition towards it chiefly in Valdés, who amuses himself with the accents rather than the locutions of his Gallicians, and Andalusians, and Cubans, spelling them with great care, and imparting a sense both of personal and local character by means of them. If we come to the Germans, we have a whole dialect fiction treated by Fritz Reuter in his Platt-Deutsch stories; but in French I cannot say how much has been done. In his earlier books Zola gave us very abundantly of Parisian slang, but I suppose this was hardly writing dialect; and in his later books I do not remember any attempt to characterize his people by their peculiar speech. I have no sense of anything of the kind in Daudet, beyond a proverb or a phrase or two in Provençal, but I have not read Daudet so much in French, and I ought not to speak of him.

I have read only in English the great Russian writers, and I cannot even guess how much they have employed dialect. One can hardly imagine Tolstoy getting on without it, in books otherwise so faithful to the simple life they deal with. I read Norwegian no more than I read Russian, but my friend Professor Boyesen tells me that the Norwegian novelists and dramatists employ dialect a great deal, and that they employ it of set purpose, with the wish not only to portray the speech of the common people, but to give the strenuous and picturesque vocables and phrases of dialect permanent place in the written language. Ibsen, he says, studies the language of his characters so minutely that he suffers them to speak only and always as a man of this or that sort would speak, in the kind of personal vocabulary which we each have more or less to himself.

III.

I do not know why I am saying all this, unless to teach the general reader here that he is not the only general reader who has been obliged to bear with popular authors in the use of dialect. I should like to persuade him that our writers have not used it out of caprice, or merely to worry him, but have genuinely felt the need of it in their endeavors to portray a life new in so many of its phases to literature. Where this has been unconscious, it has been perhaps all the more genuine, for it has been part of the world movement in fiction towards greater naturalness and lifelikeness. Without what has been done in this sort among us, I am sure we should not have the right we now undoubtedly have to a standing with the foremost of the peoples whose authors wished them to appear in literature exactly as they appear in life. I am always saying that it is not to any author singly, or even very largely, that we are to look for the proof of this, but to the whole body of our authorship. We are an intensely decentralized people in our letters as well as in our politics, and the justification of dialect is to be found not in this quarter or that, but everywhere that our authors have honestly studied the local life. Lowell in Massachusetts and Riley in Indiana have been equally artistic in its employment, and there is no section or region without some writer emulous to report its life in the terms of its peculiar parlance, when they cannot be expressed without loss in the language common to all.

The general reader, however, has got tired of dialect, and the most conscientious artist must have moments when he would like to be friends with the mammon of unrighteousness. It will be well for him, perhaps, to consider how little dialect he can get on with, and how much can be done by suggestion, without actual representation. A great deal can be done, undoubtedly; but when it comes to sacrificing a precious artistic effect, I should say that decidedly there could be no more question of the general reader's prejudices or sensibilities. In such a case, dialect must be used, and used unsparingly, and the author must trust to the recuperative forces of the general reader for a later or final appreciation. Possibly, some æsthetic anæsthetic might be discovered which would palliate the worst immediate effects of the dialect, and carry the general reader through the chapters where it prevailed in a state of unconsciousness.

32 Paul Laurence Dunbar announced
1896

Review of *Majors and Minors*, 'Life and Letters,' *Harper's Weekly*, 27 June 1896; Introduction to *Lyrics of Lowly Life*, New York, December 1896.

Howells, who was to become a founding sponsor of the National Association for the Advancement of Colored People upon its conception at the centenary of Lincoln's birth in 1909, had been reared a third-generation abolitionist in a household which suffered bankruptcy as well as obloquy for the slave. Less intimately acquainted with Negroes or Afro-American folk-ways than Clemens, he had long taken it for granted that black people were to be respected and lifted up after the Civil War without, for all evidence to the contrary, giving them or their problems much thought. But during the period of his keenest moral sensitivity and deepest creativity he had imagined a novel about certain consequences of miscegenation and published it, *An Imperative Duty*, in 1891, anticipating Clemens's *Pudd'nhead Wilson*, 1894.

How much Howells may have been sensitized imaginatively by the onslaught against black Americans of the infamous 'Jim Crow' movement to nullify the effects of the Fourteenth Amendment to the Constitution of the United States is not easy to say.[1] About all one can observe is that Howells's concern and sympathy for the black man and the black writer seemed to grow in direct relation to the rise of repression, and nothing illustrates that fact better than his relations personal and critical with the poet Paul Laurence Dunbar.

As critic Howells faced a question still more vexing in our present age of anxiety to make amends for past injustice to the Afro-American, his culture, and his contributions to our joint culture. In reviewing Dunbar's second volume, *Majors and Minors*, 1895, Howells guessed that the 'Majors' were poems in standard English and the 'Minors' poems in dialect. And he objected. Himself a registered admirer of good work in dialect, he deplored the implication that *négritude* was to be played down: he insisted, in present parlance, that 'Black *is* beautiful.' But he sensed a problem opposite, if not equal in his eyes.

The relation with Dunbar tells much about Howells's dealings with the young. It was the playwright Herne, part of the circle, who sent Howells *Majors and Minors*. When Dunbar wrote to thank Howells for the review,

243

Howells got the literary agent Ripley Hitchcock to take him on, wrote an introduction to *Lyrics of Lowly Life*, which was published in both New York and London, and interceded with the famous impresario Major Pond to put Dunbar on the lecture circuit to make himself some money. Howells's efforts were not patronizing (he had just been campaigning for Stephen Crane); they were motivated by a realizing sense of the unique worth of an art, as he said, 'which is purely and intensely black.'

Review of *Majors and Minors*

There has come to me from the hand of a friend, very unofficially, a little book of verse, dateless, placeless, without a publisher, which has greatly interested me. Such foundlings of the press always appeal to one by their forlornness; but commonly the appeal is to one's pity only, which is moved all the more if the author of the book has innocently printed his portrait with his verse. In this present case I felt a heightened pathos in the appeal from the fact that the face which confronted me when I opened the volume was the face of a young negro, with the race traits strangely accented: the black skin, the woolly hair, the thick, outrolling lips, and the mild, soft eyes of the pure African type. One cannot be very sure, ever, about the age of those people, but I should have thought that this poet was about twenty years old; and I suppose that a generation ago he would have been worth, apart from his literary gift, twelve or fifteen hundred dollars, under the hammer. My sense of all this was intensified when I came to read the little book, and to recognize its artistic quality; but I hope that the love of dramatic contrasts has not made me overvalue it as a human event, or that I do not think unduly well of it because it is the work of a man whose race has not hitherto made its mark in his art.

I do not forget what that race has done in some other arts: I know that it has achieved something worthy of more than respect on the stage; that in sculpture its attempts have been worthy of note; that in oratory, Booker Washington is the equal of the most eloquent and forcible speakers among us; that in fiction Dumas is the chief glory of the romantic school. But I do not remember any English-speaking negro, at least, who has till now done in verse work of at all the same moment as Paul Laurence Dunbar, the author of the volume I am speaking of.

Burns has long had the consecration of the world's love and honor, and I shall not do this unknown but not ungifted poet the injury of comparing him with Burns; yet I do not think one can read his negro pieces without feeling that they are of like impulse and inspiration with the work of Burns when he was most Burns, when he was most Scotch, when he was most peasant. When Burns was least himself he wrote literary English, and Mr. Dunbar writes literary English when he is least himself. But not to urge the mischievous parallel further, he is a real poet whether he speaks a dialect or whether he writes a language. He calls his little book *Majors and Minors*; the Majors being in our American English, and the Minors being in dialect, the dialect of the middle-south negroes and the middle-south whites; for the poet's ear has been quick for the accent of his neighbors as well as for that of his kindred. I have no means of knowing whether he values his Majors more than his Minors; but I should not suppose it at all unlikely, and I am bound to say none of them are despicable. In very many I find the proofs of honest thinking and true feeling, and in some the record of experience, whose genuineness the reader can test by his own.

CONSCIENCE AND REMORSE.

'Goodbye,' I said to my conscience—
  'Goodbye for aye and aye,'
And I put her hands off harshly,
  And turned my face away;
And conscience, smitten sorely,
  Returned not from that day.

But a time came when my spirit
  Grew weary of its pace;
And I cried: 'Come back, my conscience,
  I long to see thy face.'
But conscience cried: 'I cannot,
  Remorse sits in my place.'

Most of these pieces, however, are like most of the pieces of most young poets, cries of passionate aspiration and disappointment, more or less personal or universal, which except for the negro face of the author one could not find specially notable. It is when we come to Mr. Dunbar's Minors that we feel ourselves in the presence of a man with a direct and a fresh authority to do the kind of thing he is doing. I wish I could give the whole of the longest of these pieces, which he calls 'The Pahty,' but I must content myself with a passage or two.

They will impart some sense of the jolly rush of its movement, its vivid picturesqueness, its broad characterization; and will perhaps suffice to show what vistas into the simple, sensuous, joyous nature of his race Mr. Dunbar's work opens:

THE PAHTY.

Dey had a gread big pahty down to Tom's de othah night;
Was I dah? You bet! I nevah in my life see sich a sight;
All de folks f'om fou' plantations was invited, an' dey come,
Dey come troopin' thick ez chillun when dey heahs a fife an'
    drum.
Evahbody dressed dere fines'—Heish yo' mouf an' git away!
Ain't seen no sich fancy dressin' sence las' quaht'ly meetin' day;
Gals all dressed in silks an' satins, not a wrinkle ner a crease,
Eyes a-battin', teeth a-shinin', haih breshed back ez slick ez
    grease;
Sku'ts all tucked an' puffed an' ruffled, evah blessed seam an'
    stitch;
Ef you'd seen 'em wif deir mustus, couldn't swahed to which was
    which.
We had wheat bread white ez cotton an' a egg pone jes like gol',
Hog jole, bilin' hot an' steamin', roasted shoat, an' ham sliced
    cold—
Look out! What's de mattah wif you? Don't be fallin' on de flo';
Ef it's go'n to 'fect you dat way, I won't tell you nothin' mo'.
Dah now—well, we had hot chittlin's—now you'se tryin' again to
    fall;
Cain't you stan' to heah about it? 'Spose you'd been an' seed it all;
Seed dem gread big sweet pertaters, layin' by de possum's side,
Seed dat coon in all his gravy, reckon den you'd up an' died!
Mandy 'lowed, 'You all mus' 'scuse me, d'want much upon my
    she'ves,
But I've done my bes' to suit you, so set down an' he'p yo'se'ves.'
Tom, he 'lowed, 'I don't b'lieve in 'pologizin' an' perfessin',
Let 'em tek it lak dey ketch it; Eldah Thompson, ask de blessin'.'
Wish you'd seed dat colo'ed preachah cleah his th'oat an' bow his
    head;
One eye shet, an' one eye open—dis is evah wud he said:
'Lawd, look down in tendah mussy on sich generous hawts ez
    dese;
Make us truly thankful, amen. Pass dat possum, ef yo' please!'

Well, we eat and drunk ouah po'tion, twell dah wasn't nothin' lef,
An' we felt jes like new sausage, we was 'mos' nigh stuffed to def!
Tom, he knowed how we'd be feelin', so he had de fiddlah' roun',
An' he made us cleah de cabin fu' to dance dat suppah down.
Jim, de fiddlah, chuned his fiddle, put some rosum on his bow,
Set a pine box on de table, mounted it an' let huh go!
He's a fiddlah now I tell you, an' he made dat fiddle ring,
Twell de ol'est an' de lamest had to give deir feet a fling.
Jigs, cotillions, reels an' break-downs, cordrills an' a waltz er two;
Bless yo' soul, dat music winged 'em an' dem people lak to flew!
Cripple Joe, de ole rheumatic, danced dat flo' f'om side to middle,
Th'owed away his crutch an' hopped it, what's rheumatics 'ginst a
    fiddle?
Eldah Thompson got so tickled dat he lak to lose his grace,
Had to tek bofe feet an' hol' dem so's to keep 'em in deir place.
An' de Christuns an' de' sinnahs got so mixed up on dat flo'
Dat I don't see how dey'd pahted ef de trump had chanced to
    blow.
Well, we danced dat way an' capahed in de mos' redic'lous way,
Twell de roostahs in de bahn-yard cleahed deir th'oats an' crowed
    fu' day.
Y'ought to been dar, fu' I tell you evahthing was rich an' prime,
An' dey ain't no use in talkin', we jes had one scrumptious time!

One sees how the poet exults in his material, as the artist always
does; it is not for him to blink its commonness, or to be ashamed of
its rudeness; and in his treatment of it he has been able to bring us
nearer to the heart of primitive human nature in his race than any one
else has yet done. The range between appetite and emotion is not
great, but it is here that his race has hitherto had its being, with a lift
now and then far above and beyond it. A rich, humorous sense pervades his recognition of this fact, without excluding a fond sympathy,
and it is the blending of these which delights me in all his dialect verse.

WHEN DE CO'N PONE'S HOT.

Dey is times in life when Nature
    Seems to slip a cog an' go,
Jes a-rattlin' down creation,
    Lak an ocean's overflow;
When de worl' jes stahts a-spinnin'
    Lak a picaninny's top,

An' yo' cup o' joy is brimmin'
   Twell it seems about to slop.
An' you feel jes lak a racah
   Dat is trainin' fu' to trot—
When yo' mammy ses de blessin'
   An' de co'n pone's hot.

When you set down at de table,
   Kin' o' weary lak an' sad,
An' you'se jes a little tiahed,
   An' purhaps a little mad,
How yo' gloom tu'ns into gladness,
   How yo' joy drives out de doubt,
When de oven do' is opened
   An' de smell comes po'in' out,
Why, de 'lectric light o' Heaven
   Seems to settle on de spot—
When yo' mammy ses de blessin'
   An' de co'n pone's hot.

When de cabbage pot is steamin'
   An' de bacon's good an' fat,
When de chittlin's is a sputter'n'
   So's to show you whah dey's at,
Take away yo' sody biscuit,
   Take away yo' cake an' pie,
Fu' de glory time is comin',
   An' it's 'proachin' very nigh;
An' you want to jump an' hollah,
   Do' you know you'd bettah not—
When yo' mammy ses de blessin'
   An' de co'n pone's hot.

I have heerd o' lots o' sermons,
   An' I've heerd o' lots o' prayers,
An' I've listened to some singin'
   Dat has tuk me up de stairs
Of de Glory-Lan' an' set me
   Jes' below de Mahster's th'one,
An' have lef' my hawt a-singin'
   In a happy aftah tone,
But dem wu'ds so sweetly murmured
   Seem to tech de softes' spot,

When my mammy ses de blessin'
An' de co'n pone's hot.

Several of the pieces are pure sentiment, like 'The Deserted
Plantation'; but these without lapsing into sentimentality recall the
too easy pathos of the pseudo-negro poetry of the minstrel show.
There is no such suggestion in 'When de Co'n Pone's Hot', nor in the
following poem, which is purely and intensely black, as I may say, in
its feeling:

WHEN MALINDY SINGS.

G'way an' quit dat noise, Miss Lucy—
    Put dat music book away;
What's de use to keep on tryin'?
    Ef you practise twell you're gray
You cain't sta't no notes a-flyin'
    Like de ones dat rants and rings
F'om de kitchen to de big woods
    When Malindy sings. . . .

Ain't you nevah heerd Malindy?
    Blessed soul, take up de cross!
Look heah, ain't you jokin', honey?
    Well, you don't know what you los'.
Y'ought to heah dat gal a-wa'blin';
    Robins, la'ks, an' all dem things
Heish dey moufs an' hides dey faces
    When Malindy sings.

Fiddlin' man jes stop his fiddlin',
    Lay his fiddle on de she'f;
Mockin'-bird quit tryin' to whistle,
    'Cause he jes so 'shamed hisse'f.
Folks a-playin' on de banjo
    Draps dey fingahs on de strings—
Bless yo' soul—fu'gits to move 'em
    When Malindy sings.

She jes spreads huh mouf an' hollahs
    'Come to Jesus,' twell you heah
Sinnahs' tremblin' steps an' voices,
    Timid like a-drawin' neah;

Den she tu'ns to 'Rock of Ages,'
Simply to de cross she clings,
An' you fin' yo' teahs a-drappin'
When Malindy sings.

Who dat says dat humble praises
Wif de Mahster nevah counts?
Heish yo' mouf, I heah dat music
Ez hit rises up an' mounts—
Floatin' by de hills an' valleys,
Way above dis buryin' sod,
Ez hit makes its way in glory
To de very gates of God! . . .

Towsah, stop dat ba'kin'! heah me?
Mandy, make dat chile keep still;
Don't you heah de echoes callin'
F'om de valley to de hill?
Let me listen, I can heah it
Th'oo de bresh of angels' wings,
Sof' an' sweet, 'Swing Low, Sweet Chariot,'
Ez Malindy sings.

I hope the reader likes as much as I like, the strong full pulse of the music in all these things. Mr. Dunbar's race is nothing if not lyrical, and he comes by his rhythm honestly. But what is better, what is finer, what is of larger import in his work is what is conscious and individual in it. He is, so far as I know, the first man of his color to study his race objectively, to analyze it to himself, and then to represent it in art as he felt it and found it to be; to represent it humorously, yet tenderly, and above all so faithfully that we know the portrait to be undeniably like. A race which has reached this effect in any of its members can no longer be held wholly uncivilized; and intellectually Mr. Dunbar makes a stronger claim for the negro than the negro yet has done.

I am speaking of him as a black poet, when I should be speaking of him as a poet; but the notion of what he is insists too strongly for present impartiality. I hope I have not praised him too much, because he has surprised me so very much; for his excellences are positive and not comparative. If his Minors had been written by a white man, I should have been struck by their very uncommon quality; I should have said that they were wonderful divinations. But since they are expressions of a race-life from within the race, they seem to me indefinitely more valuable and significant. I have sometimes fancied that perhaps the negroes *thought* black, and *felt* black; that they were racially so utterly alien and distinct from ourselves that there never could be common intellectual and emotional ground between us, and that whatever eternity might do to reconcile us, the end of time would find us as far asunder as ever. But this little book has given me pause in my speculation. Here, in the artistic effect at least, is white thinking and white feeling in a black man, and perhaps the human unity, and not the race unity, is the precious thing, the divine thing, after all. God hath made of one blood all nations of men: perhaps the proof of this saying is to appear in the arts, and our hostilities and prejudices are to vanish in them.

Mr. Dunbar, at any rate, seems to have fathomed the souls of his simple white neighbors, as well as those of his own kindred; and certainly he has reported as faithfully what passes in them as any man of our race has yet done with respect to the souls of his. It would be very incomplete recognition of his work not to speak particularly of the non-negro dialect pieces, and it is to the lover of homely and tender poetry, as well as the student of tendencies, that I commend such charming sketches as 'Speakin' o' Christmas,' 'After a Visit,' 'Lonesome,' and 'The Spellin' Bee.' They are good, very good; and it is perhaps only the novelty of the achievement that seems to give superior value to the fine irony and neat satire of such a black piece as this:

ACCOUNTABILITY.

Folks ain't got no right to censuah uthah folks about dey habits:
Him dat give de squir'ls de bushtails made de bobtails fu' de rabbits;
Him dat built de grea' big mountains hollered out de little valleys;
Him dat made de streets an' driveways wasn't 'shamed to make de alleys.

We is all constructed diff'rent, d'ain't no two of us de same;
We cain't he'p ouah likes an' dislikes, ef we'se bad we ain't to blame,
Ef we'se good, we needn't show off, 'case you bet it ain't ouah doin';
We gits into su'ttain channels dat we jes' cain't he'p pu'suin'.

But we all fits into places dat no uthah ones cud fill,
An' we does the things we has to, big er little, good er ill.
John cain't tek de place o' Henry, Su an' Sally ain't alike;
Bass ain't nuthin' like a suckah, chub ain't nuthin' like a pike.

When you come to think about it, how it's all planned out it's
    splendid.
Nuthin's done er evah happens, 'dout hit's somefin' dat's intended;
Don't keer what you does, you has to, an' hit sholy beats de
    dickens—
Viney, go put on de kittle, I got one o' mastah's chickens.

I am sorry that I cannot give the publisher as well as the author
of this significant little book; but I may say that it is printed by
Hadley & Hadley, Toledo, Ohio. It is interesting to find it dedicated
to the author's mother.

Introduction to *Lyrics of Lowly Life*

I think I should scarcely trouble the reader with a special appeal in
behalf of this book, if it had not specially appealed to me for reasons
apart from the author's race, origin, and condition. The world is too
old now, and I find myself too much of its mood, to care for the work
of a poet because he is black, because his father and mother were
slaves, because he was, before and after he began to write poems, an
elevator-boy. These facts would certainly attract me to him as a man,
if I knew him to have a literary ambition, but when it came to his
literary art, I must judge it irrespective of these facts, and enjoy or
endure it for what it was in itself.

It seems to me that this was my experience with the poetry of
Paul Laurence Dunbar when I found it in another form, and in justice
to him I cannot wish that it should be otherwise with his readers here.
Still, it will legitimately interest those who like to know the causes, or,
if these may not be known, the sources, of things, to learn that the
father and mother of the first poet of his race in our language were
negroes without admixture of white blood. The father escaped from
slavery in Kentucky to freedom in Canada, while there was still no
hope of freedom otherwise; but the mother was freed by the events of
the civil war, and came North to Ohio, where their son was born at
Dayton, and grew up with such chances and mischances for mental
training as everywhere befall the children of the poor. He has told me

that his father picked up the trade of a plasterer, and when he had taught himself to read, loved chiefly to read history. The boy's mother shared his passion for literature with a special love of poetry, and after the father died she struggled on in more than the poverty she had shared with him. She could value the faculty which her son showed first in prose sketches and attempts at fiction, and she was proud of the praise and kindness they won him among the people of the town, where he has never been without the warmest and kindest friends.

In fact, from every part of Ohio and from several cities of the adjoining States, there came letters in cordial appreciation of the critical recognition which it was my pleasure no less than my duty to offer Paul Dunbar's work in another place. It seemed to me a happy omen for him that so many people who had known him, or known of him, were glad of a stranger's good word; and it was gratifying to see that at home he was esteemed for the things he had done rather than because as the son of negro slaves he had done them. If a prophet is often without honor in his own country, it surely is nothing against him when he has it. In this case it deprived me of the glory of a discoverer; but that is sometimes a barren joy, and I am always willing to forego it.

What struck me in reading Mr. Dunbar's poetry was what had already struck his friends in Ohio and Indiana, in Kentucky and Illinois. They had felt, as I felt, that however gifted his race had proven itself in music, in oratory, in several of the other arts, here was the first instance of an American negro who had evinced innate distinction in literature. In my criticism of his book I had alleged Dumas in France, and I had forgetfully failed to allege the far greater Pushkin in Russia; but these were both mulattoes, who might have been supposed to derive their qualities from white blood vastly more artistic than ours, and who were the creatures of an environment more favorable to their literary development. So far as I could remember, Paul Dunbar was the only man of pure African blood and of American civilization to feel the negro life æsthetically and express it lyrically. It seemed to me that this had come to its most modern consciousness in him, and that his brilliant and unique achievement was to have studied the American negro objectively, and to have represented him as he found him to be, with humor, with sympathy, and yet with what the reader must instinctively feel to be entire truthfulness. I said that a race which had come to this effect in any member of it, had attained civilization in him, and I permitted myself the imaginative prophecy that the hostilities and the prejudices which had so long constrained his race were destined to vanish in the arts; that these were to be the final proof that God had made of one blood all nations of men. I thought his merits positive and not comparative; and I held that if his black poems had been written by a white man, I should not have found them less admirable. I accepted them as an evidence of the essential unity of the human race, which does not think or feel black in one and white in another, but humanly in all.

Yet it appeared to me then, and it appears to me now, that there is a precious difference of temperament between the races which it would be a great pity ever to lose, and that this is best preserved and most charmingly suggested by Mr. Dunbar in those pieces of his where he studies the moods and traits of his race in its own accent of our English. We call such pieces dialect pieces for want of some closer phrase, but they are really not dialect so much as delightful personal attempts and failures for the written and spoken language. In nothing is his essentially refined and delicate art so well shown as in these pieces, which, as I ventured to say, describe the range between appetite and emotion, with certain lifts far beyond and above it, which is the range of the race. He reveals in these a finely ironical perception of the negro's limitations, with a tenderness for them which I think so very rare as to be almost quite new. I should say, perhaps, that it was this humorous quality which Mr. Dunbar had added to our literature, and it would be this which would most distinguish him, now and hereafter. It is something that one feels in nearly all the dialect pieces; and I hope that in the present collection he has kept all of these in his earlier volume, and added others to them. But the contents of this book are wholly of his own choosing, and I do not know how much or little he may have preferred the poems in literary English. Some of these I thought very good, and even more than very good, but not distinctively his contribution to the body of American poetry. What I mean is that several people might have written them; but I do not know any one else at present who could quite have written the dialect pieces. These are divinations and reports of what passes in the hearts and minds of a lowly people whose poetry had hitherto been inarticulately expressed in music, but now finds, for the first time in our tongue, literary interpretation of a very artistic completeness.

I say the event is interesting, but how important it shall be can be determined only by Mr. Dunbar's future performance. I cannot undertake to prophesy concerning this; but if he should do nothing more than he has done, I should feel that he had made the strongest claim for the negro in English literature that the negro has yet made. He has at least produced something that, however we may critically disagree about it, we cannot well refuse to enjoy; in more than one piece he has produced a work of art.

NOTE

1 See Martha Banta, ed., *The Shadow of a Dream and An Imperative Duty*, vol. xvii of *A Selected Edition of W. D. Howells*, Bloomington, Indiana, 1970, Introduction to *An Imperative Duty*, iii–xii.

33 'New York Low Life in Fiction'
1896

Published in the New York *World*, 26 July 1896.

The 'dramatist poet' whose name Howells forgot was Benjamin A. Baker, author of the wildly popular *A Glance at New York in 1848*. Yet they were no shallow associations which recalled the play to Howells's mind. To be sure, he had in hand to review the two first realistic studies of life in the New York depths, each written by a protégé; he loved its vulgar fun as he suffered from its agonies; he had long associated Edward Harrigan's drama with an unrealized opportunity for serious fiction devoted to low urban life. But the deep associations were personal. When Howells had seen *A Glance at New York* in Dayton, Ohio, in 1850, he was himself a child laborer among the dispossessed, overworked, and defeated poor. He never forgot those facts.

This piece to which the New York *World* gave a page-wide spread, over a large portrait of the author, was sub-headed, 'The Great Novelist Hails Abraham Cahan, the Author of *Yekl*, as a New Star of Realism, and Says that He and Stephen Crane Have Drawn the Truest Pictures of East Side Life.' It constituted Howells's definitive statement on Crane and on *Maggie, a Girl of the Streets*. Here, as in many places, the evidence mounts that those who insist that Howells was invincibly genteel may themselves be invincibly unread. Crane understood the spirit and the man so well that it was about this that he wrote to Howells, 'I always thank God that I can have the strongest admiration for the work of a man who has been so much to me personally for I can imagine the terrors of being indelibly indebted to the Chump in Art or even to the Semi-Chump in Art.'

About Cahan's relations with Howells we stand in debt for information elegantly worked out by Professors Clara and Rudolf Kirk ('Abraham Cahan and William Dean Howells,' *American Jewish Historical Quarterly*, 52 (September 1962), 27–57). Cahan's was the classic case of a young Jewish intellectual who fled Russia one jump ahead of the Czarist police, who pursued him for Socialist convictions and revolutionary activity. When in preparation for his 'Altrurian' sketches in the *Cosmopolitan* Howells wished to study a 'walking delegate,' he found Cahan—and got a surprise. His 'subject' was not only a labor militant but a Howells fan. He owned a collection of Howells volumes and had published a laudatory lecture on

256

'Realism.' Howells and Cahan became mutual admirers: Cahan was encouraged to write; Howells became the first reader of *Yekl* and, characteristically, its unpaid agent until, having failed with the Harpers and McClure, he placed *Yekl* with the Appletons. Then he was ready to push his young novelists of low life toward stardom.

Yekl, of course, became another 'first' for Howells as critic. It is the original American Jewish novel.

It is a long time since I have seen the once famous and popular play *A Glance at New York*, but I distinctly recall through the misty substance of some forty-five very faded years the heroic figures of the volunteer fireman and his friends, who were the chief persons of the piece. I do not remember the others at all, but I remember Mose, and Sikesy, and Lize. Good and once precious fragments of the literature linger in my memory, as: '"Mose," says he, "git off o' dem hose, or I'll swat you over der head wid der trumpet." And I didn't get off o' der hose, and he did swat me over der head wid der trumpet.' Other things have gone, things of Shakespeare, of Alfieri, of Cervantes, but these golden words of a forgotten dramatist poet remain with me.

I.

It is interesting to note that the first successful attempt to represent the life of our streets was in dramatic form. Some actor saw and heard things spoken with the peculiar swagger and whopperjaw utterance of the b'hoy of those dreadful old days, when the blood-tubs and the plug-uglies reigned over us, and Tammany was still almost purely American, and he put them on the stage and spread the poison of them all over the land, so that there was hardly anywhere a little blackguard boy who did not wish to act and talk like Mose.

The whole piece was painted with the large brush and the vivid pigments of romanticism, and yet the features were real. So it was many long years later when Mr. Harrigan came to the study of our low life in his delightful series of plays. He studied it in the heyday of Irish supremacy, when Tammany had become almost purely Celtic, and he naturally made his heroes and heroines Irish. The old American b'hoy lingered among them in the accent and twist of an occasional barkeeper, but the brogue prevailed, and the highshouldered sidelong carriage of the Americanized bouncer of Hibernian blood.

The treatment, however, was still romanticistic, though Mr. Harrigan is too much of a humorist not to return suddenly to nature, at times from the most exalted regions of 'imagination.' He loves laughing and making laugh, and that always saved him when he was in danger of becoming too grand, or fine, or heroic. He had moments when he was exactly true, but he allowed himself a good many friendly freedoms with the fact, and the effect was not always that of reality.

It seemed to me that so far as I could get the drift of a local drama in German which flourished at one of the East Side theatres a winter ago, that the author kept no more faithfully to life than Mr. Harrigan, and had not his sublime moments of absolute fidelity. In fact, the stage is almost as slow as criticism to perceive that there is no other standard for the arts but life, and it keeps on with the conventional in motive even when the matter is honest, apparently in the hope that by doing the stale falsehood often enough it will finally affect the witness like a fresh verity. It is to the honor of the stage, however, that it was first to recognize the value of our New York low life as material; and I shall always say that Mr. Harrigan, when he was not over-powered by a tradition or a theory, was exquisitely artistic in his treatment of it. He was then true, and, as Tolstoi has lately told us, to be true is to be moral.

II.

The fiction meant to be read, as distinguishable from the fiction meant to be represented, has been much later in dealing with the same material, and it is only just beginning to deal with it in the spirit of the great modern masters. I cannot find that such clever and amusing writers as Mr. Townsend, or Mr. Ralph, or Mr. Ford have had it on their consciences to report in the regions of the imagination the very effect of the life which they all seem at times to have seen so clearly. There is apparently nothing but the will that is wanting in either of them, but perhaps the want of the will is the want of an essential factor, though I should like very much to have them try for a constant reality in their studies; and I am far from wishing to count them out in an estimate of what has been done in that direction. It is only just to Mr. Stephen Crane, however, to say that he was first in the field where they made themselves known earlier. His story of *Maggie, a Girl of the Streets*, which has been recently published by the Appletons, was in the hands of a few in an edition which the author could not even give away three years ago; and I think it is two years, now, since I saw *George's Mother*, which Edward Arnold has brought out, in the manuscript.

Their present publication is imaginably due to the success of *The Red Badge of Courage*, but I do not think that they will owe their critical acceptance to the obstreperous favor which that has won. As pieces of art they are altogether superior to it, and as representations of life their greater fidelity cannot be questioned. In *The Red Badge of Courage* there is a good deal of floundering, it seems to me. The narration repeats itself; the effort to imagine, to divine, and then to express ends often in a huddled and confused effect; there is no repose, such as agony itself assumes in the finest art, and there is no forward movement. But in these other books the advance is relentless; the atmosphere is transparent; the texture is a continuous web where all the facts are wrought with the unerring mastery of absolute knowledge. I should say that *The Red Badge of Courage* owed its excellence to the training the author had given himself in setting forth the life he knew in these earlier books of later publication. He learned to imagine vividly from seeing clearly.

There is a curious unity in the spirit of the arts; and I think that what strikes me most in the story of *Maggie* is that quality of fatal necessity which dominates Greek tragedy. From the conditions it all had to be, and there were the conditions. I felt this in Mr. Hardy's *Jude*, where the principle seems to become conscious in the writer; but there is apparently no consciousness of any such motive in the author of *Maggie*. Another effect is that of an ideal of artistic beauty which is as present in the working out of this poor girl's squalid romance as in any classic fable. This will be foolishness, I know, to the foolish people who cannot discriminate between the material and the treatment in art, and who think that beauty is inseparable from daintiness and prettiness, but I do not speak to them. I appeal rather to such as feel themselves akin with every kind of human creature, and find neither high nor low when it is a question of inevitable suffering, or of a soul struggling vainly with an inexorable fate.

My rhetoric scarcely suggests the simple terms the author uses to produce the effect which I am trying to report again. They are simple, but always most graphic, especially when it comes to the personalities of the story: the girl herself, with her bewildered wish to be right and good; with her distorted perspective; her clinging and generous affections; her hopeless environments; the horrible old drunken mother, a cyclone of violence and volcano of vulgarity; the mean and selfish lover, a dandy tough, with his gross ideals and ambitions; her brother, an Ishmaelite from the cradle, who, with his warlike instincts beaten back into cunning, is what the b'hoy of former times has become in our more strenuously policed days. He is indeed a wonderful figure in a group which betrays no faltering in the artist's hand. He, with his dull hates, his warped good-will, his cowed ferocity, is almost as fine artistically as Maggie, but he could not have been so hard to do, for all the pathos of her fate is rendered without one maudlin touch.

So is that of the simple-minded and devoted and tedious old woman who is George's mother in the book of that name. This is scarcely a study at all, while Maggie is really and fully so. It is the study of a situation merely: a poor, inadequate woman, of a commonplace religiosity, whose son goes to the bad. The wonder of it is the courage which deals with persons so absolutely average, and the art that graces them with the beauty of the author's compassion for everything that errs and suffers. Without this feeling the effects of his mastery would be impossible, and if it went further or put itself into the pitying phrases it would annul the effects. But it never does this; it is notable how in all respects the author keeps himself well in hand. He is quite honest with his reader. He never shows his characters or his situations in any sort of sentimental glamour; if you will be moved by the sadness of common fates you will feel his intention, but he does not flatter his portraits of people or conditions to take your fancy.

In George and his mother he has to do with folk of country origin as the city affects them, and the son's decadence is admirably studied; he scarcely struggles against temptation, and his mother's only art is to cry and to scold. Yet he loves her, in a way, and she is devotedly proud of him. These simple country folk are contrasted with simple city folk of varying degrees of badness. Mr. Crane has the skill to show how evil is greatly the effect of ignorance and imperfect civilization. The club of friends, older men than George, whom he is asked to join, is portrayed with extraordinary insight, and the group of young toughs whom he finally consorts with is done with even greater mastery. The bulldog motive of one of them, who is willing to fight to the death, is most impressively rendered.

III.

The student of dialect ought to be interested in the parlance of the class Mr. Crane draws upon for his characters. They are almost inarticulate; not merely the grammar, but the language itself, decays in their speech. The Theta sound, so characteristic of English, disappears altogether, and the vowels tend to lose themselves in the obscure note heard in *fur* and *stir*. What will be the final language spoken by the New Yorker? We shall always write and print a sort of literary English, I suppose, but with the mixture of races the spoken tongue may be a thing composite and strange beyond our present knowledge. Mr. Abraham Cahan, in his *Yekl, a Story of the New York Ghetto* (Appleton's), is full of indirect suggestions upon this point. Perhaps we shall have a New York jargon which shall be to English what the native Yiddish of his characters is to Hebrew, and it will be interlarded with Russian, Polish and German words, as their present jargon is with English vocables and with American slang.

Yekl is a young Russian Jew who is very anxious to be American-ized in every way, and who takes on our smartness and vulgarity with an instinctive fitness for that degree of fellow-citizenship. He is thoroughly selfish, immoral, irreligious, cunning and vain, which does not prevent his having moments of remorse and tenderness and living in a cloud of inherited superstitions. He was Yekl Podernik at home, but in Boston, where he made his first American sojourn, his zeal for our habits and customs won him the nickname of Jake the Yankee. The action of the story all passes in the region of Hester street, where Jake works in a sweat-shop, and where he makes a home for his wife and child when they come over to him from Povodye.

As Mr. Cahan is a Russian, and as romanticism is not considered literature in Russia, his story is, of course, intensely realistic. It could not be more so indeed than Mr. Crane's stories, and it is neither more nor less faithful than these. The artistic principle which moves both writers is the same; but the picturesque, outlandish material with which Mr. Cahan deals makes a stronger appeal to the reader's fancy. He has more humor than the American, too, whose spare laughter is apt to be grim, while the Russian cannot hide his relish of the comic incidents of his story. It is mainly not at all comic, however, but tragical as the divorce of the poor little Russian wife can make it, though the reader is promptly consoled by her marriage with a man worthier of her than Jake the Yankee. He goes away and weds the Americanized 'Polish snopé' whom he had flirted with before his wife came out to him.

The tale is well told, with spirit and with artistic pleasure on the author's part, whose sense of character is as broad as his sense of human nature is subtle and deep. I cannot help thinking that we have in him a writer of foreign birth who will do honor to American letters, as Boyesen did. He is already thoroughly naturalized to our point of view; he sees things with American eyes, and he brings in aid of his vision the far and rich perceptions of his Hebraic race; while he is strictly of the great and true Russian principle in literary art. There is much that is painful in his story, as there is much that is dreadful in Mr. Crane's work, but both of these writers persuade us that they have told the truth, and that such as conditions have made the people they deal with, we see their people. If we have any quarrel with the result, we cannot blame the authors, who have done their duty as artists and for a moment have drawn aside the thick veil of ignorance which parts the comfortable few from the uncomfortable many in this city. The life they know lives before us, as we read; and the saddest thing about it is that this life as we see it after a generation of New York in Mr. Crane's stories is more hopeless than it is as we find it in Mr. Cahan's tale, which deals with the first years of his hero's contact with our civilization. Doubtless, also, temperament has something to do with this effect. Mr. Crane is essentially tragical, and Mr. Cahan, without being less serious, is essentially humorous. *Yekl* is, in fact, a charming book, and is not only delightful in itself but in its promise of future work. The author who could imagine Mrs. Kavarsky, the meddle-some, amiable neighbor of poor Githa, Jake's wife, and Mamie, 'the Polish snopé,' and Fanny, 'the Preacher,' with the scenes in the sweat-shop, at the dancing academy and, above all, in the Rabbi's parlor at the time of the divorce, has bound himself by the very excellence of what he has done to do much more that is better still.

I had almost forgotten to speak of his English. In its simplicity and its purity, as the English of a man born to write Russian, it is simply marvelous.

34 'George Du Maurier'
1896

Introduction (December 1896) to *English Society Sketched by George Du Maurier*, New York, 1897.

There was something more than a little sporting about this introduction to Du Maurier's posthumous *English Society*, 1897. As he confesses here, and often said elsewhere, the 'preposterous popularity' of *Trilby*, 1894, taught Howells that realism had lost its fight for the popular taste; but he could still love the man and admire the best of his art—and demonstrate that in fact he did not dislike Englishmen on principle—while confessing defeat.

I was thinking, with a pang, just before I put my pen to the paper, that the death of George Du Maurier must be a fact of stale interest to the reader already, and that it would be staler yet by the time my words reached him. So swiftly does the revolving world carry our sorrow into the sun, our mirth into the shade, that it is as if the speed of the planet had caught something of the impatience of age, and it were hurried round upon its axis with the quickened pulses of senility. But perhaps this is a delusion of ours who dwell in the vicissitude of events, and there are still spots on the earth's whirling surface, lurking-places of quiet, where it seems not to move, and there is time to remember and to regret; where it is no astonishing thing that a king should be a whole month dead, and yet not forgotten. At any rate, it is in the hope, if not quite the faith, of this that I venture some belated lines concerning a man whom we have lost just when he seemed beginning to reveal himself.

I.

It was my good fortune to have the courage to write to Du Maurier when *Trilby* was only half printed, and to tell him how much I liked the gay, sad story. In every way it was well that I did not wait for the end, for the last third of it seemed to me so altogether forced in its conclusions that I could not have offered my praises with a whole heart, nor he accepted them with any, if the disgust with its preposterous popularity, which he so frankly, so humorously expressed, had then begun in him. But the liking which its readers felt had not yet become loathsome to the author, and he wrote me back a charming note, promising me the mystery, and enough of it, which I had hoped for, because of my pleasure in the true-dreaming in *Peter Ibbetson*; and speaking briefly, most modestly and fitly, of his commencing novelist at sixty, and his relative misgivings, and surprises.

It was indeed one of the most extraordinary things in the history of literature, and without a parallel, at least to my ignorance. He might have commenced and failed; that would have been indefinitely less amazing than his most amazing success; but it was very amazing that he should have commenced at all. It is useless to say that he had commenced long before, and in the literary property of his work he had always been an author. The theory will not justify itself to any critical judgment; one might as well say, if some great novelist distinguished for his sense of color took to painting, that he had always been an artist. The wonder of Du Maurier's essay, the astounding spectacle of his success, cannot be diminished by any such explanation of it. He commenced novelist in *Peter Ibbetson*, and so far as literature was concerned he succeeded in even greater fulness than he has succeeded since. He had perfect reason to be surprised; he had attempted an experiment, and he had performed a miracle.

As for the nature, or the quality, of his miracle, that is another question. I myself think that in all essentials it was fine. The result was not less gold because there was some dross of the transmuted metals hanging about the precious ingot, and the evidences of the process were present, though the secret was as occult as ever. He won the heart, he kindled the fancy, he bewitched the reason; and no one can say just how he did it. His literary attitude was not altogether new; he perfected an attitude recognizable first in Fielding, next in Sterne, then in Heine, afterwards in Thackeray: the attitude which I once called confidential, and shook three realms beyond seas, and their colonial dependencies here, with the word. It is an attitude which I find swaggering in Fielding, insincere in Sterne, mocking in Heine, and inartistic in Thackeray; but Du Maurier made it lovable. His whole story was a confidence; whatever illusion there was resided in that fact; you had to grant it in the beginning, and he made you grant it gladly. A trick? Yes; but none of your vulgar ones; a species of legerdemain, exquisite as that of the Eastern juggler who plants his ladder on the ground, climbs it, and pulls it up after him into the empty air. It wants seriousness, it wants the last respect for the reader's intelligence, it wants critical justification; it wants whatever is the very greatest thing in the very greatest novelists; the thing that convinces in Hawthorne, George Eliot, Tourguénief, Tolstoy. But short of this supreme truth, it has every grace, every beauty, every charm. It touches, it appeals, it consoles; and it flatters, too; if it turns the head, if it intoxicates, well, it is better to own the fact that it leaves one in not quite the condition for judging it. I made my tacit protest against it after following Trilby, poor soul, to her apotheosis at the hands of the world and the church; but I fell a prey to it again in the first chapters of *The Martian*, and I expect to continue in that sweet bondage to the end.

II.

If I venture to say that sentimentality is the dominant of the Du Maurier music, it is because his art has made sentimentality beautiful; I had almost said real, and I am ready to say different from what it was before. It is a very manly sentimentality; we need not be ashamed of sharing it; one should rather be ashamed of disowning its emotions. It is in its sweetness, as well as its manliness, that I find the chief analogy between Du Maurier's literature and his art. In all the long course of his dealing with the life of English society, I can think of but two or three instances of ungentleness. The humor which shone upon every rank, and every variety of character, never abashed the lowly, never insulted women, never betrayed the trust which reposed in its traditions of decency and generosity. If we think of any other caricaturist's art, how bitter it is apt to be, how brutal, how base! The cruelties that often pass for wit, even in the best of our own society satires, never tempted him to their ignoble exploitation; and as for the filthy drolleries of French wit, forever amusing itself with one commandment, how far they all are from him! His pictures are full of the dearest children, lovely young girls, honest young fellows; snobs who are as compassionable as they are despicable, bores who have their reason for being, hypocrites who are not beyond redemption. It is in his tolerance, his final pity of all life, that Du Maurier takes his place with the great talents; and it is in his sympathy for weakness, for the abased and outcast, that he classes himself with the foremost novelists of the age, not one of whom is recreant to the high office of teaching by parable that we may not profitably despise one another. Not even Svengali was beyond the pale of his mercy, and how well within it some other sorts of sinners were, the grief of very respectable people testified.

I will own myself that I like heroes and heroines to be born in wedlock when they conveniently can, and to keep true to it; but if an author wishes to suppose them otherwise I cannot proscribe them except for subsequent misbehavior in his hands. The trouble with Trilby was not that she was what she was imagined, but that finally the world could not imaginably act with regard to her as the author feigned. Such as she are to be forgiven, when they sin no more; not exalted and bowed down to by all manner of elect personages. But I fancy Du Maurier did not mean her to be an example. She had to be done something with, and after all she had suffered, it was not in the heart of poetic justice to deny her a little moriturary triumph.

Du Maurier was not a censor of morals, but of manners, which indeed are or ought to be the flower of morals, but not their root, and his deflections from the straight line in the destiny of his creations must not be too seriously regarded. I take it that the very highest fiction is that which treats itself as fact, and never once allows itself to be otherwise. This is the kind that the reader may well hold to the strictest accountability in all respects. But there is another kind capable of expressing an engaging beauty, and bewitchingly portraying many phases of life, which comes smiling to you or (in vulgar keeping) nudging you, and asking you to a game of make-believe. I do not object to that kind either, but I should not judge it on such high grounds as the other. I think it reached its perfect effect in Du Maurier's hands, and that this novelist, who wrote no fiction till nigh sixty, is the greatest master in that sort who ever lived, and I do not forget either Sterne or Thackeray when I say so.

III.

When I first spoke, long ago, of the confidential attitude of Thackeray, I said that now we would not endure it. But I was wrong, if I meant that more than the very small number who judge novels critically would be impatient of it. No sooner were those fearful words printed than I began to find, to my vast surprise, that the confidential attitude in Thackeray was what most pleased the greatest number of his readers. This gave me an ill opinion of their taste, but I could not deny the fact; and the obstreperous triumph of *Trilby*, which was one long confidence, has since contributed to render my defeat overwhelming. Du Maurier's use of the method, as he perfected it, was so charming that I am not sure but I began to be a little in love with it myself, though ordinarily superior to its blandishments. It was all very well to have Thackeray weep upon your neck over the fortunes of his characters, but if he had just been telling you they were puppets, it was not so gratifying; and as for poor Sterne, his sighs were so frankly insincere you could not believe anything he said. But Du Maurier came with another eye for life, with a faith of his own which you could share, and with a spirit which endeared him from the first. He had prodigious novelties in store: true-dreaming, hypnotism, and now (one does not know quite what yet) intelligence from the neighborly little planet Mars. He had the gift of persuading you that all his wonders were true, and his flattering familiarity of manner heightened the effect of his wonders, like that of the prestidigitator, who passes round in his audience, chatting pleasantly, while he pours twenty different liquors out of one magical bottle.

I would not count his beautiful talent at less than its rare worth, and if this figure belittles that, it does him wrong. Not before in our literature has anything more distinct, more individual, made itself felt. I have assumed to trace its descent, from this writer to that; but it was only partly so descended; in what made it surprising and captivating, it was heaven-descended. We shall be the lonelier and the poorer hereafter for the silence which is to be where George Du Maurier might have been.

35 'My Favorite Novelist and His Best Book'
1897

Published in *Munsey's*, April 1897.

An ostensible 'interview,' this was in fact what it appears to be—a lively, revealing essay done on professional assignment. Since the topic turns out to be *My Literary Passions* in miniature, it is instructive to catch the allegro pace and intellectual sparkle of Howells's style here in contrast to the rather legato beat and plain palette he presented to the *Ladies' Home Journal*. Not to understand the demands of organ, audience, and context is always to miss the point of Howells's style; and there always was a point.

For several years an interviewer and for decades an interviewee, Howells appears to have enjoyed simulating a job the most skilled of journalists might envy. What wonderful questions it is implied that he has asked to draw Mr Howells out! But since Howells could silently put the queries, he deployed himself to make useful points as well as have fun. He explains how it was with him and Dickens, Tolstoi, Thackeray. He explains how one moves from Turgenev to Tolstoi. He communicates his growing disillusion with German literature—and his reasons for preferring the Scandinavians. New names creep in: Kielland, Lie, Maarten Maartens, D'Annunzio, Maeterlinck, Sienkiewicz. Thence he leaps to confide that 'Thomas Hardy is the greatest novelist, by all odds, living today in England, and next to him . . . George Moore.'

He does not forget the Americans. There are fine new ones, as in Harold Frederic, *The Damnation of Theron Ware* or Henry B. Fuller, *With the Procession* and *The Cliff Dwellers*; and great ones—Twain's *Connecticut Yankee* he feels 'in its imaginative quality . . . curiously equal' to *Don Quixote*. But really, he perseveres, nationality no longer matters. Good work matters, whether from England or Kansas, New York or Georgia. And at present his favorites are Furman's *Stories of a Sanctified Town*, Crane's *Maggie*, Cahan's *Yekl*, and Jewett's *Country of the Pointed Firs*. The first, so far as I know, is now lost in the mists. But two of the others have become classics, and *Yekl* seems of late much more visible than it used to be.

To say something concerning novels, and particularly of my favorite among them? That is a difficult thing to do, for one's point of view changes so much from youth to middle age. One's favorite at twenty would not be one's favorite later; but I am pretty sure that throughout my life there has been an increasing preference for what seems to me *real* in fiction as against what seems to me *factitious*; and whilst I have been very fond, from time to time, of the pure romance, I have never cared for the romantic novel, since I was very young.

—I used to be extremely fond of what, perhaps, was a pretty true picture of life in its way—*Handy Andy*. It was one of the first novels I read, and it was an early favorite with me; and then I read others of Lover and Lever—their names are so much alike that I confound their novels as well. But before that I had favorite novels: the Indian and pioneer romances of Emerson Bennett, and, the very first of all, a story by Lowell's friend, George F. Briggs,[1] called *The Trippings of Tom Pepper*—I fancy still a pretty good story, though it is fifty years since I read it. It was not necessary, then, however, that a novel should be good in order to be my favorite. In fact, I am rather surprised that *Don Quixote* should have been my favorite about the same time, and that Poe's tales should have been equally my favorites.

As a boy, I liked Captain Marryat's novels ever so much. I have not read any of them since except *Jacob Faithful*; I read that about ten years ago, and was very much amused to find what hard reading it was, though as a boy I had found it so easy. All this may illustrate what I mean by a changed point of view.

Later, of course, I read Dickens, and with most passionate liking, for a long time. Within a little while past I have read a good part of *Our Mutual Friend*, *Bleak House*, and *David Copperfield*, and liked them still, but not with the old, or young ardor. You are always aware in Dickens, how he is 'making it up,' but he was a great master; and I suppose that *David Copperfield* is his most representative book, though there are some of his later novels, like the *Tale of Two Cities*, which are more shapely; but the English custom of novel publication was always against form, against balance. Dickens issued his novels, until he started *Household Words*, in numbers; George Eliot published hers in the same way, and I believe wrote them from month to month as they appeared, as Mr. Hardy still writes his. A novel was not completed when its publication began. In fact, from number to number the author hardly knew what was going to happen. In a letter to Forster, Dickens tells that he was once in a stationer's shop when a lady came in and asked whether a certain number of *David Copperfield* was out; it was to be the next, and he hadn't put pen to paper, or even imagined it fully. Such conditions are fatal to symmetry. But they were the economic conditions. That was the way the author could best make his living, and the way an artist can best make his living always tells upon his art.

—If I should say that I have now no favorite novelist I might be misunderstood, because that is one of those descriptive words that do not describe. I have a great many favorite novelists. But if there is one man who seems to me better than all the rest it is Tolstoy. I mean in his work in the novel, as distinguished from his work in those little moral tales or allegories of his. Those are marred by their extreme intentionality, or what the Spaniards call 'tendenciousness'; their purpose is too large for the covering of fiction. But when he has a story to tell, or a condition of things to set forth, or a character to portray—anything of that kind—I don't know anybody who has ever equaled him.

The novelist who was my favorite all through my early manhood was Thackeray, whom I don't now think the great artist I then did; indeed, I find him very much less an artist than Dickens. The plots of Dickens, to be sure, are not such as come out of his characters. The true plot comes out of the character; that is, the man does not result from the things he does, but the things he does result from the man, and so plot comes out of character; plot aforethought does not characterize. But Dickens believed it did, and all the romantic school of writers believed it did. Bulwer, Charles Reade, and even George Eliot, in some measure, thought so; but for all that—all that faking, that useless and false business of creating a plot and multiplying incidents—Dickens was the greater artist, because he could somehow make the thing transact itself. He got it to stand upon its legs and walk off. Thackeray is always holding his figures up from behind, and commenting upon them, and explaining them. In the midst of his narration he stops and writes little essays about his characters. That is the business of the critic, not the novelist. The business of the novelist is to put certain characters before you, and keep them before you, with as little of the author apparent as possible. In a play the people have no obvious interference from the author at all. Of course he creates them, but there is no comment; there can be none. The characters do it all. The novelist who carries the play method furthest is Tourguénief, and for a long time I preferred him to any other; he was the first Russian novelist I read, and on my revulsion from Thackeray, Tourguénief became my greatest favorite.

When I came to read Tolstoy, I modified the extreme preference

that I had for the dramatic conduct of the story. Tolstoy shows you
that a great deal of drama goes on in the mind all the time, which
can never be reported in the character's own words or intimated in his
actions, and must be given by the author. He is a man without any
artifice at all, so that whatever he permits himself to do in any direction counts for very much. He gives this tacit drama very simply,
very ingenuously, and not consciously, with a wink to the reader.
Anna Karénina was the first novel of Tolstoy's that I read, and I
was struck from the very first sentence with the absolute truth of the
thing. There wasn't any question in my mind, when I read the book,
but that it was the greatest novel I had yet read. I do not know
whether I should think so now, but that was my point of view ten
years ago. Afterwards I read *War and Peace*, which confirmed me
in what I had felt concerning Tolstoy. Then I read a good many
minor novels of his, like *The Cossacks* (one of his earlier and very best
stories), and whatever else of his I could lay my hands on, with an
increasing sense of his supremacy.

There are perhaps as great talents as Tolstoy, who have written
fiction, but none in such rare combination with conscience. It is an
unspeakable comfort to come for once upon a prime talent with no
mixture of falsehood in it. He makes you feel that war is always ugly
and horrible, and that love itself is hateful when it involves untruth of
any kind, as guilty love always does. Tolstoy never preaches, in his
novels, but you cannot escape the meaning of his facts. He puts
honesty and kindness above all heroism, and while he condemns no
sinner, he never for a moment allows you to wish you were this or that
kind of sinner. Many novelists do this, and some novelists exalt
homicide and adultery.

—One reason, perhaps, why I have no favorite among German
novelists is that there do not seem to be any. Looking back into the
past, I think that *Wilhelm Meister* gave me a sense of possible largeness and scope in the novel which I had not before, but its art is imperfect and at times even crude. It was once my favorite novel; I
liked it as much at one time, as I liked *Japheth in Search of a Father* at
another. I cannot explain the fact that a great nation like Germany has
no representative novelist at present. It is very curious. There was a
German critic whom I met in Florence some years ago—an exceedingly able man, and an editor of one of their chief literary journals—
who talked of that very matter. He was inclined to attribute it to the
over education of the Germans, which extinguished their originality
and incentive in great measure, or so much so that they no longer had

the creative impulse. He was inclined, also, to attribute something to the excessive militarism of the German life, which is intensely scientific.

I should not say that a novelist can be over educated, or that he can know too much. In fact, there is nothing a novelist knows that does not 'fay in'; he cannot know too much. But he can be over trained. I suppose over training of the mind tells upon its powers just as over training of the muscles tells upon them. The muscularly over trained man is a weak man, and it is quite imaginable that there should be some such result mentally from the system of German training. Still it remains a strange thing that so vast an empire produces no fiction valued now in the literary world. The Germans translate everything, they criticise everything, they know everything; but they don't invent anything. There is that little country, Norway, just north of them, that Germany could take in the hollow of her hand and crush without feeling it more than a man in crushing a mosquito, but Norway is infinitely beyond her in fiction. What splendid things she has done in Ibsen, Kielland, Björnson, Lie!—I speak of the ones I know. Yet there are the Danes, of the same race as the Norwegians, and speaking and writing the same language, but they do not produce great fiction. There is one admirable Danish story I have read lately, but it is the only one I know of. I am told there is a large group of subordinate Danish writers who do very good work, and who feel the influence of the French very deeply, but they do not count as compared with the Norwegians, although they are essentially the same people, living under very nearly the same conditions. There is something—what you may call the new spirit—which tells. Denmark is a conservative country, where people enjoy as high a degree of liberty as we do here, for all I know. But it is quiet; everything is established; there is no change, no struggle. In Norway there has been a great upheaval; they have abolished titles; they have made the structure of society far more democratic even than ours; they are always fighting their king. Their authors went back to the sources of literature—the language of the people. They studied the diction of the peasants. They rebuilt the language from the ground up; and all that is the effect of the new spirit. Norway has become almost a new country—it has been made over.

Oddly enough, though there are no German novelists to speak of, there are very good Dutch ones. Maarten Maartens, who writes in English, is perhaps the first of them; and he is my favorite novelist while I am reading him. If you come to fiction in the form of drama, I have even my German favorites—Sudermann, for instance, and Hauptmann.

—It is rather difficult to say what nation is making the deepest impression today in the world of fiction. The Russians are rather quiescent, and the time of the Norwegian school has passed a little, though Kielland is coming forward, and every now and then Björnson publishes a book, or Ibsen brings out a play which is very important. Just at this moment I suppose the most noticeable novelist is Gabriele d'Annunzio, the Italian. I haven't read any of his books; but there is one great novelist in Italy, Giovanni Verga, whom I admire extremely. He is as good, in some of his work, as the Norwegians, and as simple. *The House by the Medlar Tree* is one of his best stories. He has written a great deal about the life of the peasants of Sicily and Naples; and nearly all that I have read of him has gone to make him my favorite.

But no nation is doing better work in fiction today than the Spanish. Of course you will allow for my liking one kind of novel and not the other; the romantic school does not count with me, for what is not true is not artistic, and so I leave out romantic fiction. Luckily for me, the Spaniards are altogether realistic. The one who pleases me best of all is Valdés, but in some respects Galdós is quite as great as he, if not greater. Valdés has much more humor; both picture the modern Spanish life and manners. Some of their stories are intolerably painful; some extremely amusing. They are all very *actual*. The Spanish novelists often touch upon the relation of the church to modern life. In his *Scum*, Valdés shows how fashionable life in Spain, as in all countries, is a life of conformity to the church and to the outward observances of religion. Galdós shows you how the old spirit remains in a good many cases, especially with women—the intolerant spirit—the cabined, cribbed, confined spirit of the old religiosity of Spain, of the Catholic Puritanism; and he contrasts that with the modern scientific spirit in some of his young men. You would be surprised at the boldness with which he treats these matters. Then, besides these two, there is a great woman living in Spain who writes excellent novels of the same kind; I mean Emilia Pardo-Bazan. These are all three my favorite novelists. They seem to have the new spirit, but just how, in their moribund country, I should be at a loss to say.

—As to the French school, I can speak only of the realistic side of it, because I do not care for the other French novels, and do not read them. It is in a sort of abeyance. My favorite Daudet does not write any more; my favorite Flaubert is long dead; and my favorite

Maupassant is lately dead. My favorite Zola lives, but he has fought his battle, and is not the force he was. The mystical dramas of Maeterlinck have a great charm for me.

Lately I got hold of a novel by a Polish novelist, Sinkiewicz, which instantly became my favorite. It is a novel of modern Polish life, and I imagine pictures very faithfully the society of Poland at this moment. It is altogether non political. It does not inquire whether the Poles are rightfully or wrongfully under the domination of Russia, but has to do with their society life. The scene is principally in Warsaw, but often again in Italy. It is a very strong novel—a huge canvas with a multitude of figures in it, all very life-like, and all acting from real motives. It is quite Russian in its artistic and ethical spirit, and it is still a favorite novel of mine. I suppose I am rather impulsive about things I like. I value them very much or not at all, and that story I liked vastly.

—I think Thomas Hardy is the greatest novelist, by all odds, living today in England, and next to him, or with him, I should put George Moore. I found *Esther Waters* one of the truest novels I had read. If you have read it, and like it, you will understand what I mean by a *real* thing as compared with a *made up* thing. As to *Trilby*, it is *sui generis*. Two thirds of the story were charming, but the last third of it was impossible—I mean as to what would probably have grown out of such a character. I do not object to the hypnotism; I like the mystical very much; what I do object to is making church and state and society bow down to *Trilby*, and making her die in the odor of sanctity! She was simple, honest, and natural, but nothing of that would have happened. Till it came to that *Trilby* was my favorite novel, as *Peter Ibbetson* was before it. I like Thomas Hardy's *Jude*. It deals very daringly with life, but it seems to me it deals honestly; it ventures far, but I believe, with Tolstoy, that anything which treats faithfully of life cannot be immoral, no matter how far it ventures.

—The novels of incident, of adventure, do not interest me. But I do not believe their authors write simply for popularity, or for the moment. I believe they do the thing they like to do; but the thing they do is worthless, as far as I am concerned. I am not sure that I am quite logical in not caring for novels of adventure, for I am very fond of the circus, and like to see people flying through the air; and I would go to a fire, any day.

—As to what I once said about our not being able to throw off the yoke of England intellectually, although we had long ago done so politically, I did not mean so much our fiction as our criticism.

American fiction is as free as it can very well be. We do not take the word from anybody; but English taste influences our criticism. If you had a vote of the critics in the United States today, it would declare by a large majority for the romantic novel, which is distinctly a second rate novel, judging it by the quality of the men who produce it. It would be the same in England, where the novel of that sort continues to be taken seriously, though there is no other country in Europe where it could possibly be taken seriously. But the English are so far behind that they prefer a novel of that sort. They are a very romantic people.

I should say that America was still coming, in fiction. Certainly it is not such a long time since we began to come that we should have stopped already. After the war there was a prodigious impulse in every direction, and it was felt in the arts as well as in affairs. We began to do new things, and, I think, some greater things than had been done here before, though not such perfect things. There has never been anything more perfect, and I doubt if there ever will be, in its way, than the romance of Hawthorne. The romance—which is not at all the romantic novel—has just as good right to be as the realistic novel, because it is just as true in its kind. The romance and the poem are of the same blood. I always liked Hawthorne because he seemed to me to be true, and to wish always to be so. I suppose I should be considered rather odd if I said that I preferred the *Blithedale Romance* to his other books, but I do.

Until after the war we had no real novels in this country, except *Uncle Tom's Cabin*. That is one of the great novels of the world, and of all time. Even the fact that slavery was done away with does not matter; the interest in *Uncle Tom's Cabin* never will pass, because the book is really as well as ideally true to human nature, and nobly true. It is the only great novel of ours before the war that I can think of. The romances of Hawthorne I do not call novels; but they are my favorite romances.

—I hardly know how much the age of a country affects fiction, but the novel does not come first in any civilization. Spain is an old country, and England is an old country, and Norway and Russia; they are all old countries, but they all have in some sort the new spirit. As I have said before, we are a condition of the English people in literature —a branch of them, just as Australia is, or as India is, so far as Kipling represents it. What we have here today, after all, is a fresh impulse of a kind in English fiction that has always existed. For instance, we haven't anything more realistic in the work of today than Defoe's novels. They are as real as anything can be; even *Robinson Crusoe* is realistically worked out. The tradition of the realistic novel has never been lost in England. Goldsmith's *Vicar of Wakefield*, up to the point where he has to make it 'end well,' is realistic. By the way, that is my favorite novel, up to the point in question.

When you come to Jane Austen, there is nothing more faithful than her work. She is one of the very greatest of English novelists, for that reason, and decidedly my favorite. She wrote very few books, but every one of them was very good. All were of the quietest, and you might say the narrowest life, the life of the small country gentry; but every fact was perfectly ascertained, every phase truthfully reflected.

—There is always a question, you know, as to what is the 'great world.' Of course there are certain novelists who prefer to deal with very poor, common people, and they are sometimes so great themselves that they make you feel that the great world is among such people. Tolstoy makes you think it is. The books of Thomas Hardy deal mostly with country life, and often with poor, common people, and when they do rise above that level they do not rise very high. He has very few lords and ladies in his books; but farmers and peasants, and tradesmen and artisans, and all kinds of people who are not of the finer world, abound; and yet I should think meanly of a man's mind who does not appreciate Hardy's books or who does not feel that he is a great novelist.

Barrie, in that little village of Thrums of which he wrote, makes you feel that the great world is there, while you are reading. There is really nothing larger than the human interest. The rest of the Scotch school *is* somewhat because Barrie *was*. I do not mean to say that the others imitated him, but his was the voice that called them into voice. They have all a dry humor at times that is very relishing. But what strikes me chiefly about all the Scotch is their extreme sentimentality, and I believe that is what makes them liked. We suppose the Scot to be a very hard headed person, but along with his hard headedness he is sentimental, just as the Englishman is romantic. We Americans are not a very sentimental people of ourselves. Only the cheaper sort of us talk sentiment, but every man likes to have his heart strings wrung, and to be made to cry; if he has cried over something he respects himself; he thinks he must be a man of very fine feelings when he cries, and it must be a fine thing that makes him cry. The Scotchmen deserve their success in a certain way, although they have not achieved all of it; a certain mood has lent itself to them. Barrie's short stories are mighty good; they have form; they have almost as good form as the American short story. But when you come to compare the short stories of the Scotch generally with those of the Americans, I don't think the Scotch are 'in it.'

—That group of our American writers is very extraordinary, and to me delightful. Their faculty—their art, their kind of writing—shows itself in every part of the country. It is not in New England alone—although they survive with great strength in New England—that you find it, but everywhere. Their forte lies in their ability to see large or little aspects of life, and to represent them on small canvases. I was talking lately with a man who has written some excellent short stories, and is always hoping to write a large story—a novel—because he thinks that he does not get himself or his subject all in; and I asked him what was his feeling about it. I said, 'Is the short story a statuette?' 'Yes,' he said, 'it is a statuette.' But we make wonderfully good statuettes. Our short story gives an impression in literature as adequate as those little things the Russians do in sculpture.

—I do not mean Bret Harte's. He belongs to the romantic period. He is a poet of rare quality, and a delightful humorist, but as a novelist he is of the time when it was felt that people must have something extraordinary happen to them or through them. The best writers recognize now that what interests us in a fellow being is some property of his mind or character. This does not appear through his dying all over the place, to save some one's life or reputation, or being taken out and hanged, or getting the drop on his neighbor. Still, Mr. Harte is a most uncommon talent, and when I think over his best work, I find him always my favorite.

—By the way, there is a kind of interest that seems, now, to be rather dropped out of the novels, except for Du Maurier's recent use of it. I mean the supernatural. Perhaps this has happened from the general decay of faith in the supernatural. Ghosts are not employed any more because people so largely disbelieve in the other life. If you do not believe men live again, where are you to get your ghosts from? Even if people still believe, they do not conjecture so much as formerly about a future life, and consequently the supernatural that used to come into fiction, comes seldom now. In the plays of Shakspere ghosts are brought in as simply as living men. The ghost of *Hamlet's* father appears; there is nothing extraordinary about that! Why not? Then in *Macbeth*, and in *Julius Cæsar*, how natural all the supernatural business is! It is done—not with artlessness, because Shakspere knew what he was about every moment—but with perfect singleness and entire faith. No doubt Shakspere himself thoroughly believed in ghosts. Most people at that time did, just as now they do not. I wish it could come again—the supernatural. I should welcome the ghosts back, though spiritualism has made them so cheap and vulgar. They ought to be some subjective sort of ghosts, though faith in the life hereafter will come again in some form or other; we are really so deeply concerned in it that we cannot give it up; and then it will be the ghosts' turn.

—I will tell you of some novels I have been recently reading, and like very much. I like *The Damnation of Theron Ware*. I think that a very well imagined book. It treats of middle New York State life at the present day, such as Mr. Frederic had treated of before, in *Seth's Brother's Wife*, and in *The Lawton Girl*. I was particularly interested in the book, for when you get to the end, although you have carried a hazy notion in your mind of the sort of man *Ware* was, you fully realize, for the first time, that the author has never for a moment represented him anywhere to you as a good or honest man, or as anything but a very selfish man. And there is a fresh and probable type of the Irish girl of the second or third American generation very well divined, who is the heroine of the novel, so far as there is one. I should not think the book would please either Catholics or Protestants, as such, and yet it is a book of great power, and, as I say of all realistic books, I think it is a very moral book. It makes you wish to be quite clean and honest if you can.

I am just now reading over again some stories of Mark Twain. There are no better books in their way than *Tom Sawyer* and *Huckleberry Finn*. They are about the honestest boys' books I know; and *A Connecticut Yankee at King Arthur's Court* is delicious. I was thinking this morning that one of the differences between the romantic and realistic was that the realistic finds a man's true character under all accidents and under all circumstances, while romanticism, even when it takes ordinary circumstances, seems to miss character; and in reading this romance of Mark Twain's—it is a pure romance—the *Connecticut Yankee*, I feel under all its impossibilities that it is true to the character of that man and true to all the conditions. You know how he imagines him—a Yankee from East Hartford, who finds himself, by some witchery, in the England of King Arthur's time. He always distinctly belongs to this period, and the Arthurian people are always their own kind of Britons. The book is not consecrated by time or by consensus of the world's liking, as *Don Quixote* is, but in its imaginative quality. I find the two curiously equal. The scheme of carrying a contemporary Yankee into the age of chivalry is just as delightful as Cervantes' conception of bringing a knight errant into his own period. In fact, it merely reverses the process.

—As to the future of this country in the field of fiction, I always say that I am no prophet, but I do not see why we should not go forward. I rather fancy that the chances are in favor of novelists who come up remote from literary centers, and who stay away from them. Partly for that reason, I think the man who has one of the best chances now, having caught the ear of the best public, is Henry B. Fuller, who wrote my favorite novels, *With the Procession*, and *The Cliff Dwellers*. I have heard that the Chicago people do not like his books, but the question with them ought to have been whether he did what he attempted truly, instead of whether he portrayed all of Chicago, or Chicago as they would have preferred to see it. It seems to me that he is distinctly part of the future, and also a very considerable part of the present.

According to my way of thinking there is no section of the United States that can claim to be the real literary center. We have two or three publishing centers, Philadelphia, New York, and Boston, and Chicago is growing to be a publishing center; but I should not call them literary centers, for if you count up the literary people that live away from those cities, you will find there are very many. There is no especial incentive to literature in any of them. Of course I do not expect anybody to agree with my speculations, and I must say I find usually that people do not agree with them in the least. One man's guessing is as good as another's when it comes to prophecy, and there is no telling but we may have a literary center tomorrow.

I do not think there is any danger of the United States falling behind in literature. There were some obvious effects of the international copyright law against us, at first, but they were temporary. There was a period of two or three years when our people preferred English authors, but the time seems to have come again now for Americans. What we want is good work, no matter where it is from. I like good work that comes from England, and I like good work that comes from Kansas or Georgia; I like it just as well as I like the good work that comes from New York, not more and not less, though it sometimes interests me a little more because it is fresher, if it comes from far.

—If I must return to the question of my favorites in fiction, *The Damnation of Theron Ware* is just now my favorite, and so is *The Connecticut Yankee*. So, for that matter, are Miss Furman's *Stories of a Sanctified Town*. So is Stephen Crane's *Maggie*, so is Abraham

Cahan's *Yekl*, so is Miss Jewett's *Country of the Pointed Firs*. But I change, or else it is the books that change, and I cannot say what my favorite will be tomorrow.

NOTE

1 Charles F. Briggs (1804–47) was the friend of Lowell who wrote *The Trippings of Tom Pepper: Or The Result of Romancing. An Autobiography by Harry Franco*, Part 1, 1847; Part II, 1850.

36 'Edward Bellamy'
1898

Published in the *Atlantic*, August 1898.

The biographer of Howells must struggle against the handicap that he outlived almost all his friends and there is, for instance, no wonderfully revealing confession by Clemens called 'Howells to Me.' Longevity permitted Howells to write the unmatched chapters of *Literary Friends and Acquaintance* (including in the Library Edition 'A Belated Guest' [Bret Harte] and *My Mark Twain*). It also enabled him to write a series of excellent critical memoirs—chapters toward what he once proposed but never completed as 'A Personal History of American Literature.' The present elegant, probing summation of Edward Bellamy stands among these, quite competent to speak for itself.

The first book of Edward Bellamy's which I read was *Dr. Heidenhoff's Process*, and I thought it one of the finest feats in the region of romance which I had known. It seemed to me all the greater because the author's imagination wrought in it on the level of average life, and built the fabric of its dream out of common clay. The simple people and their circumstances were treated as if they were persons whose pathetic story he had witnessed himself, and he was merely telling it. He wove into the texture of their sufferings and their sorrows the magic thread of invention so aptly and skillfully that the reader felt nothing improbable in it. One even felt a sort of moral necessity for it, as if such a clue not only could be, but must be given for their escape. It became not merely probable, but imperative, that there should be some means of extirpating the memory which fixed a sin in lasting remorse, and of thus saving the soul from the depravity of despair. When it finally appeared that there was no such means, one reader, at least, was inconsolable. Nothing from romance remains to me more poignant than the pang that this plain, sad tale imparted.

The art employed to accomplish its effect was the art which

Bellamy had in degree so singular that one might call it supremely his. He does not so much transmute our every-day reality to the substance of romance as make the airy stuff of dreams one in quality with veritable experience. Every one remembers from *Looking Backward* the allegory which figures the pitiless prosperity of the present conditions as a coach drawn by slaves under the lash of those on its top, who have themselves no firm hold upon their places, and sometimes fall, and then, to save themselves from being ground under the wheels, spring to join the slaves at the traces. But it is not this, vivid and terrible as it is, which most wrings the heart; it is that moment of anguish at the close, when Julian West trembles with the nightmare fear that he has been only dreaming of the just and equal future, before he truly wakes and finds that it is real. That is quite as it would happen in life, and the power to make the reader feel this like something he has known himself is the distinctive virtue of that imagination which revived throughout Christendom the faith in a millennium.

A good deal has been said against the material character of the happiness which West's story promises men when they shall begin to do justice, and to share equally in the fruits of the toil which operates life; and I confess that this did not attract me. I should have preferred, if I had been chooser, to have the millennium much simpler, much more independent of modern inventions, modern conveniences, modern facilities. It seemed to me that in an ideal condition (the only condition finally worth having) we should get on without most of these things, which are but sorry patches on the rags of our outworn civilization, or only toys to amuse our greed and vacancy. Æsthetically, I sympathized with those select spirits who were shocked that nothing better than the futile luxury of their own selfish lives could be imagined for the lives which overwork and underpay had forbidden all pleasures; I acquired considerable merit with myself by asking whether the hope of these formed the highest appeal to human nature. But I overlooked an important condition which the other critics overlooked; I did not reflect that such things were shown as merely added unto those who had first sought the kingdom of God and his righteousness, and that they were no longer vicious or even so foolish when they were harmlessly come by. I have since had to own that the joys I thought trivial and sordid did rightly, as they did most strenuously, appeal to the lives hitherto starved of them. In depicting them as the common reward of the common endeavor Edward Bellamy builded better than we knew, whether he knew better or not, and he builded from a thorough sense of that level of humanity which he was destined so potently to influence,—that American level which his book found in every Christian land.

I am not sure whether this sense was ever a full consciousness with him; very possibly it was not; but in any case it was the spring of all his work, from the earliest to the latest. Somehow, whether he *knew* or not, he unerringly *felt* how the average man would feel; and all the webs of fancy that he wove were essentially of one texture through this sympathy. His imagination was intensely democratic, it was in-alienably plebeian, even,—that is to say, humane. It did not seek distinction of expression; it never put the simplest and plainest reader to shame by the assumption of those fine-gentleman airs which abash and dishearten more than the mere literary swell can think. He would use a phrase or a word that was common to vulgarity, if it said what he meant; sometimes he sets one's teeth on edge, in his earlier stories, by his public school diction. But the nobility of the heart is never absent from his work; and he has always the distinction of self-forgetfulness in his art.

I have been interested, in recurring to his earlier work, to note how almost entirely the action passes in the American village atmosphere. It is like the greater part of his own life in this. He was not a man ignorant of other keeping. He was partly educated abroad, and he knew cities both in Europe and in America. He was a lawyer by profession, and he was sometime editor of a daily newspaper in a large town. But I remember how, in one of our meetings, he spoke with distrust and dislike of the environment of cities as unwholesome and distracting, if not demoralizing (very much to the effect of Tolstoy's philosophy in the matter), and in his short stories his types are village types. They are often such when he finds them in the city, but for much the greater part he finds them in the village; and they are always, therefore, distinctively American; for we are village people far more than we are country people or city people. In this as in everything else we are a medium race, and it was in his sense, if not in his knowledge of this fact, that Bellamy wrote so that there is never a word or a look to the reader implying that he and the writer are of a different sort of folk from the people in the story.

Looking Backward, with its material delights, its communized facilities and luxuries, could not appeal to people on lonely farms who scarcely knew of them, or to people in cities who were tired of them, so much as to that immense average of villagers, of small-town-dwellers, who had read much and seen something of them, and desired to have them. This average, whose intelligence forms the prosperity of our literature, and whose virtue forms the strength of our nation, is the environment which Bellamy rarely travels out of in his airiest romance. He has its curiosity, its principles, its aspirations. He can tell what it wishes to know, what problem will hold it, what situation it can enter into, what mystery will fascinate it, and what noble pain it will bear. It is by far the widest field of American fiction; most of our finest artists work preferably in it, but he works in it to different effect from any other. He takes that life on its mystical side, and deals with types rather than with characters; for it is one of the prime conditions of the romancer that he shall do this. His people are less objectively than subjectively present; their import is greater in what happens to them than in what they are. But he never falsifies them or their circumstance. He ascertains them with a fidelity that seems almost helpless, almost ignorant of different people, different circumstance; you would think at times that he had never known, never seen, any others; but of course this is only the effect of his art.

When it comes to something else, however, it is still with the same fidelity that he keeps to the small-town average, the American average. He does not address himself more intelligently to the mystical side of this average in *Dr. Heidenhoff's Process*, or *Miss Ludington's Sister*, or any of his briefer romances, than to its ethical side in *Equality*. That book disappointed me, to be frank. I thought it artistically inferior to anything else he had done. I thought it was a mistake to have any story at all in it, or not to have vastly more. I felt that it was not enough to clothe the dry bones of its sociology with paper garments out of *Looking Backward*. Except for that one sublime moment when the workers of all sorts cry to the Lords of the Bread to take them and use them at their own price, there was no thrill or throb in the book. But I think now that any believer in its economics may be well content to let them take their chance with the American average, here and elsewhere, in the form that the author has given them. He felt that average so wittingly that he could not have been wrong in approaching it with all that public school exegesis which wearies such dilettanti as myself.

Our average is practical as well as mystical; it is first the dust of the earth, and then it is a living soul; it likes great questions simply and familiarly presented, before it puts its faith in them and makes its faith a life. It likes to start to heaven from home, and in all this Bellamy was of it, voluntarily and involuntarily. I recall how, when we first met, he told me that he had come to think of our hopeless conditions suddenly, one day, in looking at his own children, and reflecting that he could not place them beyond the chance of want by any industry or forecast or providence; and that the status meant the same impossibility for others which it meant for him. I understood then that I was in the presence of a man too single, too sincere, to pretend that he had begun by thinking of others, and I trusted him the more for his confession of a selfish premise. He never went back to himself in his endeavor, but when he had once felt his power in the world, he dedicated his life to his work. He wore himself out in thinking and feeling about it, with a belief in the good time to come that penetrated his whole being and animated his whole purpose, but apparently with no manner of fanaticism. In fact, no one could see him, or look into his quiet, gentle face, so full of goodness, so full of common sense, without perceiving that he had reasoned to his hope for justice in the frame of things. He was indeed a most practical, a most American man, without a touch of sentimentalism in his humanity. He believed that some now living should see his dream—the dream of Plato, the dream of the first Christians, the dream of Bacon, the dream of More—come true in a really civilized society; but he had the patience and courage which could support any delay.

These qualities were equal to the suffering and the death which came to him in the midst of his work, and cut him off from writing that *one more book* with which every author hopes to round his career. He suffered greatly, but he bore his suffering greatly; and as for his death, it is told that when, toward the last, those who loved him were loath to leave him at night alone, as he preferred to be left, he asked, 'What can happen to me? I can only die.'

I am glad that he lived to die at home in Chicopee,—in the village environment by which he interpreted the heart of the American nation, and knew how to move it more than any other American author who has lived. The theory of those who think differently is that he simply moved the popular fancy; and this may suffice to explain the state of some people, but it will not account for the love and honor in which his name is passionately held by the vast average, East and West. His fame is safe with them, and his faith is an animating force concerning whose effect at this time or some other time it would not be wise to prophesy. Whether his ethics will keep his æsthetics in remembrance I do not know; but I am sure that one cannot acquaint one's self with his merely artistic work, and not be sensible that in Edward Bellamy we were rich in a romantic imagination surpassed only by that of Hawthorne.

37 'An Opportunity for American Fiction' [Thorstein Veblen]

1899

Published in *Literature*, 28 April and 5 May 1899.

In the wake of his rather odd experience with the *Cosmopolitan*, Howells wrote a series of explicit radical essays, declarations of opinion and belief which have gone strangely unmentioned in the public tradition of the author. Though there exist fifteen or twenty of these, the Altrurian 'letters' aside, the heart of his belief in a radically democratic and non-violent socialism lies revealed in four essays: 'Are We a Plutocracy?' (February 1894), 'Equality as the Basis of Good Society' (November 1894), 'The Nature of Liberty' (December 1895), and 'Who Are Our Brethren?' (April 1896). Published amid the turmoil of the second presidentiad of Grover Cleveland when the nation was swinging decisively toward the right, these were essays with an impact sought eagerly by the editors of *Forum*, *Century*, and the *North American Review*. Howells stood a significant figure in national and international circles of social concern.

When, therefore, one of the most prepotent of all American documents of social thought appeared—Thorstein Veblen, *The Theory of the Leisure Class*—Howells was alert to discover it and, as Veblen's biographer says, not only help make it 'a sensation' but help 'to set the fashion of interpreting it.'[1] Howells could do that not only because he had been making explicit his own position but because in a line of pioneering novels between *Annie Kilburn*, 1889, and *The Landlord at Lion's Head*, 1897, he had anticipated much of Veblen's mood and no few of Veblen's ideas. He was prepared to fight the Harpers' office (and did so) for the right to use his column in *Literature*, and use it twice, to announce, praise, and explain another major document in American intellectual history.

One of the most interesting books which has fallen in my way since I read *The Workers* of Mr. Wyckoff is Mr. Thorstein Veblen's *Theory of a Leisure Class* (Macmillan's). It does for the idlers in terms of cold, scientific analysis the office which Mr. Wyckoff's book dramatically performs for the workers; and I think that it is all the more

286

important because it deals, like that book, with a class newly circumstanced rather than newly conditioned. The workers and the idlers of America are essentially the same as the workers and the idlers of Occidental civilization everywhere; but there is a novelty in their environment peculiarly piquant to the imagination. In the sociological region the spectacle has for the witness some such fascination as geological stratification would have for the inquirer if he could look on at its processes; and it is apparently with as strong a zest as this would inspire that Mr. Veblen considers the nature and the growth of the leisure class among us.

His name is newer to me than it should be, or than it will hereafter be to any student of our *status*; but it must be already well known to those whose interests or pleasures have led them into the same field of inquiry. To others, like myself, the clear method, the graphic and easy style, and the delightful accuracy of characterization will be part of the surprise which the book has to offer. In the passionless calm with which the author pursues his investigation there is apparently no *animus* for or against a leisure class. It is his affair simply to find out how and why and what it is. If the result is to leave the reader with a feeling which the author never shows, that seems to be solely the effect of the facts. But I have no purpose, as I doubt if I have the qualification, to criticize the book, and it is only with one of its manifold suggestions that this notice will concern itself.

The suggestion, which is rather a conclusion, is the curious fact, noted less securely and less scientifically before, that the flower of the American leisure class does not fruit in its native air, and perhaps cannot yet perpetuate itself on our soil. In other words, the words of Mr. Veblen, 'the English leisure class being, for purposes of reputable usage, the upper leisure class of this country,' the extraordinary impulse among us toward the aristocraticization of society can as yet fulfil itself only in monarchical conditions. A conspicuous proof of this is the frequent intermarriage of our moneyed bourgeoisie with the English aristocracy, and another proof, less conspicuous, is the frequent absenteeism of our rich people. The newspapers from time to time make a foolish and futile clamour about both these things, as if they were abnormal, or as if they were not the necessary logic of great wealth and leisure in a democracy. Such things result as infallibly from wealth and leisure as indigence and servility, and are in no wise to be deprecated. They are only representations on a wider stage of the perpetual and universal drama of our daily life. The man who makes money in a small town goes into the nearest large town to spend it, that is, to waste it—waste in some form or other being the corollary of wealth—and he seeks to marry his children there into rich and old families. He does this from the instinct of self-preservation, which is as strong in classes as in individuals; if he has made his money in a large town, he goes to some such inland metropolis as Chicago to waste his wealth and to marry his children above him. The Chicago, and San Francisco, and St. Louis, and Cleveland millionaires come to New York with the same ambitions and purposes. But these are all intermediate stages in the evolution of the American magnate. At every step he discovers that he is less and less in his own country, that he is living in a provisional exile, and that his true home is in monarchical conditions, where his future establishes itself often without his willing it, and sometimes against his willing it. The American life is the life of labor, and he is now of the life of leisure, or if he is not, his wife is, his daughters and his sons are. The logic of their existence, which they cannot struggle against, and on which all the fatuous invective of pseudo public spirit launches itself effectlessly, is intermarriage with the European aristocracies, and residence abroad. Short of this there is no rest, and can be none for the American leisure class. This may not be its ideal, but it is its destiny.

It is far the most dramatic social fact of our time, and if some man of creative imagination were to seize upon it, he would find in it the material of that great American novel which, after so much travail, has not yet seen the light. It is, above all our other facts, synthetic; it sums up and includes in itself the whole American story; the relentless will, the tireless force, the vague ideal, the inexorable destiny, the often bewildered acquiescence. If the novelist were a man of very great imagination indeed, he might forecast a future in which the cycle would round itself, and our wealth would return from European sojourn, and dwell among us again, bringing its upper class with it, so that we should have a leisure class ultimated and established on our own ground. But for my part I should prefer the novel which kept itself entirely to the actualities, and studied in them the most profoundly interesting spectacle which life has ever offered to the art of fiction, with elements of equal tragedy and comedy, and a pathos through all which must be expressed, if the full significance of the spectacle were to be felt.

Mr. Thorstein Veblen does not evolve his Theory of a Leisure Class from his knowledge of that class in America alone. Until very lately we had no such class, and we rather longed for it. We thought it would edify us, or, if not that, at least ornament us; but now that we have got it, on certain terms, we can hardly be sure that it does either. The good things that we expected of it have not come to pass, and perhaps it is too soon; but in Mr. Veblen's analysis our leisure class does not seem essentially different from any of the older aristocracies, which seem not to have brought to pass the good things expected of them and often attributed to them. As with these, 'pecuniary emulation' and 'conspicuous leisure' are the first evidences of its superiority, and 'conspicuous consumption,' direct or delegated in the splendid apparelling and housing of its women and its dependents, is one of the gross means of striking the popular imagination. The 'pecuniary standard of living' is really the only standard, and the 'pecuniary canons of taste' are finally the only canons; for if the costly things are not always beautiful, all beautiful things which are cheap must be rejected because they are not costly. 'Dress as an expression of pecuniary culture' is left in our day mostly to women by the leisure class; but the men of that class share in it at least as fully as in the 'devout observances' and 'the higher learning.' Both sexes in our leisure class, as in the European aristocracies, are distinguished by the love of sport, in which they prolong their own childhood and the childhood of the race, and they are about equally devoted to the opera and the fine arts, as these minister to their magnificence. It would be hard, in fact, to draw the line between our leisure class and any aristocracy in the traits of piety, predacity, courage, prowess, charity, luxury, conservatism, authority, and the other virtues and vices which have characterized the patricians in all times. The most notable difference, and the difference which would most invite the study of the novelist, is that hitherto our leisure class has had no political standing. It has had no place in the civic mechanism; but we seem to be at the moment when this is beginning to be less apparently so. It is idle to suppose, because the leisure class, which with us is the moneyed class, does not hold public offices, that it does not control public affairs; and possibly it has always controlled them more than we have imagined. The present proof is in the fact that the industrial classes, with all the means of power in their hands, are really powerless in any contest with a group of rich men; it is almost impossible for the people to baulk the purpose of such a group; to undo what money has done has been so impossible, with all the apparatus of the elections, the Legislatures, the Courts, that there is hardly yet an instance of the kind in our history.

All this, however, makes the situation the more attractive to a novelist of imaginative force. This is the most dramatic moment, the most psychological moment which has ever offered itself to fiction; this is the supreme opportunity of the American novelist. Hitherto our politics have repelled the artist by their want of social complexity, by their rude simplicity, as a fight between parties. But if he can look at the situation from the point of view suggested, as an inevitable result from the nature of the class which Mr. Veblen has studied, I believe he will find it full of charm. If he is psychologist enough he will be fascinated by the operation of the silent forces which are, almost unconsciously, working out the permanency of a leisure class, and preparing for it in our own circumstance the ultimation it now seeks elsewhere. But I should be content if he would portray the life of our leisure class without an eye to such implications, with an eye merely to its superficial facts. If he did this he would appeal to the widest general interests in our reading public. Our appetite for everything that relates to the life removed from the life of work, from the simple Republican ideal, is almost insatiable. It strives to satisfy itself, in plays and romances, with the doings of princes and nobles in realms as surely fictitious as Lilliput and Brobdignag; it gluts itself, in the newspapers, with fables almost as gross as Gulliver's concerning the social affairs of our leisure class. Seen truly and reproduced faithfully, these would be extremely interesting, and the field they offer to inquiry is almost wholly unexplored. Our fiction has brought pretty fully into literature the country and village life of the Americans of all sections. We know this from our short stories in New England, in the South, in the middle and farther West, and on the Pacific Slope; and in a certain measure our novels have acquainted us with the lower and upper middle-class life in the minor and even the greater cities. But the attempts to deal with the life of fashion, of luxury, of leisure, have been so insufficient that they cannot be considered. This life can hardly be studied by one who is a part of it, not merely because that sort of life is not fruitful in talent, but because the procession cannot very well look on at itself. The observer must have some favorable position on the outside, and must regard it neither 'with a foolish face of praise,' nor with a satiric scorn. Like every other phase of life, it has its seriousness, its importance, and one who studies it rightly will find in it the old elements of interest so newly compounded that they will merit his most intelligent scrutiny, often his most sympathetic scrutiny. It would be easy to burlesque it, but to burlesque it would be intolerable, and the witness who did this would be bearing false testimony where the whole truth and nothing but the truth is desirable. A democracy, the proudest, the most sincere, the most ardent that history has ever known, has evolved here a leisure class which has all the distinguishing traits of a patriciate, and which by the chemistry of intermarriage with European aristocracies is rapidly acquiring antiquity. Is not this a phenomenon worthy the highest fiction?

Mr. Veblen has brought to its study the methods and habits of scientific inquiry. To translate these into dramatic terms would form the unequalled triumph of the novelist who had the seeing eye and the thinking mind, not to mention the feeling heart. That such a thing has not been done hitherto is all the stranger, because fiction, in other countries, has always employed itself with the leisure class, with the aristocracy; and our own leisure class now offers not only as high an opportunity as any which fiction has elsewhere enjoyed, but by its ultimation in the English leisure class it invites the American imagination abroad on conditions of unparalleled advantage.

NOTE

1 Joseph Dorfman, *Thorstein Veblen and His America*, New York, 1934, 196–507.

38 'A Question of Propriety'
1899

Published in *Literature*, 7 July 1899.
Perhaps it was easy, though one doubts that it was; but the accuracy of Howells's prescience as to what the drama would come to, and how critics and public would react to it in the age, let us say, of Samuel Beckett, seems uncanny.

The latest performance of Ibsen's *Ghosts* in New York has been followed by quite as loud and long an outburst of wounded delicacy in public and private criticism as the earliest provoked. Now, as then, the play has been found immoral, pathological, and revolting; and if nothing else in the case is plain, it is plain that we are not yet used to the sort of extremes to which it goes.

We are used to almost every other imaginable sort of extremes in the theatre. There is hardly anything improper or repulsive which the stage has not shown, except the repulsive impropriety of *Ghosts*, and the range outside of that play is so great that it is a little odd the author could not have been content with it. He might have deployed troops of lascivious dancers; he might have left the scene strewn with shapes of mimic murder; he might have had false wives fooling jealous husbands, and coming back for a maudlin forgiveness; he might have had seducers spreading their lures for victims; he might have had repentant prostitutes dying in the last excesses of virtue and bringing reform to their lovers and remorse to their lovers' families; he might have had heroic thieves and highwaymen doing deeds of dazzling self-sacrifice; he might have had a noble and truthful gentleman wearing a mask of crime through four acts, and tearing it off in the fifth, barely in time to baffle villainy and rescue helpless innocence; he might have had a sister devoting herself to infamy, and taking the shame, in order to save a guilty sister's good name, or her husband's honour, or her children's feelings; he might have had a saintly suicide murdering himself that his rival may marry the girl he loves; he might have had a girl contriving by every manner of lies the union of another with the man who adores her; he might have had any or all of these things, and offended no one. People are used to such things, and to any number of things like them, in the theatre, and if they are not disappointed when they do not get them, they certainly expect them.

But if all these traditions or none of them would have sufficed there is the whole printed drama from which the author might have chosen horrors freely and without the least offence. There is no form of lust, adultery, incest, homicide, cruelty, deceit, which was not open to his choice in the Greek, Spanish, English, and French drama. One Elizabethan play, the *Hamlet* of William Shakespeare, is so infinitely rich in all these motives that Ibsen could have drawn upon it alone and had every revolting and depraving circumstance which he could reasonably desire, without the least offence. That is a play which we not only see without disgust, but with the highest intellectual pleasure, and, as we believe, with spiritual edification. It is never denounced by criticism for its loathsome fable, for its bloodshed, for the atrocity with which its hero breaks the heart of a gentle girl, or for the pathological spectacle of her madness and his own. Strangest of all, it is not condemned for leaving the witness in the same sort of uncertainty as to the specific lesson that he finds himself in at the end of *Ghosts*.

The present high disdain for *Ghosts*, then, must come simply from our unfamiliarity with the sort of means employed in it to strike terror. The means are novel, that is all; when they become stale and hackneyed; when we have them in the form of hash, as we are sure, finally, to have them, no one will object, and we shall be morally nourished by them, just as we are now morally nourished by those of *Hamlet*. Then we may think no worse of the problem which a ghost leaves Mrs. Alving with regard to her son than of the problem which a ghost leaves *Hamlet* with regard to his mother. Possibly we may even come to think Mrs. Alving's problem is more important, as it is certainly more complex and profound. Compared with the question how she shall suffer to the end with the miserable boy whom his father's pleasant vices have doomed to idiocy, it is an easy matter for Hamlet to decide when and how to kill his uncle.

The psychological difference between the two tragedies is the measure of the vast space between the nerves of the seventeenth and the nineteenth centuries. In the nerves of the later time is the agonizing consciousness of things unknown to the nerves of the earlier age; and it may be this tacit consciousness which recoils from the anguish of the touch laying it bare. It is not unimaginable that in some century yet to come, say the twenty-first or twenty-second, a like consciousness will recoil from a yet subtler analysis, and cry out for the good old, decent, wholesome, sanative, dramatic means employed in Ibsen's *Ghosts*, as our consciousness now prefers to these the adulterous and vindictive motives of Shakespeare's *Hamlet*. I can fancy an indignant and public-spirited criticism demanding the 'scientific' methods of our then out-dated day as against those of some yet truer dramatist which shall hold the mirror still more unshrinkingly up to nature. That dramatist will, of course, have his party, very much outnumbered and ashamed, as Ibsen has his party in New York to-day; and I wonder in what form of revolt against the prevailing criticism this devoted little band will wreak its sense of injustice. Now, one can say that compared to the spare, severe sufficiency of *Ghosts*, the romantic surplusage of *Hamlet* is as a Wagner opera to a Greek tragedy; but what will the audacious partisan of the future dramatist say in contrasting his work with that of a then out-Ibsened Ibsen?

39 'Mr. Charles W. Chesnutt's Stories'
1900

Published in the *Atlantic*, May 1900.

As even the most recent historians of the American 1890s appear not to know, one of its significant writers was Charles Waddell Chesnutt, a pioneer in art, not theme alone, among the creators of Afro-American fiction. But Howells knew at once in 1898 and took pains to say in 1900 about Chesnutt's short stories that from them, 'Any one accustomed to study methods in fiction, to distinguish between good and bad art, to feel the joy which the delicate skill possible only from a love of truth can give, must have known a high pleasure.' It was the sort of thing he said about Mary Wilkins Freeman's short stories and denied to those of Bret Harte. And now, allowing Chesnutt to nod as well as Homer, Howells was still willing to class his best work with that of Maupassant, Turgenev, James, and Sarah Orne Jewett as well as Wilkins.

The praise is naturally not even, no more was the work. But Chesnutt was indeed an artist. And at that bitter time for the Afro-American the most influential critic in the country stood ready to deal frankly with the art, frankly and sympathetically with the racial problem as he understood it, and to commend stories of racial irony, 'Stories of the Color Line,' about issues not candidly discussed in polite white society, to the audience of the *Atlantic Monthly*.

The critical reader of the story called 'The Wife of his Youth,' which appeared in these pages two years ago, must have noticed uncommon traits in what was altogether a remarkable piece of work. The first was the novelty of the material; for the writer dealt not only with people who were not white, but with people who were not black enough to contrast grotesquely with white people,—who in fact were of that near approach to the ordinary American in race and color which leaves, at the last degree, every one but the connoisseur in doubt whether they are Anglo-Saxon or Anglo-African. Quite as striking as this novelty of the material was the author's thorough

295

mastery of it, and his unerring knowledge of the life he had chosen in its peculiar racial characteristics. But above all, the story was notable for the passionless handling of a phase of our common life which is tense with potential tragedy; for the attitude, almost ironical, in which the artist observes the play of contesting emotions in the drama under his eyes; and for his apparently reluctant, apparently helpless consent to let the spectator know his real feeling in the matter. Any one accustomed to study methods in fiction, to distinguish between good and bad art, to feel the joy which the delicate skill possible only from a love of truth can give, must have known a high pleasure in the quiet self-restraint of the performance; and such a reader would probably have decided that the social situation in the piece was studied wholly from the outside, by an observer with special opportunities for knowing it, who was, as it were, surprised into final sympathy.

Now, however, it is known that the author of this story is of negro blood,—diluted, indeed, in such measure that if he did not admit this descent few would imagine it, but still quite of that middle world which lies next, though wholly outside, our own. Since his first story appeared he has contributed several others to these pages, and he now makes a showing palpable to criticism in a volume called *The Wife of his Youth, and Other Stories of the Color Line*; a volume of Southern sketches called *The Conjure Woman*; and a short life of Frederick Douglass, in the Beacon Series of biographies. The last is a simple, solid, straight piece of work, not remarkable above many other biographical studies by people entirely white, and yet important as the work of a man not entirely white treating of a great man of his inalienable race. But the volumes of fiction *are* remarkable above many, above most short stories by people entirely white, and would be worthy of unusual notice if they were not the work of a man not entirely white.

It is not from their racial interest that we could first wish to speak of them, though that must have a very great and very just claim upon the critic. It is much more simply and directly, as works of art, that they make their appeal, and we must allow the force of this quite independently of the other interest. Yet it cannot always be allowed. There are times in each of the stories of the first volume when the simplicity lapses, and the effect is as of a weak and uninstructed touch. There are other times when the attitude, severely impartial and studiously aloof, accuses itself of a little pompousness. There are still other times when the literature is a little too ornate for beauty, and the diction is journalistic, reporteristic. But it is right to add that these are the exceptional times, and that for far the greatest part Mr. Chesnutt seems to know quite as well what he wants to do in a given case as Maupassant, or Tourguénief, or Mr. James, or Miss Jewett, or Miss Wilkins, in other given cases, and has done it with an art of kindred quiet and force. He belongs, in other words, to the good school, the only school, all aberrations from nature being so much truancy and anarchy. He sees his people very clearly, very justly, and he shows them as he sees them, leaving the reader to divine the depth of his feeling for them. He touches all the stops, and with equal delicacy in stories of real tragedy and comedy and pathos, so that it would be hard to say which is the finest in such admirably rendered effects as 'The Web of Circumstance,' 'The Bouquet,' and 'Uncle Wellington's Wives.' In some others the comedy degenerates into satire, with a look in the reader's direction which the author's friend must deplore.

As these stories are of our own time and country, and as there is not a swashbuckler of the seventeenth century, or a sentimentalist of this, or a princess of an imaginary kingdom, in any of them, they will possibly not reach half a million readers in six months, but in twelve months possibly more readers will remember them than if they had reached the half million. They are new and fresh and strong, as life always is, and fable never is; and the stories of *The Conjure Woman* have a wild, indigenous poetry, the creation of sincere and original imagination, which is imparted with a tender humorousness and a very artistic reticence. As far as his race is concerned, or his sixteenth part of a race, it does not greatly matter whether Mr. Chesnutt invented their motives, or found them, as he feigns, among his distant cousins of the Southern cabins. In either case, the wonder of their beauty is the same; and whatever is primitive and sylvan or campestral in the reader's heart is touched by the spells thrown on the simple black lives in these enchanting tales. Character, the most precious thing in fiction, is as faithfully portrayed against the poetic background as in the setting of the *Stories of the Color Line.*

Yet these stories, after all, are Mr. Chesnutt's most important work, whether we consider them merely as realistic fiction, apart from their author, or as studies of that middle world of which he is naturally and voluntarily a citizen. We had known the nethermost world of the grotesque and comical negro and the terrible and tragic negro through the white observer on the outside, and black character in its lyrical moods we had known from such an inside witness as

Mr. Paul Dunbar; but it had remained for Mr. Chesnutt to acquaint us with those regions where the paler shades dwell as hopelessly, with relation to ourselves, as the blackest negro. He has not shown the dwellers there as very different from ourselves. They have within their own circles the same social ambitions and prejudices; they intrigue and truckle and crawl, and are snobs, like ourselves, both of the snobs that snub and the snobs that are snubbed. We may choose to think them droll in their parody of pure white society, but perhaps it would be wiser to recognize that they are like us because they are of our blood by more than a half, or three quarters, or nine tenths. It is not, in such cases, their negro blood that characterizes them; but it is their negro blood that excludes them, and that will imaginably fortify them and exalt them. Bound in that sad solidarity from which there is no hope of entrance into polite white society for them, they may create a civilization of their own, which need not lack the highest quality. They need not be ashamed of the race from which they have sprung, and whose exile they share; for in many of the arts it has already shown, during a single generation of freedom, gifts which slavery apparently only obscured. With Mr. Booker Washington the first American orator of our time, fresh upon the time of Frederick Douglass; with Mr. Dunbar among the truest of our poets; with Mr. Tanner, a black American, among the only three Americans from whom the French government ever bought a picture, Mr. Chesnutt may well be willing to own his color.

But that is his personal affair. Our own more universal interest in him arises from the more than promise he has given in a department of literature where Americans hold the foremost place. In this there is, happily, no color line; and if he has it in him to go forward on the way which he has traced for himself, to be true to life as he has known it, to deny himself the glories of the cheap success which awaits the charlatan in fiction, one of the places at the top is open to him. He has sounded a fresh note, boldly, not blatantly, and he has won the ear of the more intelligent public.

40 'The New Historical Romances'
1900

Published in the *North American Review*, December 1900.

The triumph of *Trilby* and his resultant exposure to William Roscoe Thayer and company tried Howells's sense of humor. As he said to Thomas Wentworth Higginson in 1895, 'I told you that we realists should some day drive our go-cart over the hill, and so hang down the other side. God fulfills himself in many ways, but I think we must find the neo-romanticists a little difficult. He made them, however, and he knew they must sometime have their bray.' But what was he to say when the Spanish-American War, and the cult of the strenuous life, and the conduct of American imperialism in the Philippines, and a tidal wave of best-selling cloak-and-dagger romances all engulfed him at once?

As Frank Luther Mott put it, 'a series of historical and cloak-and-sword novels, ranging from serious works to hammock thrillers . . . for nearly a decade raged up and down the *Bookman*'s monthly best seller lists. . . . they prospered by falling in with the great American expansionist ideology of the turn of the century.' *The Prisoner of Zenda*, 1894, led to *Graustark*, 1901; in 1899 came *When Knighthood Was in Flower* and Winston Churchill (the Yankee), *Richard Carvel*; in 1900, *Alice of Old Vincennes*, by Maurice Thompson.[1] Howells's fight for American taste had become a rout.

What was left to him? To fight for art, for the future of the true novel, for the mind of the man whom Ezra Pound would soon make famous as 'the serious artist.' Attending, quite properly, to the serious artist, criticism has tended to forget books like *Graustark*, *Carvel*, and *Alice*. If only in relation to 'the business of authorship,' however, Howells's concern about 'The New Historical Romances' remains a document of considerable interest to literary history. The tension between stubborn Howells and neo-romanticism triumphant has a significance, for example, to American literature of the 1920s which cries for careful study.

A prophet of the kind skilled in forecasting accomplished events would have little difficulty in making himself believe that the recent deluge of historical romance, now perhaps beginning to ebb, was something he had all along expected. He might even succeed in persuading others that he had known the flood was coming; but this would be of minor importance; the great thing for the prophet, if a man of conscience, is to convince himself; the rest easily follows. At the worst, in a case like the present, the hardiest skeptic could do no more than retort that the actual fact was what everybody had foreseen.

I.

The actual fact of historical romance had been with us all through the period when the natural tendency in fiction prevailed, just as this tendency is now present amidst the welter of overwhelming romance. But some of the great masters of the natural school have ceased to be, and some have ceased to write. Flaubert and Maupassant, George Eliot and Anthony Trollope, Tourguénieff and Dostoyevsky are dead; from Björnson, Kielland and Lie we hear seldom. Of the Spaniards, Galdós, Pardo-Bazán and Valdés, Valdés alone has recently published anything. In Italy the movement that swept all before it is only apparent in the work of Matilde Serao and Fogazzaro. In England Mrs. Humphry Ward alone seems active for truth in fiction; since *Jude* Mr. Thomas Hardy has done nothing considerable, and Mr. George Moore nothing since *Esther Waters*. In France Zola confesses not merely in his abated energy, but in the sad explicitness of so many words, that he has 'fought a losing fight.' In Russia Tolstoy indeed has just spoken, after long silence in fiction, a word worthy his incomparable greatness in *Resurrection*. In our own country, where every genuine talent, young as well as old, is characterized by the instinct if not the reason of reality, nothing of late has been heard but the din of arms, the horrid tumult of the swashbuckler swashing on his buckler.

If we inquire in our own case, or the Anglo-Saxon case, what in the psychological, sociological, or meteorological conditions will account for this state of things, we are met by the ready, the too ready, the even officious suggestion, that the accumulation of riches has vulgarized and the explosion of wars has brutalized the popular mind and spoiled the taste. There may be something in that, and something more in the more subjective implication that our race, having more reason than ever to be ashamed of itself for its lust of gold and blood, is more than ever anxious to get away from itself, and welcomes the tarradiddles of the historical romancers as a relief from the facts of the odious present. It is a race which likes a good conscience so much that it prefers unconsciousness to a bad one; and there may be something in the notion thrown out and in the notion that our appetite for gross fable has been stimulated by the spread of athletics among us, and that there is an occult relation between the passion for golf, say, and the passion for historical romance. One must not press a conjecture of this sort too hard, and it is interesting rather than convincing to consider how much the prevalence of that sort of fiction has to do with the prevalence of the muscular ideals, especially among women, who especially with us are the repository of such intellectual refinement as we have attained, and whose tastes and manners have been coarsened by sharing the rude sports and boyish games of men. Apparently, women must follow men in their literary pastimes if they follow them in their other amusements: very few women probably enjoy athletics as much as they pretend, and very few women probably are fond of novels of adventure; but athletics have flourished more and more since women took to them, and the novels of adventure have supera-bounded since our reading class, or reading sex, has pretended to enjoy them.

II.

The psychologist may be interested in tracing the obscure relations of these facts; but for the present purpose it seems more useful to note that the novel of adventure, as a representation, or misrepresent-ation, of life soon exhausted the range of tolerable improbability. It had to escape into a region where comparisons and criterions could not follow it, and so we presently had that curious modern develop-ment of fiction on the lines of the old heroical romances which a few years ago filled the magazines with its phenomena. Imaginary thrones, principalities and powers in a map of Europe which the novelist changed with more than Napoleonic ease, became the ready, the eager prey of English and American soldiers of fortune, and the field of such deeds of love and war as have not been equalled since the heroes of the French seventeenth century romancers overran their airy Asias and Africas, and subdued their pretended Persias, their imaginary Egypts, and married the native rulers. The modern ad-venturers did not indeed encounter the giants, dwarfs, and magicians of the old books of chivalry, but if they had met them, no one can doubt that they would have overcome them; for these Englishmen and Americans were equipped for their forays, in that extraordinary fable land where they triumphed, with all the science and culture of the nineteenth century.

They were, of course, not the heroes of the old heroical romancers; they resembled, rather, in everything but the humility of his origin, the good Corporal Fritz of the *Grand Duchess of Gerolstein*, and the countries where they flourished were as probably ascertained as the hereditary dominions of that capricious but amusing princess. Their histories were the heroical romances come again, but with a modern difference; as the historical novels which have succeeded them are by no means the novels of Scott, of Manzoni, of Hugo, of Dumas, or even of Cooper. No reader could mistake them for the work of these authors, either collectively or severally, and yet they are as interestingly a reversion to the ideal, though not the scope of their work, as the late Gerolstein school was to that of the heroical romancers. Like the Gerolstein school, the new historical school pays its duty to the spirit of reality, up to a certain point voluntarily, and beyond that involuntarily, and its writers represent life as they have themselves seen it look and heard it talk. In one of the best of their books, built very, very carefully upon the model of Thackeray's historical fiction, and languaged with anxious scruple in the parlance of the eighteenth century as Thackeray reconstructed it, the autobiographying hero has an instant of delightful naturalness when he says he 'raised up in bed' and another when he reports a London lackey of George III.'s time as saying his master is 'some better.' We might have mistaken him for a Maryland gentleman of the colonial period, but these slight touches give him away for an up-to-date citizen of our imperial republic; and comfort us with the belief that the author, if he ever takes again to writing straight American, will not suffer from the inability to rid himself of Queen Anne English, which Trollope noted in Thackeray after his *Henry Esmond*. Another of the new historical novelists makes a Franco-American backwoodsman of the Fenimore Cooper type employ phrases drawn from our actual slang; and yet another gives vivacity if not vitality to an English princess of the sixteenth century by having her speak and act like a little Hoosier hoyden. In a fourth the heroine thees and thous the father of her country without the warrant of Quaker breeding, and misbehaves herself upon most opportunities like a schoolgirl of our familiar *fin de siècle* sort. In the fifth we have Virginia life painted in talk so tall that it can never be measured except when by some happy accident

one of the heroes forgets his lines, and tells a certain company of
miscreants that he has 'run with them long enough.'

III.

Such a lapse is rare in that book, and I am willing to own that in
citing these instances I have been testing the chain by its weakest link.
When I have said this, however, in the interest of impartiality, I am
not sure that it is true, even as regards the workmanship of the new
historical school. One must recognize the fact that its writers have
an ideal of workmanship, and that they aim at literary beauty with a
praiseworthy constancy. They mean to have style, and they have each
his or her standard to which they conscientiously devote themselves.
But nature is the only model which can be followed with the assurance
of unerring success, and literary beauty is so shy and evasive a thing
that it will respond only to a beauty of the mind, and then only if it is
not too much entreated. It does not appear from their work that these
writers have invented any memorable personage, or represented any
action that persists in the mind like an experience of the reader. In
fact, all the links seem weakest in a chain which fails to bind character
and the incident significant of character together, which does not
unite a truth to life with a nobility of ideal, or an artistic sense with an
ethical motive.

If I find the new historical romance wanting in these essentials of
good fiction, what do I find in it? That might not be easy to say without losing one's patience; for, after all, fiction is one of our most
precious possessions, and if it is not good it is one of the worst things
that can be. One cannot see it fall below the highest aim of the greatest
novelists without a pang; and this highest aim of the greatest novelists
has always been to move the reader by what he must feel to be the
truth. For the civilized man no representation of events can give
pleasure, or fail to give pain, if it is false to his knowledge of himself and
others, though effected with art indefinitely finer than that which
mainly offends the taste in our new historical romance.

If the cave dweller told tales of fighting and hunting, full of bloodshed and violence, he was probably true to life as he had known it,
and if he celebrated revenge as one of its highest aims, and homicide
as one of its noblest facts, his ethics were of the quality of his æsthetics.
But that does not form, to my mind, a reason why a twentieth century,
or even a nineteenth century, novelist should expect me to believe

and to be edified in believing his representation that this was the fact
or the ideal of life in the eighteenth, seventeenth or even sixteenth
century. I am obliged to protest that it was not, but is untrue to what
we mainly know of them. What we mainly know of those ages is that
the great mass of men, high and low, were then actuated by the wish
to be friends and at peace with other men; that they were often of
humble and contrite hearts for their sins, and wished to bear themselves gently and not violently; that they, too, like ourselves, abhorred tumult and sought their happiness in religion and industry and
learning, and often suffered for conscience' sake imprisonment and
martyrdom, that we who have come after them might be the freer
and safer and peacefuller in our lives.

But I find scarce a hint of this in the new historical romances,
which are as untrue to the complexion of the past as to personality in
any time, or rather as crudely tentative and partial. I find duels and
battles set forth as the great and prevalent human events; I find pride
and revenge worshipped as right and fine, but no suggestion of the
shame and heartache which have followed the doers of violence in all
times and countries since the stone age. There is such spilth of blood
that you might almost expect to see it drip from the printed page, and
nowhere the consciousness that it is better to suffer wrong than to
take the life of the vilest miscreant. In the several ages when the
Quaker conceived of Christ in conduct, the Puritan of the personal
conscience and the Baptist of toleration in religion, the philosopher of
positive freedom in thought, they had no part in life as it shows itself
to our new historical romancers. The moral and mental activities of
those times were apparently confined to incidents which you come
upon so often in their imaginary histories that they stamp themselves
on the memory as the only incidents.

> The ruffian against whom I was pitted began to draw his breath in
> gasps. He was a scoundrel not fit to die, . . . unworthy of a gentle-
> man's steel. I presently ran him through with as little compunction,
> and as great desire to be quit of a dirty job, as if he had been a mad
> dog.

> 'Now, I'll scalp you,' he cried in a voice terrible to hear; and with
> his words, out came his hunting-knife from its sheath. . . . In fact,
> he had taken off part of Maisonville's scalp, . . . insisting upon
> completing his cruel performance. . . . The big man wept with rage
> when he saw the bleeding prisoner protected. 'Eh bien! I'll keep
> what I've got,' he roared, 'and I'll take the rest of it next time!'

He shook the tuft of hair at Maisonville, and glared like a mad bull.

Young Brandon replied, 'Stand your ground, you coward! . . . If you try to run, I will thrust you through the neck as I would a cur. Listen how you snort.' . . . Judson tried to keep the merciless sword-point from his throat. At last, by a dexterous twist of his blade, Brandon sent Judson's sword flying thirty feet away. The fellow started to run, but turned and fell upon his knees to beg for life. Brandon's reply was a flashing circle of his steel, and his sword-point cut lengthwise through Judson's eyes and the bridge of his nose, leaving him sightless and hideous for life.

'Now, then, have you got that officer ready? . . . Up with him, then!' At the command, half a dozen men pulled on a rope which had been passed over the bough of a tree, and the young subaltern was swung clear of the ground. He struggled so fiercely for a moment that the cords which bound his wrists parted and he was able to clutch the rope above his head in a desperate attempt to save himself. It was useless, for instantly two rifles were leveled and two bullets sent through him; his hands relaxing, he hung limply save for a slight muscular quiver.

The inventors of the hideous incidents with which the new romances teem have no turn for character if they had the time for it; and possibly they do not prefer bloodshed, but are simply too busy with butchery for anything else. They are mostly gentlemen of peaceful callings and the instincts of law-abiding citizens, with probably no love of homicide in them, who would rather stay away from a slugging match than not, and would not greatly enjoy an electrocution. Any pleasure in their bloody business, if it could be realized, is still less imaginable of the young ladies who deal in its horrors. These can hardly have witnessed violence of any kind, and must sicken at the sight of blows with the fist, much more thrusts with a sword or shots with a pistol; and it may well be said that they mean no harm by their ideals of militant manhood. Very likely their ideals do not do all the harm which is their logic, but it is all the same their logic; just as the logic of the royalties and nobilities which abound in the new historical romances is that life cannot be beautiful or great without them. Their testimony, false witness as it is, is against the American life of individual worth, without titles and ranks, and only the distinction of honorable achievement.

To be sure, one must not take the books too seriously. When their

manners and their morals were the property of the dime novels, they
sometimes inspired a neighborhood of boys to make for the Western
plains in order to become or to destroy Indians; and sometimes
moved them to attempt burning one of their number as a captive at
the stake. But, after all, such things seldom happened, and now that
the dime novel has got into good literary society, and flourishes in
periodicals of the highest class, with a tradition of exacting taste in
fiction, it is not credible that its ideals will immediately affect the
conduct of its readers. The vast majority of readers will rise from the
books as guiltless of any wish to realize the ideals of conduct presented
to them as the gentle young girls and amiable gentlemen who write
them. But that such fiction will in a measure and for a while debauch
the minds and through their minds the morals of their readers, is
reasonably to be feared even by the optimist. That delicate something
which we call tone, whether intellectual or ethical, must suffer from
an orgy of the kind as it would suffer from an excess in opium or
absinthe.

IV.

Again I find myself growing too serious about a phase of fiction which
I cannot denounce unsparingly without suspecting myself of forcing
the note; and if I have borne on too hard I should like to make
amends. I am bound to say that what I think the grotesque, the ludicrous immorality of the new historical romancers does not include the
sort of immorality which we have first in mind when we use the word.
The relations of the sexes, so far as I have noticed, are mostly most
exemplary in them. There is nowhere anything but a wish to get the
lovers married at all hazards, or as many hazards as possible. Perhaps
the books would be a little truer to human experience in the past,
not to say the present, if the behavior of their heroes and heroines,
in this respect, was not so irreproachable; but I am not going to make
this a reproach to their authors, who have enough to answer for in
their inculcation of revenge, pride, anger, contempt and other bad
passions. It seems to be a condition of getting their tremendous affairs
transacted that the hero should often be a ruthless homicide; but he
really must be a tiresome ass or an impossible peacock, not to be mismated with the pert and foolish doll that passes for the heroine. He,
being what he is, is apt to be of a solemn behavior; but she is commonly very sprightly, with extraordinary social gifts for getting her-

self into trouble; she must usually have a touch of comedy, an arch manner, a habit of dropping ironical curtseys, and of making satirical speeches the wit of which she might be supposed to keep her secret, if they were not of such manifest effect upon the other characters.

Characters? Are they characters, any of those figments which pass for such in the new historical romances? They are hardly so by any test of comparison with people we know in life or in the great fictions. They are very simple souls, whose main business is to impersonate a single propensity, and immediately or remotely to do the hero and the heroine good or harm; to show them off; to die by his hand, or to cherish a baffled ambition for hers. When they are historical figures their deportment is such as would be imaginable of the historical figures of the Eden Musée if these were called upon to leave their statuesque repose and move and speak.

No pains have been spared to make them life-like, and, as I have suggested, the novelists have each been anxious to produce a literary masterpiece. The trouble with their attempt seems to be that it is only too literary. It appears that we may have some virtues in excess; that in matters of art it is possible to be so artistic as to exclude nature. I should say that the mistake of the new historical novelist, when his æsthetic intention is most admirable, was to have done just that. It is hard to get nature to take part in one's little effects when it is an affair of contemporary life; if it is an affair of life in the past, her co-operation is still more reluctant. But literature is always willing and ready to lend a hand to the literary man; it is at home when he calls; it is never previously engaged when he invites it, as nature is so often; and perhaps it is not altogether their own fault that the new historical romancers have got her help so seldom. I fancy moments when they have tried for it, and been disappointed, and so turned to the faithful friend of authorship, and got on with literature alone. At the best, the historical novelist must often do this, for the life which he wishes to portray exists only in the records, and speaks a language surviving only in the books. If he is a very great talent, he will divine that nature, especially human nature, is the same from generation to generation; and that his only hope is to put the present frankly into the clothes of the past. But he seems to me not to be a very great talent in the recent instances, or of any gift so marked as the instinct for hitting the fancy of our enormous commonplace average. Besides, what is a poor man to do with the nineteenth century in eighteenth or seventeenth century clothes, if he has at the same time to celebrate the ideals of the stone age? His difficulty is simply doubled.

V.

I do not think it by any means a despicable thing to have hit the fancy of our enormous commonplace average. Some of the best and truest books have done this. *The Pilgrim's Progress* did it; *Uncle Tom's Cabin* did it; Mr. Clemens's *Roughing It* did it; Longfellow's poetry did it; Mr. James Whitcomb Riley's poetry does it; Edward Bellamy's gospel of justice in *Looking Backward* did it. But what is despicable, what is lamentable is to have hit the popular fancy and not have done anything to change it, but everything to fix it; to flatter it with false dreams of splendor in the past, when life was mainly as simple and sad-colored as it is now; to corrupt it to an ignominious discontent with patience and humility, and every-day duty, and peace.

This, after all the allowances and exceptions, is what the new American school of historical romance must do, not of set purpose or deliberate design, but largely in obedience to the mystical law of interaction which in human affairs makes every power the agent as well as the authority. A vulgar literature is because the vulgar taste for it was, and the vulgar taste for it will be, because the vulgar literature has been. Cause and effect are so intimately associated in such things that we cannot part or distinguish one from the other; and my own failure to do so is confessed in turning from it to recognize the extraneous fact that the popularity of this sort of fiction seems already to be waning, however long its influence is obscurely to continue. There are clear signs that its immense favor is abating; there are sullen whispers in the Trade that the historical romance, as a 'seller,' has had its day; and a corresponding impatience in the simple-hearted candor of those unliterary critics who feel duped in having yielded to the temptation of reading a book because everybody else was reading it. These critics seem, if you hear them complain, not to be much comforted by the assurance of some literary critics that they were indulging a very wholesome appetite in gorging themselves at the bloody repast spread by the historical romancers; and I own that I sympathize with them in this. I do not see why the spectacle of every sort of brute adventure, even when it is not bloody, should be thought particularly wholesome. I suspect that the taste for it is not so very simple or natural in civilized and cultivated people, who might be much more simply and naturally attracted by a social situation, a moral problem, or a psychological question, and would revert to brute adventure only in their abnormal moods.

But the confession of the dupes, which, though so justly indignant,

is also so amusing, would do little more to philosophize the phenomenon than the whispers of the Trade. That work must be left,
apparently, to some synthetic student of our time, who may hereafter
get a better perspective of the fact than seems possible now. I have
tried to note such phases of it as appeal to the contemporary observer,
and there are, doubtless, others which will have caught the attention
of other inquirers, who may possibly offer some plausible explanation
of one curious fact of the situation.

While the Gerolstein school of heroical romance was almost
wholly of English origin, the new historical romance is almost
altogether native American. I can think of no new English historical
novel which has enjoyed the overwhelming popularity of so many
American romances; though the two countries seem to be moved now
by so many impulses in common, and to be swollen by the same race-
conceit, the same ignoble ideals of force. It is possibly because the
English have looked more constantly and more profoundly into the
past, and found there was nothing in it, that they have invented
imaginary realms, and left the exploitation of history to our more
ardent, more inexperienced romantic school. It is certainly simpler to
cut loose from any sort of fact, and abandon one's self to pure fake
as the English have done. One cannot, then, be brought to book, or in
any wise held responsible by the reader's knowledge; the answer to
all criticisms of manners, morals, costume, parlance, in the work of
the Gerolstein school, is that it *is* pure fake. With historical fiction it is
different and much more difficult. The novelist is obliged to keep a
conscience so far moral that he may not commit the solecisms he can
help, or make the misrepresentations that he is likely to be found out
in. He, indeed, addresses a crude and ignorant audience for the most
part, but there is always a chance, which he must guard, that some
better informed person may overhear him. He is not so free as the
heroical romancer, and hardly even as free as the poor realist who re-
stricts himself to reporting what he knows of life, and otherwise keeps
off the grass in the straight and narrow path of truth.

VI.

Do I, then, wholly dislike historical fiction as impossible and deplorable? On the contrary, I like it very much in the instances which I
can allege for the reasons I can give. I like Goldsmith's *Vicar of
Wakefield*, Richardson's *Pamela* and *Clarissa*, Frances Burney's

Evelina, Maria Edgeworth's *Belinda*, Jane Austen's *Pride and Prejudice*, *Northanger Abbey* and *Emma*, all of Anthony Trollope's novels and most of George Eliot's; my catholic affection for historical fiction embraces even Fielding's *Tom Jones* and De Foe's *Roxana*. These and the novels like them are what Mr. Kipling has somewhere declared the only historical novels, because, being true to the manners of their own times, they alone present a picture of the past, worthy to be called historical. But I go farther than this, and delight in certain retrospective novels which I find as veracious as the faithfullest circumspective novels. First and foremost among them is Tolstoy's *War and Peace*, which presents an image of the past that appeals to my knowledge of myself and of other men as unimpeachably true. There a whole important epoch lives again, not in the flare of theatrical facts, but in motives and feelings so much like those of our own time, that I know them for the passions and principles of all times. It is perhaps because the characters and events are separated from the author's day by only a generation that they are so well ascertained, or perhaps they are made equal with us in date by the author's conception of the human solidarity as always essentially the same; so that when I read a chapter of *War and Peace* it is as convincing of the external fact from the internal truth as a chapter of such a palpitant actuality as *Resurrection*. For a like reason our greatest romancer, Mark Twain, by art as unlike Tolstoy's as possible, enables one to have one's being in the sixth century with his *Connecticut Yankee at King Arthur's Court*. He, too, in an imaginative scheme as wildly fantastic as Tolstoy's is simply real, is a true historical novelist because he represents humanity as we know it must have been, since it is humanity as we know it is. His historical fiction is as nobly anarchical as most historical fiction is meanly conventional in the presence of all that wrong which calls itself vested right; and the moral law is as active in that fascinating dream world which he has created as it is in this waking world, where sooner or later every man feels its power.

I like Mark Twain's historical fiction above all for this supreme truth, just as I like Tolstoy's; but I am not above a more purely æsthetic pleasure in such an historical novel as Stendhal's *Chartreuse de Parme*, though this was written so near to the supposed time of the action that it might be called reminiscential rather than historical. In this, as in *War and Peace*, and *I Promessi Sposi*, which I like equally, a whole epoch lives again morally, politically and socially, with such entirety and large inclusion that the reader himself becomes of it.

It is by some such test that we are to know the validity of any work of art. It is not by taking us out of ourselves, but by taking us into ourselves, that its truth, its worth, is manifest; it convinces us by entering into our experience and making its events part of that, if it does not enter into our conscience and make its ideals part of that. My grief with our new historical romances is that they do neither the one nor the other; and though it is not a serious grief, the thing itself being so unserious, I must insist upon it, for it is greater than any other feeling I have concerning them. If one could go and acquire a little inexperience, or a good deal; or if one could rid one's self of one's moral sense as easily as one sometimes defies it, perhaps one might better enjoy these books; and I wish to say here, while there is yet a minute, that their badness does not seem wilful in any sort. In the literary sort, though it is often so grotesque and hopeless, it is at other moments relieved by the distinct intention of art in construction and treatment. One cannot say that there is ever much more than the intention; but such an intention is always respectable; and in some of the books there is a real feeling for nature, poetically expressed, though, so far as I have noticed, never a real feeling for human nature. In that all the rest fall below, and immeasurably below, Colonel J. W. De Forest's recent story of the revolutionary beginnings in Boston. *A Lover's Revolt* is in indefinitely smaller compass, a story akin to *War and Peace* through the moral quality of truth to universal and eternal human experience. The author makes the epoch his own by knowledge and penetrating sympathy; and the battle pieces, if less fearlessly painted than the bloody scenes in the romances which I have refrained from distinguishing by name, have the fascination of a soldier's talk about such things. It is not only from his own experience of war that Colonel De Forest paints war as it is, with Tolstoyan fidelity, but from the artistic conscience of a true novelist. This has before availed him in his novels of contemporaneous American life, though it has not availed him with a large public, which seems to be sometimes as wonderfully missed as made. It is not probable that in the wane of the historical school his book, which so easily outvalues them all in the qualities of real historical fiction, will enjoy their spectacular vogue. It has its weak points, and it is a little too thumpingly patriotic for my pleasure; but its weak points are not so many and its patriotism not so vainglorious as our public seems to like in historical romance.

The patriotism in Edward Bellamy's posthumous romance, *The Duke of Stockbridge*, is full of a misgiving which the retrospective patriot of our day always does well to acquaint himself with as a part of our national history. It is with the short and simple annals of the poor, as they may be read in the facts of that squalid period immediately following the Revolution, that this admirable book concerns itself; and if it is bare and bleak in the atmosphere to which it exposes our national pride, it is probably not less veracious for that reason. Economically it represents that terrible time when the depreciated Continental currency made the hard-working poor the easy prey of the gentleman class—the lawyers, doctors, shop-keepers, preachers and schoolmasters—all through New England, and the loathsome jails were choked with imprisoned debtors; when the poor hated the rich as never before or since in our country, and the rich ground the faces of the poor with a secure conviction of their right to do so that very few millionaires now enjoy. Politically it celebrates a phase of Shays' Rebellion, which was foredoomed to failure, and has been easily handed down to obloquy, but which is here shown as grounded in such suffering as few people have tamely undergone. On the personal side, the story is intensely vivid, and its characters live with the life that is our nature to-day, and constitute it truly historical by their truth to themselves and to us. It was by a series of chances that the book remained unpublished while the author was with us, but more than ever, in reading the story, imperfect and wanting as it is in those last touches which he would have known how to give it, one realizes how great a loss his death was not to humanity only, but to the humanities; how infinitely beyond all our other historical romancers, his fine imagination would have carried him in fiction.

VII.

In my praise of these two books I must own to having got rather far away from both the temper and the text of my sermon. After all, the sources of loving or hating in any sort will not be successfully interrogated; and I am sensible, at the end, of leaving the popularity of the present or recent historical school much the same mystery I found it. I will not risk any reputation for prophecy I may have acquired by too frankly predicting the end of that school. It may be beginning to be recent, or it may have only begun to be present. If we suppose that the young and strong, if not very sage or clear, generation now swelling the census is tired of it, there are always generations of the young and strong to come, who will perhaps be no sager or clearer than this. But we have still a republic and not yet an empire of letters, and no one is obliged to read silly books. There are plenty of wise ones which some of us have not read.

NOTE

1 Frank Luther Mott, *Golden Multitudes, The Story of Best Sellers in the United States*, New York, 1947, 207–15.

41 'Jane Austen'
1900

First published in *Harper's Bazar*, June 1900. Text taken from *Heroines of Fiction*, i, New York: Harper and Bros, 1901.

One of the necessary rules of this book has been that it shall not select from Howells's critical books except to go behind such mere collections of essays as *Literature and Life* or *Imaginary Interviews*. The reasons for such a rule seem obvious enough. *Criticism and Fiction* is invalid. To *Modern Italian Poets*, *My Literary Passions*, *Heroines of Fiction*, and *Literary Friends and Acquaintance* the author gave structural contexts and styles too special to permit one to cut out fair excerpts. Yet every rule must sometimes be broken for good cause, and this one must give way for 'Jane Austen' from *Heroines of Fiction*.

There are several compelling reasons. Howells is still one of the great Janeites. As Clemens teased him about preferring to 'be damned to John Bunyan's heaven' rather than read James's *Bostonians*, he later 'confessed' that though one might read Poe's prose 'on salary,' not so Austen's. The fun lay in the depth of Howells's adoration. Worship in the abstract is always less interesting than live ritual, and Howells's Austen analyses reveal much more than his professions of faith. These chapters stand among his finest demonstrations of mature love for British authors. And they approach close to the hidden juncture between his critical and creative imaginations.

'Elizabeth Bennet'

I.

It remained for the greatest of the gifted women, who beyond any or all other novelists have fixed the character and behavior of Anglo-Saxon fiction, to assemble in her delightful talent all that was best in that of her sisters. Jane Austen was indeed so fine an artist, that we are still only beginning to realize how fine she was; to perceive, after a

314

hundred years, that in the form of the imagined fact, in the expression of personality, in the conduct of the narrative, and the subordination of incident to character, she is still unapproached in the English branch of Anglo-Saxon fiction. In American fiction Hawthorne is to be named with her for perfection of form; the best American novels are built upon more symmetrical lines than the best English novels, and have unconsciously shaped themselves upon the ideal which she instinctively and instantly realized.

Of course it was not merely in externals that Jane Austen so promptly achieved her supremacy. The wonder of any beautiful thing is that it is beautiful in so many ways; and her fiction is as admirable for its lovely humor, its delicate satire, its good sense, its kindness, its truth to nature, as for its form. There is nothing hurried or huddled in it, nothing confused or obscure, nothing excessive or inordinate. The marvel of it is none the less because it is evident that she wrote from familiar acquaintance with the fiction that had gone before her. In her letters there are hints of her intimacy with the novels of Goldsmith, of Richardson, of Frances Burney, and of Maria Edgeworth; but in her stories there are scarcely more traces of their influence than of Mrs. Radcliffe's, or any of the romantic writers whom she delighted to mock. She is obviously of her generation, but in all literature she is one of the most original and independent spirits. Her deeply domesticated life was passed in the country scenes, the county society, which her books portray, far from literary men and events; and writing as she used, amidst the cheerful chatter of her home, she produced literature of still unrivalled excellence in its way, apparently without literary ambition, and merely for the pleasure of getting the life she knew before her outward vision. With the instinct and love of doing it, and not with the sense of doing anything un-common, she achieved that masterpiece, *Pride and Prejudice*, which is quite as remarkable for being one of several masterpieces as for its absolute excellence. There have been authors enough who have written one extraordinary book; but all Jane Austen's books are extraordinary, and *Persuasion*, *Northanger Abbey*, *Emma*, *Mansfield Park*, and *Sense and Sensibility*, are each a masterpiece, inferior only to *Pride and Prejudice*, which was written first. After the young girl of twenty had written it, she kept it half as many years longer before she printed it. In mere order of chronology it belongs to the eighteenth century, but in spirit it is distinctly of the nineteenth century, as we feel that cycle to have been when we feel proudest of it. In manners as much as in methods it is such a vast advance upon the work of her sister novelists that you wonder whether some change had not already taken place in English society which she notes, and which they fail to note.

The topics of the best fiction of any time will probably be those which decent men and women talk of together in the best company; and such topics vary greatly from time to time. There is no reason to think that Frances Burney and Maria Edgeworth were less pure-minded than Jane Austen, but they dealt with phases of human experience which she did not deal with, because their friends and acquaintances did so, without being essentially worse than hers. A tendency towards a more scrupulous tone seems to have been the effect of the general revival in religion at the close of the last century, which persisted down to that time in our own century when the rise of scientific agnosticism loosed the bonds of expression. Now again of late years men and women in the best company talk together of things which would not have been discussed during the second and third quarters of the century. One must hedge one's position on such a point with many perhapses; nothing can be affirmed with certainty; the most that can be said is that the tone if not the temper, the manners if not the morals, which have lately been called *fin de siècle*, are noticeably more akin to what was *fin de siècle* a hundred years ago, than they are to what was thought fit in polite society fifty years ago. Possibly another revival of religion will bring another change, such as the purity of Jane Austen's fiction may have forecast rather than reported. But we do not know this, and possibly again her books are what they are in matter and manner because the little world of county society which she observed was wholesomer and decenter than the great world of London society which Miss Burney and Miss Edgeworth studied.

An author is as great for what he leaves out as for what he puts in; and Jane Austen shows her mastery in nothing more than in her avoidance of moving accidents for her most moving effects. She seems to have known intuitively that character resides in habit, and that for the novelist to seek its expression in violent events would be as stupid as for the painter to expect an alarm of fire or burglary to startle his sitter into a valuable revelation of his qualities. She puts from her, therefore, all the tremendous contrivances of her predecessors, and takes her place quietly on the ground to which they were, the best of them, falteringly and uncertainly feeling their way. After De Foe and Goldsmith she was the first to write a thoroughly artistic novel in English, and she surpassed Goldsmith as far in method as she refined upon De Foe in material. Among her contemporaries she was as easily first as Shakspere among the Elizabethan dramatists; and in the high excellencies of symmetrical form, force of characterization, clearness of conception, simplicity and temperance of means, she is still supreme: that girl who began at twenty with such a masterpiece as *Pride and Prejudice*, and ended with such a masterpiece as *Persuasion* at forty-two!

II.

The story of *Pride and Prejudice* has of late years become known to a constantly, almost rapidly, increasing cult, as it must be called, for the readers of Jane Austen are hardly ever less than her adorers: she is a passion and a creed, if not quite a religion. A beautiful, clever, and cultivated girl is already piqued and interested if not in love with a handsome, high-principled, excessively proud man, when she becomes bitterly prejudiced against him by the slanders of a worthless beneficiary of his family. The girl is Elizabeth Bennet, the young man is Fitzwilliam Darcy, and they first meet at a ball, where he behaves with ungracious indifference to her, and afterwards at the dinners and parties of a small country neighborhood where persons theoretically beyond the pale of gentility are admitted at least on sufferance; the stately manners of the day are relaxed by youth and high spirits; and no doubt the academic elevation of the language lapses oftener on the lips of the pretty girls and the lively young men than an author still in her nonage, and zealous for the dignity of her style, will allow to appear in the conversation of her hero and heroine.

From the beginning it seems to Darcy that Elizabeth shines in talk beyond all the other women, though sometimes she shines to his cost. But banter from a pretty girl goes farther than flattery with a generous man; and from the first Darcy is attracted by Elizabeth Bennet's wit, as much as he is repelled by her family. In fact, he cannot get on with her family, for though the Bennets have a sufficiently good standing, in virtue of the father's quality as a gentleman, it is in spite the mother's folly and vulgarity, and the folly and vulgarity of all her sisters but one. Mrs. Bennet is probably the most entire and perfect simpleton ever drawn in fiction, and her husband renders life with her supportable by amusing himself with her absurdities. He buries himself in his books and leaves her the management of his daughters in society, getting what comfort he can out of the humor and intellectual sympathy of Elizabeth and the charming goodness of her elder sister Jane. The rest of his family are almost as impossible to him as they are to Darcy, to whom Mr. Bennet himself is rather impossible, and who resolves not only to crush out his own passion for Elizabeth, but to break off his friend Bingley's love for her sister Jane. His success in doing the one is not so great but he duly comes to offer himself to Elizabeth, and he owns in the humiliation of rejection that he believes he has failed in the other.

From this point the affair, already so daringly imagined, is one of the most daring in fiction; and less courage, less art, less truth than the author brings to its management would not have availed. It is a great stroke of originality to have Darcy write the letter he does after his rejection, not only confessing, but defending his course; and it is from the subtle but perfectly honest sense of character in her heroine that the author has Elizabeth do justice to him in what she so bitterly resents. When she has once acknowledged the reason of much that he says of her family (and she has to acknowledge that even about her adored father he is measurably right), it is a question merely of friendly chances as to the event. These are overwhelmingly supplied, to Elizabeth's confusion, by Darcy's behavior in helping save her sister Lydia from the shame and ruin of her elopement with the worthless Wickham. Lydia, who is only less entirely and delightfully a fool than Mrs. Bennet herself, is thus the means of Elizabeth's coming to such a good mind in regard to Darcy that her only misgiving is lest it may be too late. But Darcy has been enlightened as well as she: he does everything a man can to repair his wrongs and blunders, and with a very little leading from Elizabeth, he is brought to offer himself again, and is accepted with what may be called demure transport, and certainly with alacrity.

There is nothing more deliciously lover-like than the talks in which they go over all the past events when they are sure of each other; and Elizabeth, who is apt to seem at other times a little too sarcastic, a little too ironical, is here sweetly and dearly and wisely herself.

[Here follow about 300 words of quoted dialogue.]

The aunt whom Darcy means is Lady Catherine de Burgh, as great a fool as Mrs. Bennet or Lydia, and much more offensive. She has all Darcy's arrogance, without a ray of the good sense and good heart which enlighten and control it, and when she hears a rumor of his engagement to Elizabeth, she comes to question the girl. Their encounter is perhaps the supreme moment of objective drama in the book, and is a bit of very amusing comedy, which is the more interesting to the modern spectator because it expresses the beginning of that revolt against aristocratic pretension characteristic of the best English fiction of our century. Its spirit seems to have worked in the clear intelligence of the young girl to more than one effect of laughing satire, and one feels that Elizabeth Bennet is speaking Jane Austen's mind, and perhaps avenging her for patronage and impertinence otherwise suffered in silence, when she gives Lady de Burgh her famous setting-down.

[Here follow about 700 quoted words.]

In all this the heroine easily gets the better of her antagonist not only in the mere article of *sauce*, to which it must be owned her lively wit occasionally tends, but in the more valuable qualities of personal dignity. She is much more a lady than her ladyship, as the author means she shall be; but her superiority is not invented for the crisis; it springs from her temperament and character, cool, humorous, intelligent and just: a combination of attributes which renders Elizabeth Bennet one of the most admirable and attractive girls in the world of fiction. It is impossible, however, not to feel that her triumph over Lady de Burgh is something more than personal: it is a protest, it is an insurrection, though probably the discreet, the amiable author would have been the last to recognize or to acknowledge the fact. An indignant sense of the value of humanity as against the pretensions of rank, such as had not been felt in English fiction before, stirs throughout the story, and reveals itself in such crucial tests as dear 'little Burney,' for instance, would never have imagined. For when Miss Burney introduces city people, it is to let them display their cockney vulgarity; but though Jane Austen shows the people whom the Bennets' gentility frays off into on the mother's side vulgar and ridiculous, they are not shown necessarily so because they are in trade or the law; and on the father's side it is apparent that their social inferiority is not incompatible with gentle natures, cultivated minds, and pleasing manners.

'Anne Elliot and Catherine Morland'

That protest already noted, that revolt against the arrogance of rank, which makes itself felt more or less in all the novels of Jane Austen, might have been something that she inhaled with the stormy air of the time, and respired again with the unconsciousness of breathing. But whether she knew it or not, this quiet little woman, who wrote her novels in the bosom of her clerical family; who was herself so contentedly of the established English order; who believed in inequality and its implications as of divine ordinance; who loved the delights of fine society, and rejoiced as few girls have in balls and parties, was in her way asserting the Rights of Man as unmistakably as the French revolutionists whose volcanic activity was of about the same compass of time as her literary industry. In her books the snob, not yet named or classified, is fully ascertained for the first time. Lady Catherine de Burgh in *Pride and Prejudice*, John Dashwood in *Sense and Sensibility*, Mr. Elton in *Emma*, General Tilney in *Northanger Abbey*, and above all Sir Walter Elliot in *Persuasion*, are immortal types of insolence or meanness which foreshadow the kindred shapes of Thackeray's vaster snob-world, and fix the date when they began to be recognized and detested. But their recognition and detestation were only an incident of the larger circumstance studied in the different stories; and in *Persuasion* the snobbishness of Sir Walter has little to do with the fortunes of his daughter Anne after the first unhappy moment of her broken engagement.

I.

People will prefer Anne Elliot to Elizabeth Bennet according as they enjoy a gentle sufferance in women more than a lively rebellion; and it would not be profitable to try converting the worshippers of the one to the cult of the other. But without offence to either following, it may be maintained that *Persuasion* is imagined with as great novelty and daring as *Pride and Prejudice*, and that Anne is as genuinely a heroine as Elizabeth.

In *Persuasion* Jane Austen made bold to take the case of a girl, neither weak nor ambitious, who lets the doubts and dislikes of her family and friends prevail with her, and gives up the man she loves because they think him beneath her in family and fortune. She yields because she is gentle and diffident of herself, and her indignant lover resents and despises her submission if he does not despise her. He is a young officer of the navy, rising to prominence in the service which was then giving England the supremacy of the seas, but he is not thought the equal of a daughter of such a baronet as Sir Walter Elliot. It is quite possible that in her portrayal of the odious situation

Jane Austen avenges with personal satisfaction the new order against the old, for her brothers were of the navy, and the family hope and pride of the Austens were bound up with its glories. At any rate, when Sir Walter's debts oblige him to let Kellynch Hall, and live on a simple scale in Bath, it is a newly made admiral who becomes his tenant; and it is the brother of the admiral's wife who is Anne's rejected lover, and who now comes to visit his sister, full of victory and prize-money, with the avowed purpose of marrying and settling in life.

Seven years have passed since Frederick Wentworth angrily parted with Anne Elliot. They have never really ceased to love each other; but the effect has been very different with the active, successful man, and the quiet, dispirited girl. No longer in her first youth, she devotes herself to a little round of duties, principally in the family of her foolish, peevish younger sister; and finds her chief consolation in the friendship of the woman who so conscientiously urged her to her great mistake. The lovers meet in the Musgrove family into which Anne's sister has married, and Wentworth's fancy seems taken with one of the pretty daughters. Divers transparent devices are then employed rather to pique the reader's interest than to persuade him that the end is going to be other than what it must be. Nothing can be quite said to determine it among the things that happen; Wentworth and Anne simply live back into the mutual recognition of their love. He learns to know better her lovely and unselfish nature, and so far from having formally to forgive her, he prizes her the more for the very qualities which made their unhappiness possible. For her part, she has merely to own again the affection which has been a dull ache in her heart for seven years. Her father's pride is reconciled to her marriage, which is now with a somebody instead of the nobody Captain Wentworth once was. Sir Walter 'was much struck with his personal claims, and felt that his superiority of appearance might not be unfairly balanced against her superiority of rank. . . . He was now esteemed quite worthy to address the daughter of a foolish, spend-thrift baronet who had not principle or sense enough to maintain himself in the situation in which Providence had placed him.' As for Anne's mischievous, well-meaning friend who had urged her to break with Wentworth before, 'there was nothing less for Lady Russell to do than to admit that she had been completely wrong, and to take up a new set of opinions and hopes.'

II.

This outline of the story gives no just sense of its quality, which resides mainly in its constancy to nature; and it gives no sufficient notion of the variety of character involved in the uneventful, quiet action. Anne's arrogant and selfish father, her cold-hearted, selfish elder sister, and her mean, silly, empty-headed younger sister, with the simple, kindly Musgrove family, form rather the witnesses than the persons of the drama, which transacts itself with the connivance rather than the participation of Sir Walter's heir-at-law, the clever, depraved and unscrupulous cousin, William Walter Elliot; Lady Russell, the ill-advised adviser of the broken engagement; the low-born, manoeuvring Mrs. Clay, who all but captures the unwary Sir Walter; the frank, warm-hearted Admiral Crofts and his wife, and the whole sympathetic naval contingent at Lyme Regis. They brighten the reality of the picture, and form its atmosphere; they could not be spared, and yet, with the exception of Louisa Musgrove, who jumps from the sea-wall at Regis, and by her happy accident brings about the final understanding of the lovers, none of them actively contributes to the event, which for the most part accomplishes itself subjectively through the nature of Anne and Wentworth.

Of the two Anne is by far the more interesting and important personage; her story is distinctly the story of a heroine; yet never was there a heroine so little self-assertive, so far from forth-putting. When the book opens we find her neglected and contemned by her father and elder sister, and sunken passively if not willingly into mere aunthood to her younger sister's children, with no friend who feels her value but that Lady Russell who has helped her to spoil her life. She goes to pay a long visit to her sister as soon as Kellynch Hall is taken by the Croftses, and it is in a characteristic moment of her use-fulness there that Wentworth happens upon her, after their first cold and distant meeting before others.

[Here follow about 450 quoted words.]

III.

As any practised reader of fiction could easily demonstrate, this is not the sort of rescue to bring about a reconciliation between lovers in a *true* novel. There it must be something more formidable than a naughty little boy that the heroine is saved from: it must be a deadly miscreant, or a mad bull, or a frightened horse, or an express train, or a sinking ship. Still it cannot be denied that this simple, this homely scene, is very pretty, and is very like things that happen in life, where there is reason to think love is oftener shown in quality than quantity, and does its effect as perfectly in the little as in the great events. Even the most tremendous incident of the book, the famous passage which made Tennyson, when he visited Lyme Regis, wish to see first of all the place where Louisa Musgrove fell from the Cobb, has hardly heroic proportions, though it is of greater intensity in its lifelikeness, and it reverses the relations of Anne and Wentworth in the characters of helper and helped.

[Here follow about 400 quoted words.]

IV.

One of the things that Jane Austen was first in was the personal description of her heroines. Almost to her time the appearance of the different characters was left to the reader's imagination; it is only in the modern novel that the author seems to feel it his duty to tell how his people look. We have seen how meagrely and formally the heroines of *The Vicar of Wakefield* are presented. In *Sir Charles Grandison*, there is a great pretence of describing the beauty of Harriet Byron, but the image given is vague and conventional. So far as I recall them, the looks of Fanny Burney's and Maria Edgeworth's heroines are left to the reader's liking; and I do not remember any portrait even of Elizabeth Bennet in *Pride and Prejudice*. It is in her later stories that Jane Austen offers this proof of modernity among so many other proofs of it, and tells us how her girls appeared to her. She tells us not very elaborately, to be sure, though in the case of Emma Woodhouse, in *Emma*, the picture is quite finished. In *Persuasion* Anne Elliot is slightly sketched; and we must be content with the fact that she had 'mild dark eyes and delicate features,' and that at the time we are introduced to her she fully looked her twenty-seven years. But this is a good deal better than nothing, and in *Northanger Abbey* Catherine Morland is still more tangibly presented. 'The Morlands . . . were in general very plain, and Catherine was, for many years of her life, as plain as any. She had a thin, awkward figure, a sallow skin without color, dark lank hair, and strong features. . . . At fifteen, appearances were mending. . . . Her complexion improved, her features were softened by plumpness and color, her eyes gained more animation, and her figure more consequence.' At seventeen, when we make her acquaintance, her manners were 'just removed from the awkwardness and shyness of a girl; her person pleasing, and when in good looks, pretty.'

These particulars are from that delightful first chapter where the character as well as the person of the heroine is studied with the playful irony in which the whole story is conceived. From the beginning we know that it is a comedy the author has in hand; and we lose sight of her obvious purpose of satirizing the Radcliffe school of romance in our delight with the character of the heroine and her adventures in Bath and at Northanger Abbey. Catherine Morland is a goose, but a very engaging goose, and a goose you must respect for her sincerity, her high principles, her generous trust of others, and her patience under trials that would be great for much stronger heads. It is no wonder that the accomplished Henry Tilney falls in love with her when he finds that she is already a little in love with him; and when his father brutally sends her home from the Abbey where he has pressed her to visit his daughter on the belief that she is rich and will be a good match for his son, it is no wonder that Tilney follows her and offers himself to her. She prevails by her innocence and sweetness, and in spite of her romantic folly she has so much good heart that it serves her in place of good sense.

V.

The chapters of the story relating to Catherine's stay at the Abbey are rather perfunctorily devoted to burlesquing romantic fiction, in accordance with the author's original design, and they have not the easy charm of the scenes at Bath, where Catherine, as the guest of Mrs. Allen, meets Henry Tilney at a public ball.

[Here follow about 500 quoted words.]

It is plain from the beginning what must be Catherine's fate with a young man who can laugh at her so caressingly, and what must be his with a girl so helplessly transparent to his eyes. Henry Tilney is as good as he is subtle, and he knows how to value her wholesome honesty aright; but all her friends are not witty young clergymen, and one of them is as little like him in appreciation of Catherine's rare nature as she is like Catherine in the qualities which take him. This is putting it rather too severely if it conveys the reproach of wilful bad faith in the case of Isabella Thorpe, who becomes the bosom friend of Catherine at a moment's notice, and the betrothed of Catherine's brother with very little more delay. She is simply what she was born, a self-centred jilt in every motion of her being, and not to be blamed for fulfilling the jilt's function in a world where she is divined in almost her modern importance. In this character, the author forecasts the supremacy of a type which had scarcely been recognized before, but which has since played so dominant a part in fiction, and as with the several types of snobs, proves herself not only artist but prophet. Isabella is not of the lineage of the high and mighty flirts, the dark and deadly flirts, who deal destruction round among the hearts of men. She is what was known in her time as a 'rattle'; her tongue runs while her eyes fly, and her charms are perpetually alert for admiration. She is involved in an incessant drama of fictitious occurrences; she is as romantic in her own way as Catherine is in hers; she peoples an unreal world with conquests, while Catherine dwells in the devotion of one true, if quite imaginary lover. As Catherine cannot make anything of such a character, she decides to love and believe in her utterly, and she cannot well do more after Isabella becomes engaged to her brother James, and declares that she is going to withdraw from the world in his absence, and vows that though she may go to the assembly she will do it merely because Catherine asks it.

[Here follow about 450 quoted words.]

The born jilt, the jilt so natured that the part she perpetually plays is as unconscious with her as the circulation of the blood, has never been more perfectly presented than in Isabella Thorpe, in whom she was first presented; and her whole family, so thoroughly false that they live in an atmosphere of lies, are miracles of art. The soft, kindly, really well-meaning mother is as great a liar as her hollow-hearted, hollow-headed daughter, or her braggart son who babbles blasphemous falsehoods because they are his native speech, with only the purpose of a momentary effect, and hardly the hope or wish of deceit. His pursuit of the trusting Catherine, who desires to believe in him as the friend of her brother, is the farcical element of the pretty comedy. The farce darkens into as much tragedy as the scheme will suffer when General Tilney, a liar in his own way, is taken in by John Thorpe's talk, and believes her very rich; but it all brightens into the sweetest and loveliest comedy again, when Henry Tilney follows her home from his father's house, and the cheerful scene is not again eclipsed till the curtain goes down upon her radiant happiness.

'Emma Woodhouse, Marianne Dashwood, and Fanny Price'

In primitive fiction plot is more important than character; as the art advances character becomes the chief interest, and the action is such as springs from it. In the old tales and romances there is no such thing as character in the modern sense; their readers were satisfied with what the heroes and heroines did and suffered.

When the desire for character arose, the novelists loaded their types with attributes; but still there was no character, which is rooted in personality. The novelist of to-day who has not conceived of this is as archaic as any romancer of the Middle Ages in his ideal of art. Most of the novels printed in the last year, in fact, are as crudely devised as those which have amused people of childish imagination at any time in the last thousand years; and it will always be so with most novels, because most people are of childish imagination. The masterpieces in fiction are those which delight the mind with the traits of personality, with human nature recognizable by the reader through its truth to himself.

The wonder of Jane Austen is that at a time when even the best fiction was overloaded with incident, and its types went staggering about under the attributes heaped upon them, she imagined getting on with only so much incident as would suffice to let her characters express their natures movingly or amusingly. She seems to have reached this really unsurpassable degree of perfection without a formulated philosophy, and merely by her clear vision of the true relation of art to life; but however she came to be what she was, she was so unquestionably great, so unmistakably the norm and prophecy of most that is excellent in Anglo-Saxon fiction since her time, that I shall make no excuse for what may seem a disproportionate study of her heroines.

I.

Emma Woodhouse, in the story named after her, is one of the most boldly imagined of Jane Austen's heroines. Perhaps she is the very most so, for it tooks supreme courage to portray a girl, meant to win

and keep the reader's fancy, with the characteristics frankly ascribed
to Emma Woodhouse. We are indeed allowed to know that she is
pretty; not formally, but casually, from the words of a partial friend:
'Such an eye!—the true hazel eye—and so brilliant!—regular
features, open countenance, with a complexion—ah, what a bloom
of full health, and such a pretty height and size; such a firm and
upright figure.' But, before we are allowed to see her personal beauty
we are made to see in her some of the qualities which are the destined
source of trouble for herself and her friends. In her wish to be useful
she is patronizing and a little presumptuous; her self-sufficiency
early appears, and there are hints of her willingness to shape the
future of others without having past enough of her own to enable her
to do it judiciously. The man who afterwards marries her says of her:
'She will never submit to anything requiring industry and patience,
and a subjection of the fancy to the understanding. . . . Emma is
spoiled by being the cleverest of her family. At ten years old she had
the misfortune of being able to answer questions which puzzled her
sister at seventeen. She was always quick and assured . . . and ever
since she was twelve Emma has been mistress of the house and you
all.'

An officious and self-confident girl, even if pretty, is not usually
one to take the fancy, and yet Emma takes the fancy. She manages the
delightful and whimsical old invalid her father, but she is devotedly
and unselfishly good to him. She takes the destiny of Harriet Smith
unwarrantably into her charge, but she breaks off the girl's love-
affair only in the interest of a better match. She decides that Frank
Churchill, the stepson of her former governess, will be in love with
her, but she never dreams that Mr. Elton, whom she means for
Harriet Smith, can be so. She is not above a little manoeuvring for
the advantage of those she wishes to serve, but the tacit insincerity of
Churchill is intolerable to her. She is unfeelingly neglectful of Jane
Fairfax and cruelly suspicious of her, but she generously does what she
can to repair the wrong, and she takes her punishment for it meekly
and contritely. She makes thoughtless and heartless fun of poor,
babbling Miss Bates, but when Knightley calls her to account for it,
she repents her unkindness with bitter tears. She will not be advised
against her pragmatical schemes by Knightley, but she is humbly
anxious for his good opinion. She is charming in the very degree of
her feminine complexity, which is finally an endearing single-
heartedness.

Her character is shown in an action so slight that the novel of

Emma may be said to be hardly more than an exemplification of Emma. In the placid circumstance of English country life where she is the principal social figure the story makes its round with a few events so unexciting as to leave the reader in doubt whether anything at all has happened. Mr. Elton, a clerical snob as odious as Mr. Collins in *Pride and Prejudice* is amusing, indignantly resents Emma's plan for supplying him with a wife in Harriet Smith, and marries a woman who has Emma's defects without their qualities. Frank Churchill keeps his engagement with Jane Fairfax a secret till all the possible mischief can come from it, and then acknowledges it just when the fact must be most mortifying and humiliating to Emma. After she has been put to shame before Knightley in every way, she finds herself beloved and honored by him and in the way to be happily married. There are, meantime, a few dances and picnics, dinners and teas; Harriet Smith is frightened by gypsies, and some hen-roosts are robbed. There is not an accident, even of the mild and beneficent type of Louisa Musgrove's in *Persuasion*; there is not an elopement, even of the *bouffe* nature of Lydia's in *Pride and Prejudice*; there is nothing at all so tragic as Catherine Morland's expulsion by General Tilney in *Northanger Abbey*. Duels and abductions, of course, there are none; for Jane Austen had put from her all the machinery of the great and little novelists of the eighteenth century, and openly mocked at it. This has not prevented its being frequently used since, and she shows herself more modern than all her predecessors and contemporaries and most of her successors, in the rejection of the major means and the employment of the minor means to produce the enduring effects of *Emma*. Among her quiet books it is almost the quietest, and so far as the novel can suggest that repose which is the ideal of art *Emma* suggests it, in an action of unsurpassed unity, consequence, and simplicity.

It is difficult to detach from the drama any scene which shall present Emma in a moment more characteristic than other moments; but that in which Knightley takes her to task for her behavior to Miss Bates can be chosen, because it illustrates the courageous naturalness with which she is studied throughout.

[Here follow about 450 quoted words.]

It is not on such grounds, in such terms, that a heroine is often talked to in a novel, and it is not so that she commonly takes a talking-to. But it is to be remembered that Knightley is not only Emma's tacit lover; he is the brother of her sister's husband, and much her own elder, and as a family friend has some right to scold her. It is to be considered also that she is herself a singular type among heroines: a type which Jane Austen perfected if she did not invent, and in that varied sisterhood she has the distinction, if not the advantage, of being an entirely natural girl, and a nice girl, in spite of her faults.

II.

Sense and Sensibility is the most conventional, the most mechanical of the author's novels. The title, like that of *Pride and Prejudice*, implies the task of developing two opposite characters in the antithesis which suggests itself; but Elinor and Marianne Dashwood are contrasted much more directly and obviously than Darcy and Elizabeth Bennet. These, indeed, are often interchangeably proud and prejudiced; but Elinor is always a person of sense, and Marianne is always a person of sensibility. One sister always looks the facts of life in the face; the other always sees them through a cloud of romantic emotions. It is not pretended that the wise virgin escapes suffering any more than the foolish, and so far the novel attests itself the effect of Jane Austen's clear perception and faithful observation. It abounds in the truth and courage which distinguish everything she did, and it is perhaps more humorously just and more unsparingly exigent of true ideals than some other books of hers. But it is built more than her other books upon the lines of the accepted fiction of her time, or of the times before hers. In the affair of Marianne's false-hearted lover Willoughby there is almost a reversion to the novel in which young men habitually sought the love of trusting girls and betrayed it. It was in fact her earliest novel and she first wrote it in the form of letters. Then, after she had practised her 'prentice hand to mastery in *Pride and Prejudice*, she recast *Sense and Sensibility* in its present shape. It is only inferior to her other novels; compared with most of the novels that had gone before hers, this least of Jane Austen's is a masterpiece; and the romantic Marianne, even more than the matter-of-fact Elinor, is a picture of girlhood touched in with tender truth, and with the caressing irony which still leaves the character pleasing.

The story is distinctively modern in giving a description of the sister heroines, which was probably an afterthought, and occurred to the author in the making over. 'Miss Dashwood,' she says, 'had a delicate complexion, regular features, and a remarkably pretty figure. Marianne was still handsomer. Her form, though not so correct as her sister's, in having the advantage of height, was more striking. . . . Her skin was very brown, but from its transparency, her complexion was uncommonly brilliant; her features were all good; her smile sweet and attractive, and in her eyes, which were very dark, there was a life, a spirit, an eagerness, which could hardly be seen without delight.' Marianne's mother is as romantic as the girl herself, and it is by her connivance that the girl thinks it a kind of merit to be a credulous simpleton, and to believe more in the love of the cruel scoundrel who flatters and jilts her than he openly asks her to do. When she finds herself in London, shortly after their parting in the country with all the forms of tacit devotion, on his part, and he snubs her at their first meeting in society, she owns in her shame and grief, that there has been no engagement.

[Here follow about 450 quoted words.]

III.

In an earlier age of fiction, if not of society, the folly of Marianne would have meant her ruin; but in the wiser and milder æsthetics of Jane Austen it meant merely her present heart-break, with her final happiness through a worthier love. Hers is a very simple nature, studied with a simpler art than such an intricate character as Emma's. She has only at all times to be herself, responsive to her mainspring of emotionality; and a girl like Emma has apparently to be different people at different times, in obedience to inconsistent and unexpected impulses. She is therefore perhaps the greatest of Jane Austen's creations, and certainly the most modern; yet even so slight and elemental a character as Marianne is handled with the security and mastery, which were sometimes greater and sometimes less in the author's work.

Persuasion, which was the latest of her novels, is in places the poorest, and *Sense and Sensibility*, which is, on the whole, the poorest, has moments of being the greatest. There is no such meanness portrayed in all fiction as John Dashwood's, and yet you are made to feel that he would like not to be mean if only he could once rise above himself. In Marianne and her mother, who are such a pair of emotional simpletons, there are traits of generosity that almost redeem their folly, and their limitations in the direction of silliness are as distinctly shown as their excesses. Willoughby himself, who lives to realize that he has never loved any one but Marianne, and has been given to understand by the relation who leaves her money away from him, 'that if he had behaved with honor towards Marianne, he might at once have been happy and rich,' even he is not committed wholesale to unavailing regret. 'That his repentance of misconduct, which thus brought its own punishment, was sincere, need not be doubted. . . . But that he was forever inconsolable—that he fled from society, or contracted a habitual gloom of temper, or died of a broken heart— must not be depended upon, for he did neither. He lived to exert, and frequently to enjoy himself. His wife was not always out of humor, nor his house always uncomfortable; and in his breed of horses and dogs, and in sporting of every kind, he found no inconsiderable degree of domestic felicity.'

It was not Jane Austen's way to do anything wholesale; she was far too well acquainted with life, and of too sensitive an artistic conscience for that; and especially in *Mansfield Park* is one aware of the hand that is held from overdoing. As in *Sense and Sensibility*, and in fact all her other novels, the subordinate characters are of delightful verity and vitality. Mrs. Norris is of a meanness which in its sort may almost match with John Dashwood's, and Lady Bertram's indolent affections and principles form a personality of almost unique charm. These sisters of Mrs. Price who made an unhappy love marriage beneath her, are of the same quality as she, and their differentiation by environment is one of the subtle triumphs of the author's art.

It is by the same skill that a character so prevalently passive as that of sweet Fanny Price is made insensibly to take and gently to keep the hold of a heroine upon the reader. It would have been so easy in so many ways to overdo her. But she is never once overdone, either when as a child she meets with the cold welcome of charity in her uncle's family, where she afterwards makes herself indispensable, or in her return to her childhood home, which has forgotten her in her long absence. It is not pretended that she is treated by her cousins and her aunts with active unkindness, and she suffers none of the crueller snubbing which cheaply wins a heroine the heart of the witness. When she goes back to Portsmouth on that famous visit, after nine years at Mansfield Park, it is not concealed that she is ashamed of her home, of her weak and slattern mother, of her drinky, smoky, and sweary father, of her rude little brothers and sisters, of the whole shabby and vulgar household. None of the younger children remember her; her father and mother, from moment to moment, in their preoccupation with her brother, who comes with her to get his ship at Portsmouth (we are again among naval people), fail to remember her. All the circumstances are conducive to disgust and resentment in a girl who might reasonably have expected to be a distinguished guest for a while at least. But once more that delicately discriminating hand of Jane Austen does its work; it presently appears that the Price household is not so altogether impossible, and that a girl who wishes to be of use to others is not condemned to lasting misery and disgrace in any circumstances. Always the humorous sense of limitations comes in, but the human sense of good-will is there; the recognition of the effect of good-will is distinct but not elaborate. There is more philosophizing and satirizing than would be present in a more recent novel of equal mastery; but the characterization is as neat as in the highest art of any time.

Sweet Fanny Price goes back to Mansfield Park with almost as little notice from her family as when she came to Portsmouth; but she has done them good, and is the better and stronger for her unrequited self-devotion. It is not pretended that she takes any active part in supporting the family at Mansfield Park under the disgrace which has befallen them through the elopement of one daughter to be divorced and of another to be married. Her function is best suggested by the exclamation with which her aunt Bertram falls upon her neck, 'Dear Fanny, now I shall be comfortable.' To be a comfort, that has always been Fanny Price's rare privilege, and she imparts to the reader something of the consolation she brings to all the people in the story who need the help of her sympathy. Possibly there was never a heroine, except Anne Elliot, who was so passive, without being spectacularly passive, if it is permitted so to phrase the rather intangible fact; and yet who so endeared herself to the fancy.

One is not passionately in love with Fanny Price, as one is with some heroines; one is quite willing Edward Bertram should have her in the end; but she is one of the sweetest and dearest girls in the world, though these words, too, rather oversay her. She is another proof of Jane Austen's constant courage, which was also her constant wisdom, in being true to life. It is not only wit like Elizabeth Bennet's, sensibility like Marianne Dashwood's, complexity like Emma Woodhouse's, or utter innocence like Catherine Morland's that is charming. Goodness is charming, patience, usefulness, forbearance, meekness, are charming, as Jane Austen divined in such contrasting types as Fanny Price and Anne Elliot. If any young lady has a mind to be like them, she can learn how in two of the most interesting books in the world.

Some of the old English novels were amazing successes even

when compared with the most worthless novels of recent days. *Pamela*, and *Clarissa*, and *Sir Charles Grandison* were read all over the Continent. The *Vicar of Wakefield* was the gospel of a new art to Germany, where Goethe said that it permanently influenced his character. *Evelina* and *Cecilia* were the passions of people of taste everywhere, and when their trembling author was presented to Louis XVIII in Paris, he complimented her upon her novels, which were known also to the first Napoleon. No such glories attended Jane Austen in her lifetime. She found with difficulty a publisher for her greatest book, and a public quite as slow and reluctant. But her publishers and her public have been increasing ever since, and they were never so numerous as now. Whether they will ever be fewer, it would be useless to ask; what we know without asking, from the evidence of her work, is that in the real qualities of greatness she is still the most actual of all her contemporaries, of nearly all her successors.

In and out of 'The Easy Chair,'
1901–20

On the train homeward, exhausted after a lecture tour in 1899, 'one morning after the misery of a night in a sleeping-car,' Howells felt the shock of reading in the newspaper that Harper and Brothers, his House of friends and security, had gone bankrupt. To be sure, he had prospered through the decade as a free-lance, writing for S. S. McClure, for the *Cosmopolitan*, for the *Ladies' Home Journal*, for *Scribner's*, the *Youth's Companion, Century*, and the *Atlantic* once more, even *Munsey's*. But the great House had published all his new books, and his name had appeared more frequently in their magazines than everywhere else put together. He had far from ceased to belong to the Harpers' stable of authors, and he felt desolated. During the summer of 1900 he went to Cape Ann to finish *Heroines of Fiction* and came back in the autumn in a state of increasing anxiety 'for the future, which stared at me rather vacantly,' as he said in the Harper centenary book. Other publishers wanted him—McClure, L. C. Page, Dodd, Mead & Co.—but Howells hesitated until he heard from the House reorganized. What he heard at last laid pecuniary fear to rest for as long as he lived; but it employed him to do criticism for the rest of his life, too.

The key to the bargain was Colonel George Harvey, protégé of banker J. P. Morgan, wealthy in his own right, a 'president-maker' (both Woodrow Wilson and Warren G. Harding), journalist, magazine publisher, and zealous editor by avocation. For $10,000 again, plus his royalties, Howells was to write for the firm's magazines (including the ancient *North American Review*, which Harvey owned personally). He was to revive the prestigious 'Editor's Easy Chair' for *Harper's Monthly* and contribute as he saw fit elsewhere. There appears to have been quite a bit of flexibility about the arrangements, but they kept Howells writing criticism all the time.

It needs to be said, hopefully for the last time, that the tradition of 'the Dean in the Easy Chair'—of a Howells who during these years became bland, weary, chatty, innocuous, inconsequential, 'acquiescent'—does not fit all the facts. The 'Easy Chair' tradition had been that of the urbane personal essay. Howells not only revered the tradition established by George William Curtis, he had reason to know that the 'unreal editor' must now present a mask and voice different from those habitual to the 'Study.' Neither consideration, however, prevented him from dealing out

335

hard knocks. Curtis had often spoken his mind, and Howells in 'The Easy Chair' openly attacked imperialists, snobs, neo-romantics, and predatory capitalists.

But it is even more essential to recognize that other personae were available to Howells out of the 'Chair' and were strenuously employed during the 'Easy Chair' decades. In *Harper's Weekly* he published a number of editorials, often bitingly ironic, which stand out among his radical commentaries. And in the *North American Review*, the oldest, most respected vehicle of serious criticism in the United States, he held *carte blanche* to publish a series, focused any way he wished, of solid, extended essays in criticism for an audience which was by definition the best-read, most intellectually curious and responsible in the nation. For them, out of 'The Easy Chair,' Howells wrote much of the best criticism of his long career. Age, like what folk-say records of poverty, is 'no disgrace, but damned inconvenient.' Howells was nearly sixty-four when he mounted to 'The Easy Chair.' Though that excellent criticism lay ahead in the two decades of this century which remained to him, it was inevitable that almost all of it should come in the first decade, inevitable that his critical clock should begin to run down toward the end.

42 'Mark Twain: An Inquiry'
1901

Published in the *North American Review*, February 1901.

At the height of his critical powers and with the *North American Review* in hand, Howells found what journalists call a 'news-hook' to hang it on and wrote the best of his critiques on the work of Clemens. By this time almost all the best of Mark Twain had appeared and Howells could see him whole. Few critical articles more searching or valid have been written on Mark Twain as literature, and here again Howells 'set' most of the themes—and the following sheep have been jumping in his places for seventy years.

Two recent events have concurred to offer criticism a fresh excuse, if not a fresh occasion, for examining the literary work of Mr. Samuel L. Clemens, better known to the human family by his pseudonym of Mark Twain. One of these events is the publication of his writings in a uniform edition, which it is to be hoped will remain indefinitely incomplete; the other is his return to his own country after an absence so long as to form a psychological perspective in which his character- istics make a new appeal.

I.

The uniform edition of Mr. Clemens's writings is of that dignified presence which most of us have thought their due in moments of high pleasure with their quality, and high dudgeon with their keeping in the matchlessly ugly subscription volumes of the earlier issues. Yet now that we have them in this fine shape, fit every one, in its elect binding, paper and print, to be set on the shelf of a gentleman's library, and not taken from it without some fear of personal demerit, I will own a furtive regret for the hideous blocks and bricks of which the visible temple of the humorist's fame was first builded. It was an advantage to meet the author in a guise reflecting the accidental and provisional moods of a unique talent finding itself out; and the pictures which originally illustrated the process were helps to the imagination such as the new uniform edition does not afford. In great part it could not retain them, for reasons which the recollection of their uncouth vigor will suggest, but these reasons do not hold in all cases, and especially in the case of Mr. Dan Beard's extraordinarily sympathetic and interpretative pictures for *The Connecticut Yankee at King Arthur's Court*. The illustrations of the uniform edition, in fact, are its weak side, but it can be said that they do not detract from one's delight in the literature; no illustrations could do that; and, in compensation for their defect, the reader has the singularly intelligent and agreeable essay of Mr. Brander Matthews on Mr. Clemens's work, by way of introduction to the collection. For the rest one may acquit one's self of one's whole duty to the uniform edition by reminding the reader that in the rich variety of its inclusion are those renowning books, *The Innocents Abroad* and *Roughing It*; the first constructive fiction on the larger scale, *Tom Sawyer* and *Huckleberry Finn*; the later books of travel, *A Tramp Abroad* and *Following the Equator*, the multiplicity of tales, sketches, burlesques, satires and speeches, together with the spoil of Mr. Clemens's courageous forays in the region of literary criticism, and his later romances, *The Connecticut Yankee*, *The American Claimant*, and the *Joan of Arc*. These complete an array of volumes which the most unconventional reviewer can hardly keep from calling goodly, and which is responsive to the spirit of the literature in a certain desultory and insuccessive arrangement.

II.

So far as I know Mr. Clemens is the first writer to use in extended writing the fashion we all use in thinking, and to set down the thing that comes into his mind without fear or favor of the thing that went before, or the thing that may be about to follow. I, for instance, in putting this paper together, am anxious to observe some sort of logical order, to discipline such impressions and notions as I have of the subject into a coherent body which shall march column-wise to a conclusion obvious if not inevitable from the start. But Mr. Clemens, if he were writing it, would not be anxious to do any such thing. He would take whatever offered itself to his hand out of that mystical chaos, that divine ragbag, which we call the mind, and leave the reader to look after relevancies and sequences for himself. These there might be, but not of that hard and fast sort which I am eager to lay hold of, and the result would at least be satisfactory to the author, who would have shifted the whole responsibility to the reader, with whom it belongs, at least as much as with the author. In other words, Mr. Clemens uses in work on the larger scale the method of the elder essayists, and you know no more where you are going to bring up in *The Innocents Abroad* or *Following the Equator* than in an essay of Montaigne. The end you arrive at is the end of the book, and you reach it amused but edified, and sorry for nothing but to be there. You have noted the author's thoughts, but not his order of thinking; he has not attempted to trace the threads of association between the things that have followed one another; his reason, not his logic, has convinced you, or rather it has persuaded you, for you have not been brought under conviction. It is not certain that this method is of design with Mr. Clemens; that might spoil it; and possibly he will be as much surprised as any one to know that it is his method. It is imaginable that he pursues it from no wish but to have pleasure of his work, and not to fatigue either himself or his reader; and his method may be the secret of his vast popularity, but it cannot be the whole secret of it. Any one may compose a scrap-book, and offer it to the public with nothing of Mark Twain's good fortune. Everything seems to depend upon the nature of the scraps, after all; his scraps might have been consecutively arranged, in a studied order, and still have immensely pleased; but there is no doubt that people like things that have at least the appearance of not having been drilled into line. Life itself has that sort of appearance as it goes on; it is an essay with moments of drama in it, rather than a drama; it is a lesson, with the precepts appearing haphazard, and not precept upon precept; it is a school, but not always a school-room; it is a temple, but the priests are not always in their sacerdotal robes; sometimes they are eating the sacrifice behind the altar and pouring the libations for the god through the channels of their dusty old throats. An instinct of something chaotic, ironic, empiric in the order of experience seems to have been the inspiration of our humorist's art, and what finally remains with the reader, after all the joking and laughing, is not merely the feeling of having had a mighty good time, but the conviction that he has got the worth of his money. He has not gone through the six hundred pages of *The Innocents Abroad*, or *Following the Equator*, without having learned more of the world as the writer saw it than any but the rarest traveller is able to show for his travel; and possibly with his average, practical American public, which was his first tribunal, and must always be his court of final appeal, Mark Twain justified himself for being so delightful by being so instructive. If this bold notion is admissible it seems the moment to say that no writer ever imparted information more inoffensively.

But his great charm is his absolute freedom in a region where most of us are fettered and shackled by immemorial convention. He saunters out into the trim world of letters, and lounges across its neatly kept paths, and walks about on the grass at will, in spite of all the signs that have been put up from the beginning of literature, warning people of dangers and penalties for the slightest trespass.

One of the characteristics I observe in him is his single-minded use of words, which he employs as Grant did to express the plain, straight meaning their common acceptance has given them with no regard to their structural significance or their philological implications. He writes English as if it were a primitive and not a derivative language, without Gothic or Latin or Greek behind it, or German and French beside it. The result is the English in which the most vital works of English literature are cast, rather than the English of Milton, and Thackeray, and Mr. Henry James. I do not say that the English of the authors last named is less than vital, but only that it is not the most vital. It is scholarly and conscious; it knows who its grandfather was; it has the refinement and subtlety of an old patriciate. You will not have with it the widest suggestion, the largest human feeling, or perhaps the loftiest reach of imagination, but you will have the keen joy that exquisite artistry in words can alone impart, and that you will not have in Mark Twain. What you will have in him is a style which is as personal, as biographical as the style of any one who has written, and expresses a civilization whose courage of the chances, the preferences, the duties, is not the measure of its essential modesty. It has a thing to say, and it says it in the word that may be the first, or second, or third choice, but will not be the instrument of the most fastidious ear, the most delicate and exacting sense, though it will be the word that surely and strongly conveys intention from the author's mind to the reader's. It is the Abraham Lincolnian word, not the Charles Sumnerian; it is American, Western.

III.

Now that Mark Twain has become a fame so world-wide, we should be in some danger of forgetting, but for his help, how entirely American he is, and we have already forgotten, perhaps, how truly Western he is, though his work, from first to last, is always reminding us of the fact. But here I should like to distinguish. It is not alone in its generous humor, with more honest laughter in it than humor ever had in the world till now, that his work is so Western. Any one who has really known the West (and really to know it one must have lived it), is aware of the profoundly serious, the almost tragical strain which is the fundamental tone in the movement of such music as it has. Up to a certain point, in the presence of the mystery which we call life, it trusts and hopes and laughs; beyond that it doubts and fears, but it does not cry. It is more likely to laugh again, and in the work of Mark Twain there is little of the pathos which is supposed to be the ally of humor, little suffusion of apt tears from the smiling eyes. It is too sincere for that sort of play; and if after the doubting and the fearing it laughs again, it is with a suggestion of that resentment which youth feels when the disillusion from its trust and hope comes, and which is the grim second-mind of the West in the presence of the mystery. It is not so much the race-effect as the region-effect; it is not the Anglo-American finding expression, it is the Westerner, who is not more thoroughly the creature of circumstances, of conditions, but far more dramatically their creature, than any prior man. He found himself placed in them and under them, so near to a world in which the natural and primitive was obsolete, that while he could not escape them, neither could he help challenging them. The inventions, the appliances, the improvements of the modern world invaded the hoary eld of his rivers and forests and prairies, and while he was still a pioneer, a hunter, a trapper, he found himself confronted with the financier, the scholar, the gentleman. They seemed to him, with the world they represented, at first very droll, and he laughed. Then they set him thinking, and as he never was afraid of anything, he thought over the whole field, and demanded explanations of all his prepossessions, of equality, of humanity, of representative government and revealed religion. When they had not their answers ready, without accepting the conventions of the modern world as solutions or in any manner final, he laughed again, not mockingly, but patiently, compassionately. Such, or somewhat like this, was the genesis and evolution of Mark Twain.

Missouri was Western, but it was also Southern, not only in the institution of slavery, to the custom and acceptance of which Mark Twain was born and bred without any applied doubt of its divinity, but in the peculiar social civilization of the older South from which his native State was settled. It would be reaching too far out to claim that American humor, of the now prevailing Western type, is of Southern origin, but without staying to attempt it I will say that I think the fact could be established; and I think one of the most notably Southern traits of Mark Twain's humor is its power of seeing the fun of Southern seriousness, but this vision did not come to him till after his liberation from neighborhood in the vaster far West. He was the first, if not the only man of his section, to betray a consciousness of the grotesque absurdities in the Southern inversion of the civilized ideals in behalf of slavery, which must have them upside down in order to walk over them safely. No American of Northern birth or breeding could have imagined the spiritual struggle of Huck Finn in deciding to help the negro Jim to his freedom, even though he should be forever despised as a negro thief in his native town, and perhaps eternally lost through the blackness of his sin. No Northerner could have come so close to the heart of a Kentucky feud, and revealed it so perfectly, with the whimsicality playing through its carnage, or could have so brought us into the presence of the sardonic comi-tragedy of the squalid little river town where the store-keeping magnate shoots down his drunken tormentor in the arms of the drunkard's daughter, and then cows with bitter mockery the mob that comes to lynch him. The strict religiosity compatible in the Southwest with savage precepts of conduct is something that could make itself known in its amusing contrast only to the native Southwesterner, and the revolt against it is as constant in Mark Twain as the enmity to New England orthodoxy is in Dr. Holmes. But he does not take it with such serious resentment as Dr. Holmes is apt to take his inherited Puritanism, and it may be therefore that he is able to do it more perfect justice, and impart it more absolutely. At any rate there are no more vital passages in his fiction than those which embody character as it is affected for good as well as evil by the severity of the local Sunday-schooling and church-going.

IV.

I find myself, in spite of the discipline I intend for this paper, speaking first of the fiction, which by no means came first in Mark Twain's literary development. It is true that his beginnings were in short sketches, more or less inventive, and studies of life in which he let his imagination play freely; but it was not till he had written *Tom Sawyer* that he could be called a novelist. Even now I think he should rather be called a romancer, though such a book as *Huckleberry Finn* takes itself out of the order of romance and places itself with the great things in picaresque fiction. Still it is more poetic than picaresque, and of a deeper psychology. The probable and credible soul that the author divines in the son of the town drunkard is one which we might each own brother, and the art which portrays this nature at first hand in the person and language of the hero, without pose or affectation, is fine art. In the boy's history the author's fancy works realistically to an end as high as it has reached elsewhere, if not higher; and I who like *The Connecticut Yankee at King Arthur's Court* so much, have half a mind to give my whole heart to *Huckleberry Finn*.

Both *Huckleberry Finn* and *Tom Sawyer* wander in episodes loosely related to the main story, but they are of a closer and more logical advance from the beginning to the end than the fiction which preceded them, and which I had almost forgotten to name before them. We owe to *The Gilded Age* a type in Colonel Mulberry Sellers which is as likely to endure as any fictitious character of our time. It embodies the sort of Americanism which survived through the civil war, and characterized in its boundlessly credulous, fearlessly adventurous, unconsciously burlesque excess the period of political and economic expansion which followed the war. Colonel Sellers was, in some rough sort, the America of that day, which already seems so remote, and is best imaginable through him. Yet the story itself was of the fortuitous structure of what may be called the autobiographical books, such as *The Innocents Abroad* and *Roughing It*. Its desultory and accidental character was heightened by the co-operation of Mr. Clemens's fellow humorist, Charles Dudley Warner, and such coherence as it had was weakened by the diverse qualities of their minds and their irreconcilable ideals in literature. These never combined to a sole effect or to any variety of effects that left the reader very clear what the story was all about; and yet from the cloudy solution was precipitated at least one character which, as I have said, seems of as lasting substance and lasting significance as any which the American imagination has evolved from the American environment.

If Colonel Sellers is Mr. Clemens's supreme invention, as it seems to me, I think that his *The Connecticut Yankee* is his greatest achievement in the way of a greatly imagined and symmetrically developed romance. Of all the fanciful schemes in fiction it pleases me most, and I give myself with absolute delight to its notion of a keen East Hartford

Yankee finding himself, by a retroactionary spell, at the court of King Arthur of Britain, and becoming part of the sixth century with all the customs and ideas of the nineteenth in him and about him. The field for humanizing satire which this scheme opens is illimitable; but the ultimate achievement, the last poignant touch, the most exquisite triumph of the book, is the return of the Yankee to his own century, with his look across the gulf of the ages at the period of which he had been a part and his vision of the sixth century woman he had loved holding their child in her arms.

It is a great fancy, transcending in æsthetic beauty the invention in *The Prince and Pauper*, with all the delightful and affecting implications of that charming fable, and excelling the heartrending story in which Joan of Arc lives and prophesies and triumphs and suffers. She is indeed realized to the modern sense as few figures of the past have been realized in fiction; and is none the less of her time and of all time because her supposititious historian is so recurrently of ours. After Sellers, and Huck Finn, and Tom Sawyer, and the Connecticut Yankee she is the author's finest creation; and if he had succeeded in portraying no other woman nature, he would have approved himself its fit interpreter in her. I do not think he succeeds so often with that nature as with the boy nature or the man nature, apparently because it does not interest him so much. He will not trouble himself to make women talk like women at all times; oftentimes they talk too much like him, though the simple, homely sort express themselves after their kind; and Mark Twain does not always write men's dialogue so well as he might. He is apt to burlesque the lighter colloquiality, and it is only in the more serious and most tragical junctures that his people utter themselves with veracious simplicity and dignity. That great, burly fancy of his is always tempting him to the exaggeration which is the condition of so much of his personal humor, but which when it invades the drama spoils the illusion. The illusion renews itself in the great moments, but I wish it could be kept infract in the small, and I blame him that he does not rule his fancy better. His imagination is always dramatic in its conceptions, but not always in its expressions; the talk of his people is often inadequate caricature in the ordinary exigencies, and his art contents itself with makeshift in the minor action. Even in *Huck Finn*, so admirably proportioned and honestly studied, you find a piece of lawless extravagance hurled in, like the episode of the two strolling actors in the flatboat; their broad burlesque is redeemed by their final tragedy—a prodigiously real and moving passage—but the friend of the book cannot help wishing the burlesque was not there. One laughs, and then despises oneself for laughing, and this is not what Mark Twain often makes you do. There are things in him that shock, and more things that we think shocking, but this may not be so much because of their nature, as because of our want of naturalness; they wound our conventions rather than our convictions. As most women are more the subjects of convention than men, his humor is not for most women; but I have a theory that when women like it they like it far beyond men. Its very excess must satisfy that demand of their insatiate nerves for something that there is enough of; but I offer this conjecture with instant readiness to withdraw it under correction. What I feel rather surer of is that there is something finally feminine in the inconsequence of his ratiocination, and his beautiful confidence that we shall be able to follow him to his conclusion in all those turnings and twistings and leaps and bounds, by which his mind carries itself to any point but that he seems aiming at. Men, in fact, are born of women, and possibly Mark Twain owes his literary method to the colloquial style of some far ancestress who was more concerned in getting there, and amusing herself on the way, than in ordering her steps.

Possibly also it is to this ancestress that he owes the instinct of right and wrong which keeps him clear as to the conditions that formed him, and their injustice. Slavery in a small Missouri river town could not have been the dignified and patriarchal institution which Southerners of the older South are fond of remembering or imagining. In the second generation from Virginia ancestry of this sort, Mark Twain was born to the common necessity of looking out for himself, and while making himself practically of another order of things he felt whatever was fine in the old and could regard whatever was ugly and absurd more tolerantly, more humorously than those who bequeathed him their enmity to it. Fortunately for him, and for us who were to enjoy his humor, he came to his intellectual consciousness in a world so large and free and safe that he could be fair to any wrong while seeing the right so unfailingly; and nothing is finer in him than his gentleness with the error which is simply passive and negative. He gets fun out of it, of course, but he deals almost tenderly with it, and hoards his violence for the superstitions and traditions which are arrogant and active. His pictures of that old rivertown, Southwestern life, with its faded and tattered aristocratic ideals and its squalid democratic realities, are pathetic, while they are so unsparingly true and so inapologetically and unaffectedly faithful.

The West, when it began to put itself into literature, could do so without the sense, or the apparent sense, of any older or politer world outside of it; whereas the East was always looking fearfully over its shoulder at Europe, and anxious to account for itself as well as represent itself. No such anxiety as this entered Mark Twain's mind, and it is not claiming too much for the Western influence upon American literature to say that the final liberation of the East from this anxiety is due to the West, and to its ignorant courage or its indifference to its difference from the rest of the world. It would not claim to be superior, as the South did, but it could claim to be humanly equal, or rather it would make no claim at all, but would simply be, and what it was, show itself without holding itself responsible for not being something else.

The Western boy of forty or fifty years ago grew up so close to the primeval woods or fields that their inarticulate poetry became part of his being, and he was apt to deal simply and uncritically with literature when he turned to it, as he dealt with nature. He took what he wanted, and left what he did not like; he used it for the playground, not the workshop of his spirit. Something like this I find true of Mark Twain in peculiar and uncommon measure. I do not see any proof in his books that he wished at any time to produce literature, or that he wished to reproduce life. When filled up with an experience that deeply interested him, or when provoked by some injustice or absurdity that intensely moved him, he burst forth, and the outbreak might be altogether humorous, but it was more likely to be humorous with a groundswell of seriousness carrying it profoundly forward. In all there is something curiously, not very definably, elemental, which again seems to me Western. He behaves himself as if he were the first man who was ever up against the proposition in hand. He deals as newly, for instance, with the relations of Shelley to his wife, and with as personal and direct an indignation as if they had never attracted critical attention before; and this is the mind or the mood which he brings to all literature. Life is another affair with him; it is not a discovery, not a surprise; every one else knows how it is; but here is a new world, and he explores it with a ramping joy, and shouts for the reader to come on and see how, in spite of all the lies about it, it is the same old world of men and women, with really nothing in it but their passions and prejudices and hypocrisies. At heart he was always deeply and essentially romantic, and once must have expected life itself to be a fairy dream. When it did not turn out so he found it tremendously amusing still, and his expectation not the least amusing thing in it, but without rancour, without grudge or bitterness in his disillusion, so that his latest word is as sweet as his first. He is deeply and essentially romantic in his literary conceptions, but when it comes to working them out he is helplessly literal and real; he is the impassioned lover, the helpless slave of the concrete. For this reason, for his wish, his necessity, first to ascertain his facts, his logic is as irresistible as his laugh.

V.

All life seems, when he began to find it out, to have the look of a vast joke, whether the joke was on him or on his fellow beings, or if it may be expressed without any irreverence, on their common creator. But it was never wholly a joke, and it was not long before his literature began to own its pathos. The sense of this is not very apparent in *Innocents Abroad*, but in *Roughing It* we began to be distinctly aware of it, and in the successive books it is constantly imminent, not as a clutch at the heartstrings, but as a demand of common justice, common sense, the feeling of proportion. It is not sympathy with the under dog merely as under dog that moves Mark Twain; for the under dog is sometimes rightfully under. But the probability is that it is wrongfully under, and has a claim to your inquiry into the case which you cannot ignore without atrocity. Mark Twain never ignores it; I know nothing finer in him than his perception that in this curiously contrived mechanism men suffer for their sorrows rather oftener than they suffer for their sins; and when they suffer for their sorrows they have a right not only to our pity but to our help. He always gives his help, even when he seems to leave the pity to others, and it may be safely said that no writer has dealt with so many phases of life with more unfailing justice. There is no real telling how any one comes to be what he is; all speculation concerning the fact is more or less impudent or futile conjecture; but it is conceivable that Mark Twain took from his early environment the custom of clairvoyance in things in which most humorists are purblind, and that being always in the presence of the under dog, he came to feel for him as under with him. If the knowledge and vision of slavery did not tinge all life with potential tragedy, perhaps it was this which lighted in the future humorist the indignation at injustice which glows in his page. His indignation relieves itself as often as not in a laugh; injustice is the most ridiculous thing in the world, after all, and indignation with it feels its own absurdity.

It is supposable, if not more than supposable, that the ludicrous incongruity of a slaveholding democracy nurtured upon the Declaration of Independence, and the comical spectacle of white labor owning black labor, had something to do in quickening the sense of contrast which is the fountain of humor, or is said to be so. But not to drive too hard a conjecture which must remain conjecture, we may reasonably hope to find in the untrammelled, the almost unconditional life of the later and farther West, with its individualism limited by nothing but individualism, the outside causes of the first overflow of the spring. We are so fond of classification, which we think is somehow interpretation, that one cannot resist the temptation it holds out in the case of the most unclassifiable things; and I must yield so far as to note that the earliest form of Mark Twain's work is characteristic of the greater part of it. The method used in *Innocents Abroad* and in *Roughing It* is the method used in *Life on the Mississippi*, in *A Tramp Abroad* and in *Following the Equator*, which constitute in bulk a good half of all his writings, as they express his dominant æsthetics. If he had written the fictions alone, we should have had to recognize a rare inventive talent, a great imagination and dramatic force; but I think it must be allowed that the personal books named overshadow the fictions. They have the qualities that give character to the fictions, and they have advantages that the fictions have not and that no fiction can have. In them, under cover of his pseudonym, we come directly into the presence of the author, which is what the reader is always longing and seeking to do; but unless the novelist is a conscienceless and tasteless recreant to the terms of his art, he cannot admit the reader to his intimacy. The personal books of Mark Twain have not only the charm of the essay's inconsequent and desultory method, in which invention, fact, reflection and philosophy wander in after one another in any following that happens, but they are of an immediate and most informal hospitality which admits you at once to the author's confidence, and makes you frankly welcome not only to his thought but to his way of thinking. He takes no trouble in the matter, and he asks you to take none. All that he requires is that you will have common sense, and be able to tell a joke when you see it. Otherwise the whole furnishing of his mental mansion is at your service, to make such use as you can of it, but he will not be always directing your course, or requiring you to enjoy yourself in this or that order.

In the case of the fictions, he conceives that his first affair is to tell a story, and a story when you are once launched upon it does not admit of deviation without some hurt to itself. In Mark Twain's novels, whether they are for boys or for men, the episodes are only those that illustrate the main narrative or relate to it, though he might have allowed himself somewhat larger latitude in the old-fashioned tradition which he has oftenest observed in them. When it comes to the critical writings, which again are personal, and which, whether they are criticisms of literature or of life, are always so striking, he is quite relentlessly logical and coherent. Here there is no lounging or sauntering, with entertaining or edifying digressions. The object is in view from the first, and the reasoning is straightforwardly to it throughout. This is as notable in the admirable paper on the Jews, or on the Austrian situation, as in that on Harriet Shelley, or that on Cooper's novels. The facts are first ascertained with a conscience uncommon in critical writing of any kind, and then they are handled with vigor and precision till the polemic is over. It does not so much matter whether you agree with the critic or not; what you have to own is that here is a man of strong convictions, clear ideas and ardent sentiments, based mainly upon common sense of extraordinary depth and breadth.

VI.

In fact, what finally appeals to you in Mark Twain, and what may hereafter be his peril with his readers, is his common sense. It is well to eat humble pie when one comes to it at the *table d'hôte* of life, and I wish here to offer my brother literary men a piece of it that I never refuse myself. It is true that other men do not really expect much common sense of us, whether we are poets or novelists or humorists. They may enjoy our company, and they may like us or pity us, but they do not take us very seriously, and they would as soon we were fools as not if we will only divert or comfort or inspire them. Especially if we are humorists do they doubt our practical wisdom; they are apt at first sight to take our sense for a part of the joke, and the humorist who convinces them that he is a man of as much sense as any of them, and possibly more, is in the parlous case of having given them hostages for seriousness which he may not finally be able to redeem.

I should say in the haste to which every inquiry of this sort seems subject, that this was precisely the case with Mark Twain. The exceptional observer must have known from the beginning that he was a thinker of courageous originality and penetrating sagacity, even when he seemed to be joking; but in the process of time it has come to such a pass with him that the wayfaring man can hardly shirk knowledge of the fact. The fact is thrown into sudden and picturesque relief by his return to his country after the lapse of time long enough to have let a new generation grow up in knowledge of him. The projection of his reputation against a background of foreign appreciation, more or less luminous, such as no other American author has enjoyed, has little or nothing to do with his acceptance on the new terms. Those poor Germans, Austrians, Englishmen and Frenchmen who have been, from time to time in the last ten years, trying to show their esteem for his peculiar gifts could never come as close to the heart of his humor as we could; we might well doubt if they could fathom all his wisdom, which begins and ends in his humor; and if ever they seemed to chance upon his full significance, we naturally felt a kind of grudge, when we could not call it their luck, and suspected him of being less significant in the given instances than they supposed. The danger which he now runs with us is neither heightened nor lessened by the spread of his fame, but is an effect from intrinsic causes. Possibly it might not have been so great if he had come back comparatively forgotten; it is certain only that in coming back more remembered than ever, he confronts a generation which began to know him not merely by his personal books and his fiction, but by those criticisms of life and literature which have more recently attested his interest in the graver and weightier things.

Graver and weightier, people call them, but whether they are really more important than the lighter things, I am by no means sure. What I am amused with, independently of the final truth, is the possibility that his newer audience will exact this serious mood of Mr. Clemens, whereas we of his older world only suffered it, and were of a high conceit with our liberality in allowing a humorist sometimes to be a philosopher. Some of us indeed, not to be invidiously specific as to whom, were always aware of potentialities in him, which he seemed to hold in check, or to trust doubtfully to his reader as if he thought they might be thought part of the joke. Looking back over his work now, the later reader would probably be able to point out to earlier readers the evidence of a constant growth in the direction of something like recognized authority in matters of public import, especially those that were subject to the action of the public conscience as well as the public interest, until now hardly any man writing upon such matters is heard so willingly by all sorts of men. All of us, for instance, have read somewhat of the conditions in South Africa which have eventuated in the present effort of certain British politicians to destroy two free Republics in the interest of certain British speculators; but I doubt if we have found the case anywhere so well stated as in the closing chapters of Mark Twain's *Following the Equator*. His estimate of the military character of the belligerents on either side is of the prophetic cast which can come only from the thorough assimilation of accomplished facts; and in those passages the student of the actual war can spell its anticipative history. It is by such handling of such questions, unpremeditated and almost casual as it seems, that Mark Twain has won his claim to be heard on any public matter, and achieved the odd sort of primacy which he now enjoys.

But it would be rather awful if the general recognition of his prophetic function should implicate the renunciation of the humor that has endeared him to mankind. It would be well for his younger following to beware of reversing the error of the elder, and taking everything in earnest, as these once took nothing in earnest from him. To reverse that error would not be always to find his true meaning, and perhaps we shall best arrive at this by shunning each other's mistakes. In the light of the more modern appreciation, we elders may be able to see some things seriously that we once thought pure drolling, and from our experience his younger admirers may learn to receive as drolling some things that they might otherwise accept as preaching. What we all should wish to do is to keep Mark Twain what he has always been: a comic force unique in the power of charming us out of our cares and troubles, united with as potent an ethic sense of the duties, public and private, which no man denies in himself without being false to other men. I think we may hope for the best he can do to help us deserve our self-respect, without forming Mark Twain societies to read philanthropic meanings into his jokes, or studying the 'Jumping Frog' as the allegory of an imperializing Republic. I trust the time may be far distant when the 'Meditation at the Tomb of Adam' shall be memorized and declaimed by ingenuous youth as a mystical appeal for human solidarity.

43 Neo-romanticism, imperialism, and taste

1901

From 'The Editor's Easy Chair,' *Harper's Monthly*, April 1901.

It was one of Howells's insights that the popular gusto for literary swashbuckling went hand in hand with the national thirst for imperialism during and after the Spanish-American War. Critics have always supposed that bad taste meant bad morals. When bad taste ran rampant in the new world of best-sellers, Howells was shocked but not surprised. Hence his telling use of José Rizal to typify both the Filipino victims of American aggression and the good, true artist obscured by '*Gouts of Blood*' in its imaginary hundreds of thousands of copies.

As Howells aged he appears to have felt increasingly comfortable in writing criticism as dialogue, until *Imaginary Interviews*, 1910, filled a volume. Thus the evolution of his criticism tended to follow the line developed in his fiction—of which Henry James early complained that it threatened to turn into dialogue completely.

One morning, not long ago, as the light streamed in at the windows of the editor's den, taking a soft, stained-glass tone from its passage through the smoke and steam of the elevated trains, the Easy Chair had one of those Memnonian moments which experience is beginning to teach the editor to expect of it, from time to time. Of course when it actually spoke he knew that it was the tradition of the Easy Chair finding words, and he tried to answer in the reverence which he always tries to feel for a tradition: he is beginning to be a tradition himself.

I.

'Have you ever,' the Easy Chair asked, 'had your doubts whether a book was especially worth reading because its sale had reached a hundred thousand, or two, or even five hundred thousand?'

The editor looked warily about the den, and seeing that he was quite alone with the Easy Chair, he confessed, 'Yes; I have already expressed grave doubts of that sort, but nobody else seems to have them, and as I do not like to be odd, I do not keep insisting upon mine.'

'I am not sure you are right,' said the Easy Chair. 'Perhaps other people have them, and if you insisted upon them, you would not find yourself so odd, after all. Is the fact that a book has not sold half a million copies proof that it is poor literature?'

'I should be sorry to think so,' said the editor. 'I have written books, and I am afraid it would rule mine out, except in the very few cases where they have passed that figure.'

'But would you like to have written the books that sell half a million? Candidly, now!'

'Candidly, then, I wouldn't. But I would rather write them than read them; I think it would be easier. A certain kind of man would write one of the recent enormous successes, because if he wished to write at all, he would have no choice but to write that kind of book. He would be made so, but no one could be imaginably made so that he must read such a book, in the sense that the author must write it.'

'I don't know about that,' said the Easy Chair, musingly. 'The fact that there are two or three or ten or twenty men who must write trashy books possibly implies the fact that there are two or three or twenty millions who must read them. Have you any philosophy as to the vast popularity of the books that have been lately filling the world with the noise of their publicity? It used to be called advertising, but I rather like the Gallic neatness of the new word.'

'No, unless it is the publicity that does it. Only, the publicity seems not to come first, always.'

'It can't be the publicity that does it, then, though the publicity helps. The thing seems largely meteorological. It is scarcely more an affair of volition than the weather. A certain atmospheric pressure in the material world causes it to rain water, and a certain atmospheric pressure in the literary world causes it to rain rubbish. We suppose that in both cases the rain comes from the clouds, from above, but in both cases it comes primarily from the ground, from below. What you want to do in order to account for the literary rubbish which now prevails is not to analyze the authors, who are the mere modes of its discharge, but to ascertain the condition of their readers, from whom they received it as an imperceptible exhalation, and who receive it back from the authors in an appreciable form.'

'Oh, it's all very well to say that,' the editor protested. 'But the causes are so recondite that no inquiry can reach them, and one conjecture would be as good as another. The phenomenon is not only extraordinary in quality, but in quantity. The rubbish is not only rubbish, but it is rubbish in vaster amount than ever before. It is as if the rainfall should have been all at once increased tenfold over the whole territory of the United States. The rubbish-fall in the last year of the nineteenth century was greater than ever was known in the history of literature before. How do you account for that?'

'By a very simple and very obvious fact. An immeasurably greater area of humanity has been brought under cultivation or reclaimed from absolute illiteracy than ever before. In the material world the analogous sort of thing, the tilling of waste land, increases the rain-fall, and in the mental world the upturning of waste mind increases the rubbish-fall, because in both cases the clouds receive a greater exhalation from the space below, and give it back proportionately.'

'You mean, in other terms,' said the editor, 'that the number of readers has enlarged the number of writers, and the writers are trashy because the readers are.'

'Oh, you mustn't press the inference too far. Logic can always turn upon us and makes us its prey, if we do that. You will be saying next that popular education is a mistake, and that people should not be taught to read and write because they read and write rubbish.'

'Oh, no. I should not go so far as that. But I might say they had better not be taught to write.'

'And I,' said the Easy Chair, putting on its traditional air of opti-mism, 'contend that they can safely be taught to do both. You must not regard the present state as final. It is not a state at all, in fact; it is a stage, and an advance, taking in the whole body of readers, upon any former stage. We must not think the lovers of a half-million-copy novel are recreant lovers of Hawthorne, or George Eliot, or Mr. Thomas Hardy. The most part of them never heard of those authors. To leave the meteorological figure we have been working, up to this point, and try something arboricultural, we may liken our immeasur-able mental level to the prairie country, which, when men begin to plant it with trees, they first plant with the coarse, rank cottonwood. After a generation or two of cottonwood, they can grow oaks and elms and maples on the prairie, but not at first. You may be sure that the plains in which the literary cottonwoods now flourish have never grown oaks or elms or maples. Up to the time the readers of the recent successes began to read them they had read dime novels and story papers, or they went to the theatres. But the exhalation and precipitation of rubbish cannot go on forever—'

'I don't see why it shouldn't,' the editor broke in. 'Let's hear by what new metaphor you escape the logic of your postulate.'

'I have none that fits,' the Easy Chair frankly owned. 'But all the same I feel sure of my position. The forces in the mental world are not governed by the same laws as those of the material world. In the material world it must keep on raining water, but it need not rain rubbish always in the mental world. Imperceptibly the conditions will vary, and in the process of time the inspirations will be changed, and the expirations with them. On any vastly extended scale you can't expect taste for the best things; but many people of bad taste would willingly have good taste if they could. No, no,' the Easy Chair continued, 'we must never despair of the republic, in anything. We seem of late to have applied the principle of universal suffrage to the criticism of literature in an odd way, and to have decided that the book was best which got the most votes. But should you say the one which got the fewest was the best? Do you think that any half-dozen failures of the past year are as good as any half-dozen successes?'

'I am not sure,' said the editor. 'But I will own that not all the failures are good, if you will own that nearly all the successes are bad.'

'How can I help doing that?' the Easy Chair responded, and at this point it manifested by unmistakable signs such a disposition to take the word altogether that the editor willingly yielded it.

II.

'The question whether the actual prodigy is also a portent is something one may much more profitably ask one's self than those we have been putting to each other. Does publicity constitute a sort of newer criticism, and are we to form our opinions of a book from the proclamations of the advertiser, instead of the reasons of the reviewers? Is the critic, as we have hitherto had him, to pass, and is the advertiser to come and to stay? The critic as we have had him has not altogether contented us. I think I can recall some hard things you said of him yourself when you inhabited The Study. Do you say now that he, the critic, would be preferable to the expert advertiser, as an arbiter of taste?'

'Ah,' the editor evaded, 'I wish to make you observe that the advertiser rather than the critic has always been the arbiter of taste.

The novels of Tourguénief, twenty years ago, were reviewed round the land as among the most important and most artistic ever written; but they sold a thousand or two apiece in spite of the consensus of the praiseful critics. At the same time, *That Husband of Mine* and *Helen's Babies* swept the country after the advertiser began to say they were doing so.'

'I am not sure just how much such a fact proves,' the Easy Chair resumed. 'But if the great commercial successes in fiction are owing to our lack of a principled and instructed criticism, I am quite willing that the critics should go, and not continue to influence the fate of books. The reading public can quite as safely turn to the last announcements of the publishers, and if *The Flaming Sword* has sold five hundred thousand, and *Gouts of Blood*[1] has sold only four hundred and ninety-nine thousand, then go and buy *The Flaming Sword*.

'In a certain measure, the success of a book itself is a favorable criticism. The fact that it has caught the attention of a large number of people is certainly not against it in the minds of either authors or publishers. The publishers, indeed, accept the fact with general faith as a positive proof of merit, and the authors are probably waiting each one to write a book whose success shall bring the truth home to him. The author whose books have never sold more than a poor thousand or fifteen hundred would not think the worse of himself if one of his books should suddenly sell fifteen hundred thousand. But nothing in all this should disable us from asking whether, say, the merit of a book increases in the ratio of its sale.

'Certainly the fate of the enormous successes, or the most of them, in the past, is not such as to convince us that they were always of lasting worth. Who reads Tupper's *Proverbial Philosophy* now? Once it was on the marble-topped centre-table, beside the family Bible, in every Anglo-Saxon home. Has any reader of this generation heard of *The Lamplighter*? That novel sold, a brief half-century ago, as many copies as *Gouts of Blood*, if not so many as *The Flaming Sword*. It will be within the memory of middle-aged men, not to say women, that the story known, or once known, as *Called Back* ran well into a million copies; but is *Called Back* a favorite with the ingenuous youth now gorging themselves with the feast of gory collops spread for them by the neo-romanticists? The list could be extended, and brought down to that yesterday when the name of *Trilby* was on every tongue; but the few instances I have given will suffice to form the excuse of any one who hesitates a doubt of the literary quality of *The Flaming Sword* or *Gouts of Blood*, in spite of their immense acceptance with the reading, or the buying public. If these overwhelming romances are of lasting worth, the doubter may get them hereafter; and if they are not, but should happen to be wholly forgotten in six months, he will have saved his money.

'What, then, if not their merit, is the cause of their illimitable popularity? That brings us directly back to the expert advertiser, and to the modern mystery of publicity. It is apparently to the advertiser's instinct, to his prophetic soul, that the great successes are mostly owing. But just at what moment does his instinct, his prophetic soul, become operative? What intimation from the unknown enables him to declare *The Flaming Sword* the book of the season, and swiftly upon this proclaim that it has gone to ten thousand, to twenty, to a hundred thousand, to half a million? It has not reached any of these figures without his skill, but how does he know that his skill can be hopefully brought to bear upon *The Flaming Sword*? It is one of a hundred novels no worse if no better. He has the air of knowing, but perhaps he could not tell if he would. In fact that question as to what makes a book succeed can probably never be solved. A veteran publisher who used to seek my conversation, a good many years ago, before publicity became prophecy, was always puzzled to know why a book when it had sold ten thousand copies should stop selling. Had it reached in that number just the number of people who wished to read it? With the momentum it had got by such a start, why should not it keep going? What laws or chances arrested it? He gave the conundrum up in the fact of asking it; but perhaps the modern advertiser could answer it.

'In this case the only difficulty would be to get at the advertiser. He is probably not one with the publisher, but is a prophet in the publisher's pay, and is very likely a young and hustling seer who could be hired away from his employer by some one bidding more for the use of his gift. Possibly, of course, he has a conscience, and might refuse to prophesy promiscuously. When we see the extraordinary effect of his vaticinations concerning "the great novel of the year," or "the book of the season," or "the new success in fiction," we can hardly help believing that he can foresway as well as foretell literary events, and that by appealing to his conscience the children of light could enlist his interest as successfully as the children of darkness, who seem to have written most of the prodigious triumphs in the book world of late. Is not there a gleam of hope in that direction?'

III.

The editor allowed that there might be. He said that out of those triumphs he could think of one that was not half bad, and of another that was three-quarters good; and if these were the effect of a quickened conscience in the advertiser, the future was not so black as it painted itself. The first thing would be to find out whether the advertiser was one or many, or had that remarkable unity of style which distinguishes his inspirations by virtue of incorporation as a trust. When the fact was ascertained, we should know how to approach him with some good book, which we could make a test case. 'For instance,' said the editor, 'I should like to try him with a recent Filipino novel, which the American publishers have called *An Eagle Flight*, in its version from the Spanish. It was written by that beautiful soul José Rizal, whom the Spanish despatched to his last account in pure despair of finding any charge against him, a few years before we bought a controlling interest in their crimes against his country. It would have been interesting to know what we would have done with such a political prisoner, if they had handed him over to us, and whether, perplexed by the problem of a man who could be accused of nothing, but whose whole generous life accused the alien oppression, we should simply have shot him, as the Spaniards did. But he is gone, and his book remains, and though we might have a copy of it publicly burnt, that would probably not put an end to it. In fact that might inspire the advertiser to take hold of it, with the hope of getting it forbidden in the mails. I should like to suggest some such measure to him, though I am afraid he might be disappointed when he came to look at the book and found it merely an exquisite work of art, with no imaginable leze-America in it.

'I don't know whether it ought to be astonishing or not that a little saffron man, somewhere in that unhappy archipelago, should have been born with a gift so far beyond that of any or all the authors of our roaring literary successes; but those things are strangely ordered by Providence, and no one who reads this pathetic novel can deny its immeasurable superiority. The author learned his trade apparently from the modern Spanish novelists, who are very admirable teachers of simplicity and directness, with a Latin grace of their own. But he has gone beyond them in a certain sparing touch, with which he presents situation and character by mere statement of fact, without explanation or comment. He has to tell the story of a young Filipino (much like himself), well born, nurtured in luxury, and sent out to Spain to be educated, who returns to the Philippines to find his father dead and his memory dishonored by the monks whom the son supposed his friends. The son inherits their enmity; they break off his marriage with the girl to whom he has been betrothed from child-hood, involve him in a pretended conspiracy, and compass his ruin and death. A multitude of figures, men, women, and children, peasants, townsfolk, cleric and laic, of all the mixtures of race, from the pure Spanish to the pure Filipino, pour through a succession of scenes without confusion or huddling. The many different types and characters are rendered with unerring delicacy and distinctness, and the effect of all those strange conditions is given so fully by the spare means that while you read you are yourself of them, and feel their hopeless weight and immeasurable pathos, with something of the sad patience which pervades all. There are touches of comedy throughout; Rizal is a humorist as well as a poet; he has a tragedy in hand, but life has taught him that not all, or even most, spectators of tragedy are of serious make or behavior. His story has the reliefs without which a world where death is would not be habitable; but even in the extreme of apparent caricature you feel the self-control of the artistic spirit which will not wreak itself either in tears or laughter. It is a great novel, of which the most poignant effect is in a sense of its unimpeach-able veracity.'

IV.

The editor ceased, and the Easy Chair for a time was silent. Then it asked, 'And is this the sort of book you thought of commending to the ministrations of the advertiser in the hope that he could make it sell half a million copies?'

'Why not? If the advertiser should apply both skill and conscience to the task, why should not he succeed with a beautiful work of art like that, amusing, exciting, touching, heart-breaking, human—a love-story and a life-story?'

'I see,' said the Easy Chair, 'you are making your old mistake of those times in the Study when you used to argue that because a thing was good it ought to be liked. But a good thing can be liked only by those who are good enough to like it. The books that sweep the country must be of the cheapness of the average person. That book which you mentioned just now as not half bad, and that other book which was three-quarters good, succeeded each by the combination of its qualities with the defects of the great popular successes which had no qualities. Those two books had a strain of silliness or a strain of sentimentality which had the same force as the glorification of the bad passions to take people out of themselves. That is what people want, and is it any wonder, considering what people mostly are?'

'Oh come!' cried the editor. 'If you are anything at all you are a tradition of faith in human perfectibility; and you must not go saying things like that, and insinuating the most cynical despair of it.'

'Ah, there I should wish to distinguish,' said the Easy Chair. 'I am a tradition of the ethical, not the æsthetical, perfectibility of humanity. Heaven is probably full of kind souls of no taste whatever, who would not know a good novel from a bad one. No, no! You must not confound the two sorts of excellence. The advertiser couldn't hopefully take hold of your Filipino novel; but I don't lose my hopes of him on that account. I believe that he is morally perfectible too. Come! If we cannot have critical taste any longer to guide us in the choice of books, why should not we have commercial honor? Why shouldn't the literary advertiser rise to the level of the dry-goods advertiser, and a publishing-house announce its wares qualitatively; and then quantitatively, with the frankness of a department store, owning one of less value than another?'

'Because books have always been sold quantitatively and not qualitatively; and if the publishing-house discriminated in value it would have to discriminate in price, as the department store does.'

'Well?'

'Well, that is impossible. Commercial honor can do a good deal, but it cannot do that.'

'Then,' said the Easy Chair, 'we must hope that we are not in as bad a way as we seem. We probably are not. Good books are still read; names worth having are still made. Let us never despair of the Republic of Letters.'

NOTE

1 The book-titles in this section II of the essay are all ascertainably those of nineteenth-century best-sellers except *Gouts of Blood* and *The Flaming Sword*—
which are presumably satiric inventions.

44 'Professor Barrett Wendell's Notions of American Literature'

1901

Published in the *North American Review*, April 1901.

There is really no parallel in his critical writing to what Howells himself thought the unkind spirit, even the 'fury' of this attack on the first significant history of American literature and upon its author, a distinguished Harvard professor who was in some sense a friend. Therefore the long, bitter article reveals, even defines, the critic. 'Proper Boston,' Tory Cambridge, and snobby Harvard had long been subjects of Howells's intensive, ironic study. He knew them by the book; and as critic he could not bear, even to defiance of his own rule of taxonomic decorum, to let their perspectives determine the national point of view toward American literary history.

Howells had his own sense of the meaning of American literature, a moral concern as to the definition of its history. Quite naturally his feeling for the right point of view based 'Americanism' in literature upon the same ground as his feeling for the true political and social faith. The key to Howells's attitude lies not in the Henry Adams-like suspicion that some Boston swell or Cambridge Tory had snubbed him but in his complaint that Wendell had written not 'A Literary History of America' but 'A Study of New England Authorship in its Rise and Decline, with Some Glances at American Literature'—and then not understood New England.

Wendell ignored Howells and James; he pretended that Howells and his generation and school did not exist; he scouted the contribution of Howells's region and stood blind to the rise of a national literature South, West, and Far West. That was all infuriating, like the stylistic traces of patronizing lecture-hall mannerism, the tone of careless hauteur. But the heart of the essay lay in Howells's saying,

> Yet, even as a study of the New England episode of American literature, the work is not sympathetic. It is prevailingly antipathetic, with moments of kindness, and still rarer and more unexpected moments of cordial respect and admiration. Wherever Professor Wendell scents democracy or perceives the disposition to value human nature for itself and independently of the social accidents, he turns cold, and his intellectual tradition gets the better of his nature, which seems sunny

361

and light and friendly. Something, then, like a patrician view of the subject results. ... The impression ... is that American literature is not worthy the attention of people meaning to be really critical.

Posterity has ratified Howells's view. Discussing 'American Critics' in the *Times Literary Supplement* in 1920, T. S. Eliot remarked that Wendell's work constituted 'almost an admission, in a great many words, that there is no American literature.'[1] In his time at Harvard, said Van Wyck Brooks, class of 1907, 'For the Harvard imagination the country was a void,' and he was to make a career of laboring to fill it.[2] Or, in Professor Alfred Kazin's fine phrase, 'As if to mark off for all time the difference between the literature that was passing and the new literature of the twentieth century ... Wendell published in 1900 the last testament of the old school, *A Literary History of America*'[3]—except, as Howells feared, it was also the testament of a Tory school and there were Rooseveltian reasons to fear it not the last.

If the critic were to set down the psychology of his acquaintance with an important book, he would probably do a greater service to his reader than he does by merely recording his opinions of it. The best sort of criticism is that which gives the critic, as well as the author, to the reader's knowledge, so that he may judge not only the critic's opinions, but the motive behind his opinions, and value the opinions or not as he finds the motives worthy or not. I am going, therefore, to lay bare the facts of my personal history with regard to the present review, and to let the reader choose between my author and me, and enable or disable my judgment at the points where he thinks I have gone right from a just cause or wrong from an unjust cause. I do regard the book which Professor Wendell somewhat indescriptively calls *A Literary History of America* as an important book, and have found it impossible to ignore the sort of challenge it gives to one interested in the matter it treats of.

I.

I had seen, I confess at second hand, a praise of the book so sweeping, so overwhelming, from a critical authority which I value, that I at once made up my mind against it; and when, later, I came upon certain expressions from it, again at second hand, I was not distressed to find them priggish and patronizing, but fortified myself in my dislike upon evidence which, if it had been my own book, I should have thought partial. When, still later, I came to the book itself, I was not able to dispatch it so promptly as I had expected, not because I was wrong concerning its intellectual quality, but because I was not sufficiently right. It *is* priggish and patronizing, but it is several other things so very much better that one must not, on one's honor, on one's honesty, fail to recognize them. It is, throughout, the endeavor of a narrow mind to be wide, and the affair in hand receives a species of illumination in the process which is novel and suggestive. It is not the kind of mind I like, but I like it better than I did before I was so well acquainted with it. It has an elasticity which I had not suspected, and the final result is a sort of instruction which the author seems to share with the reader. One is tempted to say that if Professor Wendell had not produced in his present book the best history of American literature, he had educated himself, in writing it, to produce some such history.

His general attitude toward his subject is the attitude of superiority, but not voluntary superiority; every considered volition of his is towards a greater equality with his theme. It is as if, having been born a gentleman, he wished conscientiously to simplify himself, and to learn the being and doing of his inferiors by a humane examination of their conditions, and a considerate forbearance toward their social defects. He has his class feeling against him, but he knows it, and he tries constantly to put it aside. All this is temperamental; but, besides, Professor Wendell has certain disadvantages of environment to struggle with, and in this he exemplifies the hardship of such Bostonians as have outlived the literary primacy of Boston. A little while ago and the air was full of an intellectual life there, which has now gone out of it, or has taken other than literary forms; and, in the recent ceasing of the activities that filled it, the survivor is naturally tempted to question their greatness. The New England poets and essayists and historians who gave Boston its primacy are in that moment of their abeyance when the dead are no longer felt as contemporaries, and are not yet established in the influence of classics. It is the moment of misgiving, or of worse, concerning them; and it is altogether natural that this doubt should be most felt where their past greatness was most felt. Elsewhere, they are still measurably Emerson and Longfellow, Whittier and Holmes and Lowell; but on their native ground, where they lately walked with other men, and the other men are still walking and they not, the other men can hardly fail to ask themselves whether they were not unduly oppressed by a sense of the vanished grandeur. These other men, looking abroad, and seeing little such question elsewhere, cannot help feeling it a proof of discernment in themselves, and governing themselves accordingly. They occupy the places of those illustrious men, and though they no longer find them so very illustrious as people once fancied, still they cannot resist the belief that they inherit them and have somehow the right to administer upon their estates.

II.

The office has its difficulties, which will realize themselves to the imagination of any reader who has had the experience of looking over the papers of a person recently deceased, and has felt the insidious slight for the deceased which inevitably mingles with the conventional awe that all mankind pretend for the dead. The problem is how best to conceal the slight, not only from others, but from one's self. If one keeps silence, one may partially succeed; but if one speaks, one inevitably takes on that air of superiority which affects the witness so disagreeably, no matter how involuntary it is. Another hard condition of such a work as Professor Wendell's is, that the author, in order to widen his survey of the subject, must get a bird's eye view of it, and if the resulting map or picture is not satisfactory to an observer on the terrestrial level, he accuses the bird of strabismus or astigmatism. But such an observer ought to guard himself from hasty censure, and ought to take into account the variety of obstacles overcome, as well as the defective character of the result. He ought to consider the exhaustive athletics by which Professor Wendell, for instance, places himself in a position to get a bird's eye view of Emerson, for instance. Then, I think, the observer on the terrestrial level will allow that he has done surprisingly well, and that the great wonder is that he should not have done worse.

Much that he suggests of Emerson is just, though I doubt if he does justice to the absolute and final and august simplicity from which the greatness of Emerson rises. He sees that, on the social side, Emerson was a villager; but he does not see that this sort of social outlook is compatible with universal and secular citizenship. He complains that, to the end, Emerson 'never lost his . . . exuberantly boyish trick of dragging in allusions to all sorts of personages and matters which he knew only by name;' but he alleges no proof that Emerson was so audaciously ignorant. He bids us 'take that sentence . . . "Pythagoras was misunderstood and Socrates, and Jesus, and

Luther, and Copernicus, and Galileo and Newton." These great names he mentions with all the easy assurance of intimacy; he could hardly speak more familiarly of seven Concord farmers, idling in a row on some sunny bench.' But here, in the absence of proof from the critic, there is no internal evidence of the intimacy and familiarity ascribed to 'the juvenile pedantry of renascent New England at a moment when Yankees ... did not yet distinguish between such knowledge and the unpretentious mastery of scholarship.' He gives, upon the whole, a notion of Emerson which would be creditable to a scholarly gentleman straining a point for the sake of liberality, in the direction of things offensive to his class instincts. It is such a view as would be acceptable to one dining well with an unusually cultivated company of people, not too critical of saws or instances that seemed to glitter or illustrate, and only very amiably contrary-minded when the praise went too far.

The paper on Holmes is more adequate, because the subject is one that may be more adequately handled in the spirit of Professor Wendell's criticism; but slighter and lighter as Holmes's meaning was in literature, the criticism has not the value in the retrospect that it had in the prospect. There is always the promise of vital consideration, which somewhere, somehow, fails to fulfill itself. One perceives that little which is true in it is new; and that little which is new is true. At first, one is struck by the notion that Holmes is a sort of Bostonian Voltaire, and all the more profoundly impressed because of the critic's care in distinguishing between the authors in their conditions and temperaments. 'Yes, yes,' you say, to your neighbor at table, 'that is true; I wonder I never thought of that.' The next morning, the facts of their radical difference in feeling, thinking and saying, present themselves against the sole fact that they were both brilliant urban wits, and the notion is not at all convincing.

In the papers on Whittier and Longfellow, there is an exterior sense of their place in literature; but if the passages quoted from them as distinctive are to be taken as proof of the critic's penetration, there is little interior sense of their quality. Rather unexpectedly, the essay on Lowell satisfies one better. He was of greater intellectual range and weight than any of his contemporaries; he was more acquainted with books and with affairs; he had infinitely more humor, but on his social side as he finally lent himself more to the measurements of worldly-minded criticism. Yet, through his humor he was apt at any time to pass impalpably into his poetry, where its divining rods were of no avail.

Professor Wendell's radical disqualification for his work seems the absence of sympathy with his subject. He is just, he is honest, he is interested, he is usually civil and too sincere to affect an emotion which he does not feel; he is versed in general literature, and he knows a great deal of his chosen ground. But he does not, apparently, know all of his ground; and his facts, when he ascertains them, are the cold facts, and not the living truth. Only those of like temperament can fail to be aware of this in him, and only those of like intellectual experience can fail to perceive the error of his ideals. The chief of these ideals is distinction, which he apparently thinks a man may seek with the same effect as if it had sought him. But distinction is something that comes by nature, like personal beauty, or lofty stature, or physical courage, or a gift for poetry or art. Short of it, one may be good, or clever, or wise; but one must be born distinguished. Most members of most aristocracies, most kings and emperors, are altogether undistinguished, and no breeding can make them so. For illustration in literature, one may say, without fear of contradiction, that the writer of the most distinction now writing English is Mr. Henry James. Every page, almost every sentence, of his testifies of his intellectual distinction. The very vulgarity which none of us escapes and which he occasionally fails to escape has a sort of distinction. Contrast a passage of his criticism with a passage of Professor Wendell's, and you have the proof of what I am saying. Professor Wendell is so wanting in that distinction which is his ideal that his phrase is always in danger of wearing down to the warp of his undistinguished thought. This happens when, after some lumbering facetiation about 'those countless volumes of contemporary biography wherein successful men of business are frequently invited to insert their lives and portraits,' he goes on to assure us that 'Emerson's *Representative Men* were of a different *stripe* from these' men. His nerves do not instruct him that *stripe*, in this sense, has remained hopelessly rustic, plebeian, common, and so his ideal of distinction does not avail. It is somehow the same with his efforts for lightness; they affect one painfully as undignified, and of the sort that can be grateful only to the young gentlemen on the benches glad to relieve their overtaxed attention in a giggle.

III.

When he is serious, Professor Wendell is always interesting and he is often very respectable. The best part of his book is formed by the essays on Bryant, Poe, Longfellow, Lowell, Whittier, Holmes, Whitman, and the essay on the change from Calvinism to Socinianism in New England, all papers of such good magazine quality that an editor would think twice before declining them, as a little wanting in form and a sort of final freshness. Their group is preceded by studies, varying in fulness, of our Colonial authors. Of these, one alone survives in literature; for, though Edwards is still a theologian whom the theologians cannot ignore, Franklin is the only literary man of that period whom lovers of literature can wish to know. The rest have the interest of quaintness, and of a significance among the origins of New England literature, which seems overrated in giving them a good fourth of *A Literary History of America*. They were to be examined as the tough Calvinistic stock which flowered in the Unitarian poetry of the nineteenth century; but his notion of them, by no means original with Professor Wendell, is elaborated to the neglect of the truly American period which has followed the New England period of our literature. If he had called his book *A Study of New England Authorship in its Rise and Decline, with Some Glances at American Literature*, one could not have taxed him with neglect, though one might still have found him wanting in proportion.

As a study of New England authorship, this book *has* value, as one may freely own, without disowning its valuelessness in specific instances. Its generalizations are at times excellent; though, from the passages of their literature which he gives, he would seem to have read about his authors rather than read them, the quotations are so far from representative. One of his most notable generalizations occurs when, after long fumbling over his material, he is able to say in summing up, 'Then our ancestral America, which had so unwittingly lingered behind the mother country, awoke. In the flush of its awakening it strove to express the meaning of life; and the meaning of its life was the story of what two hundred years of inexperience had wrought for a race of Elizabethan Puritans'; and this is so well imagined, it is so challenging and suggestive, if not convincing, that, for the moment, you feel him fit to have written that history of our literature which he has not written. It is compensation and consolation for so much priggish banality that you almost forget the priggish banality, and you try to forgive him even for saying of Victoria's accession, 'When her Majesty came to the throne,' as if he were a subject of her Majesty, so devoted in his loyalty as to be insensible of the greatness of a theme essentially indignant of all ceremonial self-abasement. Still, this sort of lapse makes you doubt his fitness to treat his theme with the due breadth of feeling, as more than one page of his book makes you question his literary qualification. The man, you say, who could write such a sentence as, 'The Southerners of the fifties were far more like their revolutionary ancestors than were the Northerners,'—a sentence so slovenly, so uncouth, so really in-expressive—is surely not qualified to judge even the mechanism of literature; but presently he gives you pause by declaring that 'no one who lacks artistic conscience can write an effective short story, and . . . the artistic conscience may be called characteristic' of American authorship. He surprises you again when he declares that 'in its beginning the American literature of the nineteenth century was marked rather by delicacy than by strength, by palpable consciousness of personal distinction rather than any such outburst of previously unphrased emotion as on general principles democracy might have been expected to excite.' He surprises you still again, and still more, by his divination of the purity of soul in American literary art, as where he says: 'In the literature of every other country you will find lubricity, in that of America hardly any. Foreigners are apt to think this trait hypocritical; whoever knows the finer minds of New England will be disposed to believe it a matter not of conscientious determina-tion, but rather of instinctive preference.' He perceives that while purity has been the instinct of our literature, excellence has been its ideal, and he enforces the fact with an aptness of expression which yet once more is surprising. To be sure, none of these notions is quite novel; and you may question Professor Wendell's originality, if you like. But if you like to do so, you will not be fair. He feels them originally and he imparts them cogently.

IV.

With as much reason you could say that his point of view in the study of Hawthorne was that chosen by Mr. Henry James, and perhaps sufficiently established twenty years ago; yet Professor Wendell does some thinking of his own on the subject, and he says some things which one cannot fail to heed without loss, as: 'Comparing his work with the contemporary work of England, one is aware of its classically careful form, of its profoundly romantic sentiment, and of its admir-able artistic conscience. One grows aware, at the same time, of its unmistakable rusticity, . . . monotony, provincialism, a certain thinness. . . . He was ideal, of course, in temper; he was introspective, with all the self searching instinct of his ancestry. . . . In a dozen aspects, then, he seems typically Puritan. His artistic conscience, however, as alert as that of any pagan, impelled him constantly to realize in his work those forms of beauty which should most beautifully embody the ideals of his incessantly creative imagination. . . . Beyond any one else, he expresses the deepest temper of that New England race which brought him forth, and which now, at least in the phases we have known, seems vanishing from the earth.'

I do not think that, in my sense of the prevailing academic temper of Professor Wendell's work, I am attributing undue freshness to these remarks, though I confess that, in transferring them to my page, the freshness has seemed somehow to evaporate, and I hasten to restore my faith in their novelty by giving a passage from the paper on Irving: 'One thing is pretty clear: the man had no message. From beginning to end he was animated by no profound sense of the mystery of existence. Neither the solemn eternities which stir philosophers and theologians, nor the actual lessons as distinguished from the superficial circumstances of human experience, ever much engaged his thought. Delicate, refined, romantic sentiment he set forth in delicate, refined, classic style. One may often question whether he had much to say; one can never question that he wrote beautifully.'

I should object, of course, to the looseness and inaccuracy and tendency to tall talk in such phrasing as 'the solemn eternities,' and to a certain vagueness of statement, but I could not deny that a kind of truth about Irving, which is not the whole truth, was here strikingly expressed, while I should feel that the very perfection of his work was a sufficient 'message.'

I should be of the same divided mind, but more deeply divided, concerning Professor Wendell's saying of Poe: 'From beginning to end his temper had the inextricable combination of meretriciousness and insincerity which marks the temperament of typical actors. Theirs is a strange trade wherein he does best who best shams.' The first part of this saying appears to me true enough, and quite new; the last entirely false and wrong. The greatest actor is not he who best shams, but he who is the truest to reality. On the other hand, I should be inclined largely to agree with his saying, as far as it goes, about Longfellow: 'Whether he ever understood his mission, it is hard to say; but what that mission was is clear; and so is the truth that he was a faithful missionary. Never relaxing his effort to express in beautiful language meanings which he truly believed beautiful, he revealed to the untutored new world the romantic beauty of the old.' As far as it goes; for this saying does not get further in appreciation than the work of Longfellow's first period. As for his not knowing just what his mission was, I should hope not. Few men outside of the insane asylums are perfectly aware of what they are here for, and these are not usefully at large. In such a saying as this, however, Professor Wendell does not mean any sort of unjust limitation, and if you come to his book of a *parti pris*, with the belief that he is altogether academic, and praises or blames by rule, you will find yourself mistaken. You may say that he is narrow-minded, but that he is not open-minded you cannot say. You must own again and again that he is very open-minded, and that he is not afraid to be generous when he conceives that generosity is justice. After long years of condemnation, when there was no question of Willis's abuse of hospitality in England by turning his hosts and his fellow-guests into newspaper copy, his fame has a stout good word from an historian who does not think much of his poetry. 'Superficial as you like, his letters are vivid, animated and carefully reticent of anything which might justly have displeased the persons concerned.' But by far the most signal instance of Professor Wendell's open-mindedness is his recognition of Mark Twain's positive value as a talent almost unique, his relative importance in the literature of his country, and his representativity as a Westerner.

No man, and I least of all men, will wish to question such a characterization of a humorist whom I think the greatest that has lived; yet I strongly feel the inadequacy of Professor Wendell's general statement of the literary case as regards the region which gave Mark Twain to the world. He might defend it upon the ground that he has explicitly refused to deal with our literary history in men and women still living; but he is obliged to modify this refusal again and again. He names names and he imputes qualities in the case of writers still living quite inevitably, and it is by a volition disastrous to the completeness of his argument that he leaves unmentioned the writer in whom the brief glories of the literary movement on the Pacific slope culminated. I am not disposed to exaggerate the merits of Mr. Bret Harte, but it cannot be denied that he made one of the great impressions of his time, and that his once towering reputation was solidly based upon a real power. He still disputes European popularity with Mr. Clemens, and he long enjoyed the sort of perverse primacy on the Continent which confounds us in the case of Poe. Not to speak of such a principal writer in discussing the literature of his section is to cripple the criticism attempted, and not to speak of such another writer as Mr. James Whitcomb Riley, in dealing with Western effort in poetry, is to ignore what is most vital and indigenous in it. It is as if in treating of Scottish poetry, some Professor Wendell, contemporary with Robert Burns, should refrain from mentioning him because he was still living; and the like censure may be urged against his treatment of the chief Southern authors. The literary movement in the South since the war has been of the most interesting and promising character, and in the work of several men has been of most distinguished performance. Mr. Joel Chandler Harris's contributions to imaginative literature are of absolute novelty, and Mr. G. W. Cable has written one of the few American fictions which may be called great. These men are not fully representative of the literary advance in the South, but not to name them, not to consider their work, is to leave the vital word unsaid. But the vital word concerning the rise of American fiction since the civil war is also left unsaid, and the South only suffers with the North.

V.

As to that tendency in the North and East which, widening beyond the trend of the old New England endeavor for ideal excellence, resulted in the distinction of Mr. Henry James's work, how is any just notion of it to be given without some direct consideration of that work? Professor Wendell does not give any just notion of it, simply because he does not consider Mr. James's work either in itself or in relation to the general tendency. He has sworn to his hurt and changed not, though he swore to his hurt and changed in the case of Mark Twain with respect to the Western humor, and in the case of Miss Jewett and Miss Wilkins with respect to the New England short story. It is a pity that a critic so inconsistent should be so scrupulous, but it cannot now be helped, and Professor Wendell's history of our literature must remain so far imperfect.

If this were all, if it were imperfect only in this, it would not be so bad, but it is imperfect in so many other points as not to be a history of American literature, although it may be a literary history of America if any one can say what that is. It is not only insufficient and apparently unintelligent at the points noted, but it conspicuously ignores some incidents which even a literary history of America ought to take account of. There is, for instance, nothing in it to betray consciousness of such a resurgent spirit as produced the first *Putnam's Magazine* at New York in the early fifties, though this was a literary event of as great importance as the founding of the *Atlantic Monthly* five years later at Boston. The earlier enterprise evolved and concentrated the literary elements which gave strength to the later undertaking, and it was, perhaps, more responsive and useful to the country at large. The great New England wits were contributors to *Putnam's*, while it revived and fostered the local and general literary aspiration. It completed the intellectual development of so important an American as George William Curtis, and gave American letters the humane and manly cast which it would be a pity they should ever lose. Almost more than any other agency in their annals, it dedicated them to liberty and democracy in the best and widest sense. They ceased with its coming to be servile at their worst, and to be merely elegant at their best.

But Professor Wendell ignores an incident of such prime significance, and whether he ignores it voluntarily or involuntarily it is to be regretted that he ignores it. He scarcely offers us compensation in the story of the founding of the *Atlantic Monthly*, and its mission to our literature. That periodical was imagined by Francis Underwood, the professional literary adviser of a successful publishing house, who had no conception of it as the avenue of Harvardized genius to the American public, or even as an outlet to the culture of New England, but who had an abiding faith in Lowell as the fittest man in the world to direct such a periodical. Lowell, as the first editor, divined that Holmes could do more than any man living to 'float the *Atlantic*,' and at his strong entreaty, the 'Autocrat' papers were written, and the *Atlantic* was floated. Lowell, if any one, characterized the magazine. He gave it literary conscience and human responsibility, and the best that his successive successors could do was to keep it true to his conception of its mission. Fields, whose generous love of letters and wide intelligence Professor Wendell does not overrate, could do no more than this, and he did no more. He left the *Atlantic* what he found it, and what it has since remained with marvellous constancy to the original impulse from Lowell's great nature and liberal mind. It is ludicrously mistaken to suppose that after Fields left the magazine, it ceased to be in sympathy with Harvard. Fields had no special affinity with Harvard, and the young Harvard men—it is sufficient to name Mr. John Fiske alone—began writing for his successor in greater number than before, in proportion to their fitness or their willingness; if there was any change it was because Harvard was becoming less literary, and the country at large more literary. The good things began to come from the West and the South and the

Middle States, and the editors took the good things wherever they came from.

VI.

No one can estimate the relative value of the New England episode of our literary growth more highly than I, but I cannot ignore the fact that our literary conscience, the wish for purity and the desire for excellence, which Professor Wendell recognizes as its distinguishing qualities, was not solely of Puritan origin. Before the New England renaissance, there was an American literature dignified by these qualities, and since the New England decadence (if he insists upon an appearance in which I do not find so much fact as he) there is a far larger body of American literature illustrated by their original and prominent characteristics. Clever and charming and even 'distinguished' writing is now of an abundance in certain kinds which would have amazed the frugal sufficiency of the great New England days. In poetry only have we declined; but so has all the world.

Yet, even as a study of the New England episode of American literature, the work is not sympathetic. It is prevailingly antipathetic, with moments of kindness, and still rarer and more unexpected moments of cordial respect and admiration. Wherever Professor Wendell scents democracy or perceives the disposition to value human nature for itself and independently of the social accidents, he turns cold, and his intellectual tradition gets the better of his nature, which seems sunny and light and friendly. Something, then, like a patrician view of the subject results. Well, it is, perhaps, time that we should have the patrician view, for the patricians are usually not very articulate and it is interesting to know how they feel. The worst of it is, perhaps, that when the other patricians get this patrician view they will not care for it any more than they care for the subject. As a class, they have never, in any country, at any time, cared generally for literature, though they have been patrons of the objective arts, which could minister to their state in the decoration of their dwellings. Otherwise, they have been preoccupied with their dogs and horses, their yachts and villas; their recreations have been boyish or barbarous; their chance pleasure in a book has been almost a brevet of its badness. The American patriciate, so far as we have any, is like every other, and will not care, even unintelligently, for a patrician view of American literature. A large class of crude people, who do not know

374 IN AND OUT OF 'THE EASY CHAIR,' 1901-20

the ground, but have the belief that the things they do not know are not worth knowing, will, perhaps, in the harshness of their crudity, find Professor Wendell's history acceptable. It will not fundamentally disturb their ignorance, and it will please their vanity with the suggestion that not they alone are contemptible. The impression they will get from it is that American literature is not worthy the attention of people meaning to be really critical.

But I doubt if the American public needed any such recall as Professor Wendell has sounded from a mad pursuit of American authorship. I doubt if they have over valued it in the productions of our greatest poets, essayists, historians or novelists. I doubt if anything has been gained for a just estimation of Emerson by a patronizing allusion to his 'guileless confusion of values,' or for his interpretation by the elaborate explanation that in his saying, 'hitch your wagon to a star,' he had not in mind 'a real rattling vehicle of the Yankee country, squalid in its dingy blue,' or any such star 'as ever twinkled through the clear New England nights,' but that he used the 'incomplete symbol' to bind together for an instant 'the smallest things and the greatest.' This had always been apparent to most people; and, throughout, Professor Wendell seems unaware of the fine, quaint humor lurking at the heart of Emerson's philosophy, and amusing itself with the fire it struck from such grotesque contrasts. There seems to have been a certain fantastic wilfulness in the Seer which would account for much that Professor Wendell treats as superficiality, and even ignorance. But Professor Wendell's strong point is not humor or the perception of it. His own intentions of lightness find an expression that does not add to the reader's gaiety, and he has so little humorous conscience that he can bring out that poor old moth-eaten anecdote of Emerson and Margaret Fuller watching Fanny Elssler's dancing and the one pronouncing it poetry, and the other religion. He should have been principled against this inhumanity, but he is not probably to blame for citing, in illustration of the old New Englander's sense of human equality, the story of Father Taylor's saying of his interview with the Pope: 'So the Pope blessed me and I blessed the Pope.' Father Taylor was a saint who loved fun, and among the sailors to whom he preached there were often sinners who could take a joke. Perhaps, however, Professor Wendell knew that Father Taylor was joking, but in his need of an instance to support his position he pressed the old man's irony into the service.

One cannot often accuse him of uncandor; but no one can call his statement of the attack on Charles Sumner in the United States Senate a candid statement. 'The first blow, to be sure, was struck from behind; it was struck, however, in the most public place in America,' he says; and he gives the impression that Brooks's attack was made in full session of the Senate, in the midst of a crowd of spectators, when he ought to have known that the blow from behind was dealt a man sitting at his desk and busy over his papers, with only a few unfriendly people by. This distortion of the fact is wholly needless, even to the unhandsome effect which the literary historian of America achieves. No man, except some such angelic minded man as Longfellow, ever met Charles Sumner without feeling the impact of his gross egotism almost like a blow in the face; and there can be no question that the speech which provoked Brooks's attack was insufferably outrageous in its insolence. One is amazed in reading it that any one should permit himself such brutal terms with an opponent; but the wish to minimize the far greater atrocity which it provoked cannot be justified, even in the interest of a patrician view of American literature. Mostly, however, Professor Wendell's uncandor goes no farther than that sort of noble aloofness with which self-conscious gentlemen begin their letters to editors in the formula, 'Sir, my attention has been called to an article in your paper,' and so forth. In the spirit of this fine detachment he acknowledges the persistent vitality of *Uncle Tom's Cabin*, by owning that, 'to this day, dramatized versions of it are said to be popular in the country,' when he must have known, at first hand, that they were popular not only in the country, but in the suburbs of Boston itself, and wherever a summer pleasaunce large enough for the scene lent itself to the representation of a play requiring real bloodhounds in pursuit of fugitives escaping across a river of real water. At the moment I write, it is filling one of the largest New York theatres.

VII.

Is it, then, the tone of Professor Wendell's book, rather than the matter of it, that I am finding fault with? I think it is largely the tone; for I believe that I have already done justice to the recurrent excellence of its matter. When he can keep himself from instances, he deals interestingly and often convincingly with his subject. It is when he illustrates his meaning by a quotation, and interprets the passage given by comment on it, that he is least fortunate. Then you see that he has judged the poet with a narrow mind, and has failed of his real significance through natural disability, or that he has wilfully obscured it. An unpleasing instance of this sort is his remark upon that poem of Longfellow's on the dead slave:

> Beside the ungathered rice he lay,
> His sickle in his hand;

of which he says, 'One may fairly doubt whether, in all anti-slavery literature, there is a more humorous example of the way in which philanthropic dreamers often constructed negroes by the simple process of daubing their own faces with burnt cork.' Here the misconception of the artistic intention of the poet is so offensive, and put in terms of such jaunty vulgarity, that it is hard not to believe it a wilful misrepresentation. You ask yourself: 'Could any one sincerely take that view of it?' and, for the credit of the human mind, you prefer to think not, bad as the insincerity would be.

Downright vulgarity Professor Wendell is not often guilty of; but something one must call commonness is rather common with him. His language is without distinction, as his thought is without precision, not always, but regrettably often. One finds it hard to forgive a writer who can suffer himself such a figure as, 'Coal and oil, too, and copper and iron began to sprout like weeds.' No writer of artistic sensitiveness could have written that sentence, and no critic of ultimate civility could say of Walt Whitman's 'mad kind of rhythm' that it 'sounds as if hexameters were trying to bubble through sewage.' That is not graphic; it is simply disgusting. Yet the paper on Walt Whitman is almost the best of the whole collection, and is notable for some of the sanest and frankest and kindest criticism of a most difficult subject:

> One begins to see why Whitman has been so much more eagerly welcomed abroad than at home. His conception of equality, utterly ignoring values, is not that of American democracy, but rather that of European. ... The saving grace of American democracy has been a tacit recognition that excellence is admirable. ... The glories and beauties of the universe are really perceptible everywhere, and into what seemed utterly sordid Whitman breathed ennobling imaginative fervor. ... The spirit of his work is that of the old-world anarchy; its form has all the perverse oddity of old world decadence; but the substance of which his poems are made— their imagery, as distinguished from their form or spirit—comes wholly from our native country. In this aspect, then, though

probably in no other, he may, after all, throw light on the future of literature in America.

VIII.

But what is literature in America? Almost any one can tell us what it will be, but it wants a prophet to tell us what it is and has been, and I doubt if Professor Wendell is that prophet. In the first place, it does not appear to me that a prophet beginning to prophesy would give you the feeling that the things he is about to divine are not quite worthy of his powers, and I think that Professor Wendell gives you this feeling. In the next place, it does appear to me that he mistakes the nature of our literature, or seems to do so, in contrasting from time to time what we were doing in America with what they were doing in England at the same moment, and minifying our performance accordingly. Such a method might be the means of useful spiritual exercise for those vain Americans who suppose that our literature is the rival or the sister of English literature. It is the daughter or the granddaughter of that literature, or, in terms less flowery, it is a condition of English literature; and it is not interesting in its equality or likeness to the other conditions, but in its inequality or unlikeness. It has differenced itself from the mother or grandmother literature involuntarily, so far as it has differenced itself valuably, and it is an error either in friend or foe to put it in the attitude of rivalry. It would fail in that rivalry so far as it was like English literature, just as English literature would show itself inferior where it was like American literature. Professor Wendell, therefore, has not dealt wisely or kindly with it in the contrasts he makes; and, largely speaking, I should say he was not a kind or wise critic of it.

This is, of course, solely to his own disadvantage; the literature will remain for every future student, while his criticism may, perhaps, pass; and I should be sorry to pronounce him inimical where the proof would be difficult. The best I could do toward convincing the reader would be to recur again to his tone. 'And what,' the reader might ask, 'is his tone? Come,' he might continue, 'you have had your flings at his tone; you have tried to disable his supposed point of view; you have accused him of this, that and the other; but where is your proof?' I might retort that I preferred to leave the proof to Professor Wendell himself; but this seems rather sneaking, and I will not make that retort. I will allege the things I have quoted from him, and I may fairly, also, allege the impression of slight for his subject which he leaves with the reader. His subject is not, as I have represented, American literature, but that episode of our literary history which he calls the New England Renaissance. It cannot be questioned by any one who observes his attitude that he has the effect of looking down upon it. I will not suppose him capable of the charlatanry of wishing to surprise or shock his readers, or of the mistaken notion that they could be awakened to a just sense of New England literature by an occasionally rude or supercilious behavior to it. Clearly, he is sincere in not valuing it as it has been hitherto critically valued, and as it is still popularly valued. I cannot blame him for that; I myself have had my misgivings as to its perfection; and I have freely confessed them, but what I wish to make Professor Wendell observe is, that the New England literature uttered with singular adequacy the spirit of its time and place. I could also desire him to note that this spirit was generous and even sublime in its faith in humanity. He might answer me that it was weakened and intellectually dwarfed by this faith in humanity. In that case, I should say that I did not believe it, and I should like to ask what we should have faith in, if not in humanity. That would brings us to the *impasse* which people of different opinions must always come to.

NOTES

1 Quoted in Richard Ruland, *The Rediscovery of American Literature*, Harvard, 1967, x.
2 *Scenes and Portraits*, New York, 1954, iii.
3 *On Native Grounds*, New York, 1942, 57.

45 The problem of Longfellow
1902

From 'The Editor's Easy Chair,' *Harper's Monthly*, April 1902.
Though one of Howells's most admired essays was 'The White Mr. Longfellow' written for *Literary Friends and Acquaintance*, he was well aware that criticism as memoir is not the same as explication or judicial criticism but rests, like literary history, on evaluative assumptions. And he was aware that new generations were raising critical questions dangerous to Longfellow's prestige. The present 'Easy Chair' is the best of his answers. Like the best of recent Longfellow critics, the late Professor Newton Arvin for example, Howells recognizes the difference between the most permanent and the most popular of Longfellow. Like them, he sees that the best is the poetry relatively little known, the poetry written relatively late. He found an effective strategy for arguing Longfellow's artistic authenticity and wrote it well.

It is a sad condition of criticism that the critic, when he has striven faithfully to do his part by an author, may be as little pleased with his censure as some reader who likes it least. His reasons for discontent will not always be the same as the reader's, but they will be good reasons, and probably better than the reader's, for criticism is always oversaying or undersaying the thing it means with a fatality which might well incline the critic, upon second thought, to the contrary of his own opinions. This, at any rate, has been the long experience of the Easy Chair as a critic in various guises; and what is one's experience for if it is not to form the background on which one may imagine the predicament of another as if drawing from the fact? The result may not be like the fact at all, it may be nothing but a semblance which is more like the artist than the subject, but in that case the artist has the consolation of knowing that he has paid the subject the greatest possible compliment.

I.

We have been reading Mr. George Rice Carpenter's all too little life of Longfellow with a pleasure which we will not conceal from our own readers, any more than the fact that our pleasure in it would have been greater if we could have constantly agreed with the author. We like agreeing with people, not merely because it makes us feel they are right, but because it saves trouble; it saves the labor of convincing them they are wrong; and we are sorry to find ourselves agreeing with people so seldom: it seems to put mankind at a disadvantage. Not that we should disagree with Mr. Carpenter as to his manner of telling the tale of the poet's life. Rarely does a little book like a little brook run so limpidly along, reflecting the shores in its course, and taking the skies overhead into the depths of the water-grasses, the rocks, the sands underneath. It portrays admirably the poet in his environment, in his time and place, in his companionships as he chose them, and as they chose him; we could hardly wish it better done. But when it comes to the poet's work, its worth and place among other poets' work, our misgivings, our differences, our distinctions begin; and they insist the more because a hundred years hence, or a thousand, there will still be the same misgivings, differences, distinctions in the varying minds of men according to their several ways of thinking and feeling.

Speaking roughly, (and yet not roughly, we hope,) Mr. Carpenter's thinking and feeling about the poetry of Longfellow is that it is the poetry of sentiment; that it is the poetry of the library and not of the street or field; that its pictorial effects are compositions of generalized phases rather than the representation of actual features; that it is imageryative (the adventurous word is ours, not Mr. Carpenter's) rather than imaginative; that it is didactic rather than artistic; smooth and pleasing rather than strong and moving; gentle, cultivated, refined, rather than bold, native, and robust. All this he says or intimates, while recognizing the unique value of such poems as *Evangeline*, *Hiawatha*, and *The Courtship of Miles Standish*; and all this in a certain measure we may allow, while denying that it is the measure of Longfellow's work, except in a partial and occasional sense. In a partial and occasional sense it is true of his work; and it is also true of his work that it was partially and occasionally prosaic when it ought to have been always poetic. But this is true, partially and occasionally, of the work of all poets, except perhaps Keats alone, and he was not one of the greatest poets.

Lowell once said to the present Easy Chair that coming into a room where some one was reading aloud to a company of people, he thought that he was listening to prose, till presently it turned out to be the poetry of Tennyson's *Idyls of the King*. He held that Shakspere had set a pace of poetry which few others could keep up with; and one may be forgiven for adding that Shakspere did not always keep up with it himself. The highest poets in all languages lift to the skies long levels of prose with here and there peaks of song. Goethe abounded in prose; Dante renders his moments of poetry precious by his hours of prose; Wordsworth was terribly prosaic, and Shelley at times was worse; as for Byron, he was at times worse still, he was journalistic. Yet all these were great poets, and the presence of prose in verse is no proof that the verse on the whole is not poetry. It is certainly present in Long- fellow's *New England Tragedies*, and in *The Golden Legend*; and only the diction of the New Testament saves *The Divine Tragedy* from being largely prose. Nevertheless these pieces severally express with the high authority of poetry the spirit of the supreme human event, the travail of the darkened mediæval soul, and the emergence of the world out of theologic darkness into religious liberty and light.

II.

By the conditions of production what a man writes remains the man; not part of what he writes but all of what he writes, just as all that he is is he, and not merely his fine moments. Critics have sometimes vainly supposed that time would so sift or winnow a man's work that only the pure grain would be left, but it seems to be the law that though the grain be separated from the chaff and tares, the chaff and the tares endure with it. If a man could be kept from setting down anything but poetry when he wrote verse, then the world would not be littered with so much metrical prose; but apparently he never could, and so we have had to take the bad along with the good. The question with most is what they shall judge him by, and whether they shall condemn him for the bad or acquit him for the good. We think they should do neither the one nor the other. The only justice we can render is not to forget his poetry in the midst of his prose, and we must make inquiry of our conscience and our consciousness whether there has been more of the one or more of the other. This will not be simple, for the two are sometimes as inextricably mixed in his lines as they are in our own lives.

Mr. Carpenter seems to us unusually well equipped for the inquiry, for he has shown himself in this little book able beyond most other critics to understand Longfellow through a sense of his art, and has known how to suggest what may not be precisely defined, as 'an impersonal artistic product, having a form and individuality of its own, apparently separate from the author's experience, though created by it.' Yet having so admirably intimated the nature of the thing, Mr. Carpenter is sometimes, as we think, insensible of it where its effect is apparent, especially among the poems of Longfellow's later period. In other words, the balance of this scrupulous critic's mind is on the side of the criticism which makes the poet now suffer rejection because of the acceptance that came to him too widely before his best work was done.

The art of Longfellow is something too precious among our heritages from the past not to be valued at its full worth. It was the hardly saving grace which Hawthorne owned in the American literature of his time, and it is the art of Longfellow which takes from the American poetry of his generation the aspect of something fragmentary and fugitive. Whatever else it had from others, from Emerson, from Bryant, from Whittier, from Holmes, from Lowell, it had standing and presence and recognition among the world literatures from the art of Longfellow. We had other poets easily more American than he, but he was above all others the American poet, and he was not the less American because he accepted the sole conditions on which American poetry could then embody itself. As far as he ever came to critical consciousness in the matter he acted upon the belief, which he declared, that we could not be really American without being in the best sense European; that unless we brought to our New World life the literature of the Old World, we should not know or say ourselves aright. It seems to us, therefore, that Mr. Carpenter's speculations as to what sort of poet Longfellow might have been if he had been differently environed, or had been obliged in the West, or elsewhere, to enter more hardly into the struggle of life, are beside the question. Longfellow was what he was, and as it is probable that no man is idly or unmeaningly born of certain parents and not of certain others, so it seems reasonable to suppose there is some sort of order in a man's place and time which he can scarcely be even imagined outside of. Longfellow's place was in Cambridge among apparently smooth things, and his life was apparently tranquil and even, but these appearances cannot conceal the fact that his life included in its course all the sorrow and all the tragedy that can educate a man to sympathy with other human lives. Longfellow's time was that period which Mr. Carpenter calls sentimental, but which we should rather call ethical and emotional, and which Longfellow certainly reflected in the poetry of his early and middle manner. But beneath its surface aspects his art was instinctively seeking the meanings of its aspects. These were what the meanings of humanity are in every time, whether the time is optimistic or pessimistic, ethical or scientific; they were very simple meanings, the eternal desire of the race to orient itself aright with love and death, with sin and sorrow, with hope and despair. The soul is apparently busy with many other things, with war, money, office, letters, arts, ambitions, interests, but it is really the mind that is busy with such things; the soul, the very man, moves in the round of those elemental meanings, and it is the affair of poetic art to find them out and report them in the language of the day. Its task is a process of translation out of the old dialects of the past; and he who shows himself aptest in the new version is the greatest poet of his age. Did Tennyson add anything to the thinking and feeling of England in his day, or did he merely surprise his fellow-Englishmen with a new gloss of the thoughts and feelings which have always been in the world, but which the time required in terms more intelligible than those of the past? If Tennyson expressed the most of thinking and feeling Englishmen to themselves, in the same measure Longfellow expressed the like Americans.

If he was emotional and ethical, it was because they were so. His art of that period had the color and complexion of the contemporary mood; but the most interesting fact concerning Longfellow is one of the least recognized, and appears to have been scarcely recognized at all by Mr. Carpenter. He did not remain of any given time. He grew from his youth to his manhood, and from his manhood to his age, and his art won a greater fineness and firmness with the passing of the years. It responded to the temper of his later time as it had responded to the temper of his earlier time. It was senescent as the century itself was, and it was saddened with the wisdom of science, as once it had been cheered with the wisdom of faith. It is difficult, it is dangerous to allege proofs; the instance which you summon to your help, to prove your case and stand your stead, may turn upon you and play you false when it comes to testifying. But there are some of Longfellow's sonnets which seem to us such trustworthy evidence of what we have been saying that we shall venture to call them into court, and to ask certain of them to testify. Shall the first be, among the three sonnets to three dead friends of the poet, that perfect one in which his grief

has a pathos as of some lament caught and fixed in antique bronze—
shall it be that unsurpassable sonnet to the memory of Agassiz?

> I stand again on the familiar shore.
>> And hear the waves of the distracted sea
>> Piteously calling and lamenting thee,
> And waiting restless at thy cottage door.
> The rocks, the seaweed on the ocean floor,
>> The willows in the meadow, and the free
>> Wild winds of the Atlantic welcome me;
> Then why shouldst thou be dead, and come no more?
> Ah, why shouldst thou be dead, when common men
>> Are busy with their trivial affairs,
>>> Having and holding? Why, when thou hadst read
> Nature's mysterious manuscript, and then
>> Wast ready to reveal the truth it bears,
>>> Why art thou silent, why shouldst thou be dead?

Here is fancy, if you will, but here is imagination too, if there is any
unforced difference between the two; and here is the last effect of a
most instructed art. The thing is single, adequate, absolute; it has
the unmoralized completeness of a sigh. It is very personal; it is grief
that is speaking, and grief is personal; but if any critic objects to
having it so, then the sonnet on Agassiz, which should fit no other, is
at fault in sentiment for that critic. Personality, in fact, is the note of
all these noble sonnets, and perhaps for that reason, which so enriches
them, they will not prove our case. Then let us summon this one,
which expresses as electly a more universal, but not more generous
pang:

> 'A soldier of the Union mustered out,'
>> Is the inscription on an unknown grave
>> At Newport News, beside the salt sea wave,
> Nameless and dateless; sentinel or scout
> Shot down in skirmish, or disastrous rout
>> Of battle when the loud artillery drave
>> Its iron wedges through the ranks of brave
> And doomed battalions, storming the redoubt.
> Thou unknown hero sleeping by the sea
>> In thy forgotten grave, with secret shame
>> I feel my pulses beat, my forehead burn,
> When I remember thou hast given for me

> All that thou hadst, thy life, thy very name.
> And I can give thee nothing in return.

The plainness of the words, the utter simplicity of the mental pose, the passion of unselfish regret, constitute the terms on which an emotion of the noblest poetry here imparts itself. There is no pretence of consolation where consolation is impossible; there is no didactic or homiletic endeavor; there is only the explicit acceptance of the human case within the strict bound of human experience. We doubt if there is anything more simple or direct in the language. The note struck is the dominant of all Longfellow's later song, in which the wisdom of the man humbled him to the universal conditions, and the imperative sincerity of his nature forbade him to feign the hope and faith he no longer felt. The form is to our thinking faultless, but we are aware that all our saying so cannot make it so to others, and that any insistence to such an effect would be unworthy of the art itself.

46 'Émile Zola'

1902

Published in the *North American Review*, November 1902.
Having paid his dues in public obloquy for an unswerving public admiration of Zola and his work from 1886 forward, Howells felt free to cite him as one of the great minds of his own age and, in broad terms, school. It should be remarked that in the last analysis Howells's ideal of the perfect realist let only Tolstoi through the heavenly gate. Everybody else, including himself, was sometime, somehow romanticistic. Once again, his obituary summation of Zola became a superb critique.

In these times of electrical movement, the sort of construction in the moral world for which ages were once needed, takes place almost simultaneously with the event to be adjusted in history, and as true a perspective forms itself as any in the past. A few weeks after the death of a poet of such great epical imagination, such great ethical force, as Émile Zola, we may see him as clearly and judge him as fairly as posterity alone was formerly supposed able to see and to judge the heroes that antedated it. The present is always holding in solution the elements of the future and the past, in fact; and whilst Zola still lived, in the moments of his highest activity, the love and hate, the intelligence and ignorance, of his motives and his work were as evident, and were as accurately the measure of progressive and retrogressive criticism, as they will be hereafter in any of the literary periods to come. There will never be criticism to appreciate him more justly, to depreciate him more unjustly, than that of his immediate contemporaries. There will never be a day when criticism will be of one mind about him, when he will no longer be a question, and will have become a conclusion.

A conclusion is an accomplished fact, something finally ended, something dead; and the extraordinary vitality of Zola, when he was doing the things most characteristic of him, forbids the notion of this in his case. Like every man who embodies an ideal, his individuality partook of what was imperishable in that ideal. Because he believed with his whole soul that fiction should be the representation, and in no measure the misrepresentation, of life, he will live as long as any history of literature survives. He will live as a question, a dispute, an affair of inextinguishable debate; for the two principles of the human mind, the love of the natural and the love of the unnatural, the real and the unreal, the truthful and the fanciful, are inalienable and indestructible.

I.

Zola embodied his ideal inadequately, as every man who embodies an ideal must. His realism was his creed, which he tried to make his deed; but, before his fight was ended, and almost before he began to forebode it a losing fight, he began to feel and to say (for to feel, with that most virtuous and veracious spirit, implied saying) that he was too much a romanticist by birth and tradition, to exemplify realism in his work. He could not be all to the cause he honored that other men were—men like Flaubert and Maupassant, and Tourguenieff and Tolstoy, and Galdós and Valdés—because his intellectual youth had been nurtured on the milk of romanticism at the breast of his mother-time. He grew up in the day when the great novelists and poets were romanticists, and what he came to abhor he had first adored. He was that pathetic paradox, a prophet who cannot practise what he preaches, who cannot build his doctrine into the edifice of a living faith.

Zola was none the less, but all the more, a poet in this. He conceived of reality poetically and always saw his human documents, as he began early to call them, ranged in the form of an epic poem. He fell below the greatest of the Russians, to whom alone he was inferior, in imagining that the affairs of men group themselves strongly about a central interest to which they constantly refer, and after whatever excursions definitely or definitively return. He was not willingly an epic poet, perhaps, but he was an epic poet, nevertheless; and the imperfection of his realism began with the perfection of his form. Nature is sometimes dramatic, though never on the hard and fast terms of the theatre, but she is almost never epic; and Zola was always epic. One need only think over his books and his subjects to be convinced of this: *L'Assommoir* and drunkenness; *Nana* and harlotry; *Germinale* and strikes; *L'Argent* and money getting and losing in all its branches; *Pot-Bouille* and the cruel squalor of poverty; *La*

Terre and the life of the peasant; *Le Debâcle* and the decay of imperialism. The largest of these schemes does not extend beyond the periphery described by the centrifugal whirl of its central motive, and the least of the Rougon-Macquart series is of the same epicality as the grandest. Each is bound to a thesis, but reality is bound to no thesis. You cannot say where it begins or where it leaves off; and it will not allow you to say precisely what its meaning or argument is. For this reason, there are no such perfect pieces of realism as the plays of Ibsen, which have all or each a thesis, but do not hold themselves bound to prove it, or even fully to state it; after these, for reality, come the novels of Tolstoy, which are of a direction so profound because so patient of aberration and exception.

We think of beauty as implicated in symmetry, but there are distinctly two kinds of beauty: the symmetrical and the unsymmetrical, the beauty of the temple and the beauty of the tree. Life is no more symmetrical than a tree, and the effort of art to give it balance and proportion is to make it as false in effect as a tree clipped and trained to a certain shape. The Russians and the Scandinavians alone seem to have risen to a consciousness of this in their imaginative literature, though the English have always unconsciously obeyed the law of our being in their generally crude and involuntary formulations of it. In the northern masters there is no appearance of what M. Ernest Dupuy calls the joiner-work of the French fictionists; and there is, in the process, no joiner-work in Zola, but the final effect is joiner-work. It is a temple he builds, and not a tree he plants and lets grow after he has planted the seed, and here he betrays not only his French school but his Italian instinct.

In his form, Zola is classic, that is regular, symmetrical, seeking the beauty of the temple rather than the beauty of the tree. If the fight in his day had been the earlier fight between classicism and romanticism, instead of romanticism and realism, his nature and tradition would have ranged him on the side of classicism, though, as in the later event, his feeling might have been romantic. I think it has been the error of criticism not to take due account of his Italian origin, or to recognize that he was only half French, and that this half was his superficial half. At the bottom of his soul, though not perhaps at the bottom of his heart, he was Italian, and of the great race which in every science and every art seems to win the primacy when it will. The French, through the rhetoric of Napoleon III., imposed themselves on the imagination of the world as the representatives of the Latin race, but they are the least and the last of the Latins, and the Italians are the first. To his Italian origin Zola owed not only the moralistic scope of his literary ambition, but the depth and strength of his personal conscience, capable of the austere puritanism which underlies the so-called immoralities of his books, and incapable of the peculiar lubricity which we call French, possibly to distinguish it from the lubricity of other people, rather than to declare it a thing solely French. In the face of all public and private corruptions, his soul is as Piagnone as Savonarola's, and the vices of Arrabbiati,[1] small and great, are always his text, upon which he preaches virtue.

II.

Zola is to me so vast a theme that I can only hope here to touch his work at a point or two, leaving the proof of my sayings mostly to the honesty of the reader. It will not require so great an effort of his honesty now, as it once would, to own that Zola's books, though often indecent, are never immoral, but always most terribly, most pitilessly moral. I am not saying now that they ought to be in every family library, or that they could be edifyingly committed to the hands of boys and girls; one of our first publishing houses is about to issue an edition even of the Bible 'with those passages omitted which are usually skipped in reading aloud'; and it is always a question how much young people can be profitably allowed to know; how much they do know, they alone can tell. But as to the intention of Zola in his books, I have no doubt of its righteousness. His books may be, and I suppose they often are, indecent, but they are not immoral; they may disgust, but they will not deprave; only those already rotten can scent corruption in them, and these, I think, may be deceived by effluvia from within themselves.

It is to the glory of the French realists that they broke, one and all, with the tradition of the French romanticists that vice was or might be something graceful, something poetic, something gay, brilliant, something superior almost, and at once boldly presented it in its true figure, its spiritual and social and physical squalor. Beginning with Flaubert in his *Madame Bovary* and passing through the whole line of their studies in morbid anatomy, as the *Germinie Lacerteux* of the Goncourts, as the *Bel-Ami* of Maupassant, and as all the books of Zola, you have portraits as veracious as those of the Russians, or those of Defoe, whom, indeed, more than any other master, Zola has made me think of in his frankness. Through his epicality he is Defoe's inferior, though much more than his equal in the range and implication of his work.

A whole world seems to stir in each of his books; and, though it is a world altogether bent for the time being upon one thing, as the actual world never is, every individual in it seems alive and true to the fact. M. Brunetière says Zola's characters are not true to the French fact; that his peasants, working-men, citizens, soldiers are not French, whatever else they may be; but this is merely M. Brunetière's word against Zola's word, and Zola had as good opportunities of knowing French life as M. Brunetière, whose æsthetics, as he betrays them in his instances, are of a flabbiness which does not impart conviction. Word for word, I should take Zola's word as to the fact, not because I have the means of affirming him more reliable, but because I have rarely known the observant instinct of poets to fail, and because I believe that every reader will find in himself sufficient witness to the veracity of Zola's characterizations. These, if they are not true to the French fact, are true to the human fact; and I should say that in these the reality of Zola, unreal or ideal in his larger form, his epicality, vitally resided. His people live in the memory as entirely as any people who have ever lived; and, however devastating one's experience of them may be, it leaves no doubt of their having been.

III.

It is not much to say of a work of literary art that it will survive as a record of the times it treats of, and I would not claim high value for Zola's fiction because it is such a true picture of the Second Empire in its decline; yet, beyond any other books I just now think of, his books have the quality that alone makes novels historical. That they include everything, that they do justice to all sides and phases of the period, it would be fatuous to expect, and ridiculous to demand. It is not their epical character alone that forbids this; it is the condition of every work of art, which must choose its point of view, and include only the things that fall within a certain scope. One of Zola's polemical delusions was to suppose that a fiction ought not to be selective, and that his own fictions were not selective, but portrayed the fact without choice and without limitation. The fact was that he was always choosing, and always limiting. Even a map chooses and limits, far more a picture. Yet this delusion of Zola's and its affirmation resulted in no end of misunderstanding. People said the noises of the streets, which he supposed himself to have given with graphophonic fulness and variety, were not music; and they were quite right. Zola, as far as his effects were voluntary, was not giving them music; he openly loathed the sort of music they meant just as he openly loathed art, and asked to be regarded as a man of science rather than an artist. Yet, at the end of the ends, he was an artist and not a man of science. His hand was perpetually selecting his facts, and shaping them to one epical result, with an orchestral accompaniment, which, though reporting the rudest noises of the street, the vulgarest, the most offensive, was, in spite of him, so reporting them that the result was harmony.

Zola was an artist, and one of the very greatest, but even before and beyond that he was intensely a moralist, as only the moralists of our true and noble time have been. Not Tolstoy, not Ibsen himself, has more profoundly and indignantly felt the injustice of civilization, or more insistently shown the falsity of its fundamental pretensions. He did not make his books a polemic for one cause or another; he was far too wise and sane for that; but when he began to write them they became alive with his sense of what was wrong and false and bad. His tolerance is less than Tolstoy's, because his resignation is not so great; it is for the weak sinners and not for the strong, while Tolstoy's, with that transcendent vision of his race, pierces the bounds where the shows of strength and weakness cease and become of a solidarity of error in which they are one. But the ethics of his work, like Tolstoy's, were always carrying over into his life. He did not try to live poverty and privation and hard labor, as Tolstoy does; he surrounded himself with the graces and the luxuries which his honestly earned money enabled him to buy; but when an act of public and official atrocity disturbed the working of his mind and revolted his nature, he could not rest again till he had done his best to right it.

IV.

The other day Zola died (by a casualty which one fancies he would have liked to employ in a novel, if he had thought of it), and the man whom he had befriended at the risk of all he had in the world, his property, his liberty, his life itself, came to his funeral in disguise, risking again all that Zola had risked, to pay the last honors to his incomparable benefactor.

It was not the first time that a French literary man had devoted himself to the cause of the oppressed, and made it his personal affair, his charge, his inalienable trust. But Voltaire's championship of the persecuted Protestant had not the measure of Zola's championship of the persecuted Jew, though in both instances the courage and the persistence of the vindicator forced the reopening of the case and resulted in final justice. It takes nothing from the heroism of Voltaire to recognize that it was not so great as the heroism of Zola, and it takes nothing from the heroism of Zola to recognize that it was effective in the only country of Europe where such a case as that of Dreyfus would have been reopened; where there was a public imagination generous enough to conceive of undoing an act of immense public cruelty. At first this imagination was dormant, and the French people conceived only of punishing the vindicator along with the victim, for daring to accuse their processes of injustice. Outrage, violence, and the peril of death greeted Zola from his fellow-citizens, and from the authorities ignominy, fine, and prison. But nothing silenced or deterred him, and, in the swift course of moral adjustment character-istic of our time, an innumerable multitude of those who were ready a few years ago to rend him in pieces joined in paying tribute to the greatness of his soul, at the grave which received his body already buried under an avalanche of flowers. The government has not been so prompt as the mob, but with the history of France in mind, remem-bering how official action has always responded to the national impulses in behalf of humanity and justice, one cannot believe that the representatives of the French people will long remain behind the French people in offering reparation to the memory of one of the greatest and most heroic of French citizens. It is a pity for the govern-ment that it did not take part in the obsequies of Zola; it would have been well for the army, which he was falsely supposed to have de-famed, to have been present to testify of the real service and honor he had done it. But, in good time enough, the reparation will be official as well as popular, and when the monument to Zola, which has already risen in the hearts of his countrymen, shall embody itself in enduring marble or perennial bronze, the army will be there to join in its consecration.

V.

There is no reason why criticism should affect an equal hesitation. Criticism no longer assumes to ascertain an author's place in literature. It is very well satisfied if it can say something suggestive concerning the nature and quality of his work, and it tries to say this with as little of the old air of finality as it can manage to hide its poverty in.

After the words of M. Chaumie at the funeral, 'Zola's life work was dominated by anxiety for sincerity and truth, an anxiety inspired by his great feelings of pity and justice,' there seems nothing left to do but to apply them to the examination of his literary work. They unlock the secret of his performance, if it is any longer a secret, and they afford its justification in all those respects where without them it could not be justified. The question of immorality has been set aside, and the indecency has been admitted, but it remains for us to realize that anxiety for sincerity and truth, springing from the sense of pity and justice, makes indecency a condition of portraying human nature so that it may look upon its image and be ashamed.

The moralist working imaginatively has always had to ask himself how far he might go in illustration of his thesis, and he has not hesitated, or if he has hesitated, he has not failed to go far, very far. Defoe went far, Richardson went far, Ibsen has gone far, Tolstoy has gone far, and if Zola went farther than any of these, still he did not go so far as the immoralists have gone in the portrayal of vicious things to allure where he wished to repel. There is really such a thing as high motive and such a thing as low motive, though the processes are often so bewilderingly alike in both cases. The process may confound us, but there is no reason why we should be mistaken as to motive, and as to Zola's motive I do not think M. Chaumie was mistaken. As to his methods, they by no means always reflected his intentions. He fancied himself working like a scientist who has collected a vast number of specimens, and is deducing principles from them. But the fact is, he was always working like an artist, seizing every suggestion of experience and observation, turning it to the utmost account, piecing it out by his invention, building it up into a structure of fiction where its origin was lost to all but himself, and often even to himself. He supposed that he was recording and classifying, but he was creating and vivifying. Within the bounds of his epical scheme, which was always factitious, every person was so natural that his characters seemed like the characters of biography rather than of fiction. One does not remember them as one remembers the characters of most novelists. They had their being in a design which was meant to represent a state of things, to enforce an opinion of certain conditions; but they themselves were free agencies, bound by no allegiance to the general frame, and not apparently acting in behalf of the author, but only from their own individuality. At the moment of reading, they make the impression of an intense reality, and they remain real, but one recalls them as one recalls the people read of in last week's or last year's newspaper. What Zola did was less to import science and its methods into the region of fiction, than journalism and its methods; but in this he had his will only so far as his nature of artist would allow. He was no more a journalist than he was a scientist by nature; and, in spite of his intentions and in spite of his methods, he was essentially imaginative and involuntarily creative.

VI.

To me his literary history is very pathetic. He was bred if not born in the worship of the romantic, but his native faith was not proof against his reason, as again his reason was not proof against his native faith. He preached a crusade against romanticism, and fought a long fight with it, only to realize at last that he was himself too romanticistic to succeed against it, and heroically to own his defeat. The hosts of romanticism swarmed back over him and his followers, and prevailed, as we see them still prevailing. It was the error of the realists whom Zola led, to suppose that people like truth in fiction better than false-hood; they do not; they like falsehood best; and if Zola had not been at heart a romanticist, he never would have cherished his long delusion, he never could have deceived with his vain hopes those whom he persuaded to be realistic, as he himself did not succeed in being.

He wished to be a sort of historiographer writing the annals of a family, and painting a period; but he was a poet, doing far more than this, and contributing to creative literature as great works of fiction as have been written in the epic form. He was a paradox on every side but one, and that was the human side, which he would himself have held far worthier than the literary side. On the human side, the civic side, he was what he wished to be, and not what any perversity of his elements made him. He heard one of those calls to supreme duty, which from time to time select one man and not another for the response which they require; and he rose to that duty with a grandeur which had all the simplicity possible to a man of French civilization. We may think that there was something a little too dramatic in the manner of his heroism, his martyry, and we may smile at certain turns of rhetoric in the immortal letter accusing the French nation of intolerable wrong, just as, in our smug Anglo-Saxon conceit, we laughed at the procedure of the emotional courts which he compelled to take cognizance of the immense misdeed other courts had as emotionally committed. But the event, however indirectly and involuntarily, was justice which no other people in Europe would have done, and perhaps not any people of this more enlightened continent.

The success of Zola as a literary man has its imperfections, its phases of defeat, but his success as a humanist is without flaw. He triumphed as wholly and as finally as it has ever been given a man to triumph, and he made France triumph with him. By his hand, she added to the laurels she had won in the war of American Independence, in the wars of the Revolution for liberty and equality, in the campaigns for Italian Unity, the imperishable leaf of a national acknowledgment of national error.

NOTE

1 Though Howells had read a deal of Italian history in Italian, he probably expected his reader to feel the force of these allusions to the history of Florence during the age of Savonarola (esp. 1492–8) through a general knowledge of George Eliot's *Romola*, 1863. The *Piagnoni*, 'they that mourn,' were first Savonarola's puritanical followers and thence the 'popular' or anti-Medici party. The opposition *Arrabbiati*, 'the infuriate,' were first cavalier opponents of Savonarola and thence the 'aristocratic' pro-Medici party.

47 'Frank Norris'

1902

Published in the *North American Review*, December 1902.

It was Howells's tragedy and tragic for American literature that the two finest of his American heirs died young—Stephen Crane in 1900, aged twenty-nine; Frank Norris in 1902, aged thirty-two. Howells's standard of discipleship was strikingly Emersonian: the aim was not replication, a clan of little Howellses, but self-discovery, self-realization, devotion to the truth honestly seen. Crane and Norris, each after his fashion, joined the 'beautiful war,' wrote astonishingly, and died much too young. Their contemporary, Theodore Dreiser, offered allegiance to Howells, failed to win approval for *Sister Carrie*, lived long, wrote much, denied the biographical facts, and became a symbol of 'emancipation' from Howells.

Dreiser, in whom by his own standards Howells could not have believed, did not matter to him. But Crane and Norris mattered terribly, and this essay, intimately informed about both, is a dirge.

The projection which death gives the work of a man against the history of his time, is the doubtful gain we have to set against the recent loss of such authors as George Douglas, the Scotchman, who wrote *The House with the Green Shutters*, and Frank Norris, the American, who wrote *McTeague* and *The Octopus*, and other novels, antedating and postdating the first of these, and less clearly prophesying his future than the last. The gain is doubtful, because, though their work is now freed from the cloud of question which always involves the work of a living man in the mind of the general, if his work is good (if it is bad they give it no faltering welcome), its value was already apparent to those who judge from the certainty within themselves, and not from the uncertainty without. Every one in a way knows a thing to be good, but the most have not the courage to acknowledge it, in their sophistication with canons and criterions. The many, who in the tale of the criticism are not worth minding, are immensely unworthy of the test which death alone seems to put into their power. The few, who had the test before, were ready to own that Douglas's study of Scottish temperaments offered a hope of Scottish fiction freed the Scottish sentimentality which had kept it provincial; and that Norris's two mature novels, one personal and one social, imparted the assurance of an American fiction so largely commensurate with American circumstance as to liberate it from the casual and the occasional, in which it seemed lastingly trammelled. But the parallel between the two does not hold much farther. What Norris did, not merely what he dreamed of doing, was of vaster frame, and inclusive of imaginative intentions far beyond those of the only immediate contemporary to be matched with him, while it was of as fine and firm an intellectual quality, and of as intense and fusing an emotionality.

I.

In several times and places, it has been my rare pleasure to bear witness to the excellence of what Norris had done, and the richness of his promise. The vitality of his work was so abundant, the pulse of health was so full and strong in it, that it is incredible it should not be persistent still. The grief with which we accept such a death as his is without the consolation that we feel when we can say of some one that his life was a struggle, and that he is well out of the unequal strife, as we might say when Stephen Crane died. The physical slightness, if I may so suggest one characteristic of Crane's vibrant achievement, reflected the delicacy of energies that could be put forth only in nervous spurts, in impulses vivid and keen, but wanting in breadth and bulk of effect. Curiously enough, on the other hand, this very lyrical spirit, whose freedom was its life, was the absolute slave of reality. It was interesting to hear him defend what he had written, in obedience to his experience of things, against any change in the interest of convention. 'No,' he would contend, in behalf of the profanities of his people, 'that is the way they *talk*. I have thought of that, and whether I ought to leave such things out, but if I do I am not giving the thing as I *know* it.' He felt the constraint of those semi-savage natures, such as he depicted in *Maggie*, and *George's Mother*, and was forced through the fealty of his own nature to report them as they spoke no less than as they looked. When it came to *The Red Badge of Courage*, where he took leave of these simple æsthetics, and lost himself in a whirl of wild guesses at the fact from the ground of insufficient witness, he made the failure which formed the break between his first and his second manner, though it was what the public counted a success, with every reason to do so from the report of the sales.

The true Stephen Crane was the Stephen Crane of the earlier books, the earliest book; for *Maggie* remains the best thing he did. All he did was lyrical, but this was the aspect and accent as well as the spirit of the tragically squalid life he sang, while *The Red Badge of Courage*, and the other things that followed it, were the throes of an art failing with material to which it could not render an absolute devotion from an absolute knowledge. He sang, but his voice erred up and down the scale, with occasional flashes of brilliant melody, which could not redeem the errors. New York was essentially his inspiration, the New York of suffering and baffled and beaten life, of inarticulate or blasphemous life; and away from it he was not at home, with any theme, or any sort of character. It was the pity of his fate that he must quit New York, first as a theme, and then as a habitat; for he rested nowhere else, and wrought with nothing else as with the lurid depths which he gave proof of knowing better than any one else. Every one is limited, and perhaps no one is more limited than another; only, the direction of the limitation is different in each. Perhaps George Douglas, if he had lived, would still have done nothing greater than *The House with the Green Shutters*, and might have failed in the proportion of a larger range as Stephen Crane did. I am not going to say that either of these extraordinary talents was of narrower bound than Frank Norris; such measures are not of the map. But I am still less going to say that they were of finer quality because their achievement seems more poignant, through the sort of physical concentration which it has. Just as a whole unhappy world agonizes in the little space their stories circumscribe, so what is sharpest and subtlest in that anguish finds its like in the epical breadths of Norris's fiction.

II.

At the other times when I so gladly owned the importance of this fiction, I frankly recognized what seemed to me the author's debt to an older master; and now, in trying to sum up my sense of it in an estimate to which his loss gives a sort of finality for me, I must own again that he seemed to derive his ideal of the novel from the novels of Zola. I cannot say that, if the novels of Zola had not been cast in the epic mould, the novels of Frank Norris would not have been epical.

This is by no means certain; while it is, I think, certain that they owe nothing beyond the form to the master from whom he may have imagined it. Or they owe no more to him, essentially, than to the other masters of the time in which Norris lived out his life all too soon. It is not for nothing that any novelist is born in one age, and not another, unless we are to except that aoristic freak, the historical novelist; and by what Frank Norris wrote one might easily know what he had read. He had read, and had profited, with as much originality as any man may keep for himself, by his study of the great realists whose fiction has illustrated the latter part of the nineteenth century beyond any other time in the history of fiction; and if he seemed to have served his apprenticeship rather more to one of them than to another, this may be the effect of an inspiration not finally derived from that one. An Italian poet says that in Columbus 'the instinct of the unknown continent burned;' and it may be that this young novelist, who had his instincts mostly so well intellectualized, was moved quite from within when he imagined treating American things in an epical relation as something most expressive of their actual relation. I am not so sure that this is so, but I am sure that he believed it so, and that neither in material nor in treatment are his novels Zolaesque, though their form is Zolaesque, in the fashion which Zola did not invent, though he stamped it so deeply with his nature and his name.

I may allow also that he was like Zola in his occasional indulgence of a helpless fondness for the romantic, but he quite transcended Zola in the rich strain of poetry coloring his thought, and the mysticism in which he now and then steeped his story. I do not care enough, however, for what is called originality in any writer to fatigue myself greatly in the effort to establish that of a writer who will avouch his fresh and vigorous powers to any one capable of feeling them. I prefer, in the presence of a large design left unfulfilled, to note the generous ideal, the ample purpose, forecast in the novel forming the first of the trilogy he imagined.

In one of those few meetings which seem, too late, as if they might have been so many, but which the New York conditions of overwork for all who work at all begrudge, I remember how he himself outlined his plan. The story of the Wheat was for him the allegory of the industrial and financial America which is the real America, and he had begun already to tell the first part of this story in the tragedy of the railroad-ridden farms of California, since published as *The Octopus*. The second part, as he then designed, was to carry the tale to Chicago, where the distribution of the Wheat was to be the theme, as its production had already been the theme in the first. The last part was to find its scene in Europe, among the representative cities where the consumption of the Wheat was to form the motive. Norris believed himself peculiarly qualified for the work by the accidents of his life; for he was born in Chicago and had lived there till he was fifteen years old; then he had gone to California, and had grown up into the knowledge of the scene and action which he has portrayed so powerfully; later, he had acquainted himself with Europe, by long sojourn; and so he argued, with an enthusiasm tempered by a fine sense of his moral and artistic responsibility, that he had within himself the means of realizing the whole fact to the reader's imagination. He was aware that such a plan could be carried out only by years of ardent and patient study, and he expected to dedicate the best part of his strong young life to it.

III.

Those who know *The Octopus* know how his work justified his faith in himself; but those who had known *McTeague* could not have doubted but he would do what he had undertaken, in the spirit of the undertaking. Norris did give the time and toil to the right documentation of his history. He went to California and renewed his vital knowledge of his scene; he was in California again, studying the course of the fact which was to bring him to Chicago, when death overtook him and ended his high emprise. But in the meantime he had given us *The Octopus*, and before that he had given us *McTeague*, books not all so unlike in their nature as their surfaces might suggest. Both are epical, though the one is pivoted on the common ambition of a coarse human animal, destined to prevail in a half-quackish triumph, and the other revolves about one of the largest interests of modern civilization. The author thought at first of calling *McTeague*, as he told me, *The Golden Tooth*, which would have been more significant of the irregular dentist's supremacy in the story, and the ideal which inspired him; but perhaps he felt a final impossibility in the name. Yet, the name is a mere mask; and when one opens the book, the mask falls, and the drama confronts us with as living a physiognomy as I have seen in fiction. There is a bad moment when the author is overcome by his lingering passion for the romantic, and indulges himself in a passage of rank melodrama; but even there he does nothing that denies the reality of his characters, and they are always of a reality so intense that one lives with them in the grotesquely shabby San Francisco street where, but for the final episode, the action passes.

What is good is good, it matters not what other things are better or worse; and I could ask nothing for Norris, in my sense of his admirable achievement, but a mind freed to criticism absolute and not relative. He is of his time, and, as I have said, his school is evident; and yet I think he has a right to make his appeal in *The Octopus* irrespective of the other great canvases beside which that picture must be put. One should dissociate it as far as possible from the work of his masters—we all have masters; the masters themselves had them—not because it is an imitation, and would suffer from the comparison, but because it is so essentially different, so boldly and frankly native, that one is in danger of blaming it for a want of conformity to models, rather than for too close a following. Yet this, again, does not say quite the right thing, and what I feel, and wish others to feel, in regard to it, is the strong security of its most conscientious and instructed art. Here is nothing of experiment, of protest, of rebellion; the author does not break away from form in any sprawling endeavor for something newly or incomparably American, Californian, Western, but finds scope enough for his powers within the limits where the greatest fiction of our period 'orbs about.' The time, if there ever was one, for a prose Walt Whitman was past; and he perceived that the indigenous quality was to be imparted to his work by the use of fresh material, freshly felt, but used in the fashion and the form which a world-old art had evolved in its long endeavor.

McTeague was a personal epic, the Odyssey of a simple, semi-savage nature adventuring and experiencing along the low social levels which the story kept, and almost never rose or fell from. As I review it in the light of the first strong impressions, I must own it greater than I have ever yet acknowledged it, and I do this now with the regret which I hope the critic is apt to feel for not praising enough when praise could have helped most. I do not think my strictures of it were mistaken, for they related to the limits which certain facts of it would give it with the public, rather than to the ethical or æsthetic qualities which would establish it with the connoisseur. Yet, lest any reader of mine should be left without due sense of these, I wish now to affirm my strong sense of them, and to testify to the value which this extraordinary book has from its perfectly simple fidelity: from the truthfulness in which there is no self-doubt and no self-excuse.

IV.

But, with all its power, *McTeague* is no such book as *The Octopus*, which is the Iliad to its Odyssey.

It will not be suggesting too much for the story to say, that there is a kind of Homeric largeness in the play of the passions moving it. They are not autochthons, these Californians of the great Wheat farms, choking in the folds of the railroad, but Americans of more than one transplantation; yet there is something rankly earthy and elemental in them, which gives them the pathos of tormented Titans. It is hard to choose any of them as the type, as it is hard to choose any scene as the representative moment. If we choose Annixter, growing out of an absolute, yet no gross, materiality, through the fire of a purifying love, into a kind of final spirituality, we think, with misgiving for our decision, of Magnus Derrick, the high, pure leader of the rebellion against the railroad, falling into ruin, moral and mental, through the use of the enemy's bad means for his good cause. Half a score of other figures, from either camp, crowd upon the fancy to contest the supreme interest, men figures, women figures; and, when it comes to choosing this episode or that as the supreme event, the confusion of the critic is even greater. If one were to instance the fight between the farmers and the sheriff's deputies, with the accompanying evictions, one must recall the tremendous passages of the train-robbery by the crazy victim of the railroad's treachery, taking his revenge in his hopeless extremity. Again, a half-score of other scenes, other episodes rise from the remembered pages, and defy selection.

The story is not less but more epical, in being a strongly inter-wrought group of episodes. The play of an imagination fed by a rich consciousness of the mystical relations of nature and human nature, the body and the soul of earthly life, steeps the whole theme in an odor of common growth. It is as if the Wheat sprang out of the hearts of men, in the conception of the young poet who writes its Iliad, and who shows how it overwhelms their lives, and germinates anew from their deaths. His poem, of which the terms are naked prose, is a picture of the civilization, the society, the culture which is the efflorescence of the wheaten prosperity; and the social California, rank, crude, lusty, which he depicts is as convincing as the agricultural California, which is the ground of his work. It will be easily believed that in the handling nothing essential to the strong impression is blinked; but nothing, on the other hand, is forced in. The episode of Vanamee and

Angèle, with its hideous tragedy, and the long mystical epilogue ending almost in anti-climax, is the only passage which can be accused of irrelevance, and it is easier to bring than to prove this accusation.

As I write, and scarcely touch the living allegory here and there, it rises before me in its large inclusion, and makes me feel once more how little any analysis of a work of art can represent it. After all the critic must ask the reader to take his word for it that the thing is great, and entreat him to go see for himself; see, in this instance, the breadth and the fineness, the beauty and the dread, the baseness and the grandeur, the sensuality and the spirituality, working together for the effect of a novel unequalled for scope and for grasp in our fiction.

V.

Fine work we have enough of and to spare in our fiction. No one can say it is wanting in subtlety of motive and delicate grace of form. But something still was lacking, something that was not merely the word but the deed of commensurateness. Perhaps, after all, those who have demanded Continentality of American literature had some reason in their folly. One thinks so, when one considers work like Norris's, and finds it so vast in scope while so fine and beautiful in detail. Hugeness was probably what those poor fellows were wanting when they asked for Continentality; and from any fit response that has come from them one might well fancy them dismayed and puzzled to have been given greatness instead. But Continentality he also gave them.

His last book is a fragment, a part of a greater work, but it is a mighty fragment, and it has its completeness. In any time but this, when the air is filled with the fizz and sputter of a thousand pin-wheels, the descent of such a massive aërolite as *The Octopus* would have stirred all men's wonder, but its light to most eyes appears to have seemed of one quality with those cheap explosives which all the publishing houses are setting off, and advertising as meteoric. If the time will still come for acknowledgment of its greatness, it will not be the time for him who put his heart and soul into it. That is the pity, but that in the human conditions is what cannot be helped. We are here to do something, we do not know why; we think it is for ourselves, but it is for almost anyone but ourselves. If it is great, some one else shall get the good of it, and the doer shall get the glory too late; if it is mean, the doer shall have the glory, but who shall have the good?

This would not be so bad if there were life long enough for the processes of art; if the artist could outlive the doubt and the delay into which every great work of art seems necessarily to plunge the world anew, after all its experience of great work.

I am not saying, I hope, that Frank Norris had not his success, but only that he had not success enough, the success which he would have had if he had lived, and which will still be his too late. The two novels he has left behind him are sufficient for his fame, but though they have their completeness and their adequacy, one cannot help thinking of the series of their like that is now lost to us. It is Aladdin's palace, and yet,

> The unfinished window in Aladdin's palace
> Unfinished must remain,

and we never can look upon it without an ache of longing and regret.

Personally, the young novelist gave one the impression of strength and courage that would hold out to all lengths. Health was in him always as it never was in that other rare talent of ours with whom I associate him in my sense of the irretrievable, the irreparable. I never met him but he made me feel that he could do it, the thing he meant to do, and do it robustly and quietly, without the tremor of 'those electrical nerves' which imparted itself from the presence of Stephen Crane. With him my last talk of the right way and the true way of doing things was saddened by the confession of his belief that we were soon to be overwhelmed by the rising tide of romanticism, whose crazy rote he heard afar, and expected with the resignation which the sick experience with all things. But Norris heard nothing, or seemed to hear nothing, but the full music of his own aspiration, the rich diapason of purposes securely shaping themselves in performance.

Who shall inherit these, and carry forward work so instinct with the Continent as his? Probably, no one; and yet good work shall not fail us, manly work, great work. One need not be overhopeful to be certain of this. Bad work, false, silly, ludicrous work, we shall always have, for the most of those who read are so, as well as the most of those who write; and yet there shall be here and there one to see the varying sides of our manifold life truly and to say what he sees. When I think of Mr. Brand Whitlock and his novel of *The Thirteenth District*, which has embodied the very spirit of American politics as American politicians know them in all the Congressional districts; when I think of the author of *The Spenders*, so wholly good in one half that one

forgets the other half is only half good; when I think of such work as
Mr. William Allen White's, Mr. Robert Herrick's, Mr. Will Payne's
—all these among the younger men—it is certainly not to despair
because we shall have no such work as Frank Norris's from them.
They, and the like of them, will do their good work as he did his.

48 'Mr. Henry James's Later Work'
1903

Published in the *North American Review*, January 1903.
The Howells who had led, advised, and consoled James since 1866 also followed him with avidity. Nothing, not even the effective insights into the work of James's 'major phase,' is more interesting in this essay than Howells's calculated effort to persuade the *North American Review* audience that James is an absolutely first-rate artist, a master to whom they *must* open their hearts and minds.

Howells's humor here about feminine psychology and ratiocination portrays himself at a most typical game. An ardent feminist, he thought women superior to men intellectually and aesthetically. But he deplored their lack of education and the incapacity to be impersonal which cultural conditions had forced upon them. Believing in women's superior moral sensitivity, he felt critical of their immorality in not seeking or coping with responsibility. Attacked by their answering chauvinism, their demand that he create a lofty, faultless heroine, he had long since taken refuge in the remark, here paraphrased, that he was waiting for the Almighty to begin.

It has been Mr. James's lot from the beginning to be matter of unusually lively dispute among his readers. There are people who frankly say they cannot bear him, and then either honestly let him alone, or secretly hanker for him, and every now and then return to him, and try if they cannot like him, or cannot bear him a little better. These are his enemies, or may be called so for convenience' sake; but they are hardly to be considered his readers. Many of his readers, however, are also his enemies: they read him in a condition of hot insurrection against all that he says and is; they fiercely question his point of view, they object to the world that he sees from it; they declare that there is no such world, or that, if there is, there ought not to be, and that he does not paint it truly. They would like to have the question out with him personally: such is their difference of opinion that, to hear them talk, you would think they would like to have it out with him pugilistically. They would, to every appearance, like to beat also those who accept his point of view, believe in his world, and hold that he truly portrays it. Nothing but the prevailing sex of his enemies saves them, probably, from offering the readers who are not his enemies the violence to which their prevailing sex tempts them. You cannot, at least, palliate his demerits with them without becoming of the quality of his demerits, and identifying yourself with him in the whole measure of these. That is why, for one reason, I am going to make my consideration of his later work almost entirely a study of his merits, for I own that he has his faults, and I would rather they remained his faults than became mine.

I.

The enmity to Mr. James's fiction among his readers is mostly feminine because the men who do not like him are not his readers. The men who do like him and are his readers are of a more feminine fineness, probably, in their perceptions and intuitions, than those other men who do not read him, though of quite as unquestionable a manliness, I hope. I should like to distinguish a little farther, and say that they are the sort of men whose opinions women peculiarly respect, and in whom they are interested quite as much as they are vexed to find them differing so absolutely from themselves.

The feminine enmity to Mr. James is of as old a date as his discovery of the Daisy Miller type of American girl, which gave continental offence among her sisters. It would be hard to say why that type gave such continental offence, unless it was because it was held not honestly to have set down the traits which no one could but most potently and powerfully allow to be true. The strange thing was that these traits were the charming and honorable distinctions of American girlhood as it convinced Europe, in the early eighteen-seventies, of a civilization so spiritual that its innocent daughters could be not only without the knowledge but without the fear of evil. I am not going back, however, to that early feminine grievance, except to note that it seems to have been the first tangible grievance, though it was not the first grievance. I, with my gray hairs, can remember still earlier work of his whose repugnant fascination was such that women readers clung to it with the wild rejection which has in a measure followed all his work at their hands.

It has been the curious fortune of this novelist, so supremely gifted in divining women and portraying them, that beyond any other great novelist (or little, for that matter) he has imagined few heroines acceptable to women. Even those martyr-women who have stood by him in the long course of his transgressions, and maintained through thick and thin, that he is by all odds the novelist whom they could best trust with the cause of woman in fiction, have liked his anti-heroines more,—I mean, found them realer,—than his heroines. I am not sure but I have liked them more myself, but that is because I always find larger play for my sympathies in the character which needs the reader's help than in that which is so perfect as to get on without it. If it were urged that women do not care for his heroines because there are none of them to care for, I should not blame them, still less should I blame him for giving them that ground for abhorrence. I find myself diffident of heroines in fiction because I have never known one in life, of the real faultless kind; and heaven forbid I should ever yet know one. In Mr. James's novels I always feel safe from that sort, and it may be for this reason, among others, that I like to read his novels when they are new, and read them over and over again when they are old, or when they are no longer recent.

II.

At this point I hear from far within a voice bringing me to book about Milly Theale in *The Wings of a Dove*, asking me, if *there* is not a heroine of the ideal make, and demanding what fault there is in her that renders her lovable. Lovable, I allow she is, dearly, tenderly, reverently lovable, but she has enough to make her so, besides being too good, too pure, too generous, too magnificently unselfish. It is not imaginable that her author should have been conscious of offering in her anything like an atonement to the offended divinity of American womanhood for Daisy Miller. But if it were imaginable the offended divinity ought to be sumptuously appeased, appeased to tears of grateful pardon such as I have not yet seen in its eyes. Milly Theale is as entirely American in the qualities which you can and cannot touch as Daisy Miller herself; and (I find myself urged to the risk of noting it) she is largely American in the same things. There is the same self-regardlessness, the same beauteous insubordination, the same mortal solution of the problem. Of course, it is all in another region, and the social levels are immensely parted. Yet Milly Theale is the superior of Daisy Miller less in her nature than in her conditions.

There is, in both, the same sublime unconsciousness of the material environment, the same sovereign indifference to the fiscal means of their emancipation to a more than masculine independence. The sense of what money can do for an American girl without her knowing it, is a 'blind sense' in the character of Daisy, but in the character of Milly it has its eyes wide open. In that wonderful way of Mr. James's by which he imparts a fact without stating it, approaching it again and again, without actually coming in contact with it, we are made aware of the vast background of wealth from which Milly is projected upon our acquaintance. She is shown in a kind of breathless impatience with it, except as it is the stuff of doing wilfully magnificent things, and committing colossal expenses without more anxiety than a prince might feel with the revenues of a kingdom behind him. The ideal American rich girl has never really been done before, and it is safe to say that she will never again be done with such exquisite appreciation. She is not of the new rich; an extinct New York ancestry darkles in the retrospect: something vaguely bourgeois, and yet with presences and with lineaments of aristocratic distinction. They have made her masses of money for her, those intangible fathers, uncles and grand-fathers, and then, with her brothers and sisters, have all perished away from her, and left her alone in the world with nothing else. She is as convincingly imagined in her relation to them, as the daughter of an old New York family, as she is in her inherited riches. It is not the old New York family of the unfounded Knickerbocker tradition, but something as fully patrician, with a nimbus of social importance as unquestioned as its money. Milly is not so much the flower of this local root as something finer yet: the perfume of it, the distilled and wandering fragrance. It would be hard to say in what her New Yorkishness lies, and Mr. James himself by no means says; only if you know New York at all, you have the unmistakable sense of it. She is New Yorkish in the very essences that are least associable with the superficial notion of New York: the intellectual refinement that comes of being born and bred in conditions of illimitable ease, of having had everything that one could wish to have, and the cultivation that seems to come of the mere ability to command it. If one will have an illustration of the final effect in Milly Theale, it may be that it can be suggested as a sort of a Bostonian quality, with the element of *conscious* worth eliminated, and purified as essentially of pedantry as of commerciality. The wonder is that Mr. James in his prolonged expatriation has been able to seize this lovely impalpability, and to impart the sense of it; and perhaps the true reading of the riddle is that such a nature, such a character is most appreciable in that relief from the background which Europe gives all American character.

III.

'But that is just what does not happen in the case of Mr. James's people. They are merged in the background so that you never can get behind them, and fairly feel and see them all round. Europe *doesn't* detach them; *nothing* does. "There they are," as he keeps making his people say in all his late books, when they are not calling one another dear lady, and dear man, and prodigious and magnificent, and of a vagueness or a richness, or a sympathy, or an opacity. No, he is of a tremendosity, but he worries me to death; he kills me; he really gives me a headache. He fascinates me, but I have no patience with him.'

'But, dear lady,' for it was a weary woman who had interrupted the flow of my censure in these unmeasured terms, and whom her interlocutor—another of Mr. James's insistent words—began trying to flatter to her disadvantage, 'a person of your insight must see that this is the conditional vice of all painting, its vital fiction. You cannot get behind the figures in any picture. They are always merged in their background. And there you are!'

'Yes, I know I am. But that is just where I don't want to be. I want figures that I *can* get behind.'

'Then you must go to some other shop—you must go to the shop of a sculptor.'

'Well, why isn't *he* a sculptor?'

'Because he is a painter.'

'Oh, that's no reason. He ought to be a sculptor.'

'Then he couldn't give you the color, the light and shade, the delicate *nuances*, the joy of the intimated fact, all that you delight in him for. What was that you were saying the other day? That he was like Monticelli in some of his pastorals or picnics: a turmoil of presences which you could make anything, everything, nothing of as you happened to feel; something going on that you had glimpses of, or were allowed to guess at, but which you were rapturously dissatisfied with, any way.'

'Did I say that?' my interlocutress—terrible word!—demanded. 'It was very good.'

'It was wonderfully good. I should not have named Monticelli, exactly, because though he is of a vagueness that is painty, he is too much of a denseness. Mr. James does not trowel the colors on.'

'I see what you mean. Whom should you have named?'

'I don't know. Monticelli will do in one way. He gives you a sense of people, of things undeniably, though not unmistakably, happening, and that is what Mr. James does.'

'Yes, he certainly does,' and she sighed richly, as if she had been one of his people herself. 'He does give you a sense.'

'He gives you a sense of a tremendous lot going on, for instance, in *The Wings of a Dove*, of things undeniably, though not unmistakably, happening. It is a great book.'

'It is, it is,' she sighed again. 'It wore me to a thread.'

'And the people were as unmistakable as they were undeniable: not Milly, alone, not Mrs. Stringham, as wonderfully of New England as Milly of New York; but all that terribly frank, terribly selfish, terribly shameless, terribly hard English gang.'

'Ah, Densher wasn't really hard or really shameless, though he was willing—to please that unspeakable Kate Croy—to make love to Milly and marry her money so that when she died, they could live happy ever after—or at least comfortably. And you cannot say that Kate was frank. And Lord Mark really admired Milly. Or, anyway, he wanted to marry her. Do you think Kate took the money from Densher at last and married Lord Mark?'

'Why should you care?'

'Oh, one oughtn't to care, of course, in reading Mr. James. But with any one else, you would like to know who married who. It is all too wretched. Why should he want to picture such life?'

'Perhaps because it exists.'

'Oh, do you think the English are really so bad? I'm glad he made such a beautiful character as Milly, American.'

'My notion is that he didn't "make" any of the characters.'

'Of course not. And I suppose some people in England are actually like that. We have not got so far here, yet. To be sure, society is not so all-important here, yet. If it ever is, I suppose we shall pay the price. But *do* you think he ought to picture such life because it exists?'

'Do you find yourself much the worse for *The Wings of a Dove*?' I asked. 'Or for *The Sacred Fount*? Or for *The Awkward Age*? Or even for *What Maisie Knew*? They all picture much the same sort of life.'

'Why, of course not. But it isn't so much what he says—he never *says* anything—but what he insinuates. I don't believe that is good for young girls.'

'But if they don't know what it means? I'll allow that it isn't quite *jeune fille* in its implications, all of them; but maturity has its modest claims. Even its immodest claims are not wholly ungrounded in the interest of a knowledge of our mother-civilization, which is what Mr. James's insinuations impart, as I understand them.'

'Well, young people cannot read him aloud together. You can't deny that.'

'No, but elderly people can, and they are not to be ignored by the novelist, always. I fancy the reader who brings some knowledge of good and evil, without being the worse for it, to his work is the sort of reader Mr. James writes for. I can imagine him addressing himself to a circle of such readers as this *Review*'s with a satisfaction, and a sense of liberation, which he might not feel in the following of the family magazines, and still not incriminate himself. I have heard a good deal said in reproach of the sort of life he portrays, in his later books; but I have not found his people of darker deeds or murkier motives than the average in fiction. I don't say, life.'

'No, certainly, so far as he tells you. It is what he *doesn't* tell that is so frightful. He leaves you to such awful conjectures. For instance, when Kate Croy—'

'When Kate Croy—?'

'No. I *won't* discuss it. But you know what I mean; and I don't believe there ever was such a girl.'

'And you believe there was ever such a girl as Milly Theale?'

'Hundreds! She is true to the life. So perfectly American. My husband and I read the story aloud together, and I wanted to weep. We had such a strange experience with that book. We read it half through together; then we got impatient, and tried to finish it alone. But we could not make anything of it apart; and we had to finish it together. We could not bear to lose a word; every word—and there were a good many!—seemed to tell. If you took one away you seemed to miss something important. It almost destroyed me, thinking it all out. I went round days, with my hand to my forehead; and I don't believe I understand it perfectly yet. Do you?'

IV.

I pretended that I did, but I do not mind being honester with the reader than I was with my interlocutress. I have a theory that it is not well to penetrate every recess of an author's meaning. It robs him of the charm of mystery, and the somewhat labyrinthine construction of Mr. James's later sentences lends itself to the practice of the self-denial necessary to the preservation of this charm. What I feel sure of is that he has a meaning in it all, and that by and by, perhaps when I least expect it, I shall surprise his meaning. In the meanwhile I rest content with what I do know. In spite of all the Browning Clubs—even the club which has put up a monument to the poet's butler-ancestor—all of Browning is not clear, but enough of Browning is clear for any real lover of his poetry.

I was sorry I had not thought of this in time to say it to my inter-locutress; and I was sorry I had not amplified what I did say of his giving you a sense of things, so as to make it apply to places as well as persons. Never, in my ignorance, have I had a vivider sense of London, in my knowledge a stronger sense of Venice, than in *The Wings of a Dove*. More miraculous still, as I have tried to express, was the sense he gave me of the anterior New York where the life flowered which breathed out the odor called Milly Theale—a heartbreaking fragrance as of funeral violets—and of the anterior New England sub-acidly fruiting in Mrs. Stringham. As for social conditions, predicaments, orders of things, where shall we find the like of the wonders wrought in *The Awkward Age*? I have been trying to get phrases which should convey the effect of that psychomancy from me to my reader, and I find none so apt as some phrase that should suggest the convincingly incredible. Here is something that the reason can as little refuse as it can accept. Into quite such particles as the various characters of this story would the disintegration of the old, rich, demoralized society of an ancient capital fall so probably that each of the kaleidoscopic fragments, dropping into irrelevant radiance around Mrs. Brooken-ham, would have its fatally appointed tone in the 'scheme of color.' Here is that inevitable, which Mr. Brander Matthews has noted as the right and infallible token of the real. It does not matter, after that, how the people talk,—or in what labyrinthine parentheses they let their unarriving language wander. They strongly and vividly exist, and they construct not a drama, perhaps, but a world, floating indeed in an obscure where it seems to have its solitary orbit, but to be as solidly palpable as any of the planets of the more familiar systems, and wrapt in the aura of its peculiar corruption. How bad the bad people on it may be one does not know, and is not intended to know, perhaps; that would be like being told the gross facts of some scandal which, so long as it was untouched, supported itself not unamusingly in air; but of the goodness of the good people one is not left in doubt; and it is a goodness which consoles and sustains the virtue apt to droop in the presence of neighborly remissness.

I might easily attribute to the goodness a higher office than this; but if I did I might be trenching upon the ethical delicacy of the author which seems to claim so little for itself. Mr. James is, above any other, the master of the difficult art of never doing more than to 'hint a fault, or hesitate dislike,' and I am not going to try committing him to conclusions he would shrink from. There is nothing of the clumsiness of the 'satirist' in his design, and if he notes the absolute commerciality of the modern London world, it is with a reserve clothing itself in frankness which is infinitely, as he would say, 'detached.' But somehow, he lets you know how horribly *business* fashionable English life is; he lets Lord Mark let Milly Theale know, at their first meeting, when he tells her she is with people who never do anything for nothing, and when, with all her money, and perhaps because of it, she is still so trammelled in the ideal that she cannot take his meaning. Money, and money bluntly; gate-money of all kinds; money the means, is the tune to which that old world turns in a way which we scarcely imagine in this crude new world where it is still so largely less the means than the end.

But the general is lost in the personal, as it should be in Mr. James's books, earlier as well as later, and the allegory is so faint that it cannot always be traced. He does not say that the limitless liberty allowed Nanda Brookenham by her mother in *The Awkward Age* is better than the silken bondage in which the Duchess keeps her niece Aggie, though Nanda is admirably lovable, and little Aggie is a little cat; that is no more his affair than to insist upon the loyalty of old Mr. Longdon to an early love, or the generosity of Mitchett, as contrasted with the rapacity of Mrs. Brookenham, who, after all, wants nothing more than the means of being what she has always been. What he does is simply to show you those people mainly on the outside, as you mainly see people in the world, and to let you divine them and their ends from what they do and say. They are presented with infinite pains; as far as their appearance (though they are very little described) goes, you are not suffered to make a mistake. But he does not analyze them for you; rather he synthetizes them, and carefully hands them over to you in a sort of integrity very uncommon in the characters of fiction. One might infer from this that his method was dramatic, something like Tourguénieff's, say; but I do not know that his method is dramatic. I do not recall from the book more than one passage of dramatic intensity, but that was for me of very great intensity; I mean the passage where old Mr. Longdon lets Vanderbank understand that he will provide for him if he will offer himself to Nanda, whom he knows to be in love with Vanderbank, and where Vanderbank will not promise. That is a great moment, where everything is most openly said, most brutally said, to American thinking; and yet said with a restraint of feeling that somehow redeems it all.

Nothing could well be more perfected than the method of the three books which I have been supposing myself to be talking about, however far any one may think it from perfect. They express mastery, finality, doing what one means, in a measure not easily to be matched. I will leave out of the question the question of obscurity; I will let those debate that whom it interests more than it interests me. For my own part I take it that a master of Mr. James's quality does not set out with a design whose significance is not clear to himself, and if others do not make it clear to themselves, I suspect them rather than him of the fault. All the same I allow that it is sometimes not easy to make out; I allow that sometimes *I* do not make it out, I, who delight to read him almost more than any other living author, but then I leave myself in his hands. I do not believe he is going finally to play me the shabby trick of abandoning me in the dark; and meanwhile he perpetually interests me. If anything, he interests me too much, and I come away fatigued, because I cannot bear to lose the least pulse of the play of character; whereas from most fiction I lapse into long delicious absences of mind, now and then comfortably recovering myself to find out what is going on, and then sinking below the surface again.

The Awkward Age is mostly expressed in dialogue; *The Wings of a Dove* is mostly in the narration and the synthesis of emotions. Not the synthesis of the motives, please; these in both books are left to the reader, almost as much as they are in *The Sacred Fount*. That troubled source, I will own, 'is of a profundity,' and in its depths darkles the solution which the author makes it no part of his business to pull to the top; if the reader wants it, let him dive. But why should not a novel be written so like to life, in which most of the events remain the meaningless, that we shall never quite know what the author meant? Why, in fact, should not people come and go, and love and hate, and hurt and help one another as they do in reality, without rendering the reader a reason for their behavior, or offering an explanation at the end with which he can light himself back over the way he has come, and see what they meant? Who knows what any one means here below, or what he means himself, that is, precisely stands for? Most people mean nothing, except from moment to moment, if they indeed mean anything so long as that, and life which is full of propensities is almost without motives. In the scribbles which we suppose to be imitations of life, we hold the unhappy author to a logical consistency which we find so rarely in the original; but ought not we rather to praise him where his work confesses itself, as life confesses itself, without a plan? Why should we demand more of the imitator than we get from the creator?

Of course, it can be answered that we are *in* creation like characters in fiction, while we are outside of the imitation and spectators instead of characters; but that does not wholly cover the point. Perhaps, however, I am asking more for Mr. James than he would have me. In that case I am willing to offer him the reparation of a little detraction. I wish he would leave his people more, not less, to me when I read him. I have tried following their speeches without taking in his comment, delightfully pictorial as that always is, and it seems to me that I make rather more of their meaning, that way. I reserve the pleasure and privilege of going back and reading his comment in the light of my conclusions. This is the method I have largely pursued with the people of *The Sacred Fount*, of which I do not hesitate to say that I have mastered the secret, though, for the present I am not going to divulge it. Those who cannot wait may try the key which I have given.

But do not, I should urge them, expect too much of it; I do not promise it will unlock everything. If you find yourself, at the end, with nothing in your hand but the postulate with which the supposed narrator fantastically started, namely, that people may involuntarily and unconsciously prey upon one another, and mentally and psychically enrich themselves at one another's expense, still you may console yourself, if you do not think this enough, with the fact that you have passed the time in the company of men and women freshly and truly seen, amusingly shown, and abidingly left with your imagination. For me, I am so little exacting, that this is enough.

The Sacred Fount is a most interesting book, and you are teased through it to the end with delightful skill, but I am not going to say that it is a great book like *The Awkward Age*, or *The Wings of a Dove*. These are really incomparable books, not so much because there is nothing in contemporary fiction to equal them as because there is nothing the least like them. They are of a kind that none but their author can do, and since he is alone master of their art, I am very well content to leave him to do that kind of book quite as he chooses. I will not so abandon my function as to say that I could not tell him how to do them better, but it sufficiently interests me to see how he gets on without my help. After all, the critic has to leave authors somewhat to themselves; he cannot always be writing their books for them; and when I find an author, like Mr. James, who makes me acquainted with people who instantly pique my curiosity by 'something rich and strange,' in an environment which is admirably imaginable, I gratefully make myself at home with them, and stay as long as he will let me.

V.

'But,'—here is that interlocutress whom I flattered myself I had silenced, at me again,—'do you like to keep puzzling things out, so? I don't. Of course, the books *are* intensely fascinating, but I do not like to keep guessing conundrums. Why shouldn't we have studies of life that are not a series of conundrums?'

'Dear lady,' I make my answer, 'what was I saying just now but that life itself is a series of conundrums, to which the answers are lost in the past, or are to be supplied us, after a long and purifying discipline of guessing, in the future? I do not admit your position, but if I did, still I should read the author who keeps you guessing, with a pleasure, an edification, in the suggestive, the instructive way he has of asking his conundrums beyond that I take in any of the authors who do not tax my curiosity, who shove their answers at me before I have had a chance to try whether I cannot guess them. Here you have the work of a great psychologist, who has the imagination of a poet, the wit of a keen humorist, the conscience of an impeccable moralist, the temperament of a philosopher, and the wisdom of a rarely experienced witness of the world; and yet you come back at me with the fact, or rather the pretence, that you do not like to keep puzzling his things out. It is my high opinion of you that you precisely do like to keep puzzling his things out; that you are pleased with the sort of personal appeal made to you by the difficulties you pretend to resent, and that you enjoy the just sense of superiority which your continual or final divinations give you. Mr. James is one of those authors who pay the finest tribute an author can pay the intelligence of his reader by trusting it, fully and frankly. There you are; and if you were not puzzling out those recondite conundrums which you complain of, what better things, in the perusal of the whole range of contemporary fiction, could you be doing? For my part I can think for you of none. There is no book like *The Awkward Age*, as I said, for it is sole of its kind, and no book that at all equals it, since Mr. Hardy's *Jude*, for the intensity of its natural-ness. I don't name them to compare them; again I renounce all comparisons for Mr. James's work; but I will say that in the deeply penetrating anguish of *Jude*, I felt nothing profounder than the pathos which aches and pierces through those closing scenes of *The Awkward Age*, in Nanda's last talk with Vanderbank, whom she must and does leave for her mother's amusement, and her yet later talk with old Mr. Longdon, to whom she must and does own her love for Vanderbank so heartbreaking. What beautiful and gentle souls the new-fashioned young girl and the old-fashioned old man are, and how beautifully and gently they are revealed to us by the perfected art of the book in which they continue to live after we part with them! How—'

'Ah, there,' my interlocutress broke in, as if fearful of not having the last word, 'I certainly agree with you. I wish you were as candid about everything else.'

49 The rise of psychologism
1903

From 'The Editor's Easy Chair,' *Harper's Monthly*, June 1903.
As I have argued for some years, it was inevitable that realism should transform itself toward psychological and stream of consciousness fiction. It would have done so had there been no Sigmund Freud; it had largely done so before Freud's work transpired. Howells not only began to work in that direction as early as 1889, he had been taking cognizance of the shift toward psychologism in the intellectual history of his age for a decade before he announced the transition definitively. The old agnostic in Howells said, 'What really endures is mystery, which is the prime condition of existence, and will doubtless be its ultimate condition.' But newly he sees that the doubt once rooted in 'science' now roots itself in 'psychology' and a new species of imagination rules the modern world.

Among the means of amusing us mortals on the way where we know so little to the end where we shall know everything or nothing, the favorite with the Supreme Wisdom seems to be the simple action of the pendulum. It is not the employment of the pendulum in noting the passage of time, which we have now grown so used to as hardly to notice it, but its perpetual oscillation, its agreeable and persuasive swing from side to side, and its promise of pause at the extremes, which beguile the spirit. No doubt, if the pendulum were really to stop at the farthest right or the farthest left, and hang there, it would fatigue the sensibilities; but it is the nature of the pendulum to return from the one to the other, and it is the nature of man to desire this reversion.

It is with the nature of both that Providence deals in ordering that perpetual change which seems the one absolute law of life here, and if life persists, then not imaginably less the law of life otherwise. The very faith in this life otherwise is subject to the law, and perhaps more notably subject than any other principle of our being. No sooner has the pendulum swung in the direction of faith, and dogma has got its little nail and hammer ready to rivet the pendulum there in a creed, than the pendulum begins to drop, and to slide down, and to swing slowly up to the opposite point, where doubt is foiled in a like attempt to fasten it. What really endures is mystery, which is the prime condition of existence, and will doubtless be its ultimate condition.

Sometimes the mystery seems pervaded with despair, and sometimes with hope, but it is at no time without incentive for the mind and soul. We must still seek to fathom it; but if we could plunge the lead of our learning to its bottom we might bring up from those rayless depths only the sands of our familiar shores; and it is in our highest interest that we are kept within the familiar bounds of surmise, and safe from positive knowledge. Till we know everything we are rich in the possibility of knowing something that may outvalue everything, and we reconcile ourselves to our ignorance, if we are wise. If we are not wise, we are all the same held to it until the time appointed for its dispersion has come.

I.

The question of the life hereafter, which at a certain dreadful moment seemed reduced to a formula of alphabetical rappings, has again resumed the dignity of those conjectures in which our longing to be assured had patiently dwelt from the beginning, and must doubtless dwell to the end. At another dreadful moment, our conjectures were forbidden us by the savants who found in them none of the tangible results confessedly impossible to them; but that moment passed too, and now again we have the comfort of our conjectures, which divine much or little according to the mood we are in, but which modestly refuse to conclude anything. They form the atmosphere in which we must acquaint ourselves with a good deal of the latest thinking, and in which most of his sympathetic readers will turn the sibylline leaves of such a book as Mr. John Bigelow's on *The Mystery of Sleep*, which, after his careful revision and enlargement, we now have from him in a new edition; and perhaps they will create that common ground on which they will feel themselves safer with him in his speculations than in his documents. What is speculative, what is hypothetical, in his essay, is somehow more convincing than what is documentary.

The proof that the soul may have here in the dreams of sleep a life concurrent and contemporaneous with the life that the mind has in the facts of waking, lies in the impalpable impressions, the almost

obliterated experiences of each reader, rather than in the testimony of
sacred and profane literature. This, when it is alleged, seems forced
to an unwilling office, and it is the part of Mr. Bigelow's work which
we care for so little that in the interest of his thesis we could wish
to dispense with it except in those instances where it is least absolute.
The point he seeks to carry can be carried only through the intimate
self-knowledge, the recondite self-question of each reader, and cannot
be avouched by any accumulation of testimony, which in the very act
of being summoned turns irrelevant and inacceptable.

Dreams, like apparitions, are quite inalienably personal. They are,
when they are most significant, so entirely for the dreamer alone, that
if he repeats them he has one chance of convincing his hearer against
a thousand chances of merely boring him; the twice-told tale is not
nearly so tedious as the once-told dream. The fabric of one's visions
is so insubstantial that it shrivels in one's hands, if one attempts to
show it, to so little that the temptation to eke it out with invention is
almost irresistible. We each know from our own experience that there
are wonderful dreams, but we do not find the dreams of another
wonderful without suspecting him of romancing. These are the terms
on which the documentation of the mystery of sleep becomes the very
material of misgiving, and the facts have the effect of incredulously
questioning themselves in the act of affirmation.

Yet the mystery and the wonder and the infinite intimation
remain, and it is in touching them that the essay of Mr. Bigelow has
its fascination. Why we spend a third of our lives in the realm of
inexorable mystery; how sleep becomes one of the vital processes
of spiritual regeneration and the renewal of mental vigor; why sleep
diminishes as life becomes more complex; how the experiences of
sleep are stored up in the internal memory, so that we are not permitted to remember them in waking; how we die daily in sleep, and
how death and sleep are of the same essential effect: these are theses
which approve themselves to our reason through the simple appeal
to our consciousness, and fail to convince in proportion as they are
accompanied by the evidences necessary for conviction in other
things. What we rather ask of our author than his instances, his
dreams of Agassiz, or Cicero, or Scipio, is the report of some such
augustly solemn and authoritative passage as 'In a dream, in a vision
of the night, when deep sleep falleth upon men, in slumberings upon
the bed; then he openeth the ears of men, and sealeth their instruction.' For it is in words like these, and not in incident and circumstance, that mystery dwells, and everything that seems to dispel or

explain or diminish the mystery of sleep, or renders it the property of exact knowledge, seems to make us the poorer and not the richer.

II.

The mystery of sleep is, after all, a little thing beside the mystery of waking. We may, if we like, or if it comforts or amuses us to do so, believe or make believe that in the silence of sleep, where, as in death, 'beyond these noises there is peace,' the soul has her life more absolute than in 'the midst of men and day,' but the mystery is not greater there, not more palpable or more awful than here where the mind is knowingly alive and the body vividly sentient. In fact, every pulsation of conscious experience deepens the mystery in which we are conditioned. Nothing happens to us or from us which does not suggest question of our inscrutable origin and destiny. We cannot suppose ourselves underived or undestined; that is not thinkable; but why was any particular one of us selected from potentiality to become actuality, and what will be the effect of each thing done to us or by us? The questions press from every point, and there is no answer to the most elemental, such as why do we enjoy and why do we suffer, or to what useful end, in a universe where all other functioning seems to have its obvious use? When did consciousness become conscience, and how did thoughts and desires and deeds which in themselves seem natural and harmless, and in yet unconscienced millions of the race are without the effect of depravity, define themselves as sinful? Why should some of us be in light and some in darkness, and why should the children of light seem to grieve rather more than the children of darkness? Why should there be beauty and ugliness, and how was it decided which was which? Why should the leaf of clover be exquisitely decorated to match the other two of its group, and so many forms of life be left hideous and repulsive?

What is the source of happiness that we should desire it, or is happiness, as it seems, the true end of life? What is the essential quality of love? Is it finally the most exquisite egoism, or the very reverse of that?

If the answers to these riddles are known to our dreaming, as they are certainly not known to our waking, then they are securely folded away from our knowledge in that internal memory which keeps record of the life of the soul, and shall be disclosed to us only when the soul has its life free of the body. What Mr. Bigelow's inquiry suggests is that in certain moments of rapture, in that ecstasy of consciousness when consciousness seems to cease, we have intimations of supernal things in waking, which are of the property of our habitual experiences in dreaming. We recover from these intimations with a start, and are what we call ourselves again; and perhaps we have been no nearer the solution of the puzzle than we are when we are immersed in affairs, and employed with matter-of-fact concerns. Yet there is an effect of authority in these intimations, which does not suffer us to contemn their message, if we may give a name so positive to the ethereal communication which they seem to open between our inner and outer selves. We are not necessarily nearer knowledge of their secret now, when men send word to one another on the viewless currents of the air, than we were when the conception of wireless telegraphy was as remote from the race as the conception of deity still is. Still we are in an age when science has opened up the realms of wonder so illimitably and the surprises of the known are so far beyond anything which the unknown once seemed to hide, that we cannot quite forbid ourselves the hope of appreciable consolations from mystery itself.

III.

At any rate there has been a swing of the pendulum from one of those extremes to the other, and now from denying ourselves all such consolations, as unscientific and unworthy, we are turning to them with a zest scarcely known before in the history of man. We read eagerly a book like this book of Mr. Bigelow's, and the only grief we have with it is that it does not leave us entirely to its conjectures, to its suggestions of parity in all human experience in the occult, to its speculations that cannot be established, but offers us documents in corroboration of its conjectures, suggestions, speculations. We read eagerly whatever Mr. William James writes upon his favorite themes because it similarly abounds in the substance of things hoped for, the evidence of things not seen. All psychology, which disclaims its putative relation to the soul, is alive with fresh interest for those who seek to know it through the mind, and a whole order of literature has arisen, calling itself psychological, as realism called itself scientific, and dealing with life on its mystical side. This, in fact, now includes what is best known in fiction, and it is not less evident in Tolstoy, in Gorky, in Ibsen, in Björnson, in Hauptmann, and in Mr. Henry James, than in Maeterlinck himself.

It would not be possible to say with which of these eminent authors the reaction from science, from realism, began. Which talent so strongly weighted the pendulum, then, when it began to slide from the scientific extreme, and gave it the momentum which carried it to the mystical extreme? Maeterlinck's weird dramas, in which, as we have said before, the persons are not so much men and women as mortals, are not more mystical than certain passages of Tolstoy, whose psychologism is rooted in a realism as rank and palpable as Gorky's own. It is not necessary, as it is not possible, to discover the origin of the present condition, but that it is an actual condition no one can doubt, who looks at any current magazine, and notes the psychologic coloring of the dramatic thinking in it. We have indeed, in our best fiction, gone back to mysticism, if indeed we were not always there in our best fiction, and the riddle of the painful earth is again engaging us with the old fascination. The old insoluble problems of life and death, of good and evil, present themselves to us with a novel promise of comfort, inviting us to repose in their insolubility with the patience which each must use, and with the faith that this patience shall be rewarded in each. So far from being taught by the new inspiration, coming no one knows whence, the old desolating doctrine of denial, we are somehow authorized, or encouraged, each in the belief that—

> Something is, or something seems,
> That touches me with mystic gleams,
> Like glimpses of forgotten dreams—
> Of something felt, like something here;
> Of something done, I know not where;
> Such as no language may declare.

It can be said that this is not very much, that it is no better than a form of agnosticism, but then it can also be said that agnosticism is not an unpromising or unhopeful frame of mind. It may be only one remove, as it is only one syllable, from a Gnosticism wiser and not less trusting than the old; and perhaps the present psychologism is the beginning of it. At any rate, we have the psychologism, in many phases, and we may justifiably fancy that we are encountering it at many points where we are ostensibly confronting every-day, matter-of-fact things. In spite of all the hello-girls, and the frightful jargon which the daily use of the telephone has created, the telephone is still a very respectable mystery, which is really as impossible to the imagination as it is practicable to experience. As for the wireless telegraph, that is still too remote from familiar custom to have lost the bewilderment which the mere concept of it has; it is still much more a miracle than any manifestation of the outdated spiritism which for half a century has prospered on its commerce with another world. The beneficent discoveries of science in many other directions are so wonderful that though the recent report of the blind seeing without the direct agency of the optic nerve is already discredited, there is much reason to believe that the deaf can be made to hear in many cases once thought hopeless.

The reasoning used by Lord Byron in the lines—

> When Bishop Berkeley said there was no matter,
> And proved it, 'twas no matter what he said—

no longer holds with the force which it had at the beginning of the nineteenth century, 'when the thoughts that shake mankind' were not yet fairly in motion. The question so smilingly put by, repeats itself now with novel force; and how much or little of the universe is subjective, is again matter of speculation which does not seem so altogether idle. It recurs with peculiar force in the presence of such a wonderful book as the *The Story of My Life*, where the blind deafmute, Helen Keller, tells the fairytale of her emergence from the darkness and silence of her infancy into the full radiance of such being as all the senses bring to few of us. We may account for it by the extraordinary native powers evident in her, and still leave ourselves a wide margin for marvelling at the scope of the knowledge which has reached her through one sense alone; still lose ourselves in the maze of surmise which her unparalleled experience suggests. The world of color and form and sound seems to exist as appreciably for her, by force of her creative imagination, as for any who hear and see the things that can only be known intellectually to her; and as one reads, the mystical purport of the saying, 'The Kingdom of God is within you,' avouches itself in new significances, or at least new suggestions. Of course one knows that Helen Keller's development from a child, bereft of all the ordinary means of learning, into a woman as rarely accomplished as endowed, has been through the infinitely patient teaching of the friend whose devotion is one of the richest strains of the poem embodied in their joint record. All the facts which constitute her mental experience have been imparted to her by the indefatigable touch, the innumerable touches, of the faithful friend whose witness of her life is by no means the least interesting, the least wonderful, share of their work; for the autobiography of Helen Keller would be incomplete without the contributions of Miss Anne M.

Sullivan to the knowledge of her history and character. Her friend had first to create a language of touch, had somehow, in whatever miraculous wise, to invent a primary understanding, by which she could convey meanings through the only avenue open between them, and then slowly, and with incredible assiduity, communicate to the imprisoned intelligence such a knowledge of the form of words that the child could feel it not only from the touch of the finger, but in the motion of the lips, and even in its inarticulate rise through the throat. It all seems impossible, but it has become the commonplace of two lives united as none have been before. By virtue of their union, Helen Keller, blind, deaf, dumb, speaks the words she has never heard, reads and writes the words she has never seen, not alone in English, but in French and German, Greek and Latin. She is admirably accomplished, far beyond the wont of young ladies who have the use of their eyes, ears, and tongues, and she knows something of the best of all literatures, with an inappeasable hunger for learning.

IV.

The lesson of such a life, apparently so fatally blighted in the bud, so brilliant and glorious in the flower, can be single only for intelligences more limited than Helen Keller's was before her illumination began. On its surface the story is that of a being as rarely gifted as hopelessly bereft, surmounting every disadvantage and arriving at a fulness of consciousness, a passionate interest in the universal frame of things, known to the very few; but below the surface it is rich in intimations yet dearer to the race than any hints toward the perfectioning of its existence here. We seem to know the outer world from the world within us. Somehow there, in the dim, inmost of life seems the test of material things; and the question which will oftenest recur to some readers of Helen Keller's wonderful story is how much her knowledge of the inaudible and invisible world around her was guessed by her exquisite nerves from the conscious intuitions and the unconscious moods of her devoted friend, and how much has been revealed from the sources which again we are beginning to interrogate with renewed courage, if not with renewed hope. The swing of the pendulum is once more toward the highest point in the direction from which a little while ago it seemed to have fallen forever.

50 Shaw and Shakespeare
1905

From 'The Editor's Easy Chair,' *Harper's Monthly*, September 1905.

Howells was Shakespearian enough to have broken all records for number of book-titles derived from the Bard. But he was also iconoclast enough so that he and Shaw enjoyed each other and he could take an instance from Shaw to set up one of his happiest achievements in criticism as humor. To play Shavian games with Shaw was no mean thing; but to turn the game to effective communication at once of Howells's love for Shakespeare and his contempt for bardolators, of his disbelief in genius and his professional insight into Shakespeare's art, of his adoration of democracy and humanity yet appreciation for the actualities of Shakespeare's world—to do all this and never lose the light touch was the work of a master.

In a world so busy as this it is well that even Shakespearian controversies should be rapidly superseded by other interests, and that so important a contention as Mr. Bernard Shaw's that he can and does write, when he likes, as good poetic drama as Shakespeare, or better, should have ceased, in four short months, to occupy the public mind. His dissentients (for they were hardly anything so unfriendly as antagonists) mostly took his frankness, delightful and refreshing always amidst the prevalent mock-modesties, in the right spirit, and whether they were convinced or unconvinced, did not quite hold him to the letter of his contention. So far as we remember, the deadly parallel was not used against him; there was no comparison, as there might have been, of passages from the plays of the two dramatists to prove that the elder was the finer poet; and we shall certainly attempt nothing of the kind at so late a day as this, when, as we have been rejoicing, the whole matter is forgotten. If we relume in September the charred wick of the brief candle which burnt itself out in April, it is to turn its fitful ray on a point or two not in dispute between Mr. Shaw and his dissentients. We find ourselves directly little concerned in the question whether he is, at will, greater than Shakespeare or not, though we should be glad to have him or any other greater, for we can never have too many men actually or potentially outdoing Shakespeare. Hitherto it has been thought difficult, but that is no reason why it should be impossible, and at the present time the need of some such superiority is pressing among the dramatists who have almost driven Shakespeare from the stage.

Mr. Shaw's assurance that he has repeatedly surpassed Shakespeare, we provisionally accept as blithely as it is given. But what is perhaps more cheering, and perhaps less susceptible of dispute, is Mr. Shaw's indirect and impersonal affirmation of the manifold imperfections of a poet who is, in spite of them, probably first among the immortals. The wise uneasiness of Ben Jonson, who wished that, instead of never blotting a line, Shakespeare had blotted a thousand, has unfortunately been lost in the idolatrous zeal of the succeeding generations of his worshippers. Unless you have the bold gayety of Mr. Shaw to charm their fury, you incur the penalty of sacrilege in saying, for instance, that there are certain plays of Shakespeare's which you would rather not have written, though you would be willing to have written some passages in them. With the Shakespearolaters, all he has done is consecrated by the best he has done, which is, indisputably, the best that has ever been done, whatever Mr. Shaw may do hereafter.

This is measurably the case with every classic. When a saint is canonized, his sins are not, so to say, transnatured; they remain sins, and never become part of the devotion of the religious. But when a poet is immortalized, in anything like the Shakespearian fulness, his blemishes are seen beauties, or at least blinked; and then, instead of a majority of mild agnostics, who say they do not know whether his blemishes are beauties or not, we have a multitude of insensate zealots adoring in him an unqualified perfection, with here and there a furious unbeliever raging forth blasphemies, or a boisterous sceptic breaking into Homeric laughter at the expense of Homer himself, if he happens to be the classic question. This is very unseemly, but it probably does not inconvenience Homer; he continues to nod in comfort; it is the worshippers of his impeccable perfection who suffer, not from the scoffing of the others, but from their own praying. Their mental attitude, so far as it is conscious, is wholly immoral. It is not only the privilege, it is the duty of any one whose heart misgives him of a classic, to own his lapse of faith. Far from persecuting the doubter, the worshippers should lend him part of the praise they lavish upon their idol.

There is no harm in the classics, as there is none in the saints, so long as it is clearly understood that they became what they are largely in spite of themselves, and are, so to speak, almost as innocent of their virtues as they are guilty of their vices. Shakespeare probably did not know it when he was writing what is Shakespeare, but he was fully aware when he was writing what is not Shakespeare. Probably he could not have said where his best came from, or honestly claimed it for his own. He would have known that it was not Ben Jonson's, because it could not have been; but he might have thought it Marlowe's, or Webster's, or Beaumont and Fletcher's. He might have ended by recognizing it as the effect of one of those subliminal processes in himself, which may well restore to a poet the faith in inspiration.

We do not say, to every poet, for Mr. Shaw in his claim of an actual and potential superiority to Shakespeare, the minor Shakespeare, seems to have had a very present sense of creating the surpassing passages when he was at it, with, as it were, one hand tied behind him. His ultimate difference from Shakespeare may be found to lie in the fact that when he was excelling Shakespeare he knew he was doing it; while Shakespeare, when he was excelling Mr. Shaw, did not know he was doing it. But this mystical detail must not keep us, especially as it implies a seriousness out of harmony with the general tone of our inquiry.

We should lose half the delightfulness of what Mr. Shaw has said of Shakespeare as a rival poet if we took it altogether seriously, but we think we may without so much loss allow ourselves to be more seriously, if still not quite seriously, interested in what he says of Shakespeare as a fellow citizen. It was certainly Shakespeare's business to amuse the houses at the Globe theatre, and Mr. Shaw does no more than affirm, at the utmost compass of his excess, that Shakespeare was strictly *business*. From all the little we know of him he was a poor player, but he was a very good actor-manager and actor-dramatist, and whether or not he kept the other eye on the temple of fame, he certainly kept one eye on the box-office when meditating his immortal scenes. The divine light of Utopia had then scarcely dawned upon the world, and it is not for us who now bask in its effulgence to blame him for a hard, low, individualistic ideal of life. From all the little we know of him, we cannot be so sure as Mr. Shaw seems, 'that like most middle-class Englishmen bred in private houses . . . he took it for granted that all inquiry into life began and ended with the question, Does it pay?' But it appears certain that he was not in the

Globe theatre for his health, and it looks very much as if he ran the Elizabethan drama for what there was in it. From all the little we know of him we cannot, with any great alacrity, join Mr. Shaw in blaming him for his wish to get back to Stratford, and there having purged himself of his Bohemian past, to live cleanly like a gentleman in the shelter of a very respectable family tree. We will not deny ourselves the pathos of supposing a poetical heart-hungering, a divinely implanted home-sickness in him, working his return from his London exile. But there is nothing in the plays which, with their manifold imperfections, remain the mightiest and beautifulest work of man, to show the sort of feeling for other men which Mr. Shaw denies in him, when he affirms 'his complete deficiency in that highest sphere of thought, in which poetry embraces religion, philosophy, morality and the bearing of these on communities, which is sociology.'

Here, indeed, it might be urged in Shakespeare's behalf that the sociologist and the poet have seldom been one to their common advantage, and in the most signal instance of their union, say, Victor Hugo, they have not been a supreme success. Something more of assent might be given to the position that Shakespeare was a pessimist, though one might hesitate Mr. Shaw's epithet of vulgar. It would be easier, if one were of obscure origin and humble employ, and found oneself always heaped with scorn and never helped with sympathy in one's hard conditions by Shakespeare, to add cynic to pessimist. Hearts before Shakespeare's time, as well as hearts in his time, had been and were touched by the sorrow wrought to common men by their betters, and even stirred to revolt by the man-made inequalities which never moved Shakespeare to a kind or brave word.

He could say that if he had spoken the word it would spoil the pleasure of the time, and he might be very right. He could contend against Mr. Shaw that if 'his characters have no religion, no politics, no conscience, no hope, no convictions of any sort,' that he was putting it extremely, but that allowing for much truth within the extremes, it was not in this or that plan of his to deal with people so qualified. To this Mr. Shaw, as another artist, could have nothing to say. He would have to allow that, quite as much as the artist chooses his theme, his theme chooses the artist, and that then the artist's duty is to do his best by it. Still, in that half of the case in which the artist and not the theme does the choosing, Mr. Shaw might insist upon his accusation, and Shakespeare could only reply that if he was lacking in that sort of humanity which men now call altruism, he was not without compassion for princes, and pity for unfortunate persons in high places. If he had nothing but contempt for tinkers and weavers and joiners, and commonly attributed low traits to low conditions, he could say that he was strictly of his period in this, and that it took quite three hundred years to fix a different point of view for the poet. No man, he might urge, could be for all times without being distinctly of his own time, and he could not have become so sufficingly a Victorian Englishman without having been so perfectly an Eliza-bethan Englishman. Actuality, which his plays are so full of, was, he could say, subjective as well as objective, and he could not show forth so wonderfully what Mr. Shaw calls the blackguardly and the bom-bastic as he saw it all around him, without also seeing it within him. He might add that this was measurably true of every literary artist.

Shakespeare would probably own, if personally brought to book by our finer morality, that he was, with all his infinity, extremely limited. He might confess that there were things he had not dreamt of in the philosophy of life. Perhaps he would allow that in his pre-occupations as actor-manager and actor-dramatist, consorting habitually with the literary Bohemians of his London, and occasion-ally graced with the company of courtiers and the notice of royalty, there were certain aspects of his fellow men which had escaped him. But he could say, that so far as he had been advised by the theory and practice of literature, princes and nobles were alone worthy of tragedy, and that he had behaved rather handsomely in admitting persons of lower condition into their company in the same action, as foils to their dignity, and that this innovation was analogous to what in Mr. Shaw's time would be anarchistic. As to the unreligious, unpolitical, unconscientious, unhopeful, unconvictioned, and unsociological nature of his characters, again, he could say that he had supposed they would do their office for the edification of the spectator, and ulti-mately the reader, all the better for being warnings rather than ex-amples. He might add that he hoped Ruskin was entirely right in noting that there were no heroes in his plays, and that he took this censure as a testimony to their truth, there being no heroes in life, or none at least that life was not the worse for.

In his poor, seventeenth-century sort, Shakespeare could make out a case, and his case should not be invalidated by the foolish fanaticism of his worshippers, who would see no defect in him. He might well stoop from his altar and entreat that ridiculous rabble to be done with their service of praise, and to own him human and full of errors, not inconsistent with the merits of what he had had the luck to do, or the chance to do. If he could once drive his thick and thin adorers from his presence, a saner concourse might replace them, and in this it would not be surprising to find Mr. Bernard Shaw himself. After all, it is the greatest human presence, and in it is the highest exaltation, the serenest repose. In it, one can lose oneself as in no other, and to lose oneself is the greatest possible gain. No mere hedonist can work the miracle for us, and if the actor-manager, actor-dramatist of the Globe theatre can do it three hundred years after his mortal day, we shall not begrudge him his gate-money, and his getting back to the comfort of it at Stratford. He may have been of a low ideal, the mere hedonist Mr. Shaw imagines him (for the confusion of the Shake-spearolators as we imagine), and in immediate effect he may have been only the master of the revels that Emerson reproaches him for being, but unconsciously and mediately he is such an interpreter of man to himself as we have not yet looked on the like of.

51 'Henrik Ibsen'
1906

Published in the *North American Review*, July 1906.
First-rate and pioneering Ibsen criticism, this also became a compact, eloquent self-analysis by a critic working passionately to wake up his audience.

It is within the memory of people still young that a change has come over the mood of the world concerning great men who die. The time was, before this time, that the commemoration of a great man began with his death. In ceasing to be an activity he became an increasingly important interest. But in the recent change of the world's mood this seems to be no longer so. A great man in dying, nowadays, goes out of the minds of the living much more rapidly than he once went. His passing is still a human event, and for a day, a week, a month, a year, his name reverberates in the newspapers and the magazines; his biography revives the fading curiosity; and then, according to the convention, which we still respect, his place in history is supposed to be ascertained. But in fact a subtle neglect steals upon his fame almost with the publication of the fact that he is dead, and this deepens and deepens into forgetfulness with a swiftness quite in keeping with the pace of all things in our hurried age.

It is probably because our age is hurried, and not because we have so many great men, that we forget them with increasing ease when they die. In any case, it seems certain that the renown of few or none is destined to widen with the lapse of years. After all, there has been but one Shakespeare in literary history, and the attempts of historians to rehabilitate the fame of other sorts of great men who have passed out of remembrance, or to vindicate the right of any to the interest which they inspired while living, have not been of a success encouraging to great men in the enjoyment of an actual obscurity. The rewards of writing for posterity are more and more uncertain; if one

433

is not a classic in one's own day, it is not probable that he will become so later.

I.

Whether Henrik Ibsen has been and is a classic is a question which the generation passing with him could not answer dispassionately, and one would not wish to kindle the fires of controversy from his funeral pyre. I will merely note that, if having the praise of the first minds in all countries is to the effect of being a classic, then Ibsen is and has been a classic; for there can be no doubt that the highest criticism has everywhere recognized his greatness as a dramatist. With this criticism in Germany, France, Italy, Spain, England and these States, there could hardly be any longer a misgiving as to his primacy, there could hardly be a hesitation. There is no one whom it would put beside him, and few whom it would put near him, in a time when there has been a universal revival of the dramatic art, and when, among every civilized people, the theatre has been of a performance, and not a promise merely, unsurpassed except in the supreme moment incarnated in Shakespeare. Yet with this universal recognition by the highest criticism, which ought to have the power of classicizing, it must be owned that there is wanting to Ibsen's towering repute that breadth of base which apparently gives security and perpetuity. It is no

> star y-pointing pyramid,

with foundations spreading as far as its upward reach, but a lonely column climbing the skies from a pedestal almost as narrow as itself. In every country, where the first intelligences have given him their unanimous acclaim, the second intelligences have as unanimously refused him theirs; and these intelligences, though second, are still of a quality which commands respect. In their refusal they hold by tradition, by convention, by what may be called the vested ideals, those collaterals by which men enjoy a mental increment without the labor of original thinking. Such intelligences will always have the regard of the majority, and a vast influence. They stand between the majority and the first intelligences, who mostly fail to reach the popular mind; and perhaps they usefully protect it from the shock of innovation until it is able to bear a novel truth. At any rate, Ibsen, whom the highest criticism of our time regards as the greatest dramatist of our time, is altogether without popular standing. His name, indeed, is almost as widely known to the multitude as that of Tolstoy himself, and in much the same sort; but his work is almost quite unknown to it. The multitude has heard of his name, and it has a derivative from it, and uses the word 'Ibsenism' convertibly with 'pessimism'; it is not impossible that, if a strong appeal were made by the second intelligences, the multitude would approve the exclusion of his works from the mails. If we trusted to the popular knowledge of the nature and intention of *Ghosts*, it would then be as useless to order a copy of it through the post as it would once have been to order a copy of *The Kreutzer Sonata*.

This is the anomalous situation one must face; these are the distracting contradictions one must recognize, before hoping to impart any just conception of Ibsen. The difficulty is very great; perhaps it is insuperable; and yet Ibsen is always a problem of such interest that one cannot turn from him in despair, without a sense of intolerable loss to one's self and to others. One cannot quite hope to make him clear, but there is a cloudy significance in all his work that charms and edifies; the light breaks through in flashes, but though it is resumed again in the stormy sky, it is a precious light, and one's vision is forever purified of certain mists by it.

II.

What this cloudy significance is, however, I do not find myself much helped to say by any of those prime critics who have joined in declaring Ibsen's importance to the modern drama, to the modern life. Unaided, I should say what I have already said elsewhere, and re-affirm that the great and dreadful delight of Ibsen is from his power of dispersing the conventional acceptations by which men live on easy terms with themselves, and obliging them to examine the grounds of their social and moral opinions. This cruel joy, this '*höchst angenehmer Schmerz*,' as Heine would call it, is not welcome to all; it is welcome to so very few that the vast majority will shrink from the mere rumor of it, and it is with no hope of winning favor or following for him that I suggest it as the prevailing effect of his peculiar talent. But I believe that this effect is the sum of all his other excellencies, and of a value higher than that of any one of them.

To my experience he is a dramatist of such perfection, he is a poet of such absolute simplicity and veracity, that when I read him or see him I feel nothing wanting in the æsthetic scheme. I know that there are graces and beauties abounding in other authors which are absent from him, but I do not miss them; and I perceive that he abundantly fulfils his purpose without them. I am sensible of being moved, of being made to think and feel as no other has made me think and feel, and I think that sufficient; I do not care what is left out of the means to the end. For illustration, we will say, what I believe, that *Macbeth* is the supreme play of conscience, of that spirit in us that censures conduct. The means to its end are of an opulence which renders *Ghosts*, in the contrast, bare and poverty-stricken. Yet I do not miss in *Ghosts* any of the means that richly edified me in *Macbeth*, and I am aware of a spirit in it that censures conscience itself. Shakespeare in Macbeth and in Lady Macbeth has made me shudder for their guilt; Ibsen in Manders and Mrs. Alving makes me tremble for their innocence. The difference measures the advance from the mediæval to the modern man, and accounts for the hardihood of those who have declared that Ibsen says more to them now than Shakespeare says. They are right if they mean that Shakespeare makes them question the evil, while Ibsen makes them also question the good. The time has come, apparently, when we are to ask ourselves not of the justice of our motives, so much as of the wisdom of our motives. It will no longer suffice that we have had the best motive in this or that; we must have the wisest motive, and we must examine anew the springs of action, the grounds of conviction.

That is what Ibsen invites us to do, not in *Ghosts* alone, but in most of the plays which may be called his most realistic. Some of his dramas deal typically with human, with Norwegian, life—as *Brand*, as *Peer Gynt*, as *The Lady from the Sea*; others deal personally with Norwegian, with human, life—as *Ghosts*, as *Pillars of Society*, as *The Wild Duck*, as *Hedda Gabler*, as *Little Eyolf*, and it is these last which Ibsen valued himself most upon, and which, I think, form the richest part of his legacy to literature. It has been conjectured that when they have had their full ethical effect, and the world has come more or less to the ground where they challenge conscience for its reasons, they will be of less interest and less significance than the more idealistic dramas; but if the representation of character, and the study of personality, form the highest office of art, as I believe they do, I think Ibsen will not be finally found mistaken in his preference. I am quite willing to own that I agree with him, perhaps because I like the real better than the ideal, though I find abundant reality in his idealistic dramas.

III.

As to the ethical effect of the plays which I permit myself, in the company of their author, to like best, I have my doubts whether it is so directly and explicitly his intention as some of the highest critical intelligences have imagined. He is, first of all, not a moralist, and far less a polemicist, but an artist, and he works through instruments, as the creative force always works, in which he is himself intangible, and, as it were, absent. His instruments are of course the characters of the drama in hand, and it is not to be inferred that the end to which any of these comes is Ibsen's conclusion, any more than it is to be inferred that what any one of them says is Ibsen's opinion. You are not to take this thing or that as the point of the moral, but to consider the whole result left with you, and to use your reason, not your logic, upon it. In *Ghosts*, Mrs. Alving upbraids her old lover for not letting her stay when she took refuge with him from the horror of her marriage, and for making her go back to her husband; she upbraids herself for not having sympathized with the life-lust in her husband, which mainly manifested itself in love-lust outside of their marriage; she seems willing, rather than make the same mistake again, that her son shall have his half-sister for wife, or even for mistress. But in her case, as in every other, Ibsen does not wish to teach so much as he wishes to move, to strike with that exalted terror of tragedy which has never hesitated at its means; which in Shakespeare confronts us with a son forced to bring his mother to shame for her incestuous union with his uncle, and to study the best moment for the murder to which his father's revengeful spirit urges him, and from which his own faltering temperament withholds him, though the spectator is made to feel it is his sacred duty, and shares the truculent impatience of the spectre at his delay. It would be no sillier to suppose that Shakespeare meant to inculcate such bloody deeds as that which Hamlet shrinks from doing, than to suppose that Ibsen means in Mrs. Alving's distraction to teach libertinage, or that complicity with suicide in which the play apparently ends. The moral is far back of all this, and involved by her violation of duty in marrying for the worldly ends of her family a man she does not love, for this is the wrong-doing which no after duteousness in her mismarriage can catch up. Here is the source of all the sorrow that ensues; and the lesson, so far as the play is lessoned, is that you must be true from the start, if you would not be false in the truth itself afterwards. But probably Ibsen meant nothing so explicit as that. He was writing a play, not a sermon.

He was offering a bitter and poisonous flower of life as he had found it growing; not a botanical medicine that he had dried and pressed for the ethicist's herbarium.

Ghosts is the most tragical of Ibsen's plays, and it is none the less tragical because it is a tremendous effect of the author's peculiar humor. He is a humorist in the presence of its dreadful facts not because he is a hard-hearted cynic, but because he sees that the world which a wise and merciful and perfect God has created seems full of stupidity and cruelty and out of joint to utter deformity, and he shows it as he sees it. If he is apparently inconsistent, it is because the world is really inconsistent; and if we hold him to any hard and fast rule of logic, we may indeed *have* him, but his best meaning will escape us. In *Pillars of Society*, that tragedy of his which comes nearest being a satirical comedy, or for the most part is so, the misery comes because Bernick will be a hypocrite and a liar; and the inference is, that any sort of truth, or anybody's, would be better than the falsehood in which he lives. In *The Wild Duck*, the truth is brought home from the outside to a wretched creature unable to bear it, who has existed through the lie become vital to him, and who goes to pieces at the touch of the truth, and drags those around him to ruin and death in his fall; and the inference is that the truth is not for every one always, but may sometimes be a real mischief. The two plays seem to contradict each other, but they do not; they are both true to different predicaments and situations of life, and can no more be blamed for inconsistency than God's world which they faithfully mirror. There is in fact a divine consistency running through them and through *Ghosts*, where you shall learn, if you will pay due heed, that the truth once denied avenges itself in the dire necessity of falsehood, and renders all after-truth mechanical and of the effect of a lie. When Mrs. Alving had once been false to herself in marrying for money and position a man she did not love, while she loved another man, she never could again be true to herself without doing him harm. She lent herself to his evil as long as she could bear it, and when she could bear it no longer the worst had been done. She had borne a son on whom his father's sins must be visited, and had pledged herself to falsehood against which she revolted in vain and forever too late. If she had revolted earlier, and made known the facts of her life to all the world, still it would not have availed. People who saw in *Ghosts* merely a heredity play, based upon a questionable assumption of science, never saw it whole, and they who saw in it merely a destiny play, in which fate relentlessly brooded as in Greek tragedy, as little fathomed its meaning. This, as I think we have found, is very simple, and is not discordant with any dictate of religion or reason, and it is always Ibsen's meaning. Do not be a hypocrite, do not be a liar, do not be a humbug; but be very careful how and when you are sincere and true and single, lest being virtuous out of time you play the fool and work destruction.

This is what he is always saying, but this is not the effect to which he is always working. It is his prime business and his main business to show things as they are so that you shall not only be edified, but also stirred and charmed in such sort as you never were before, and in the measure that you are capable of emotion. But when I say that the representation of life is his prime business and his main business, I do not mean that he works always in the same way, or that he convinces us of the reality of what he shows us by the same methods. Some of his plays are more allegorical than others, and in these he finds the reality far below the surface ideality which we see; and he makes us find it if we are capable of so much; if we are not capable of so much he must leave us to the obvious facts. This will account for a very general supposition that in *A Doll's House* he teaches that a wife who finds her husband a priggish fraud ought to abandon her home and go away, somewhere or anywhere, so only that she may be freed from her false relation to him. The moral in that play, and in every other play of Ibsen's, is that certain actions result in certain tendencies, and that from these tendencies certain things happen. If the actions are selfish, they eventuate in misery; if they are false, they hold the doer in a bondage to falsehood from which no truth can avail to free him later. It might appear that Ibsen believes with the Preacher that the heart is above all things deceitful and desperately wicked, but in showing this, he cannot justly be accused of inculcating its immoralities and iniquities, as they follow in an endless train of evil from the first evil. Yet I can quite understand how people who feel so intensely the tragic effect of his plays, accept the catastrophe as if it were a solution which the dramatist offered. Never was human nature shown so nakedly as in his tremendous scene; it is stripped as bare of all its disguises as it could be at the Judgment Day; yet the dramatist does not deliver judgment. He leaves every wretched being, whether before or behind the footlights, to pronounce sentence upon himself. His homily is acted on the stage, not preached from the pulpit, and its applications are made by the people who go home and think it over.

IV.

In the awful moment of Hawthorne's romance, when Dimmesdale stands with his paramour and their child on the scaffold, and declares his guilt before the people, he hopes for mercy only through the fulness of his public ignominy; and in the closing chapter, where the author gathers up the threads of his story, and tries to make his meaning clear, he bids his reader 'Be true! Be true! Be true! Show freely your worst to the world or some trait by which the worst may be known.' Yet, in spite of this sublime and, as it seems to a later art, only too obvious simplicity of motive, *The Scarlet Letter* was in its time fiercely denounced as an attack on the character of the Puritan clergy of New England, made with the satirical motive of bringing them into contempt. It is not very strange, then, that Ibsen should have been as widely and wildly mistaken, and should have been honestly believed a malignant cynic, with no higher motive than mockery, and no aim but to pervert and to corrupt. As an artist, he could not say what ought to be plain to every one who reads him or sees him played, that his increasing purpose, from first to last, has been to confront selfishness and conceit and falsehood with themselves. His view of human nature is the humorist's; but it amuses him sorrowfully, and his view of human life is far above the satirist's. It is the realist's view, the view of the honest man, the only honest man; and in this view he sees that selfishness, conceit and falsehood form that sin of hypocrisy on which modern civilization is founded. It is this which he is always allowing to expose itself on his scene, and he has no other agency in the affair than to let it. He does not praise this action or blame that one; he has nothing to do with any inference which the wrong-headed or weak-minded may draw from any fact or trait represented. His sole business is to make us feel that the basis of society, as we now have it, is hypocrisy, though an hypocrisy now grown almost involuntary and helpless, and it is not his business to do this by precept, but by example. You may say that he is right, or you may say that he is wrong, but you cannot say that he does not believe in what he is doing, or that he is trying to do something else, or that he is not trying to do anything, but is only diabolically delighting in the spectacle of human weakness. If he takes the world as he finds it, certainly he does not leave it so, as each witness will own who feels himself unmasked in the presence of those terrible sufferings and shames. With Hawthorne he says, 'Be true, be true, be true!' but he adds, 'Be true in time, be true from the beginning; for later you shall be true in vain, and your very truth shall become part of that great lie, that world-hypocrisy, in which civilization lives and moves and has its being.'

I do not pretend that Ibsen is a comfortable companion, or that a play of his is something to take up and while away a pleasant hour with, or that if seen upon the stage it will take a tired business man's mind off himself, or help a society woman forget the manifold vexations of the day. His plays were probably never intended to do anything of the kind, and probably they were as little meant to be seen by the inexperienced young people who go to the theatre in pairs, with or without a chaperon. But neither of these probabilities has anything to do with the question of their literary value, or their effect, though both of them have everything to do with the question of their popularity in all Anglo-Saxon countries. They will never have a great or a small popularity with our race, in any of the seven seas; and yet, for all the reasons against them, however furiously urged, we should be the better for their wide acceptance, honester and cleanlier.

It is one of the conventions of our hypocritical civilization that young people are ignorant of certain matters because they do not speak of them to their elders, and that their minds will be tainted or corrupted by others' open recognition of them. Ibsen's recognition of the fact is not, indeed, as open as it might be, but it is unmistakable, and its purport is wholly sanative. He addresses himself most terribly to those who have committed the mistakes or the misdeeds which he puts before them; but, if the hopes of reform are always with the young, he more usefully addresses himself to those who are no longer ignorant but are still innocent. I say this, not because I see any chance of his being presently suffered to do so, on the popular scale, but because I think it a pity that art should not be allowed to enforce the precepts of religion, in regard to matters of which the young drink in knowledge from the very fountain of our religion.

Such a play as *Little Eyolf* is awful, no one can deny that. It wrings the heart with grief and shame, but any one who refuses to see the hope which it holds out, that if you will do right you are safe from wrong, must be wilfully blind. It proclaims, in terms that humiliate and that almost disgrace, the truth which Tolstoy preaches in other terms when he declares that there is and can be no such thing as personal happiness. Both of these just men perceive that, in the scheme of a just God, there is no room for such happiness; and that, wherever it tries to force itself in, it pushes aside or crushes under it the happiness of some other human creature. In *Little Eyolf*, where the wife and mother vainly hopes to perpetuate the passion of her first married years, and wishes to sacrifice to that idolatry herself, her husband and her child, we have something intolerably revolting; but the lesson is, alike from Ibsen and from Tolstoy, that you must not and you cannot be happy except through the welfare of others, and that to seek your bliss outside of this is to sin against reason and righteousness both.

As for the fact involved, and put in words so plain that it can scarcely be called hinting, it is one of those things which they who shrink from such wicked and filthy things as the drama has commonly dealt with may shrink from having handled, and these will be shocked quite as much by the diabolism of Hedda Gabler as by the animalism of Rita Allmers. Obsession is an easy name for the state of such women, but if it is the true name then it is time men should study the old formulas of exorcism anew.

V.

I do not say that this is what Ibsen means men to do, or that he finally thinks some of them better than such women. Upon the whole he holds the balance between the sexes pretty evenly in portraying the actions in which their not so very different natures eventuate. In fact, they seem in his handling rather different temperaments than different natures. We see women-natured men, and we see men-natured women, and the first are no better than the last. Both are obviously included in human nature, and their variations of temperament are not more convincing of good in men of feminine temperament than of evil in women of masculine temperament. We distinguish there the quality of their sins, by our common, thumb-fingered morality; but, to the more delicate touch of Ibsen's ethics there is no distinction in the quality of the sinners.

He does not affirm this more strenuously than some other things, and it is not his habit to affirm anything very strenuously. Georg Brandes sums up his attitude toward life in a saying of Ibsen's own: 'My calling is to question, not to answer,' and this is what all of those who have tried to divine him have paraphrased in one way or another. It is the essence of Mr. Bernard Shaw's *Quintessence of Ibsenism*, a fascinating but by no means always convincing book; it is the effect of the several admirable things that Mr. William Archer has written about Ibsen; it is the somewhat desperate and faltering conclusion of

Brandes; it was substantially the mind of one of his best critics, the too early dead Hjalmar Hjorth Boyesen. We are instinctively dissatisfied with this attitude of Ibsen's; we demand something more of the only partially, or not at all, developed. It is because we are still creatures of instinct, or still children with reasoning powers only partially developed, or not at all. It is because we are irreverent of the divine mystery in which we are posited here, the whole mystery of life. If we took thought in making our foolish demand, we should realize that nothing is answered here; not one of the things that are worth knowing is answered. Not one passion explains itself; not one principle will be traced back to the source where it gets its name as principle. In the mean time, there are abundant explanations and researches.

In some sort Ibsen can be personally and even intellectually accounted for, and I commend to those whom his death has interested in his life a very interesting critical biography of him by Henrik Jaeger, which Mr. William Morton Payne has translated better than I know, for I do not know Norwegian, with all my airs of knowing Ibsen. But he seems an author very little dependent on his native vehicle in his prose dramas; he gets there, as far as concerns the effect with the reader or spectator, as well in English as in his mother-speech; and from Mr. Payne's Jaeger-biography my equally little Norsed reader can learn fully enough how Ibsen found his way to mastery while continuing singularly aloof from circumstance. With fair beginnings early blighted by adversity, he grew strong by standing alone in a small Scandinavian seaport, where to have been first could not have been much, and to be last was to be the sort of outcast that Ibsen afterwards rather chose being. The son of the broken merchant became an apothecary's apprentice, and then, by steps inevitable, if not natural, a poet, a journalist, and a playwright; but we need not trace the steps. It is enough that he arrived in Norway at the position he held in Skien, an eminence of unpopularity and misunderstanding accorded to few but the greatest. All this and more is apparent from the recently published letters of Ibsen, in which we hear him speaking replylessly, as one through a telephone, for there are no answers printed with his letters. They confirm the impression of the biographies that he was the victim of his disadvantages, and from being forced to stand too much alone became too conscious of the claim of his genius, too much devoted to its development as the prime, if not the sole, interest of his being. As the world is now built, a man can no more live to himself than he can live to others exclusively; one is bound selfishly as well as unselfishly to one's fellows in the competitive conditions which are so far from final, and Ibsen's life has not the grandeur of his gift, one of the rarest and finest bestowed upon mortal, though not the most definite in effect.

In a sort he was ultimately reconciled to Norway; but it would not be strange if he kept a grudge to the end. The citizen of a small country must suffer at short range the wounds dealt afar to high spirits in wider lands; and, doubtless, there was something peculiarly embittering to Ibsen in his close acquaintance with his misunderstanders and maligners. But, after all, his hardships were not very different from the hardships of most literary men; and his dislike of Norway was founded upon public as well as private grounds. The grief between them was that Norway was provincial and Ibsen was not, though some of the more ignorant of the Anglo-Saxonry have supposed him provincial because he always put the scenes of his realistic dramas among the people he knew best. He went from these early enough, and stayed away long enough to learn the great world as it is known in the chief German, French and Italian cities, and he returned to them only after he was high above their control. He was then fairly enough a cosmopolitan, such as it is difficult to be in London or even New York, and spiritually he seems to have been pretty much always the same Ibsen.

That is to say, he lived as he has died, 'a very imperial anarch,' for, more even than agnosticism, the note of this mighty solitary, hermited in the midst of men, was anarchism. Solidarities of any sort he would not have. The community was nothing to him, and, if not quite so despicable as the majority, was still a contemptible substitute for the individuality. That was alone precious, and it was like some medicines, in doing good in proportion as it disagreed with the taste of the patient, of the fellow man. Ibsen had really a dread of being acceptable, for in the popular favor he feared the end of his usefulness. In some way or other he was often saying that, both directly and dramatically; and he lived it as nearly as civility would let him. He had not differenced himself so much from the generality of his kind as not to have married; he had become a husband and father, and his domestic life was of a physiognomy undistinguished by the experiences which stimulate the conjectures of criticism as to the personal sources of an author's most impersonal inspirations.

Since his early allegories and romances there has been a wonderful unity in his work. It has been constantly a challenge to thought from the instances of life. His very last drama is the most mystical of these challenges; but never has any literary man looked life so squarely in the face, except perhaps Flaubert or Tolstoy, though he has confronted her on such very different terms that he cannot very well be compared with these widely parted masters. If he found her countenance full of terrible and insoluble mysteries, and rendered her likeness so as to impart the most piercing sense of tragedy, it can scarcely be imputed to him for a fault. It is at worst his characteristic, his habit, his business. He was, if not born to it, trained to it; and it seems very much as if he were born to it. In a way, he is himself the greatest proof, if any besides common experience were needed, of the truth of what he tells. Faculties like his were given him to be employed, and they could not be employed if there were not facts to use them upon. Let us suppose him created for some wise purpose, and keep on trying to make him out.

As to how long we shall keep on, now he is dead, I have already hinted my doubt. As I have said, he has always been as he is now, more known than read, and more read than seen. Even in his own country, even in Germany, in France, his pieces have been comparatively seldom played, though the plays that he has inspired others to write have been very much played. If we can call him a force, we can still better call him an influence. It can be said, quite short of exaggeration, that but for him we should hardly have had, just as they are, Sudermann, Hauptmann and others in Germany, Echegaray in Spain, D'Annunzio in Italy, and Pinero, or that unhappy Oscar Wilde, in England; perhaps not Mr. Henry Arthur Jones. He is one of those masters, by no means surprisingly rare, who are more accepted through those they have influenced than in themselves. The public knows the name of Ibsen in an ignorance of his work in really stupendous measure. It would not be altogether impossible that the future should know him on some such terms, just as it would not be altogether impossible that some in the future should know him with the passionate joy with which a few in the present have had the courage to know him.

52 Of originality and imitation

1907

From 'The Editor's Easy Chair,' *Harper's Monthly*, February 1907.

Howells's word on this chimera of criticism seems so nearly final one can only mourn that the tireless source-stalkers of the next academic generation did not take it to heart.

In Art as in Life, there are apparently no tangible beginnings. Endings, there may be, which you can put your finger on, and say, Here the man ceased to breathe; or, Here the thing was no longer done. But is death the close of life? Religion says it is not. Is the prevalence of bad taste the end of art? History would not seem to think so. In either life or art, except at the divine source of both, there is no creation; there is only recreation. Or, we may reverse the paradox and say there are no fathers, there are only forefathers. As for art alone there is no such thing as positive originality in it, there is only comparative originality. You can never say this or that manner, or method, or achievement, is quite original. You can only say it is rather original, or pretty original. It germinates simultaneously in many widely separated minds, it matures and decays in the same way over the same range. But when you fancy it has wholly disappeared it is really awaiting regeneration, renascence, resurrection. The good kinds in it can never perish; only the fashions, the affectations, the caprices are perishable; and even these have their palingenesis, and reappear age after age.

The patient reader of the Easy Chair will bear it witness that it does not often abound in sayings so Orphic as these, which have been suggested to it by a passage in the life of Tolstoy by Paul Birukoff. Nothing could well be flatter or tamer than that work; in the self-abnegation of the author it is of much the moral quality of the sheet on which the events of the kinematograph play; but it leaves you with the question whether that is not, after all, the very best ground on

446

which the history and personality of a great man can be projected. For such a purpose you do not so much want a medium as a blank space, and this is what Tolstoy's authorized biographer supplies. He has had all the material which Tolstoy could give him, and he offers the texture of a perfectly subordinate mind, as the surface on which the materials may arrange themselves. But possibly this is the biographer's humble triumph, or his subtle triumph, and is the fashion he chooses of showing himself an artist. We will not be sure, and we will not go further in our inquiry, for this is not to be a review of the book, but only a means of asking the reader's interest in a single fact of far the most impressive literary career of our time, or, for the matter of that, any time. To our mind, Tolstoy is without a rival in the whole history of the art of fiction, or rather without an equal; rivals enough he certainly has, but they are defeated rivals. He dwarfs them to the dimensions of artifice which it takes when it is confronted with nature. He alone and for the first time since fable began to moralize the human story seems to have set frankly and directly about his work. As he has said, he made Truth his hero, and he has had no aim but to find out the truth, and let his reader see it as clearly as he did. Yet this unequalled artist, this wonderful creator, this unrivalled original, owns himself a follower of another master, especially in that power of realizing war to the most unwarlike reader, so that it seems as if no one had honestly written of battles before.

'As to Stendhal,' Tolstoy says, 'I will speak of him only as the author of the *Chartreuse de Parme* and *Rouge et Noir*. These are two great, inimitable works of art. I am, more than any one else, indebted for much to Stendhal. He taught me to understand war. Read once more—*Chartreuse de Parme*—his account of the battle of Waterloo. Who before him had described war—*i.e.*, as it is in reality? Do you remember Fabricius crossing the battle-field, and "understanding nothing," and how the hussars threw him with ease over the back of his horse, his splendid general's horse? ... Soon afterward in the Crimea I easily verified all this with my own eyes. I repeat, all I know about war I learned first of all from Stendhal.'

If this magnificently generous tribute to an elder author shall do no more than send the reader of Tolstoy's page to Stendhal's, it will do enough, for it will renew for him the great joy which the later master gave him. The *Chartreuse de Parme* is of something like the noble physical proportions of *War and Peace*, while it reveals something like the vast political and spiritual grasp of that matchless study of mankind, something like its astounding insight into the motives and the intentions of men. Of course it halts immeasurably behind it in the moral, or if the reader is not tired of that poor shabby, lying word, the unmoral treatment of persons and events. It cannot be said of the *Chartreuse de Parme*, as it can be said of *War and Peace*, that the most innocent mind can receive no stain from the knowledge of good and evil in which it abounds, and the difference is probably that quality of originality which Tolstoy adds to the lesson of his master.

But leaving this aside, is it to be supposed that Stendhal was the first to depict war truthfully ? Tolstoy, who ought to know, seems to think that he was. But probably if literature could be thoroughly searched there would be found long and often before Stendhal, true pictures of war, if not in fiction, verse, or prose, then in memoirs, letters, local histories, such sources as fiction, often unknowingly, draws its inspirations, or gets its suggestions from. But even in fiction it is probable that there was some obscure author, long since read and forgotten, whom Stendhal consciously imitated as Tolstoy consciously imitated Stendhal. The arts borrow from one another, and it might have been from the study of some of those horrible old pictures of medieval warfare that Stendhal conceived the notion of painting war as it really was. Those who saw the awful canvases of Verestchagin, portraying in our time the cruel and hideous disaster of war, saw the transliteration of Tolstoy's battle-pieces, and had a proof of how the arts borrow from one another.

The subjective experience of the reader who takes up the master of a greater master is sometimes very curious, and in reading *Chartreuse de Parme* we were ourselves bewildered with the sense of knowing it already, which must have been a remote effect of earlier intimacy with *War and Peace*. It might be said that Tolstoy had not imitated Stendhal, but as a modern Italian dramatist has said of his study of Goldoni, he had learned from Stendhal how to imitate nature, imitate reality. The worst thing is, the only bad thing is, when one author learns from another, how to imitate unnature, how to imitate unreality. But for good or for evil it is impossible that artists should not imitate one another, so long as one is born earlier and another later. As far as this goes, there is no such thing as originality in art. From Cimabue and Giotto we have Botticelli, from Mino da Fiesole we have Donatello, from Giovanni Bellini we have Titian, Tintoretto, Paolo Veronese, and so on, all measurably, none entirely, like his master. It is so in the literary arts, as, for instance, Dryden—Pope, Cowper—Wordsworth, Keats—Tennyson, Goldsmith—Irving, George Eliot—Mrs. Hum-

phry Ward, Zola—Mr. George Moore, Miss Edgeworth—Miss
Austen, Sterne—Heine. There is occasionally an author so overwhelmingly himself, after a certain time of being some one else, that
he cannot be imitated except for a very short time and in a very few
things, and it would not be easy to couple with another name the name
of Shakespeare, or Dickens, or Thackeray. But probably no authors
have so widely affected or infected authorship as these.

It does not follow that the earlier author is greater than the later.
In his battle-pieces Tolstoy is immeasurably greater than Stendhal.
Once, in coming to a volume of Pushkin's short stories, we had a
teasing sense of familiarity in them, a tormenting sense of been-there-
before, such as one sometimes has when confronted with a new scene
or action. Presently we were aware of Tourguénief, and we realized
that Tourguénief had learned from Pushkin how to imitate nature;
but he had carried the art so far beyond the art of his master that
Pushkin seemed the disciple and Tourguénief the preceptor. The
work appeared a weak reflex of a stronger work, but the reflex was
from a light that had followed, not preceded. In eternity, Swedenborg
teaches, there is no such thing as time and space, and in the immortality of art there would seem to be at least no such thing as time, neither
first nor last except in excellence.

Of course what the later artist does is to add his temperament to the
example of the earlier, and if he is the greater personality, to become
the original when he finds himself. There is in every considerable
author the instinct, more or less latent, more or less patent, of what
we must call originality till there is some other word which will better
define our meaning. The very fact that each is drawn through this
instinct to one master rather than another is proof of originality. The
overpowering love of doing a thing is a sort of proof of the power to do
it; not infallible proof, but proof such as shakes the presumption
against it. With this love of doing a thing must come the love of doing
it in a certain way—a way that has delighted the lover more than any
other in the whole wide world of doing. It would be impossible for
him even to try doing it in any other; he must liken himself in his
endeavor to that master who did that thing in that way. This universe
is a universe of similarities as well as differences:

Du gleichst dem Geist dem du begreiffst.[1]

You cannot help being like and wishing to be like the spirit which you
so passionately, so perfectly divine. There seems an understanding
between the two, and in the mystic eternity of art, where there is no

time, the apprentice imagines that the master is as privy to the understanding as he. It is an emulation in which they strive together for the interpretation of the truth which has come to both. The first did not invent that truth, the last did not purloin it, did not even borrow it. They are contemporaries in its possession. This, at least, is what the last says to himself of the matter, but whether the first would say so, if *he* had his say, is not so clear. He might have his hesitations in owning their contemporaneity, just as sometimes the last has his hesitations in owning their similarity.

Not all disciples have had Tolstoy's noble bravery in proclaiming the name of their prophet. Perhaps Tolstoy himself would not have done it in the hour of his discipleship. When he had gone far beyond Stendhal it was easier to say that Stendhal had taught him how to be true about war than it would have been when he was studying the truth in him. Very likely it will always be so, and we cannot expect the poet who is getting together the materials of his laurel crown to acknowledge that he plucked the leaves from this or that bush. The thing is not so simple; and yet, would not it be well for every author who has reasonable expectations of immortality to leave a sealed confession, to be read, say, with his will, when the people come back from his funeral, where it shall be owned before his family and friends, if not the world, that up to a certain moment he tried as hard as he could to write like this master or that; and that all along in his career he was in the habit of snatching a phrase here, a turn there, that seemed fortunate, and weaving it into the web of his work long after the material and texture had become effectively his own? It would be better for the peace of his soul if he could make this confession, and it would immeasurably help the contention that in art there is no such thing as originality to become the general recognition of the fact.

After all, what we want is not originality but excellence. To better your instruction is the highest achievement of which you are capable. It was long the superstition of us poor Americans that sometime we were to be called to the invention of new forms of art, if not of some art wholly unimagined before the discovery of our hemisphere. This was expected of us as well as expected by us, and we believed that we owed it to ourselves and the rest of the world to fulfil the supposed purposes of the deity with regard to us. But when we worked out of the ethics in which our intellects were swaddled into esthetic freedom, and began to walk on our own feet, it was by holding on to the knees and arms of the parent race. If we had any distinct wish in the matter, it was to better our English instruction, to refine upon it, to outdo the most delicate and exquisite effects of the ancestral art. All the ignorance of our vast, vacant world could not avail to render us original, or even aboriginal. When Walt Whitman first cropped the prairie mind and offered mankind his Leaves of Grass in the long windrows into which the hay was tedded, it did seem to the inner and outer expectation that at last here was something doing. Here, apparently, was a poet who was bettering no man's instruction, who was richly beginning master, and not poorly beginning prentice, like the other hands in the shop. But if any worshipping critic had turned to his Bible half as often as the good Walt Whitman himself must have done, he would have found the Psalmist of the King James version writing a good deal like Walt Whitman at his best. Of course the subjects were different. The American poet celebrated Man and adored himself; the Hebrew poet celebrated God and deplored himself. But there are some passages in the Song of Solomon which recall passages in *Leaves of Grass*, and there are passages in the beautiful rhythms of the imaginative books of the Old Testament, that are apparently reminiscent of the writers' acquaintance with the Long Island Bard. Of course this is an illusion to which the dweller in the timeless regions of art is subject, and we have been careful to say apparently reminiscent. The prophets were really as anterior to the poet as Babylon on the Pharpar was anterior to Babylon on the Great South Bay. The effect is such as bewitches the reader with a sense of Tolstoy in Stendhal, of Tourguénief in Pushkin. But we do not say that you feel as if the Psalmist and the Proverbial Philosopher were imitating the Long Island Bard. That would be going too far. It would be going too far even to say that the Long Island Bard had bettered his instruction from them. What is certain is that he like every other master had his instruction.

NOTE

1 Goethe, *Faust*, i. Howells's succeeding sentence is an expanded translation: literally, 'Thou'rt like the Spirit thou comprehendest.'

53 'Lyof N. Tolstoy'

1908

Published in the *North American Review*, December 1908.

The new names of the new century drifted into Howells's criticism: Gorky, Hauptmann, Maeterlinck, Shaw, Henry Arthur Jones, Pinero, Wilde, Echegaray, D'Annunzio. Nevertheless, his ultimate men were his own men, the great men of his own time: Clemens, James, Ibsen, Zola, and Tolstoi—always, first and last, the author who came to him with the force of religion, Tolstoi. The best of all his Tolstoi pieces, therefore one of his best critical pieces, is this, written almost late enough to be, like 'Edward Bellamy,' 'Émile Zola,' and *My Mark Twain*, an obituary summing up.

In the long perspective since the turmoil of 1885 and without polemic constraint, Howells here can see and say what cannot be accepted. By the same tokens he is free to name exactly what he thinks best in the greatest mind and art of the age.

At eighty a man has so well-nigh finished his work that it may be considered as something definite. He then 'has lived,' as the Romans preferred to phrase the great final fact, and if he continues to exist, it is because his work lives for him in such praise and blame as the nearer future may then give it as fitly as the further future. In such commemoration of Lyof N. Tolstoy's eightieth birthday as any friend of his may offer, this study of the reasons of his fame may not be the least tribute of affection and gratitude.

The century in which Tolstoy mostly lived and mostly wrought had among its many great names few more memorable than his, if it had any. There was Napoleon and there was Lincoln, and then there was Tolstoy in an order which time may change, though it appears to me certain that time will not change the number of these supreme names.

Since I have set them down here they have suggested to me a sort of representative unity in their relation to one another. If you fancy

Napoleon the incarnation of the selfish force which inspired and supported his own triumphant enemies in their reaction against progress; if you suppose Lincoln the type of humanity struggling toward the ideal in the regeneration of the world's polity, you may well conceive of Tolstoy as the soul's criticism of the evil and the good which, however wholly or partially they knew it, the others imperfectly did. The work of Lincoln was no more final than the work of Napoleon; and like Napoleon's and like Lincoln's, Tolstoy's work has been without finality. So far as I can perceive, it has even been without effect in a civilization which calls itself Christian, but which has apparently been no more moved by the human soul as it was in Tolstoy than by the divine spirit as it was in Christ. At first, indeed, the world was startled by the spectacle of a man of the highest rank, of a most ancient lineage, of great wealth, of renown in arms and in letters, putting from him fame and ease and honor, and proposing literally to obey the word of God, by making himself as one of the least of the brethren of Christ. It was a very curious sight, a bit droll, rather mad, wholly extraordinary. The world could hardly believe its eyes. It rubbed the sleep of two thousand years out of them at the sound of this voice crying in the wilderness, this voice that had so charmed it in fable, and bidding it prepare the way of the Lord and make His paths straight. Some tears came into its eyes, and some smiles; but after a while its lids fell again, and all was as before. The event, one of the greatest in the history of mankind, has been without perceptible effect in civilization.

On this side the teaching and the living of Tolstoy have been a failure so utter, so abject, that the heart sickens in considering it. An enemy might say that it could come to nothing better, for it was altogether lacking in originality; it was merely the living and the teaching of Christ over again, or if it had initiative in anything it was in the eschewment of some eases and pleasures in life which Christ permitted himself, or others, as harmless. An enemy might reason that this new ascetic was as illogical in the terms upon which he proposed regeneration as he was in the means he employed; and, in fact, the position of Tolstoy was full of illogicality. He proposed to himself poverty, but poverty without the fear of want is the least of hardships; he would give himself to work with his hands, but that was, so far as it went, taking the bread out of the mouths of those who needed the pay for the work of their hands; he dedicated himself to the good of others, as if it could be well to bestow the happiness which he refused; he would deny himself a soft bed and a luxurious board, but how many in all ages had fared simply and lain hard! He was defended from the consequences of his precept and his practice by the inalienable wealth of his family, the inalienable affection of the sovereign for the name and memory of his race. He was safe amidst his renunciations, and his protestations; he could freely do and say things for which the really poor and humble must suffer hunger and prison and exile. It was undeniably grotesque, but it was also pathetic, almost the most pathetic predicament in history for a noble and sincere and unselfish man. Yet it excited mainly derision, though the actor in the involuntary drama again and again disclaimed and deplored it, and humbly besought those who witnessed it at close range not to regard it as his ideal. Once to an interviewer, out of those scores and hundreds of interviewers who have swarmed upon him and reported his willing or unwilling words, he turned with the entreaty that he should not be taken as supposing that his life was comfortable to his doctrine. It was what he could make it, the best he could make it, on the conditions he had accepted. He has said that he sometimes regretted not having really impoverished himself, though to do it he must have compelled the assent of those whom he had not the heart or perhaps the right to compel. He asked to be regarded as a man staggering through the dark, and often stumbling and falling down, but struggling up and staggering on again.

In this he showed a humility more genuine and precious than all that his simplification, his vowed and voluntary poverty, had graced him with. But the prophet who owns to human weakness, to human frailty of will and action, while he preaches fortitude and renunciation, will hardly have a following. There is no sect of Tolstoyans, there are no disciples or apostles. A few just people in England have gathered in a small community for the practice and the publication of his teaching, his interpretation and application of the doctrine of Christ. But I know of no other embodied acceptance of Tolstoy in an age when Mormonism holds its own, and Eddyism spreads among millions of comfortable people, cheerful in the least and lowest of the least spiritual precepts of the gospel, and more eager to save their bodies than their souls alive. There may be, indeed, a tacit and occult effect from the Tolstoyan morality for which it is yet too early to look, but which may hereafter show itself in a renewed and revitalized Christianity. That end is all that he could hope or wish; and there must have come to him from many hearts a response, oftenest despairing and self-accusing, where his words have awakened a conscience which—

Not poppy or mandragora
Nor all the drowsy syrups of the world
Can ever medicine to that sweet sleep

which they 'owed yesterday.' This conscience is the sense of fealty to
the eternal and universal human brotherhood, in which there is no
high, no low, no better, no worse, no worthy, no unworthy, but only
the bond of duty and the tie of love; and in whomsoever Tolstoy's
words have awakened it, there is awakened the wish to do plainly and
simply the plain and simple will of Christ.

In the hours of disappointment and impatience which he must
have passed through, such a result, if he had been aware of it, must
have been his sufficient consolation. Being supported in his self-
sacrifice and his mission of self-sacrifice by no fanatical frenzy, by no
pretence to divine authority which the gospel of Christ does not
confer upon all, he doubtless needed this consolation. It has been
stupendous, but not wonderful, how his precept and his practice have
been misconstrued. Some such misconstruction is the lot of all the
prophets whether they convince or confound their time. The greatest
of them, Christ Himself, was misconstrued, first in His defeat and
then in His triumph. The earliest Christians, who endeavored only for
a life of love, peace and purity, were reputed guilty of every wickedness and filthiness. The world has got so far beyond this shabby state
of suspicion and accusal, that nothing wrong could be believed of the
life of this latest of the earliest Christians, but of his faith all things
were misimagined. If any one, with the cloudy impression which most
people have of this, will go to Tolstoy's books, he will be hardly less
than astonished to find how little is expected of him there in the much
that is asked of him. What Tolstoy asks of any one is that he shall keep
trying to be like Christ; that he shall make this his ideal and perpetually endeavor to realize it in his conduct, though he shall and
needs must fail to attain it. He asks this as Christ Himself asked His
followers to be perfect even as their Father in heaven was perfect,
knowing that more than the constant endeavor for that perfection was
impossible. Tolstoy is otherwise apparently self-contradictory
enough. In one place he supposes a devoted pair, who dedicate themselves to a life of good works, renouncing their worldly wealth and
going down among the very poorest and foulest and basest, whom in
the relentless logic of their self-sacrifice, they suffer to prey upon them
and befoul them and infect them, till they end by being effectively in
hell: hell here, though heaven hereafter. In another place he declares

that he 'peacefully and joyously lives, and peacefully and joyously is approaching death' because he professes the Christianity which coincides with truth; yet so far as he may he is practising the precepts by which that devoted pair end in hell upon earth: the hell of futile endeavor for the good of others, which still he urges as the supreme object of the Christian life. That is, he urges it as the ideal, which must never be lost sight of though it may never be attained.

If you will read this saying in the light of his essay on *Life* it will not be hard, for there he shows the impossibility of the personal happiness which we are always longing for and striving for. Personal happiness is an unworthy end, which you fail of as you fail of personal righteousness, the worthiest end, the supreme ideal, the identification of the human with the divine. Yet this identification will be the destiny of the righteous man after death, when his human shall be merged in the divine; though what becomes of the unrighteous man we are not told. Perhaps it is felt that we are not concerned with the bad, the good being bad enough. Perhaps the way of the unrighteous man to such immortality is through his identification with all humanity first, and in his unity with the worst or the indifferent good, the righteous will prevail for the unrighteous. Tolstoy does not say that; he is chary of promising reward; but he says and he shows that the selfish life, the individual, the personal life, is always misery and despair, and, except for some moments of mad oblivion, is constant suffering. Some of the most beautiful, the most wonderful, passages of his fiction, both that which is real and that which is ideal in terms, embody events in which he seizes and perpetuates the heavenly rapture of a supreme act of self-sacrifice, of identification. The imagination has never gone farther than in these portrayals of mystical ecstasy; in them, indeed, the human consciousness of the original and final divine is suggested as no polemic could urge it.

Those who with Tourguénief regret that Tolstoy did not leave prophesying and resume imagining may say that here is proof of the greater power he could have had even for righteousness if he would have stayed to sugar his unpalatable truth with fiction. I do not think so, though I do not think that in fiction he has any peer or even any rival, because from the beginning he 'took truth for his sole hero,' and would have no other in any extremity, or for any end. But even with his devotion to reality in the study of life, which, so far as I can note, was absolute, the prime affair was to captivate the reader, to lead his fancy, not to convince and persuade his reason. A

great gulf, never to be bridged, divides the ethical and the æsthetical
intention, though,—

> Beauty is truth, truth beauty,—

and though when the æsthetic intention presently becomes unconscious, and the creation of the truly beautiful may make for righteousness, still it is latent, still it serves two masters with the effect
declared of old. But when once the call of Religion came to Tolstoy
it came so powerfully, so loudly, that it must shut from his senses
every voice that called before; there he stood; so help him God, he
could no other than obey it, and it alone, testifying for it with all his
heart and all his soul and all his mind. The moral spectacle is of unsurpassed sublimity, and no riches of fiction is conceivable, fiction
even from him, the supreme master, which would console our poverty
if we had failed of such books as *My Confession, My Religion, The
Kingdom of God, What is Art?, What is Religion?, Life, What is to be
Done?*, and the many briefer essays, and occasional appeals to the
world in signal events and emergencies against its blindness and
cruelty and folly.

Suppose that he had never written these things, or such novels as
Resurrection and *The Kreutzer Sonata* and *The Death of Ivan Ilyitch*
where the purpose of captivating the imagination is renounced from
the outset and a terrible story is nakedly told, with no ray of the
prettiness or lure to curiosity in which the fictionist clothes his
invention, and there is no appeal but to the agonizing conscience,
would the world even of literature now be the better? I do not believe
it. Before he came to his awakening Tolstoy had done enough for
fiction and the art of it, for he had done incomparably more for it than
any other master of it. He himself says that *War and Peace* is like
Stendhal's *Chartreuse de Parme* in some of its battle-pieces, and he
would not say that if it were not his belief; but Stendhal was to
Tolstoy, in the ripeness of his art, as a beginner, and of the effect of
some anterior imitator. Above all, he lacked Tolstoy's abounding and
abiding moral sense, which is so one with that qualifying all human
experience that in Tolstoy's work it needs no explicit application; it
is interwoven there with the tissue of every motive and every action
for the reader to feel and own.

Yet it is not enough. The prodigious fascination of the tale is such,
its interest is so powerful, its current is so compelling, that the inner
purpose and meaning are hidden from some at times, and perceptible
only to a few at all times. The escape from the exercise of his power

upon the fancy is vital to the wizard himself. If he would become and remain a human being, in obedience to the call that he heard above the applause of his admirers, and the sighs and sobs of the hearts he wrung, he must renounce his world of art, the world he had won and held subject to his spell, and seek only that other world in which he must be as the least of the brethren except in the power to bear and to transmit its heavenly light.

No doubt Tolstoy was qualified and fortified for his ethical work by his æsthetic achievement. But he descended to the labor of teaching from such heights of art in fiction as no man had reached before. From *War and Peace*, from *Anna Karenina*, he humbled his art to such 'prentice-work as those little fables and allegories and sketches adapted to the understanding of peasants and peasants' children, as he humbled his life to the level of theirs. But he could not keep his charm out of the least of his writings, and he could not remain within the bounds of the narrow duteousness that he had set himself. From time to time he rose out of his self-prescribed limit, and then the whole world had masterpieces from him again: such masterpieces as *The Death of Ivan Ilyitch*, as *Master and Man*, as *The Kreutzer Sonata*, as *Resurrection*. He could not put his gift away; his mastery mastered even him; his own power made him its instrument, so that if he had continued directly to exercise his art we might not have had greater effects from it. His will was overruled in the simplification of his literature as in the simplification of his life; he could not make himself one with the lowliest in either. The event was in his literature a compromise as it was in his life, when he sat in a ploughman's dress eating a ploughman's fare at one end of the table, and at the other the world, economic and æsthetic, sat served with costly viands. Midway, the succession of interviewing and reviewing witnesses criticised and censured his hospitality and acclaimed or condemned according to their respective make, while in the hours saved from his rude toil he continued his sublime work. The event was a compromise or it was a defeat, if you choose to think it so; but it was no more a compromise or a defeat than that of any other human career. Compared with the event of any other career in this time, the career of the greatest warrior, statesman, king, priest or poet, it is a flawless triumph.

Tolstoy's example is of the quality of his precept, which with the will to be all positive is first notable for what is negative in it. To have renounced pride and luxury and idleness, and the vain indulgence of the tastes and passions, but not to have known want or the fear of it, not to have felt cold, hunger, houselessness, friendlessness, is to have done something which for the spectator lacks its corollary in practice, as the proposition of certain truths lacks its corollary in precept. That is, your reason is convinced and your soul is moved by what you are persuaded is right in the one as in the other, while as yet the necessary deduction from either does not enforce itself. Tolstoy says, in summing up the results of his gospel studies, that he 'believes in Christ's teachings,' and that 'happiness on earth is possible only when all men fulfil Christ's teaching,' which is 'possible, easy and pleasant.' 'I understand now,' he says, 'that he alone is above others who humbles himself before others, and makes himself the servant of all. I understand now how those that are great in the sight of men are an abomination to God. . . . Everything that once seemed to me right and important—honor, glory, civilization, wealth, the complications and refinements of life, luxury, rich food, fine clothing, etiquette—has become for me wrong and despicable. Rusticity, obscurity, poverty, austerity, simplicity of surroundings, of food, of clothing, of manners, all have become right and important to me. . . . Now I can no longer give my support to anything that lifts me above, or separates me from, others. I cannot, as I once did, recognize in myself or others titles or ranks of qualities aside from the title or quality of man. . . . I cannot help striving for what will not separate me from others' in knowledge, fame and riches, 'but will unite me to the majority of men. . . . I cannot encourage or take part in licentious pastimes, novels, plays, operas, balls and the like, which are so many snares for myself and for others. I cannot favor the celibacy of persons fitted for the marriage relation. . . . I cannot help considering as sacred and absolute the sole and unique union by which a man is once for all indissolubly bound to the woman with whom he has been united,' for this union he deems the sole marriage, whatever it is called. He cannot discriminate between his own country and others, or maintain his rights of property, or obey the authorities against his conscience, or take oaths, or resist evil with violence, or fail to work hard with his hands for his bread and for the subjection of his flesh and its lusts.

The catalogue of what he may not do, and does not believe, is longer than that of the things which he believes and may do; for as I have more than once noted, the variety of evil in this strangely constituted world of ours is far greater than the variety of good; the vices outnumber the virtues two to one. His precept, therefore, is mainly negative, as his practice is mainly negative, and the corollary of the good life is wanting as it is not wanting in the gospel creed, for there is implicated in this the promise of everlasting happiness, of personal, individual happiness such as we long for here all our hungry disappointed lives, but shall elsewhere have our fill of with rest to our souls.

In the Tolstoyan interpretation of the gospel religion this promise is not implicit. What we are to hope for is reunion with the divine source of our being; which may suffice the self-wearied worldling turned peasant, but which is not the simple hope of the peasant born, who has never yet had enough of himself in even those commonest things which constitute the bliss of conscious being, the every-day joys, the delight of beauty, the rapture of repose, even the low content of a full stomach.

'It cannot be that the instincts which are implanted in us and which are in themselves not more vicious than virtuous shall become and forever remain the means of our mortification and disappointment,' the reader of Tolstoy says. He feels without impiety that he may not regard ultimate absorption into the source of being as the supreme end of being, and that in so far as he has lived rightly and cleanly he may justly hope for a future life of conscious blessedness. All the more simply and fully does he hope for this if his life on earth has involuntarily been that ideal life of toil, hardship, denial, which Tolstoy sought when he left the world. The reader, even if he is not of that level, but some level nearer the intellectual and social level of the prophet, feels like asking him whether he has not made a mistake in his premise. He follows him consentingly enough in his *Confession*, and he owns tacitly to many, or most, or all of Tolstoy's transgressions, according as he knows himself to have lived selfishly. But at the same time, unless he is of an exceptionally gloomy temperament he is aware of living in a world which at its worst is not hopelessly wicked or unhappy. In the midst of its immoralities he believes that he has known many who were true and kind and chaste, but who had yet no thought of abandoning it to its comforts and conventions and seeking salvation at the plough-tail. 'Salvation,' he would say, 'is indeed there; but it is also here in the midst of the easy-going world in which some things seem almost innocuous even when not innocent.' He would say that the moral universe was not governed by logic in its events; that consequences often failed to follow causes, and that there was a divine unreason in the Oversoul which was supreme in the affairs of men. He might say that grapes from thorns and figs from thistles were necessarily no more impossible in the divine economy than the entry of a rich man into the kingdom of heaven. He might say with Tolstoy himself that if it was a question of ideal perfection at which we were to aim, though we knew we could never attain it, then neither were we without this aim, and that far or near was the same if the intent was the same.

In all this I think that the reader would be measurably or entirely wrong; but whether they would be wrong who said they remained in and of the world in the hope and belief that man was to be redeemed socially and not individually, by rescuing Christianity from the church and state to which it was devoted by the first Christian emperor when he conquered in its sign, and by making it the economic and political life, I am not so sure. All this, however, is something aside from the literary inquiry which I proposed to myself in writing about Tolstoy. The excuse for such an excursion is that the literature, especially the critical literature of Tolstoy, is not separable from the religion of Tolstoy, in whom ethics and æsthetics are one. This is apparent in all that he has written, so far as I know it, and there is but little of his writing that I do not know, that I have not felt to the full depth of my being. His literature both in its ethics and æsthetics, or its union of them, was an experience for me somewhat comparable to the old-fashioned religious experience of people converted at revivals. Things that were dark or dim before were shone upon by a light so clear and strong that I needed no longer grope my way to them. Being and doing had a new meaning and a new motive, and I should be an ingrate unworthy of the help I had if I did not own it, or if I made little of it. The voluntary and involuntary allegiance I had been paying to the truth which is beauty and beyond art, and to an ideal of goodness and loveliness in the commonest and cheapest lives, was here reasoned and exampled in things beyond refutation or comparison. What I had instinctively known before, I now knew rationally. I need never again look for a theme of fiction; I saw life swarming with themes that filled my imagination and pressed into my hands. I had but to look about me, and there was my drama, comic or tragic, here, yonder and everywhere, with the meaning that could not fail my inquiry.

I first saw his book, *My Religion*, in the house of two valued friends who spoke of it bewilderedly, as something very strange, which they could not quite make out. They were far too good to deny its strong appeal, but they were too spiritually humble, with all their reason for intellectual pride, to be quite sure of themselves in its seemingly new and bold postulates, which were, after all, really so old and meek. They showed me at the same time the closely printed

volumes of the French version of *War and Peace*, for it was long before
its translation into English, and they were again apparently baffled, for
a novel so vast in scale, and so simple and sincere in the handling of
its thronging events and characters, was something almost as alien to
modern experience as the absolute truthfulness of *My Religion*. The
incident was quite forgotten, and seven or eight years passed, in
which I had for four or five years *The Cossacks* of Tolstoy on my
shelves, unread and almost unlooked at. One day I took it down,
wholly oblivious of the Russian author who had bewildered and baffled
my friends, and dipped into it. To dip into it was to pass through its
mystical depths, but I do not know that I yet received a definite impression of the greatness of a novelist who wrote so unlike other
novelists, even other Russian novelists. By that time I had long
known nearly all of Tourguénief, and something of his master
Pushkin, but Tolstoy was a new name to me, and presently again it
was a forgotten name. It was recalled to me by yet another friend,
who lent me *Anna Karenina* with the remark, 'It is the old Seventh
Commandment business, but it is not treated as the French treat it.
You will be interested.' The word was poor and pale for the effect of
the book with me. The effect was as if I had never read a work of the
imagination before. Now for the first time I was acquainted with the
work of an imagination which had consecrated itself, as by fasting and
prayer, to its creative office and vowed itself to none other service
than the service of the truth. Here was nothing blinked or shirked or
glossed, nothing hidden or flattered, in the deepest tragedy of
civilized life. It was indeed the old Seventh Commandment business,
not only not treated as the French treat it, but rightly placed as to the
prime fact in its relation to all the other experiences of a sinning and
agonizing soul. Nothing was disproportionately insisted upon; as the
story moved forward as with the steady pace of time, and the capital
events in its progress were no more distinguished from the minor
events by the author than the hours are distinguished from one
another by the mechanism of a clock. It would be hard to say what was
most searching in it; one scene, one incident, was as penetrating as
another. If I name the moment when Anna defiantly, recklessly
declares her love for Vronsky to her husband; or the moment when
she steals into his house after she had abandoned it to wreak her
mother soul in hopeless tenderness upon their child; or the moment
of sleep when she escapes the agony of her guilt in the dream that she
has two husbands and is crazily happy in it; or the moment in which
she begins to be jealous of Vronsky and to suffer not only the ignominy

of her social rejection, but the fear that he will leave her, and yet cannot help tormenting him out of sufferance; or that final moment, when she lays herself down before the heavy train, and when its wheels crush over her breast would have saved herself from the death she sought; if I name these moments it is because they recur to me at random and not because I esteem them the effect of greater art than some others. I am not sure that the supreme effect of art in the book is not that moment when the dull, anti-pathetic Karenin perceives that he cannot forgive with dignity and yet forgives. Such a drama within the soul where the actor is the only spectator is something in its powerfulness beyond any overt action or experience.

It is now long since I read that story, and no doubt if I now looked into it instance upon instance would start from its page to make me think my remembrance of the particulars of its greatness had served me ill. But I cannot be mistaken as to the greatness of its art as a whole; I recall no flaw in it, and its negative perfection is a truer witness of its art than anything positive could be. The happy story of the Levines in its parallel current with the dark stream of Anna's and Vronsky's tragical love is not to my sense the rift or seam in the perfection which some feel it. Rather it is an effect of the author's full sense of life, in which many diverse fates move parallel and inevitably contrast in the significance, the obviousness, which only a supreme artist can keep from seeming mechanical.

But I wish, in paying my eager homage to Tolstoy as an artist, not to appear only to treat of his art as technique. It is, so far as I know it, and I think I have left none of his fiction unread, always most spiritual; it is so far from seeking beauty, or adorning itself with style, as to be almost bare and plain. His art is from his conscience, and you feel his conscience in it at every moment. This was perhaps only implicit in his earlier work, but in his later work it becomes more and more explicit. He is never false to his reader because he is never false to himself; it would be foolish to suppose that he could not misrepresent or wrongly color a given notion or action in his tale, but you may trust your soul to him in the assurance that he will not.

Since I began to write these pages, I have read his critical study of De Maupassant, and though I cannot say that it has heightened my sense of his æsthetics, I cannot deny that it has clarified my knowledge. In this piece of criticism he tells us how, as he read the tales and novels of that great talent, who, he says, could consider of any piece of life so closely and long and deeply, as to see it in the 'light that never was' before, he perceived a very great difference in the author's relations to his subjects and his characters. The subjects were, as we know, nearly always the old Seventh Commandment business, and the characters were the guilty lovers, the more guilty who overcame, and the less guilty who succumbed. In some cases, in some books, De Maupassant hated the evil in the seducers, and portrayed them with truth and conscience; in others he rather liked it and amused himself with their pleasures; in others he attempted to be Greek, as the Greek is supposed to have been, but probably was not, to regard good and evil with a conscienceless indifference, and in the 'creation of beauty' to be immoral, or as we vainly try to call it, unmoral. It is only when he was true to himself, to the sense of right and wrong which is innate in a man with his spiritual birth, that Maupassant is capable of that penetrating and absorbing attention which discovers the new meaning in things, and constitutes him to Tolstoy's mind a 'genius.'

Apparently from the very beginning of his fiction Tolstoy was capable of this penetrating and absorbing attention. From the beginning, therefore, he had but two questions to ask himself: Is this the fact? and, Have I represented the fact truly? If he had represented the fact truly, as in his conscience and intelligence he had known it really to be, he had treated it ethically and of necessity æsthetically; for, as you cannot fail to feel in every piece of his fiction, the perfect æsthetics result from the perfect ethics. I cannot otherwise explain that greatness which I recognize in every page of his where he has not wilfully abdicated his artistry to do the work of the allegorist. Where the artist and the moralist work together for righteousness, there is the true art; for it is the business of the moralist to feel and the business of the artist to portray. Otherwise you have a sermon, or you have a romance, and not the homily in which your own soul is mirrored in that of some fellow man. When he had recognized and appropriated the principle that to see the fact clearly by the inner light, and to show it as he saw it, was his prime office, all other things were added unto Tolstoy. In the presence of his masterpiece, you forget to ask for beauty, for style, for color, for drama; they are there, so far as they are not of naughtiness, in such measure as no other novelist has compassed. Every other novelist, therefore, shrinks and dwindles beside him; behind him, in the same perception, but not the full perception or the constant perception, come Maupassant and Zola and Flaubert, Galdós and Pardo-Bazán, Verga, Björnson, and perhaps Hardy,—yes, certainly, Hardy in *Jude*,—with, of course, Hawthorne from a wholly different air.

I like to call the names of his stories for the pleasure of recalling the pleasure I have had in them; it was oftenest the pleasure-pain which the truth gives; but I cannot call them in the order of my reading or of their relative greatness. I remember as paramount, of course, *War and Peace*, and *Anna Karenina*; but only of less scope and not less truth, to my feeling and thinking, were *The Cossacks, Kostia, The Death of Ivan Ilyitch, Two Generations, Polikushkta, Master and Man, The Kreutzer Sonata, Resurrection, Scenes of the Siege of Sebastopol, The Invaders, The Russian Proprietor*. Some of these are scarcely more than short stories, and there are other short stories, mere sketches, such as left the wide and deep impression of masterpieces, alike whether they were large masterpieces or little masterpieces. The equality of their art is wonderful, for it is always the same, through the æsthetics deriving from the ethics with the clear insight and the truthful utterance. For this, I have never, in my profoundest gratitude for it, thought that Tolstoy was to be praised any more than most other artists, his inferiors, were to be blamed for their mechanical obtuseness. The world is full of ugly things made for people who seem to want ugly things; and literature abounds in foolish and futile fiction because the vast majority of readers seem sure to want foolish and futile fiction. Perhaps their systems need it; they might revolt, in their mental infancy, from the food that nourishes the minds of grown men and women. But for art's sake, criticism should recognize the supreme value, the prime quality, of the art which comes purified and strengthened to its office through the devout scrutiny of life and the religious will to tell the truth of it.

If one were called upon to say in a word what Tolstoy and what his art was, one could not do better than to say that they were religious: the man, and the art that was the man. The art was more the man than the man knew. Out of the twelve volumes which represent his activity in the edition before me, nine are works of fiction, that is, works of art, and in the remaining three the artistic nature of the man is recurrently, if not constantly, shaping the religious utterances of his spirit. To enforce this point or that, he supposes a case so vividly that it lives at his touch; he invents a parable; he recalls an incident, an experience which he involuntarily clothes in drama, but so as to show its human reality the more and not to hide or to disqualify it. When he halts wilfully in this natural tendency and holds stubbornly to the business of laying down the law, or the gospel, he repeats himself again and again, both in theme and in phrase; he addresses himself to compelling rather than persuading his reader.

It is then that ceasing to take the natural, the spiritual view of the world and its waywardness, he takes the temperamental view, and in the gloom of his mood gropes for a hopeless reversion to innocence through individual renunciation of society instead of pressing forward to the social redemption which the very ecstasy of error must help effect. The state of mankind is bad, but it is not so bad as he sees it in this temperamental view, for then he sees it within and not without, and though the world is within each of us, it is always a little different in each one from the world in another. Essentially it is the same, its good and its evil are always the same; these divinely established constituents of our being no human difference can change; but from youth to manhood, from manhood to age, the world within changes, so that evil will be more at one time and less at another, or if not that, then more or less pardonable; and good will be more or less virtuous. As for the great world without, which is the sum of all the little worlds within, we judge it temperamentally and provisionally as we do these. We may be sure that, bad as it is, it is not hopelessly a mistake, and with all our mistaking we cannot make it so. It seems to me, though I say this with due submission, that it is not altogether or always the world that Tolstoy sees in his polemics; it is not intolerably bad. For youth there is abundant joy in it, for manhood there is abundant reward of hard working and right doing, for age there is still comfort and the peace of a life well spent. There is not enough of these things, not nearly enough, to go round, so that much merit misses of them; and there is untold sin and selfishness and misery. But at one time the balance will be on one side and at another time on another; and often it will seem as if the effect were altogether subjective, and there were really nothing of what our senses reported to us.

It is impossible not to believe what Tolstoy in his primarily ethical works tells us is the fact; he shows it, he proves it; he traces the cause, he points the consequences; you cannot refuse your assent. Those books, *My Confession, My Religion, Life, What is to be Done?* and the rest, if you have once read them, may have passed out of your surface memory, and they may have seemed as dead as the hundreds and thousands of other books which you have read; but open one of them and you find it all alive, glowing with the fire in which your irresponsibility was consumed, and the light from which you hid yourself, but which again shines unquenched around you. Undeniably, however, the second effect of the ethical books is not as powerful as the first. They have changed you; never can you look on life as you looked on it before you read them; but it must be that in the nature of it the ethics which are not æstheticized are of less permanent impression than the æsthetics which are ethicized. Very likely few of my readers are such inveterate readers of *War and Peace* as I am, but there must be one or two among them who have read it half a score of times and who yet come to it with an unjaded sense of its beauty and truth. If such a one will take, say, *My Religion* and contrast its effect upon him with the effect of *War and Peace*, I think he will own the more lasting power of the fiction. It is not only as a drama incomparably vaster than has filled the imagination before, but as a homily, comprehensive and penetrating beyond any direct sermoning, that it moves and stirs the heart. It is one of Tolstoy's earliest books, but already his ethics were realized if not formulated. He already hated the evil in his characters and loved the good, but with an artistic toleration which was also an ethical tolerance of the evil-doers. It appears fatalistic, but it does not, in its panoramic view of the vast trend of human affairs, ignore the personal responsibility of every actor in the spectacle, great or small: you are made to feel that there was a moment in the history of each when he or she, pressed but not forced by destiny, consciously lent himself or herself to the evil done in them. We behold a multitudinous movement of human beings, each of whom is a strongly defined character in himself and is a type of innumerable like characters. Every passion is portrayed, every affection, every propensity, not because the author wished to include all in his scheme, but because the scheme was so vast that they could not be excluded. It seems superfluous to say that it is a conspect of the Russian world (which in its human side is the world we always know everywhere) as it was affected by the wars of Napoleon's aggression; but no minute fact of any personal situation escapes the vigil of this prodigious study of life. If the proportions of the scheme are vast, the density of the constituent incidents, in which there are always free motive and purpose, is not less astonishing. It is as if the story were built upon the divination of atomic activity in the moral as in the material universe where stocks and stones are the centres of motion as unceasing, unresting, as blind, as that of the stars in their courses, but not less guided and intended. Where from time to time the author pauses and tries to tell why the things happened that he makes us see happening, neither he nor we are the wiser for his exegesis. What we do seem to be the wiser for is a toleration for the actors, not the actions, of the drama commensurate with the scene of the drama.

This toleration is what stays us and consoles us for the sorrows and sins of people who seem so terribly like ourselves, but for whose evils we are much abler to forgive ourselves than we are for those evils which in his religious books Tolstoy brings home to our own doors. It was inevitable that he should finally do this; it was the logic of what he had already done. For him it was not enough that he should create fiction far beyond his preaching in its appeal; he must tell us what he was doing and leave us to determine what in view of the facts enforced we mean to do.

Probably we mean to do very little, however much we have determined. In the mean time he has given many of his readers a bad conscience, and a bad conscience is the best thing a man can have. It may be the best thing that the world can have. At any rate, it can never be the same world it was before Tolstoy lived in it. Worse it may be, in mere shame and despair, or better in mere shame, but not imaginably the same. Such men do not die for all time. To the end of time they have their recurring palingenesis.

54 Arnold Bennett

1911

From 'The Editor's Easy Chair,' *Harper's Monthly*, March 1911.

Though Howells continued, as we have seen, to write criticism to the end, and some of it was still very good, it was never so strong again after the first decade of the century—as indeed it had seldom been before. But there came a special felicity in the moment when he could say that, at least in half his work, there had appeared a British novelist after his own heart. Arnold Bennett the realist suited Howells at last, never mind Bennett the romancer: could there be two men? asked smiling Howells. Never mind. Bennett the truth-teller was epic like Norris, like Tolstoi, 'at once intensely realistic and insurpassably imaginative, as the realistic always and alone is.'

With Hardy turned to poetry, with Tolstoi and Björnson gone, 'and Flaubert, and Zola, and the Goncourts, and Frank Norris' all gone, and 'no more books from Perez Galdós or Palacio Valdés, there is no writer living in whose reality we can promise ourselves greater joy than Mr. Bennett.' No doubt it was gratifying to have Bennett write and testify that he had trained himself in youth on Howells's fiction, even his criticism; but it was Bennett's existence, the evidence of the 'Five Towns' fiction, which brought a last victory—with a last absurdity—to an old ironist.

One of the slighter trials of the adventurer in the uncharted seas of literature is to have tardier navigators hailing him under their laggard sails, or the smoke-stacks of their twin-screw, turbine, separate-tabled, thirty-thousand-tonner, and bellowing through their trumpets, so that all the waste may hear, the insulting question whether he has ever sighted such and such islands or sojourned on the shores of such and such continents: islands where he has loitered whole summers away, continents where he has already founded colonies of enthusiastic settlers. Probably the most vexing thing in the whole experience of Columbus was having Vespucius ask him whether he had happened to notice a new hemisphere on his way to India; though it could have been no such trial as having people come to you with

books of Mr. Arnold Bennett, and urging you to read *The Old Wives'*
Tale, as if the places and persons of it were entirely novel to you half a
dozen years after you had read *The Grim Smile of the Five Towns*.
Still, it shall not spoil our pleasure in speaking of Mr. Bennett, now,
when everybody else knows him or knows about him.

Perhaps they do not know all about him. Perhaps they do not know,
even if they know that he began writing fiction in partnership with
Mr. Eden Phillpotts, that he united his own with that other uncommonly sincere and original talent in writing romances as ungenuine as any we happen to think of at the moment. Yet one ought to
distinguish, one ought to say that the joint output of the firm was
brilliantly ungenuine, though perhaps it was the worse for being so. It
may have deceived them as to its real nature so, and kept them the
later from finding their true selves.

Lights that do mislead the morn

are fires more fatally ineffectual for good than none. But Mr. Bennett
seems to have trusted longer to their will-o'-the-wisps than Mr.
Phillpotts. The generation of his real and true work is partially *A Man
from the North*, 1898; *Anna of the Five Towns*, 1902; *Whom God
Hath Joined*, 1906; *The Grim Smile of the Five Towns*, 1907; *The Old
Wives' Tale*, 1908; *Clayhanger*, 1910. The generation of his romantic
novels, since he left writing them together with Mr. Phillpotts, is
partially *The Great Babylon Hotel*, 1902; *Buried Alive*, 1904; *The
Gates of Wrath*, 1908; *Hugo, The Glimpse, The Ghost*, fantasticalities of
dates not precisely ascertainable by us, but evidently coeval with the
contrasting realities cited. There are two or three of his books which
we have not read, and which we cannot classify, but apparently he
has found a comfort, or a relaxation, or an indemnification in writing a
bad book after writing a good one. It is very curious; it cannot be from
a wavering ideal; for no man could have seen the truth about life so
clearly as Mr. Bennett, with any after doubt of its unique value; and
yet we have him from time to time indulging himself in the pleasure of
painting it falsely.

As far as we have noted, his former partner, since their dissolution,
has not yielded to the same sort of temptation. Alike in their truer work
they have preferred the spacious limit; they have tended to the gigantic, the one in height, the other in breadth; and they have tended alike
to the epical in motive, to the massive in form. The mass of Mr.
Bennett is wrought over with close detail, which detracts nothing from
its largeness, though in his latest work he has carried largeness to the

verge of immensity, without apparently reflecting that immensity may be carrying largeness too far. If he does not break under it himself, his reader may; though it is only honest to say that we are not that sort of reader. In fact, *Clayhanger* has left us wishing that there were more of it, and eager, or at least impatient, for the two other parts which are to complete the trilogy promised; an enemy might say threatened; but we are no enemy, and we rather admire the naïve courage of the author in giving so brave a warning, especially at a moment when the reader may be doubting whether he can stand any more of Hilda. For ourselves we will say that we can stand a great deal more of Hilda, and that we should like very much to know how or why, having just engaged herself to Clayhanger, she should immediately marry another man. We should like to have the author's explanation. We are sure that it will be interesting, that it will be convincing, even if it is not satisfactory. That is his peculiar property: to be convincing if not satisfactory, and always to be interesting. We would not spare the least of his details, and as we have suggested, his mass is a mass of details, not only superficially but integrally.

If it shall be demanded how, since he is a mass of details, his work can also be epical, we will say that the central motive of his fiction—that is, his good fiction—is the collective life of those Five Towns, and that his fiction revolves round this, falling back into it by a force as of gravitation, when it seems finally thrown off from it. It is epical, not with the epicality of the *Odyssey*, but of the *Iliad*, and its hero is a population of Achaian homogeneity; yet it is not Homeric so much as it is Tolstoyan, and its form, its symmetry, its beauty is spiritual rather than plastic. For this sort of epical grandeur, which we find in high degree in Mr. Bennett's true fiction, the supreme Russian gave once for all the formula when he said, 'The truth shall be my hero,' and it was not necessary for the Englishman, when he took the Five Towns for his theme, to declare that he was going to act upon it; you could not read a dozen paragraphs of his book without seeing what he meant to do, what he was already about. Tolstoy's inspiration was his sense of the essential equality of men, and the essential value of every human being, who in any scheme of art must be as distinctly recognized as every other, whether prominently shown or not. Something must be said or done to let you into the meaning of every soul in the story; none could be passed over as insignificant; each presence contributed to the collective effect, and must be proportionately recognized. Life may seem to consist of a few vast figures, of a few dramatic actions; and the representation of life may reflect this appearance; but for the artist there can be no seeming except as the result of being, and his design, in fiction at least, must be so Pre-Raphaelite that the reader can always see the being within the seeming. The nakedness of humanity under its clothes must be sensible to the painter or he will not be able to render the figure, even if apparently it is no more part of the drama than a table or a chair; really, it can never help being part of the drama.

We do not say that the perception of this is always evident in what Mr. Bennett does, or the consciousness of it; but we do say that without it, latent or patent, his work would lack mastery, the mastery which we feel in it. He has by means of it made his Five Towns, just wherever or whatever they are, as actually facts of the English map as if their names could be found in the gazetteer. The towns are so actual, in fact, that we have found their like in our own country, and when reading the *Grim Smile* of them, we were always thinking of certain American places. Of course one always does something of this sort in reading a book that convinces, but here was a book that studied unexpected traits of English life, and commended them so strongly to our credence that we accepted them for American, for New England, for Connecticut. Afterward in reading more of the author's work, say *The Old Wives' Tale* and *Clayhanger*, we were aware of psychical differences in those manufacturing-town, middle-class English people from our own, which we wish we could define better than we shall probably be able to do. Like our own they are mostly conscientious, whether still sunk in their original Dissent, or emancipated by the Agnostic motions of modern science; they are of a like Puritan conscience with our own New-Englanders; they feel, beyond the help of priest or parson, their personal responsibility for wrongdoing. But it appears that they accept Nature rather more on her own terms and realize that human nature is a part of her. They do not prize respectability less; they prize it rather more; but they do not stretch accountability so far as our Puritanized wrong-doers; they know when to stop atoning, when to submit, and, without any such obsolete phrasing, leave the rest to God. Those conscientious, manufacturing-town, middle-class English outlive their expiation; they serve their terms; but with our corresponding penitents the punishment seems a life sentence.

Of the sort of vital detail in which the author abounds it would be only too easy to multiply instances, but we will take only one, one so luminous, so comprehensive, that it seems to us the most dramatic incident, like, say, a murder, or an elopement, or a failure in business, could not be more so, or so much so, in so little space. When Sophia, in *The Old Wives' Tale*, after her long sojourn in Paris, had come back to her sister in one of the Five Towns, and they were both elderly, ailing women, they were sitting one night waiting for supper. 'The door opened and the servant came in to lay the supper. Her nose was high, her gaze cruel, radiant, and conquering. She was a pretty and an impudent girl of about twenty-three. She knew she was torturing her old and infirm mistresses. She did not care. She did it purposely. . . . Her gestures as she laid the table were very graceful, in the pert style. She dropped forks into their appointed places with disdain; she made slightly too much noise; when she turned she manoeuvred her swelling hips as though for the benefit of a soldier in a handsome uniform.'

Here is not only a wonderful bit of detail, a pinch of mother earth precious beyond rubies, but a cosmical implication in which a universe of circumstance and condition and character is conveyed. Here is not only a lesson in art beyond the learning of any but the few honest men and women presently writing fiction, but an illustration of the truth which commonplace detail alone can give. It is at once intensely realistic and insurpassably imaginative, as the realistic always and alone is; but more than anything it is interesting and poignantly pertinent to the affair in hand, which is not to ascertain or establish the excellence of Mr. Arnold Bennett's work, but to put the reader upon the trail of a psychological inquiry often, not to say constantly, engaging the curiosity of the Easy Chair, and moving it to speculation which it has had no great difficulty in keeping trivial, at least in appearance. We mean the question of that several self, which each of us is sensible of in his own entity, without much blushing, or, in fact, anything but a pleasing amaze, but which he perceives in others with stern reprobation as involving a measure of moral turpitude.

We have already noted not only the wide disparity, but the absolute difference of nature in the two varieties of Mr. Arnold Bennett's fiction, parallel in time and apparently of like deliberate intention. So far as our knowledge of it goes, and we do not say it goes the whole way or quite inclusively, every alternate book of his is ungenuine in material, false in make, and valueless in result, so far as any staying power with the reader is concerned. We can think of but one such story which seems to summon a measure of reality to the help of its structural hollowness; in *A Great Man* there is something like human comedy in the unhuman farce; a good deal of living detail in the persons and situations from time to time forces your faith in the general scheme of make-believe. It is an amusing book; it is good farce; but it is essentially farce, and things do not happen in it, but are made to happen. For the rest, we may safely say, the author's different books are as unlike as so many peas: peas out of the pod, and peas out of the can; you have but to taste, and you know instantly which is which.

It is not less than wonderful, the difference in the product which is apparently always green peas; we use the figure respectfully and for its convenience, and not in any slight of a writer whose serious perform-ance no one can pass us in prizing and praising. Since Tolstoy is gone, and Björnson is gone, and Flaubert, and Zola, and the Gon-courts, and Frank Norris, and all the early naturalists are gone, and we have no more books from Perez Galdós or Palacio Valdés, there is no writer living in whose reality we can promise ourselves greater joy than Mr. Bennett. For one thing, we can instantly know it from his unreality; we lose no time in doubt; the note of truth or the note of untruth is struck with the first word; in one case we can securely lend our whole soul to listening to the end; in the other, we can shut the book, quite safe from losing anything.

But again the question is not so much æsthetical or ethical (the one always involves the other) as psychological. Apparently there are two selves of the one novelist who are simultaneously writing fiction entirely opposed in theory and practice. Can there, outside of the haunts of the Advertising Muse, be any possible comparison between *The Gates of Wrath*, say, and *The Old Wives' Tale*, say? If we are right in holding that there can be none, then is not it within the force of hypnotic suggestion to constrain the self of Mr. Bennett writing such books as *The Gates of Wrath* to write such books as *The Old Wives' Tale*, and to do this invariably? The self which we here propose to constrain may reply that it addresses an entirely different public, which does not care for *Old Wives' Tale*, but wants *Gates of Wrath*, and continually more of them. To any such argument we should re-turn that a public of this sort is profitably negligible; and in our con-tention we believe we shall have the earnest and eager support of that self of Mr. Bennett's which writes only, and can write only, *The Old Wives' Tale*, and the like, and to which we are now looking impatiently for the two remaining parts of the *Clayhanger* trilogy.

Of course there is always the chance that there may be two Mr. Arnold Bennetts, rather than two selves of one. Or it may be that there is a pseudo-Mr. Arnold Bennett who is abusing the name of a master to foist his prentice inventions upon the public. In this case we hardly know what to suggest in the way of remedy. It would be difficult to bring such a matter into court, or if it could be got there it might result in giving an undesirable extension to the publicity of the prentice work. Otherwise, we should hope that something in the nature of an injunction might be made to apply to the practices of the pseudo-Mr. Arnold Bennett, which are clearly *contra bonos mores*. After all, however, it may be best simply to let the genuine author write the ungenuine down. He is unquestionably competent to do so, or at least there is no author now living who is more competent. It is scarcely the moment, here at the foot of our fourth page, to state his qualifications in full, but we may say that the genuine Mr. Arnold Bennett writes with a directness which is full of admirable consciousness. Slowly, carefully, distinctly, he accumulates the evidences of situation and character, and then sets them forth so steadily, so clearly, that your mind never misgives you as to their credibility. In the long stretches of time covered by the action, the persons of the drama grow up from childhood to youth, from youth to age, and when they die it is no more theatrically than when the immense majority of the race daily attests its mortality. More important than all this, it is shown how each seed of character bringeth forth fruit of its kind, and does not turn into some other kind because of the weather, the drought, the frost, the tempest; no nature is changed in a single night from black to white, or the reverse. We do not allege instances because the books are all instance, but what is certain, without any such trouble, is that here once more, and in the years that we might have feared would be years of famine, we have a harvest of fiction, such as has not been surpassed in any former season, and the field of it is so wide that no one of wholesome appetite need hunger. Whether the reaper shall finally stand out against the sky as vast as the reapers of other days, does not matter. Probably he will not. Along with other kinds of heroes, the author-hero has probably gone forever. At least, in the interest of literature, we hope so.

Bibliography

Primary reference

The indispensable *vade mecum*, a pillar of fire in an otherwise benighted wilderness, is William M. Gibson and George Arms, *A Bibliography of William Dean Howells*, New York: Arno Press, 1948, now available in a reprint edition (1971) with an additional note by the compilers. Its companion is James Woodress (ed.), 'A Bibliography of Writing About William Dean Howells,' *American Literary Realism, 1870-1910*, Special Number, 1969, which is in process of updating.

In work among the volumes to come in *A Selected Edition of W. D. Howells* are a multi-volume edition of Letters; three volumes of criticism (to 1881, ed. Ulrich Halfmann; 1881-1900, ed. Donald Pizer; 1901-20, ed. Ronald Gottesman); and, at the very end (perhaps 1980?) a definitive bibliography.

Meanwhile see:

ARMS, GEORGE *et al.*, *Prefaces to Contemporaries (1882-1920) by William Dean Howells*, Florida: Scholars' Facsimiles, 1957.

BALDWIN, MARILYN AUSTIN (ed.), *My Mark Twain by William Dean Howells*, Baton Rouge: Louisiana State University Press, 1967.

GIBSON, WILLIAM M. (ed.), 'W. D. Howells On Novel-Writing and Novel-Reading,' *Howells and James: A Double Billing*, New York Public Library, 1958.

HOWELLS, MILDRED (ed.), *Life in Letters of William Dean Howells*, 2 vols, New York: Doubleday, Doran, 1928.

KIRK, CLARA MARBURG, and KIRK, RUDOLF (eds), *Criticism and Fiction and Other Essays by W. D. Howells*, New York University Press, 1959.

MESERVE, WALTER J. (ed.), *The Complete Plays of W. D. Howells*, New York University Press, 1960.

MORDELL, ALBERT J. (ed.), *Discovery of a Genius: William Dean Howells and Henry James*, New York: Twayne, 1961.

SMITH, HENRY NASH, and GIBSON, WILLIAM M. (eds), *Mark Twain–Howells Letters: The Correspondence of Samuel L. Clemens and William D. Howells, 1870-1910*, 2 vols, Cambridge: Harvard University Press, 1960.

Secondary reference

Books on Howells

BENNETT, GEORGE NEIL, *William Dean Howells: The Development of a Novelist*, Norman, Oklahoma: University of Oklahoma Press, 1959.

476

CADY, EDWIN H., *The Road to Realism: The Early Years, 1837–1885, of William Dean Howells*, Syracuse University Press, 1956.

CADY, EDWIN H., *The Realist at War: The Mature Years, 1885–1920, of William Dean Howells*, Syracuse University Press, 1958.

CADY, EDWIN H., and FRAZIER, DAVID L. (eds), *The War of the Critics Over William Dean Howells*, Evanston, Illinois: Row, Peterson, 1962.

CARTER, EVERETT, *Howells and The Age of Realism*, Philadelphia: J. B. Lippincott, 1954.

EBLE, KENNETH E. (ed.), *Howells: A Century of Criticism*, Dallas: Southern Methodist University Press, 1962.

FRYCKSTEDT, OLOV W., *In Quest of America: A Study of Howells' Early Development as a Novelist*, New York: Russell & Russell, 1971 (originally 1958).

GIBSON, WILLIAM M., *William D. Howells*, University of Minnesota Press, 1967.

KIRK, CLARA MARBURG, *W. D. Howells: Traveller from Altruria, 1889–1894*, New Brunswick, New Jersey: Rutgers University Press, 1962.

KIRK, CLARA MARBURG, *W. D. Howells and Art in His Time*, New Brunswick, New Jersey: Rutgers University Press, 1965.

KIRK, CLARA MARBURG, and KIRK, RUDOLF, *William Dean Howells*, New York: Twayne, 1962.

LYNN, KENNETH S., *William Dean Howells: An American Life*, New York: Harcourt, Brace, Jovanovich, 1971.

MCMURRAY, WILLIAM, *The Literary Realism of William Dean Howells*, Carbondale: Southern Illinois Press, 1967.

VANDERBILT, KERMIT, *The Achievement of William Dean Howells*, Princeton University Press, 1968.

WAGENKNECHT, EDWARD, *William Dean Howells: The Friendly Eye*, New York: Oxford University Press, 1969.

WOODRESS, JAMES L., JR, *Howells and Italy*, Durham, North Carolina: Duke University Press, 1952.

Books on theme, theory, or period

AARON, DANIEL, *Men of Good Hope*, New York: Oxford University Press, 1951.

ÅHNEBRINK, LARS, *The Beginnings of Naturalism in American Fiction*, Cambridge: Harvard University Press, 1950.

BECKER, GEORGE J. (ed.), *Documents of Modern Literary Realism*, Princeton University Press, 1963.

BERTHOFF, WARNER, *The Ferment of Realism: American Literature, 1884–1918*, New York: Free Press, 1965.

CADY, EDWIN H., 'The Gentleman as Socialist: William Dean Howells,' *The Gentleman in America*, Syracuse University Press, 1949.

CADY, EDWIN H., *The Light of Common Day: Realism in American Fiction*, Bloomington: Indiana University Press, 1971.

CURRENT-GARCIA, EUGENE, and PATRICK, WALTON R. (eds), *Realism and Romanticism in Fiction*, Chicago: Scott, Foresman, 1962.

FALK, ROBERT, 'The Rise of Realism, 1871–1891,' *Transitions in American Literary History*, Harry Hayden Clark (ed.), Durham, North Carolina: Duke University Press, 1953.

FALK, ROBERT, *The Victorian Mode in American Fiction, 1865–1885*, East Lansing: Michigan State University Press, 1965.

HARLOW, VIRGINIA, *Thomas Sergeant Perry*, Durham, North Carolina: Duke University Press, 1950.

HOLMAN, CLARENCE HUGH (ed.), *The American Novel through Henry James*, Goldentree Bibliographies, New York: Appleton-Century-Crofts, 1966.

JONES, HOWARD MUMFORD, *The Age of Energy: Varieties of American Experience, 1865–1915*, New York: Viking, 1971.

KAZIN, ALFRED, *On Native Grounds: An Interpretation of Modern American Prose Literature*, New York, Reynal & Hitchcock, 1942.

KOLB, HAROLD, *The Illusion of Life: American Realism as a Literary Form*, Charlottesville: University Press of Virginia, 1969.

LEVIN, HARRY, *The Gates of Horn: A Study of Five French Realists*, New York: Oxford University Press, 1963.

MCMAHON, HELEN, *Criticism of Fiction: A Study of Trends in the Atlantic Monthly, 1857–1898*, New York: Bookman Associates, 1952.

MARTIN, JAY, *Harvests of Change: American Literature, 1865–1914*, Englewood Cliffs, New Jersey: Prentice-Hall, 1967.

PERKINS, GEORGE B. (ed.), *The Theory of the American Novel*, New York: Holt, Rinehart & Winston, 1970.

PIZER, DONALD, *Realism and Naturalism in Nineteenth-Century American Literature*, Carbondale: Southern Illinois University Press, 1966.

PIZER, DONALD (ed.), *American Thought and Writing: The 1890's*, Boston: Houghton, Mifflin, 1972.

RUBIN, LOUIS D., and MOORE, JOHN REES (eds), *The Idea of an American Novel*, New York: Crowell, 1961.

STOVALL, FLOYD (ed.), *The Development of American Literary Criticism*, Chapel Hill: University of North Carolina Press, 1955. See esp. Fogle, Richard H., 'Organic Form in American Criticism, 1840–1870', and Falk, Robert, 'The Literary Criticism of the Genteel Decades, 1870–1890,' and Raleigh, John J., 'Revolt and Revolution in Criticism, 1900–1930.'

WALCUTT, CHARLES CHILD, *American Literary Naturalism: A Divided Stream*, Minnesota University Press, 1956.

WIENER, PHILIP P., *Evolution and the Founders of Pragmatism*, Cambridge: Harvard University Press, 1949.

ZIFF, LARZER, *The American 1890's*, New York: Viking, 1966.

Selected articles

ARMS, GEORGE, 'The Literary Background of Howells's Social Criticism,' *American Literature*, 14 (November 1942), 260–76.

ARMS, GEORGE, 'Howells' English Travel Books: Problems in Technique,' *PMLA*, 82 (March 1967), 104–16.

BENNETT, SCOTT, 'David Douglas and the British Publication of W. D. Howells' Works,' *Studies in Bibliography*, 25 (1972), 107–24.

BUDD, LOUIS J., 'William Dean Howells' Debt to Tolstoy,' *American Slavic and East European Review*, 9 (December 1950), 292–301.

BUDD, LOUIS J., 'W. D. Howells's Defence of the Romance,' *PMLA*, 67 (March 1952), 32–42.

BUDD, LOUIS J., 'Altruism Arrives in America,' *American Quarterly*, 8 (Spring 1956), 40–52.

CARTER, EVERETT, 'William Dean Howells' Theory of Critical Realism,' *Journal of English Literary History*, 16 (June 1949), 151–66.

CARTER, EVERETT, 'Taine and American Realism,' *Revue de Littérature Comparée*, 26 (July–September 1952), 357–64.

CLARK, HARRY HAYDEN, 'The Role of Science in the Thought of W. D. Howells,' *Transactions of the Wisconsin Academy of Science, Arts and Letters*, 42 (1953), 263–303.

DOWLING, JOSEPH A., 'William Dean Howells' Literary Reputation in England, 1892–1897,' *Dalhousie Review*, 45 (Autumn 1965), 277–88.

EDWARDS, HERBERT, 'Howells and the Controversy Over Realism in American Fiction,' *American Literature*, 3 (November 1931), 237–48.

EDWARDS, HERBERT, 'Zola and the American Critics,' *American Literature*, 4 (May 1932), 114–29.

FOSTER, RICHARD, 'Frankly I Like Criticism,' *Antioch Review*, 22 (Fall 1962), 273–83.

GIBSON, WILLIAM M., 'Mark Twain and Howells, Anti-Imperialists,' *New England Quarterly*, 20 (December 1947), 435–70.

GOLDFARB, CLARE R., 'From Complicity to Altruria: The Use of Tolstoy in Howells,' *University Review*, 32 (Summer 1966), 311–17.

LINNEMAN, WILLIAM R., 'Satires of American Realism, 1880–1900,' *American Literature*, 34 (March 1962), 80–93.

LUTWACK, LEONARD, 'William Dean Howells and the "Editor's Study,"' *American Literature*, 24 (March 1952), 195–207.

MATTHEWS, BRANDER, 'Mr. Howells as a Critic,' *Forum*, 32 (January 1902), 629–38.

MONTEIRO, GEORGE, 'The New York *Tribune* on Henry James, 1881–2,' *Bulletin of the New York Public Library*, 67 (February 1963), 71–81.

STRONKS, JAMES B., 'Paul Laurence Dunbar and William Dean Howells,' *Ohio Historical Quarterly*, 67 (April 1958), 95–108.

TRILLING, LIONEL, 'W. D. Howells and the Roots of Modern Taste,' *Partisan Review*, 18 (September–October 1951), 516–36.

WESTBROOK, MAX, 'The Critical Implications of Howells' Realism,' *University of Texas Studies in English*, 36 (1957), 71–9.

WOODRESS, JAMES L., 'The Dean's Comeback: Four Decades of Howells Scholarship,' *Texas Studies in Literature and Language*, 2 (Spring 1960), 115–23.

Index